John Lemp • The Beer Baron of Boise
Millionaire Brewer of Frontier Idaho

Also by Herman Wiley Ronnenberg:

Disciples of King Gambrinus VOLUME I:
Twenty-Five Unfortunate Lives

Disciples of King Gambrinus VOLUME II:
Capitalists and Town Fathers

Material Culture of Breweries (Guides to Historical Artifacts)

Beer and Brewing in the Inland Northwest

Pioneer Mother on the River of No Return:
The Life of Isabella Kelly Benedict Robie

Jeanette Manuel:
The Life and Legend of the Belle of Fabulous Florence

The Politics of Assimilation

John Lemp
The Beer Baron of Boise
Millionaire Brewer of Frontier Idaho

By Herman Wiley Ronnenberg

HWR
Heritage Witness Reflections Publishing
Troy, Idaho

John Lemp: The Beer Baron of Boise
by Herman Wiley Ronnenberg
Copyright © 2014 Herman Wiley Ronnenberg
All rights reserved

Paperback ISBN: 978-0-9895967-3-2
Hardback ISBN: 978-0-9818408-1-9
Ebook ISBN: 978-0-9895967-4-9
Hardback LCCN: 2008943305

Heritage Witness Reflections Publishing
P.O. Box 356
Troy, Idaho 83871

Book design by Robert and Erik Jacobson
www.LongfeatherBookDesign.com

This book is dedicated to the decendents of John Lemp

Foreword

Settlement of early Boise coincided with the well-known rush for gold in nearby Boise Basin. The City's growth and considerable prosperity after the mine's decreased production and the mainline of the railroad passed it by bring an anomaly to the development of population centers in the early West. Boise's very amenable climate and topography account for its success to a degree. Moreover, the attitude of her most prosperous citizens played a very large role. They appointed themselves to boost the fortunes of the settlement as their own wealth grew, determining the nascent city's growth and future. A few dozen men who wanted to stay in what is now called "Treasure Valley" to raise their families and enjoy the fruits of their labors kept reaching into their own pockets to finance its development. They dug irrigation ditches and watered the arid out of the Boise River. They held meetings to determine potential alternative railroad routes to connect Boise to the outside world. They sponsored the arts, built churches, and ran flourishing businesses in this isolated place.

Among these men, John Lemp stood significantly. He arrived when the town began and cut a larger-than-life figure in every aspect of community life. His main occupation was to brew beer. However, his business life also included owning the ditch later called Settler's Ditch, the Capitol Hotel, the Lemp Dry Goods Store, the Star mine, a number of cattle ranches, the Lemp addition in the North End of Boise, and corrals and livery for excellent horses, including draft horses that delivered his prize beer. His legacy extended beyond business to include decades of work on the city council, a term as mayor, an "eternal" position as treasurer of his IOOF lodge, a charter member of the Turn Verein Society for German-Americans, a charter member of the El Koran Shrine, and board membership for several banks, the Boise Rapid Transit Company, and the Artesian Hot and Cold Water Company. At over two hundred pounds, Lemp literally cut a large figure, and his family's size reflected his appetite and optimism: he and his German wife had thirteen children!

Aware of their place in history, early Boiseans formed their own Historical Society of Idaho Pioneers, of which John Lemp was a charter member. Yet, until Herman Ronnenberg's thorough and excellent research, a biography on this early Boise beer baron has been missing. No newspaper article, census report, exchange of deed, letter, or report on or during John Lemp's life has escaped Ronnenberg's attention.

Known affectionately as "Doctor Beer" among his friends, Ronnenberg's many articles on liquor, and especially on beer, have addressed drinking from the time of the Romans to the present day. His dissertation on the "History of the Brewing Industry in Idaho" gave him adequate background to collect biographical information on Idaho's most famous and prolific brewer, John Lemp. Yet Ronnenberg knows that Lemp's life speaks to a larger subject than providing pioneers of the city between the high desert and the high mountains in the valley of the Boise River with good beer. Lemp contributed time and money to the city's growth.

In isolated Boise key figures shared their prosperity for the growth and development of the community. They imbued Idaho's capital city with values that have persisted to render greater dividends than the size of the population would indicate. Boise's being a good place to live today started with these hardy individuals. They gleaned their wealth from the area's mines, farms, timber, ranches, and each other's needs, and they reinvested it into a culturally rich city apart from the mainstream of the developing West. Either voluntarily or according to the law, they built Boise with their money and time. As Ronnenberg states, "When Boise improved itself, a large share of the bill always went to John Lemp." Many years running, Lemp was second or third in assessment of personal wealth and, therefore, payment of property taxes. His estate upon death totaled $1,000,000, and astronomical sum in 1912.

For those interested in Boise's past, Boise's values, and Boise's colorful citizens, Ronnenberg's book will reveal rich insights and information.

Carol Lynn MacGregor, PhD

Acknowledgments

During the two plus decades this research of the Lemp family and Idaho's other brewers has gone on there has been a myriad of people who have offered their help in so many ways. I especially owe a big thank you to Delos and Mary Ann Newcomer who so graciously and so often offered room and board and friendship while I was researching in Boise.

Many historians of Idaho, a few of which specialize in brewing history, have given me many bits of information I would never have found on my own. These include Kendall Lee Ballard for information on his collection of Idaho alcohol tax stamps; Steve Armstrong for beer labels, letters from Idaho brewing companies and his general knowledge of Idaho brewing history; Rose Graham who kept the microfilm readers working at the University of Idaho library for me and others. I'll offer a collective thank you to the members of the Idaho Token Collectors Club, and particularly Greg Manos, John Mutch for the photos of6 the Capitol Hotel token, Dan Lute for the Lemp Addition plat map. The members of this club know more about Idaho early businesses than anyone else. Thanks to Karl Lemp of St. Louis, great grandson of the subject, and his father, for photos and information about his ancestors.

Idaho and regional libraries, librarians and historical societies aided me at many times beyond the call of duty; especially, the Special Collections staff, past and present, at the University of Idaho—Terry Abraham, Dick Davis, and Judy Nielson, in particular. Lillian Heytvelt of the Deny Ashby Memorial Library, Pomeroy, Washington, helped with research assistance and endless inter-library loans,

Dennis Gillis of Pomeroy High School, Pomeroy, Washington, nursed my computer through its illnesses and my technical limitations. Dr. Elizabeth Hess helped with photography and Dr. William Swagerty gave research advice and encouragement. Dr. John Sullivan, foreign language professor emeritus of the University of Idaho, helped with German translations. My Grandson, Corey Robbins, accompanied me on research trips. Mr. Rich Lenhard of Wentzville, Missouri, came up with a Lemp beer bottle for my collection, and indirectly to illustrate the text. He gets a big thanks.

My long-time friend, Dr. Carol Lynn MacGregor, expert on Boise history, did an enormous amount of editing on the manuscript. If it is at all readable give her the credit, if it is not, blame me.

If I've left any one out, I apologize.

Prosit, my friends! I could not have finished without you.

TABLE OF CONTENTS

Foreword vii
Acknowledgments xi
Illustrations xvii
Lemp Family Charts xxi
Introduction xxv

Part I

1838 to 1890. 3
Lemp's Early Life 5
1865 10
1866 13
1867 13
1868 14
John and Catherine. 15
Lemp The Lodge Brother 16
1869 18
The 1870's 20
1871 27
1872 29
1873 30
1874 32
1875 34
The South Mountain Brewery. 35
Boise Mayor John Lemp 37

1876 37
1877 40
1878 44
1879 47
Education in Boise 48
Non-Education Matters 51
1880 53
1881 56
1882 61
A Railroad for Boise? 63
Back to Other Business 1883 69
1884 70
An Aside about George Leyerzaph 73
1885 76
1886 78
Lemp's Canals, ... 80
20 years of irrigation leadership 80
1887 84
1888 89
1889 92
End Notes 96

Part II

1890 to 1900 119
The Bitter Election of 1891 125
1892 131
The Star Mine, Hailey, Idaho 134
Other Business, 1892 138
The Lemp-Pence War 140
Back to Non-War Matters 142
The Samuel Adolph Family of Salem, Oregon 147
Back to Boise 149
The Lemp-Pence War: Round Two 150
Other Business 151
The Death of John Emil Lemp 155
Richards, Gordon et al vs. John Lemp and W.B. Connor 166
Other Business 168

1899	170
End Notes	179

PART III

1901 to 1912	197
The Lemp Dry Goods Store	201
Back to 1901	205
1902	209
Gibbard vs. Lemp	209
1903	215
The Slow, Painful, Unlamented Death of the Lemp Brewery	217
1903	227
1904	228
1905	234
The Lemp Triangle	243
1906	247
1907	251
The Death of Catherine Lemp	255
Lemp Park	260
1908	261
1909	261
1910	264
1911	268
Polo	271
1911	273
1912	273
The Death of John Lemp	275
End Notes	279
The Legacy of John Lemp	297
John Lemp's Place Among Idaho's Brewers	297
Edward H. Lemp	300
Augusta Julia Margaret Lemp Grant	301
Herbert Frederick Lemp	301
Daughter-in-Law Marguerite Ann Nolan (Mrs. Herbert) Lemp	313
Granddaughter Mary Catherine Lemp	313
John Frederick Lemp (Son of Emil)	314
Louise Bernice Lemp Simonson	314

Martha Elizabeth Lemp Conner............... 314
Albert C. Lemp........................ 315
Bernard Louis Lemp..................... 315
Leona Marie Lemp...................... 316
Ada Anna Lemp Hurt.................... 316
Colonel John Lemp...................... 317
Lemp Brewery of St. Louis................. 319
End Notes........................... 320

Appendices

Appendix I........................... 323
John Lemp's Will....................... 323
Appendix II........................... 325
Lemp's Positions of Trust
A. Lemps Service as a Business Trustee, Director, or Officer, Etc. 325
B. Public Committees.................... 327
C. Political Delegate and Committee Member......... 327
D. Jury Duty.......................... 328
E. Court Cases of Any Type................. 328
F. Lodge Offices and Activities................ 330
G. Political Offices...................... 331
H. Community Involvement................. 331
I. Charity Work and Donations............... 332
J. Religious Affiliations of Lemp Family Members...... 332
K. Mines and Mining Claims Owned by Lemp........ 333
L. Other Brewers Who Were Affiliated with John Lemp... 334
M. John Lemp's Minor Real Estate Transactions....... 334
End Notes........................... 336

Bibliographical Comment.................... 339

Referrences.......................... 340
I. Books, periodicals, interviews, letters to the author, bylined newspaper articles, cd-roms, maps, dissertations and historical files . 340
II Newspapers......................... 344
III. Manuscript Material................... 345
IV. Internet Sites....................... 346

Illustrations

John Lemp as a young man 4
Future Montana Senator William A. Clark 7
Monument marking the approximate site of the original fur
    trade post of Fort Boise. 9
Advertisement placed in the Statesman when the partners
    went separate ways. 11
A newspaper ad for the bank partially owned by the
    beer-loving Ridgeby Greathouse. 12
Catherine Kohlepp Lemp 15
Lemp was immediately involved in the operation of the Odd
    Fellows lodge, as his committee work attests.. 17
John Emil Lemp 19
These were among the first newspaper ads placed by the new
    Turnverein. Everyone, including non-Germans were invited.
    Lemp's name was listed on both of these 20
Ads for Lemp and Misseldt were adjacent, in the same
    column of the newspaper 21
George William Jacob Lemp. 22
Julia (Jennie) Lemp Leyerzapf, Sister of John Lemp 23
Margarethe Lemp Bach, Sister of John Lemp. 25
Jacob Lemp, John's brother as a young man. 26
Martha Elizabeth Lemp, Sister of John Lemp 31
George, Martha and John, children of John and Catherine Lemp 33
Augusta Julia Margaret Lemp 38

Ida Catherine Lemp and Ada Anna Lemp, the first
   twins born in Boise 39
The Lemp home as depicted in Elliot's History of
   Idaho Territory, 1884.. 41
Photo of the Lemp home with family members
   identified by name. 43
Albert Carl Lemp 47
William Adam Lemp, Tombstone in Pioneer Cemetery 64
Lemp liquor store, as shown in Elliot's History of Idaho
   Territory, 1884. 71
Herbert Frederick Lemp 75
Bernard Louis Lemp 85
Louise Bernice Lemp 87
William Brower Conner 91
Marie Anna Lemp. Thirteenth child of John and Cathrine . . . 131
Plat of the Lemp addition to Boise. 152
The revolver owned by John Emil Lemp. 157
The Samuel Adolph home, Salem Oregon,
   in the early 21st Century.. 159
1893 fire insurance map showed the Capitol Hotel. 160
Lemp's brewery as it was on the fire insurance map
   of Boise in 1893. 162
Lemp advertised the Wiener beer of San Francisco
   that he sold in his saloon. 165
Ida Catherine Lemp 199
Typical newspaper ad for Lemp's Dry Goods store. 200
Newspaper ad for Lemp's Dry Goods store. 203
Lemp brewery as it appeared on the fire insurance map of 1903. 222
Newspaper photo that was published after the fire. 226
A group portrait of Boise Pioneers 237
Section of fire insurance map showing the Lemp Triangle. . . . 245
Louise Lemp. 249
Site where the Lemp brewery had previously stood.. 274
Lemp Lane road sign 277
emp family plot in Pioneer Cemetery. 278
Lemp Street remains a part of Boise. 298
Letterhead of the St. Louis Lemp Brewing Company. 299

Six descendants of John Lemp, all named John Lemp 300
Undated resume for Herbert F. Lemp 302
Newspaper Ad for the loans Lemp offered 306
Herbert Lemp on his favorite polo pony, Scrambled Eggs,
    on the steps of the Idaho State Capitol building 307
Newspaper mentioning Herbert's accident. 311
Edna and Marie Lemp, daughters of Bernard and
    Leona Tucker Lemp. 317
Grave marker for Mary Catherine Lemp 318

LEMP FAMILY CHARTS

1. Ancestors and siblings of John Lemp

John Jacob Lemp (?-1850)
Anna Elizabeth Jung (1813—19 January 1899)
John (12 April 1838—18 July 1912)
Johann Adam Lemp (?)
Julia Lemp (September 1844—1922)
Margarethe (4 May 1848—31 January 1926)
Martha Elizabeth (28 May 1849—1929)
Jacob (1850—5 December 1896)

2. Ancestors and Siblings of Catherine Kohlepp

William Kohlepp (21 May 1813—21 May 1869)
Martha E. ???? (7 March 1813—7 February 1881)
George William (1848—4 May 1923)
Henry J. (1844—???)
Mattie (???)
William (??—1870)
Mary (ca 1842—17 September 1893)
Catherine (20 Nov 1850—10 Jan 1908)

3. Children of John Lemp and Catherine Kohlepp Lemp

John Lemp (12 April 1838—18 July 1912)
Catherine Kohlepp (20 Nov 1850—10 Jan 1908)
John Emil (30 December 1866—March 1895)
George William Jacob (16 December 1868—1 January 1900)
Martha Elizabeth (11 September 1870—23 September 1928)
Augusta Julia Margaret (1 August 1872—10 May 1926)
Ida Catherine (11 October 1874—7 July 1904)
Ada Anna (11 October 1874—8 June 1959)
Albert Carl (7 February 1877—28 March 1937)
William Adam (10 August 1879—28 July 1881)
Edward Henry (31 October 1881—6 September 1912)
Herbert Frederick (24 June 1884—6 May 1927)
Bernard Louis (8 November 1886—July 1950)
Louise Bernice (24 October 1888—3 November 1966)
Marie Anna (5 March 1892—6 January 1896)

4. Descendants of John Lemp and Cathererine Kohlepp—their grandchildren (Five of the Lemp children had children of their own for a total of ten grandchildren for John and Catherine)

John Emil Lemp (30 Dec 1866—Mar 1895)
Caroline Zeitmann (4 Jun 1869—13 Dec 1954)
John Frederick Lemp (21 Feb 1894—16 Jul 1977)

Albert Carl Lemp (7 February 1877—28 March 1937)
Lucille L. Weaver
Katherine Ida Lemp (9 Apr 1902—??)

Herbert Frederick Lemp (24 June 1884—6 May1927)
Marguerite Ann Nolan (14 Feb 1882—8 Jul 1967)
John Frederick (19 Feb 1907—Oct 1974)
Mary Catherine (13 Apr 1908—7 Aug 1969)

Bernard Louis Lemp (8 November 1886—July 1950)
Leona Caroline Tucker (2 Apr 1884—2 Mar 1932)
Bernard Louis, Jr. (6 Apr 1910—7 Nov 1986)
George Tucker (26 Nov 1915—?????)
Leona Marie (20 Mar 1920—26 Mar 1976)
Edna (20 Mar 1920—24 Jan 1970)

Louise Bernice Lemp (24 October1888—3 November 1966)
Marshall Cantine Simonson (17 Oct 1882—12 Feb 1966)
Marshall Lemp Simonson (6 Oct 1912—16 Jun 1988)
Louise Bernice Simonson (26 Jan 1915—???)

INTRODUCTION

Dionysus brought wine to the Greeks; Johnny Appleseed spread apple cider production into the old Northwest territory of America; and a multitude of German brewers brought lager beer to the far western frontier of the United States. Politically, philosophically, and militarily Germany tried to conquer the world twice in the twentieth century. The military attempts were a failure. In the nineteenth century, however, German lager beer had already conquered the world. From Mexico to Singapore to Boise, Idaho, "beer" meant lagerbier brewed with a special yeast in a process evolved in Germany. The concept, the technology, and the skilled labor behind the beer came from Germany.

Tell me what a man drinks and I will tell you, at a metaphysical level, who he is. If a beer lacks character, it was because the brewer had none; if your beer is the finest product of the brewers' art, the man who brewed it was the among the finest products of the human condition. Here is the story of one extraordinary brewer among thousands of ordinary ones.

John Lemp was the most successful brewer in the history of Idaho but, as befits a business leader of the Gem state, he cut a multitude of other facets into his personal and professional identity. As an early Idaho businessmen, his story gives insights into the early development of the state and, particularly, of Boise. His biography could be interpreted as fitting into the literature of various individual businessmen in the West. Most of the West's brewers were, like Lemp, of German ancestry. From that view point Lemp can be studied as an example of his ethnic group. As a brewer, Lemp can be lumped with liquor manufacturers and sellers of all types and these can be considered a separate, perhaps even disrespectable, group within society. I am unable to find a study of any American brewer that does not emphasize liquor control, politics, and prohibition. These are strong themes in Lemp's life too. Lemp had magnanimous personal traits no fair person could do anything but laud, but he also had a hard-edged side that never shied from conflict.

The association of the name Lemp with beer was very strong in the nineteenth century West, but this was due to the large amount of beer shipped from the Lemp Brewery of St. Louis, not the small amount brewed in Boise. Nevertheless, the association was noteworthy.

Most of the information about Lemp is from the newspapers of the era. Nearly all Idaho towns had newspapers from their earliest days and they covered the most minute comings and goings in some cases. The Boise Statesman began publication soon after Lemp arrived in town. Many other Boise newspapers came and went, and Lemp was mentioned in dozens of other papers in Idaho, particularly when he visited their localities. Indexes to Idaho newspapers are limited. I gathered this material by uncountable days and nights scanning faint, poorly focused, old microfilmed newspapers. There is a great deal of genealogical information available on the internet. U. S. Census records, state court cases, and county judicial records are vital. No letters, diaries, business records or other such private sources have come to light. There are some Idaho historical documents on the internet that particularly pertain to Lemp's life and career. With many prominent men, the biographer's job is to sort through the overwhelming amount of information to reach a synthesis. However, the search for sufficient details of Lemp's life was the central research issue in this instance.

The U.S. Census surveyed Idaho several times in the 1860s, and of course there were the regular enumerations for each decade. As of this writing, 1930 is the most recent Census available. Census material in the text has the source mentioned. I believe footnoting it would be pedantic. Some of these are indexed by specialized companies, which is of great help. Lemp and family were on the 1860, 1870, 1880, 1890, 1900, and 1910 enumerations. His descendants and relatives were on the 1920 and 1930 censuses. There are also indexes of marriage records, death records, cemetery records, etc., which makes such information more available than ever before. There are many books on Idaho history or local history that mention Lemp and other brewers. Early histories of the state often had many biographical sketches appended which are helpful. These short biographies tend to be all very positive due to the fact that most subjects had to pay or buy a certain number of copies of the book to be listed. John Lemp had many such biographies and similar sketches in newspaper special editions. Professional brewing journals and books cover Idaho as they cover every other state and emphasize business events relative to Lemp's life. Lemp was involved in a vast number of court cases, the records of which tell a great deal about his life, business dealings, and even his personal philosophies. I have attempted to cover his extended family and genealogy as much as possible. In particular, events in the lives of Lemp's relatives that could not avoid affecting him are discussed.

I originally wrote *Beer and Brewing in the Inland Northwest* (University of Idaho Press, 1993) as a history of an industry, with a small amount of biographical information on Idaho's brewers as a whole. The possibilities of recovering and evaluating detailed life stories of some of the brewers was obvious. I have been working on a collective biography of these many individuals for over a decade. As that work has neared completion, I have more than three times as much information available on Lemp than on any other individual Idaho brewer. This was true simply because he had invested in so many businesses, made so much money, joined so many fraternal lodges, took an active part in so many events, and fathered so many children. His life story could and should stand alone.

My many friends who have heard me tell and retell these biographical stories for a decade or more know that I often refer to Lemp and other individuals as "my brewers ." Forgive the Schmaltz ; I apologize, but I have earned the right. A friend once asked me why I did not just find these people's relatives and ask them what I needed to know and save myself so many countless hours of research. Today, I know more about their mundane daily activities than anyone's family remembers. I have recovered the brewers' day-to day trials and tribulations as well as enough of the large picture to allow generalizations. John Lemp, brewer, millionaire, and kingpin of early Boise, deserves to be remembered and understood.

Herman Ronnenberg
Troy, Idaho

John Lemp • The Beer Baron of Boise
Millionaire Brewer of Frontier Idaho

Part I

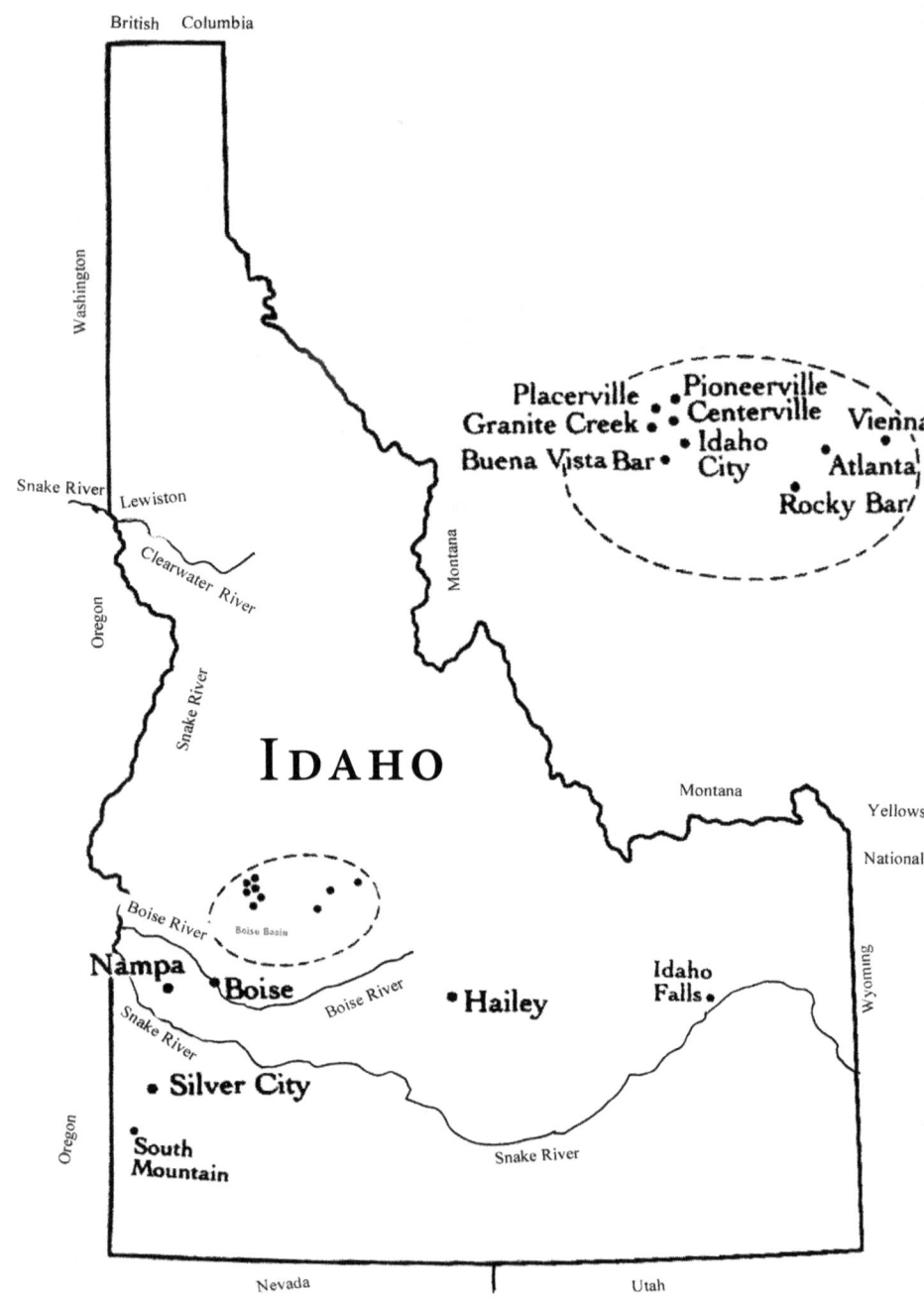

1838 to 1890

MANY AMERICAN IMMIGRANTS with dreams of building a fortune have sought to make that dream come true by quenching the thirsts of other men. If Rumpelstiltskin could spin straw into gold, a brewer could ferment malted barley into a golden-colored elixir that would magically endow its creator with golden wealth. The dream was heady and its realization difficult. Many failed. The few successful ones became rich, powerful, and famous; these became legends of American enterprise; Beer Barons. Adolphus Busch followed this plan in St. Louis and became the greatest brewer of all; Adolph Coors of Colorado was the most successful brewer in the Rocky Mountains; Frederick Pabst and Joseph Schlitz both made Milwaukee famous; Theodore Hamm was a city patron of St. Paul; and Henry Weinhard was a pillar of Portland; each a brewing entrepreneur, all wealthy, socially and politically powerful Nineteenth Century American businessmen. Each of these men was born in a Germanic area of Europe but instrumental in the development of the American city where he immigrated and made a fortune in the brewing business.

Idaho also had its nineteenth century brewing magnate; John Lemp. Lemp did not become a national figure but he was certainly the kingpin, or beer king, of early Boise. As with the other great brewing entrepreneurs, Lemp began in brewing but spread his financial interests far and wide. He had greater involvement in more Idaho businesses, and broader interaction with more Idaho citizens, than any of his contemporaries. He was a major, yet unrecognized,

Lemp as a young man. Photo from Idaho Daily Statesman, 15 November 1908, Section II, P. 5.

figure in the history of the American West. John Lemp was the Beer Baron of Boise.

If one were to write a history of Idaho banking, as has been done, Lemp would figure prominently in the story; a history of Idaho canal building must include a big chapter on Lemp's contributions; a history of beer brewing in the state, necessarily includes much of Lemp's life story; likewise, any projected histories of mines, land development or subdivisions, hotels, horse racing, retailing, cattle ranching, fraternal organizations, especially the Odd Fellows, would have to include major sections on Lemp's contributions. Lemp's enterprises, philosophies, and business practices molded early Idaho, and his imprint remains on the state's foundations.[a] Here is the life of John Lemp in all its hectic, multi-faceted detail.

In 1852, a wide-eyed German lad of fourteen went through the maze of the New York immigration facility. His father had been dead for two years and he had decided that there was no opportunity for him in his village of Niederweisel. The liberal revolutions of 1848 had failed. Central Europe had fallen into an era of ever-increasing rigidity and undemocratic authoritarianism. Young Lemp burned with an inner determination to escape the confines of the Old World and seek his fortune far from the Hesse-Darmstadt area of his boyhood. He vowed to subdue this new land despite its strange customs, and unfamiliar tongue.[b] The large number of German refugees arriving in America in the late 1840s and early 1850's have been called the "Forty-Eighters," or the "Refugees of Revolution." Thousands came to America, quite a few of these continued to Idaho, but only one, John Lemp, was considered the wealthiest man in Idaho just thirty years later.

Lemp's financial triumphs paralleled and reflected the opportunities for wealth and status the Idaho frontier offered. His success also demonstrated what a German immigrant could accomplish in a new homeland. Lemp never found a major gold strike, never received a government subsidy, and never relied on luck. Instead he applied hard work, a solid business sense, and a full measure of the toughness the new land required of its would-be tamers. He built a small empire and the corner stone of his empire—a corner stone that endured forty-five years—was his brewery on Main Street in Boise. The wealth Lemp built went beyond money. He had a wealth of family, a wealth of lodge brothers, a wealth of business associates, and a wealth of political influence.

LEMP'S EARLY LIFE

John was born at Niederweisel, in the principality or grand dukedom of Hesse-Darmstadt (later part of the German Empire) on 21 April 1838.[c] This village was near the city of Frankfurt am Main. Niederweisel survived the thirty Years War to emerge with a debt of 26,000 florins.[d] A 1643 list of the 139 taxpayers liable for this debt has "Lemp" among the 61 family names included. A Mr. Hanns Jung, a member of John's maternal lineage, was also a prominent individual about this time. Beer brewing became important enough in the village in the decades to come that a cooperage was established to make the beer barrels. A list of town residents for the period of the early 19th century had thirty-six families named Jung and nine named Lemp. John Lemp's ancestors were in this village for at least several centuries before he was born.

Our future Idaho capitalist was the son of John Jacob and Anna Elizabeth (Jung) Lemp. His siblings were Jacob, Johann Adam, Julia, Martha Elizabeth, and Margarethe. John was educated in his native village and confirmed as a member of the Lutheran church in 1850.[e] Two years later, John somehow procured a German passport without serving the required time in the army. He was off to America.

The records of the immigrants leaving Nieder in the 18th century list Elisabetha Lemp (1841-1875), Johann Konrad Lemp (1833-1889), Maria Elisabetha (1834-1923), and Susanna Lemp (1839-1917). There was also an Anna Elisabetha Jung (1807-1875), and fourteen other individuals with that same sir name who left the village. Their exact familial relationship to John is problematic, but they were extended family.

Future St. Louis brewer Johann Adam Lemp, born 1798 in Eschwege, arrived in America in 1836, two years before John was born.[f] These two Lemp families were both branches from one older trunk. In America they kept loose contact with each other. J. Adam Lemp owned a business in St. Louis by 1838, and was on his way to owning one of the largest breweries in America.

Through contacts in the German-American community—for John Lemp remained loyal to his homeland and fellow Germans throughout his life—young Lemp, shortly after arriving in America, went from the port of New York to Louisville, Kentucky. Louisville had a substantial community of people from the Fatherland and the young boy was aided in getting a clerking position in a leading store of the city. The seven years he clerked in Louisville must have given him training in business matters to replace the formal education he was never able to acquire. He also mastered the English language.

Lemp had little to say about his experiences in Louisville. The numerous sketches of his life that appeared in print usually give only passing mention. By 1855 about 30 percent of the citizens of Louisville were Germans.[g] By 1859 sixteen of Louisville's seventeen breweries were run by Germans (including Swiss and Alsatians). Life was not necessarily easy for a German there during that decade. In August 1855 mobs of Know Nothings attacked Irish and German neighborhoods, burned one brewery and tried to burn another. At last twenty-four and maybe as many as 200 died in the violence. John Lemp was in his formative teenage years at this time. Perhaps very painful memories of Louisville were what caused him to never volunteer any reflections on his time there.

A vigorous adult of twenty-one, John heard the cry of "go west young man." Tales promising another California lured him to the Colorado gold rush of 1859.[h] He prospected and mined there but without success. His informal education kept pace though, as he realized that only lucky miners got rich, but astute businessmen made their own luck. The U. S. Census of 1860 found him at South Park, Arapaho County, Kansas [Colorado had not yet been officially formed] on the 14th of July. He was listed as a miner with $200 in personal estate and from Kentucky.

Margarethe Lemp, 23, accompanied by Johannes Lemp, 12, arrived in New York that same year of 1859 from the port of Bremen, Germany.[i] Her residence was listed as Frais (sic). These were probably relatives. On 23 August 1862, Adam Lemp, the man who first brought lager beer to St. Louis and possibly to America, died. His son William Lemp took full control of the Western Brewery in that great Missouri City. John Lemp was aware of the development of the brewery owned by his distant cousins.

Colorado was not the El Dorado John Lemp sought, so when a new gold rush to the Idaho/Montana area ignited in 1863, he headed farther west. John led a team of oxen that pulled his worldly possessions, and he joined a group of other gold seekers. Later in life Lemp remembered this trek well and all the historical sketches of his life record the journey, but offer scarce details. The party heading for Montana included William A. Clark, who later became Senator Clark of Montana and one of the wealthiest men in America.[j] Also with the group was W. C. Tatro who settled at Boise, and, like Lemp, became prominent in local business for decades to come.[k]

Clark once told the story of their trek in great detail and his biographer recorded the tale. Clark was working at Bob Tail Hill in Colorado when he heard tales from prospectors returning form the northwest. One day, Jack Reynolds arrived in Blackhawk, a town nearby, having ridden all the way from Montana, and he told of the great strike on Grasshopper Creek, near the new town of Bannack. Clark resolved to go and his companions at Bob Tail decided to join him. "All of us were imbued with the same ambition, to endeavor to better our condition in the world if possible."[l] On May 4, the party set out

Future Montana Senator William A. Clark

with a light Schuttler wagon loaded with food, picks, shovels and gold pans and drawn by two yoke of oxen that could be sold for food after they arrived in Montana. Seven hundred miles of wilderness stretched before them as they followed the Cherokee Trail. If they escaped the Arapahoe and Cheyenne, they still had to deal with swollen streams and challenging mountain passes. The usual route west from Colorado was to head north out of the Denver area, then go west and cross the Rockies at Bridger Pass, just south of the usual Oregon trail route through South Pass, and then intersect the main California/Oregon trail at Fort Bridger.

At Fort Bridger they were warned not to go further alone due to Indian danger. They waited for other travelers until a party of twenty-five wagons had been formed. This strong group saw Indians but was never attacked. The fresh graves they encountered along the trail made them believe the wagons that preceded them had experienced trouble. At Fort Hall on the Snake River, which would one day be eastern Idaho, the party heard of the rich discoveries in Boise Basin.

The group split at this point, with Clark's and three other wagons going north to Bannack, Montana, and Lemp and his group continuing west to "West Branch," soon to be renamed Boise, Idaho.[m] Clark's group was near the Continental Divide, site of present day Lima above Monide Pass, on the Fourth of July and they celebrated Independence and their two month journey with a "small keg of pretty good Old Rye whiskey." Four days later, July 8th, they entered Bannack.

Lemp's group went on toward Fort Boise, which had been established on the Snake River some distance from the modern city of that name back in 1834 as a fur trading center that, a decade or so later, became an important stop on the Oregon Trail. The fort itself was closed in 1855. A Mr. Jeff Thompson had allegedly built the first house in the Boise valley a number of miles away from the old fort site in the Fall of 1861 and the settlement of the new area had begun.[n] Abraham Lincoln signed an act of Congress on March 4, 1863 creating the Territory of Idaho. Lemp reached Boise on July 8, 1863, four days after Major Pinkney Lugenbeel of the United States engineer corps located the site on which to build Boise barracks, a military fort that would endure for decades.[o]

Back east, in a little-known town of Gettysburg, Pennsylvania,

Confederate General Robert E. Lee had been defeated. Never again would the South invade the North and the eventual outcome of the Civil War now seemed determined. Two days after Lemp's arrival in Boise, on July 10, far to the north in Lewiston, the new territory of Idaho was organized. Lemp's arrival was also just one day after Idaho's—or at least Boise's— founding fathers had met in a log cabin to plat the future capital city.p Lemp was in Idaho almost early enough to witness its birth.

William Clark said he arrived in Bannack with just $5.00 in "Bob Tail" dust. This was an amalgam made in the mills of Colorado and was the sole currency in circulation in that area. One can speculate that Lemp was not measurably better off financially.

Boise was a tiny frontier settlement then with only a post office, a few stores and a few simple houses but this was the embryo for its future as a supply center to the mining areas, a seat of territorial government, and the largest city in the state. While the Civil War raged in the far off East, the army post was constructed as planned. From this site Idaho's gold shipments, which were financing the Civil War, could be protected; the settlers could be protected from the Indians; and no coup with southern sympathies could threaten northern sovereignty in the territory. That summer of 1863 Boise replaced Lewiston and became the second Capital of the Idaho Territory. The city named for the French word for trees officially became the permanent state capital on 24 December 1864.

Early Boise had at least two very small breweries which can be seen

This monument marks the approximate site of the original fur trade post of Fort Boise. This is near the Snake River, a number of miles from the modern city of Boise.
Photo by author, June, 2006

on the oldest known photo of the settlement dated 1863 and on the oldest known painting of the city from about the same time.[q]

John Lemp could not be content until he had seen the mining camps and tried his luck with prospecting, so he set out for Idaho City—forty or so miles away in the high Boise Basin—which was booming and on its way to the temporary distinction of being the largest city in the Pacific Northwest. John Lemp stayed nearly a year, surveyed the situation there, earned some gold, and then made a momentous personal decision. He was not addicted to the wanderlust and the boom and bust financial cycle of the mining camps; it was stability he craved—stability he had not enjoyed since he was 12. Boise, not Idaho City, would be his new home. When Lemp eventually died he had been a continuous Boise resident longer than any other person.

Lemp came down from the mountains and went to work at Felix Collins' Boise Brewery for a month before buying it on 5 September 1864.[r] This was Lemp's first business activity in Boise, and he paid Collins with a now-legendary tea cup full of gold dust.[s] The brewery was small but adequately equipped. Lemp's brewing capacity at first was two barrels—62 gallons—per day.[t] Whatever his other business fortunes and ventures were from time to time, Herr brewer Lemp stayed firmly in the brewery business with his plant on Main Street between Third and Fourth until 1907. It was a steadfast fixture among the transient businesses in the early days of Boise.

1865

Lemp briefly took a business partner, Samuel Adolph, during the early years. Adolph's future wife and Lemp's future wife were both daughters of the William Kohlepp family which came to Boise from Iowa. Adolph had also been a partner with Boise brewer John Krall after Krall and Thomas Paulson had dissolved their partnership in August of 1864.[u] On the Federal Tax Records of May 1865, Lemp & Co. paid their fermented liquor license fee; in June 1865 the brewed 9 1/2 barrels; in July and August 1865 Lemp and Co. brewed 16 barrels at Boise City; in Sept 1865, Lemp and Co. paid Federal Tax; in October 1865, Lemp & Co. brewed 6 barrels; in November 1865 they paid on 6 barrels of beer, and in December 1865 Lemp & Co. paid tax on 6 1/2 barrels of beer brewed.[v] There is also a listing for Lemp,

Krall & Co. brewers in Boise City in June 1865.ʷ Krall was a pioneer brewer but this is the only reference ever found to the two of them being in business together. In March 1866, Lemp and Co. paid tax on five barrels brewed that month, and in May 1866 the partners paid for their fermented liquor license. On another page they paid their brewers' license and retail liquor license; in June 1866 Lemp and Adolph at Boise paid tax on twelve barrels of beer.ˣ On the records for September, 1866, they paid for 15 barrels of beer; in October 1866 Lemp and Adolph paid tax for brewing 16 1/2 barrels of beer.ʸ These seem like small quantities of beer but they were similar to the other breweries of the territory.

In 1866, after his marriage, Adolph moved on to Salem, Oregon, and remained a successful brewer there for nearly three decades. Lemp and Adolph announced their dissolution of partnership on 22 October 1866 with Lemp to receive all accounts due.ᶻ

In 1866, back east in St. Louis, Missouri, the gateway to the West, William J. Lemp built a large new brewery that year located over the natural limestone caves his father had first used for lagering (aging) his beer in cold storage. John Lemp may well have known of these development and been inspired to emulate them. Brewing could be an avenue to success.

The young city of Boise was deep in the lawless, negative rebellion of its political and cultural youth during the 1860s. Minimal law enforcement and legal institutions made for a general attitude of reliance on self, not government. "Roughs," who had probably come

The advertisement place in the Statesman when the partners went separate ways.

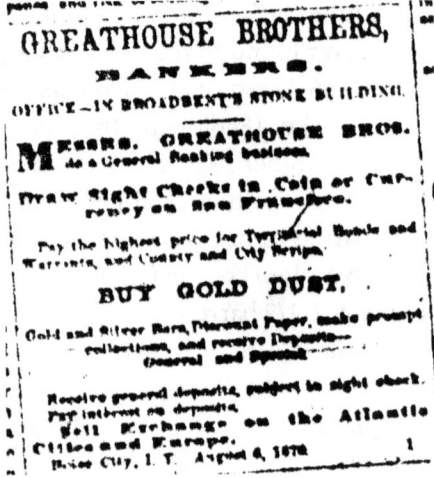

A newspaper ad for the bank partially owned by the beer-loving Ridgeby Greathouse.

West to avoid honest labor, lived by theft and bullying and, sometimes, by gaining political office. Honest men banded together for protection. Dave Updyke, Boise livery stable owner, managed to get elected sheriff of Ada County. Many believed he was involved in an informal conspiracy with the outlaw forces. He was forced to resign when money under his control disappeared. In April of 1865, Updyke and his chief henchman Jake Dixon were hanged by vigilantes near the gold camp of Rocky Bar.[aa] W. H. Bush in 1910 told the tale that the vigilance committee that lynched sheriff Updyke in the early days of Boise had "a man named Collins," among the seven. This may well have been the brewery owner from whom Lemp purchased his business.[ab]

The sign left on Dixon's corpse said "Horse thief, counterfeiter and road agent generally. A dupe and tool of Dave Updyke. Updyke's sign read: "Accessory after the fact to the Port Neuf stage robbery. Accessory and accomplice to the robbery of the stage near Boise City in 1864. Chief conspirator in burning property of the Overland stage line. Guilty of aiding and assisting West Jenkins, the murderer to escape, while you were sheriff of Ada County. Accessory and accomplice to the murder of Raymond. Threatening the lives and property of an already outraged and suffering community. Justice has overtaken you."[ac] Not everyone was an opponent of Updyke. The editor of the Capital Chronicle in March of 1870 called the vigilantes "a murdering, thieving set of highwaymen."[ad] A portion of the tension in the early days was a reflection of the North vs. South tension in the war raging in the killing fields of the East.

1866

Even discounting the dangers of outlaws, life as a brewer still did not start smoothly for John Lemp. On 1 August 1866, less than two years into his new career, a lumber mill caught fire in central Boise. According to the Statesman, two hundred men fought the fire for an hour and saved the mill office, the saw logs, and the adjacent brewery of Adolph and Lemp, but only after the brewery's "front end was pretty much burned out."[ae] Repairs were made and the beer-making business resumed.

Another completely different problem with the brewing business came up at this time. Questions about how to handle the actual mechanics of the beer tax were settled with the rule that a stamp had to be attached to the spigot on every barrel removed from a brewery, effective September 1, 1866.[af] National rules applied even to distant Idaho, and Lemp would have been affixing tax stamps at that time.

During those very early days in business Lemp had high costs and small profits and counted his money closely. One Ridgeby Greathouse and his brother started a bank just a few doors from the brewery. Ridgeby came in often to quench his noteworthy thirst. Instead of paying the standard two-bits per large glass he always paid with two dimes. In frontier parlance this was a short two-bits, and acceptable in payment. Greathouse, however, did it every time instead of once in a while. Lemp was losing a nickel on every beer but he "put on a good face and dished up the beer as if he were making a clean profit on every drink."[ag] Ridgeby drank so much under-priced beer that Lemp thought him intent on bankrupting the brewery. After a year or two the bank closed, and the banker with his thirst moved elsewhere.[ah] Two decades later Lemp said that he often reflected about the narrow escape from financial disaster he had endured at the hands and lips Mr. Greathouse.

1867

A new rival in the brewing business opened its doors in 1867. John Fortman and George Gurting rented the City Brewery and "intend to sustain its former reputation by furnishing the best Lager Beer to the citizens of Boise City and vicinity that is made in Idaho Territory. We use pure water, the best material, and employ European brewerymen to do our work."[ai] These gentlemen placed the first advertisement for a brewery ever to appear in the Statesman, and also wanted to buy clean brewing barley.

The year after his brewery purchase, Lemp erected an "extensive" brewery on the site. The concept of reinvestment of profits was a mainstay in the philosophy that led to the Lemp fortune. Four years later the Tri-Weekly Statesman glowed with praise over a cellar that Professor James Hurd had just built for the Lemp brewery.[aj] It was 16 by 42 feet with an arch of "11 feet in the clear" of native stone from the bluffs east of town and "superior to anything of its kind in the territory." The term "cellar" was applied to above ground storage buildings as well as underground structures in those days.

1868

Also in 1868, from August to December, Lemp had a new partner, Peter Stuzenacker. Their ads said "Lemp and Stuzenacker, Main St. opposite the Overland House, Boise Brewery and Saloon/ . . .lager beer."[ak] Stutzenacher was on the Boise City Common Council after the elections of 6 January 1868.[al] In December, there was a dissolution of partnership notice as Lemp bought the interest of his partner.[am] They advertised for all outstanding accounts to settle up at that time. All else I know of Peter is that in 1869 he filed for divorce against his wife Elizabeth charging "natural impotency" existed at the time of the marriage.[an] They had been married on the 13th of December 1868 about the time his career as brewery owner ended. Sol Hasbrouck, Clerk of the District Court, published a summons for Elizabeth in several local newspapers.[ao]

In 1868 there were still five breweries in Boise, according to the town census in the Statesman.[ap] By frontier standards these breweries were large businesses but compared to modern beer plants, they seem absurdly small. Idaho's beer production totals were available in 1866 for the first time when the territory brewed 1,679 barrels. A barrel was 31 gallons. In 1868 production reached a temporary record with 2,347 barrels. Production fell statewide for the next 14 years and was at only 1,926 barrels in 1880.[aq] By 1882 it was back in true growth territory with 2,747 barrels. Government tax records indicate Lemp sold 329 barrels of beer sold in 1878 and 492 in 1879, totals just ahead of the second largest Idaho brewery in Lewiston.[ar] A decade before this, before placer mining played out, sales may have differed significantly. Idaho's population actually dropped in the 1870s and beer sales may have been higher in the late 1860s.

Though brewing was a source of steady cash flow, it was inadequate to be a sole source of income. Lemp had to reach out into other ventures. Another large Boise brewery of this time was run by John Krall who took on newcomer Joseph Misseldt, lately of California, as a partner in 1868.[as] Misseldt became a friend, as well as a rival, to Lemp. Another of these rivals was the Central Brewery and Bakery of Ford and Co. Other brewers have escaped the historical record.

The 1868 Revenue Act required wholesale liquor dealers, and brewers who sold from their warehouses to pay a $100 special tax.[at] The government continued to tax the working man's drink, though indirectly in this case.

JOHN AND CATHERINE

Soon after arrival in Boise, Lemp branched out into other non-business activities. Behind every successful man stands a woman, the saying goes, and John Lemp married a stalwart German girl perfectly suited for him. Catherine Kohlepp was born in Marburg, Hesse-Cassel, Germany, but raised in Muscatine, Iowa.[au] New York Passenger Lists Records indicate the family arrived on 14 September 1854 on the Northumberland out of London having originated in Germany. Her father William brought the whole family to America when Catherine was only four. In 1864, at the age of fourteen, she started across the plains with her family to the Northwest. William and his wife Martha, both 51 years old, daughters Catherine (Kate) and Mary, probably son George and others

Catherine Kohlepp Lemp
20 November 1850 to 7 January 1908
Photo, Idaho State Historical Society

came West, while one or more older children remained in Iowa. This immigrant party brought a herd of cattle that they were afraid would prove too attractive to Indians.[av] Their fears increased because the wagons preceding them had allegedly been attacked. The unnamed previous wagon train being attacked seems to be an element in an excessively high number of frontier legends. Young Kate was not easily frightened and secured friendship with the Indians along the trail by inviting them to eat, and particularly by sharing with them her prize biscuits.

The Kohlepp family safely made their journey to Boise where Catherine soon caught John's eye. They were married on the 6th of May 1866, six months before the bride's 16th birthday.[aw] John was mature enough to cross the Atlantic Ocean at 14, and Catherine was mature enough to cross the Great Plains and begin married life at 15. Their first child, John Emil, was born 30 December 1866—the first of no less than 13 children born to this union.

Lemp The Lodge Brother

Beside having a family, a successful man of that era needed memberships in fraternal organizations. Lodge brothers were less than kin but more than friends and they were the source of business contacts and alliances in a newly settled area where almost no one had extended family or old friends to fulfill that roll. Lemp became an Odd Fellow in 1868. He eventually was state-level treasurer for 13 years, a member of the state board of trustees, and Past Grand Patriarch. That first year of 1868 he was already one of three on the committee to arrange the annual ball.[ax] In 1870 he was first installed as treasurer.[ay] He was also a member of the Masonic Lodge and filled all the offices including Worshipful Master. He was made a Master Mason in Shoshone Lodge No. 3 which later consolidated with Boise Lodge No. 2.[az] Late in life he also joined the Mystic Shrine, a Masonic affiliate.

The Masons were on the rebound after the anti-Masonic hysteria of the 1830s had damaged the brotherhood. Many Idaho men were Masons, and the presence of these men in the territorial vigilante movement has been noted in several studies.

Lemp was one of the founders of the Boise Turnverein. A German-American organization dedicated to athletics and German culture, it was originally formed in Germany by one Father Frederich Ludwig Jahn in the early 19th Century. Jahn's goal was to restore the German people to the level of physical vigor they enjoyed when their warriors first bounded from the forest to terrify the Roman legionnaires. Also known as the Turner Bund, it began in America in 1848 in New York. In America the organization soon adopted social and political goals and had activities for every member of the family. Anti-slavery, anti-prohibition and anti-nativism were the principles of the movement in its American branch.

They also trained men to physically defend the immigrant Teutons from the threats of Know Nothings and other violent nativists.

Turnen translates as gymnastics, and *Verein* means a union or club. Turnverein—pronounced toorn-fair-ine— means "athletic club." Chapters were started in many cities after the Civil War. It than began to move west with the immigrant population. Lemp remained a member the rest of his life.

In late February of 1870 *The Capital Chronicle* introduced the organization.[ba] "We are pleased to know our German citizens have organized a society called the 'Harmony Society.'" The first officers were: president, John Lemp; vice-president, Louis Heyd; Secretary, Jacob Schmidt; treasurer, George Bayhouse; vocal leader, Louis Steidel; turn leader, Moses Moritz. "A Society of this character has long been needed in our community. There is no finer exercise than that of a Turn Verein society and we are glad an organization has been perfected." Their first ball was planned for February 22 and the public was invited. They planned to build a fine brick building in the fall with a large front room for dancing, reading, and with portable exercise

Lemp was immediately involved in the operation of the Odd Fellows lodge, as his committee work attests.

equipment so it could be truly multi-purpose. Some money was already in their treasury.

In January of 1871, the group evolved to a new level. Lemp was re-elected president and William Bayhouse vice-president of the new Turn Verein (or Turnverein) Society.[bb] They were now officially affiliated with the nation-wide organization.

In April of 1907, the Turners celebrated their 35th anniversary with a gala event; the featured speaker was local attorney Gustave Kroeger, lawyer to brewers and spokesman against the forces of prohibition.[bc] Kroeger told how a meeting between William Bayhouse and Julius Ostheimer led to the founding of the Boise Wesangverein (singing group) in 1870.[bd] In a year it blossomed into the Boise Turnverein, and among the charter members, still living, were John Lemp and John Krall. Kroeger looked forward on that special night—erroneously, it turned out—to a 70th or 80th anniversary of the organization.

1869

Two weeks short of two years since John Emil was born, John and Catherine Lemp added a second new German-American to Boise in the person of offspring number two, George William Jacob Lemp, born 16 December 1868. Both parents had their father's names attached to the new son.

William Kohlepp, Catherine Lemp's father, died on Sunday 21 February 1869 of heart disease, less than two months after the birth of his grandson.[be] He was only 54 years old. The newspapers contained no mention of a funeral, nor gave anything resembling an obituary. They even misspelled his name.

Brewer Lemp remained busy with his business concerns. By late February of 1869, barley was mentioned as becoming a scarce item in the Boise valley.[bf] The price was going up in response. One farmer had 3,000 bushels left in his bin and was offered 4 1/2 cents at that place with the buyer offering to sack it himself. The farmer refused the offer. Barley for malting is the one voluminous ingredient brewers must have. Lemp may have been hard pressed to keep brewing materials on hand. The many other sundry items a brewer needs daily were advertised in the Boise newspaper. Casmier Winter and Company of San Francisco, "Importers of Hops, Corks and Brewers Stock," and

"Agency of the South Park Malt House," solicited business in the Statesman from "any part of the Pacific coast." [bg] They would have been a source of materials for Lemp.

Getting freight into Boise was a related question. The first transcontinental railroad was completed on 10 May 1869 when the tracks joined at Promontory Point, Utah. Goods from the whole world—even malt and hops—could now be taken by rail to Nevada or Utah and hauled north by wagon or pack train to Idaho. Also telegraph lines followed the rails. This created the possibility of running a branch telegraph line north to Idaho to bring the news of the world, and allow rapid transmission of messages to many American locations.

While Walla Walla and Umatilla on the Columbia River had been the source of most of the freight heading into and ultimately through Boise north to the Boise Basin or South to the Silver City area, now Kelton, Utah, on the railroad became the main source.

Of the many breweries started in Idaho during the 1860s only the Lemp brewery of Boise and the Weisgerber brewery of Lewiston would survive over 30 years and be able eventually to welcome the Twentieth Century. Lemp obviously had an ability to survive that nearly no others shared.

The technological marvels of the Nineteenth Century were on a relentless trek toward the isolated territory of Idaho, and with the help of John Lemp, Boise would be the site where modernity made its initial and greatest inroads into the Gem of the Mountains.

John Emil Lemp
Born 30 December, 1866
Photo, Idaho State Historical Society

The 1870s

In 1870 there were 1,972 active breweries in the United States. A small one on the far western frontier in Boise, Idaho, was a minuscule bubble in the foaming collar of the American brewing industry. On the local and personal level, however, Lemp was using his brewery to anchor his blossoming economic empire. To welcome 1870, Lemp did some very direct beer advertising. He tapped a keg in front of the Statesman newspaper office to pour the public a free New Year's treat, and he won suitable praise from the Boise journalists for his largess[bh] The new decade was baptized in Boise with a proper libation of Boise's own locally brewed lager.

At the meeting of Ada Lodge No. 3 of the I.O.O.F. that month, Lemp was elected treasurer and was put on the board of trustees along with W. James and Gus Kohlberg.[bi] The quite new Turn Verein organization gave a great ball on 2 May 1870 at Slocum's Hall.[bj] Tickets were $3 in coin. John Lemp was one of the floor managers for the dance. Lemp was cementing his position in the fraternal world.

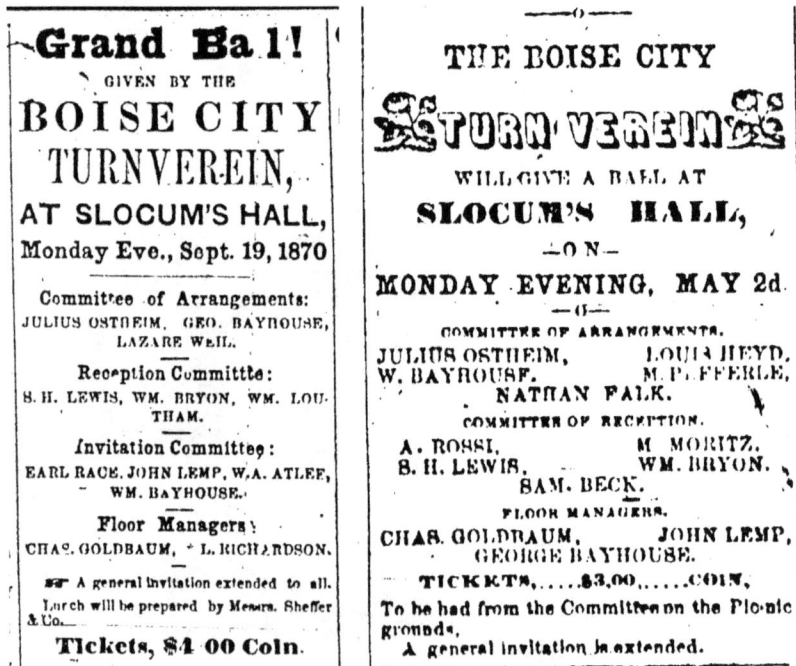

These were among the first newspaper ads placed by the new Turnverein. Everyone, including non-Germans were invited. Lemp's name was listed on both of these.

Lemp was, in fact, doing well on all fronts. The 1870 U.S. Census recorded Lemp having $12,000 in real estate and $2,000 in personal estate.[bk] Wife Kate was 20 years-old, Amel (sic) [Emil] was 3, George 1. They also had Ai Schin, 20, a cook from China living with them. Their first daughter Martha Elizabeth (Lizzie) was born 11 September 1870, too late for the June 1 cut-off of the Census, and 21 months after baby George's birth. Schin was probably the German family's phonetic spelling of a name usually transliterated as "Shin." [bl] He was one of eight Chinese cooks listed in the Census in Boise at the time.

Ads for Lemp and Misseldt were adjacent, in the same column of the newspaper.

The people of the frontier contributed many a damaged liver and nauseous morning while garnering reputations for unrestrained alcohol abuse, but there were also tenacious contrasting forces almost from the beginning of European settlement in Boise seeking the prohibition of alcohol. There were three great waves of prohibition sentiment in American history. The first great wave of rose and fell in the 1850s. Maine, in 1846, was the first state to go dry and begin the movement. In 1858, it went wet again to end this first wave. Idaho was not yet a territory at this point and not involved. The second wave may have symbolically begun when Kansas went dry in 1867 and Massachusetts in 1869. In 1870 the Good Templars—the leading dry group to date—came to Idaho to preach abstinence from liquor and to get men to sign the pledge to abstain. Signers were derisively known as "Water Tanks,' or just tanks. The doorman at the lodge meetings shouted after each arrival "admit the brother if he is duly sober." The revival spirit the Templars employed was so effective in Idaho City that after a visit by Jonas W. Brown, esquire, the Idaho apostle

*George William Jacob Lemp
16 December 1868 to 1 January 1900
Photo, Idaho State Historical Society*

of temperance, every saloon in town but one had soon closed. The local paper opined that shortly "they will all be found opening gorgeously."[bm] As the emotion of the moment dissipated, thirst returned.

The Good Templar movement never seemed to be able to project the same degree of momentary zeal in Boise City. This movement could have posed trouble for a brewer, but many men who swore off liquor viewed beer as an acceptably mild candidate to be their new social beverage. Beer sales were little affected, and Lemp never seemed to be in any financial danger. The temperance movement was focusing on whiskey at this time although it officially opposed beer also.

In June of 1870, Lemp made his first try at public office. He ran for Ada county treasurer as a Republican against Charley Himrod, a Democrat. As the Statesman said at the time, most Germans were Republicans.[bn] Although Lemp carried the Boise precinct 255 to 238, and the Union precinct 24 to 22, he ultimately lost to Himrod by 43 votes.[bo]

Early rival John Krall sold his brewery to partner Joseph Misseldt in September of 1870, and pursued other business interests in Boise the rest of his long life.[bp] Misseldt carried on a brief, friendly rivalry with Lemp.

In September, 1870, there was a fire in the wooden building between Lemp's wholesale liquor store and John Early's saloon.[bq] Col. Orlando "Rube" Robbins, the city Marshall—and the most romantic, larger-than-life figure in early Idaho law enforcement—was helping stages arrive and depart at quarter to three in the morning. He noticed the fire, gave the alarm and thus saved the adjacent buildings—including Lemp's—with his quick action. Lemp's long time interest in the Fire department of Boise was probably created by these early close calls with disaster.

The newspaper advertisement for Lemp in 1870 read: "Boise Brewery and Saloon, Main street, opposite Overland House. John

Julia (Jennie) Lemp Leyerzapf September 1844 to 1922. Sister of John Lemp, lived in Boise. Photo, Idaho State Historical Society

Lemp, . . . Proprietor. Finest and Best Brewed Lager constantly on hand, as well as the best wines, liquors and cigars! Nothing kept except what is first-class in quality. Fore (sic) those who favor me with their patronage can rest assured that they will not be disappointed in their expectations. A cold lunch, with all kinds of nice Cheese served at any hour. John Lemp."

At a meeting of the Ada County Jockey Club, John Lemp was put on a committee of three (including Charley Himrod who had just defeated him for county treasurer) to solicit new members. His lifelong interest in horses became evident.

Also, in the busy month of September of 1870 Lemp was made a trustee in the new corporation formed to bring a telegraph line from the nearest railroad into Idaho.[bt] The contemplated route to Idaho was from Elko, Nevada, to Placerville, Idaho, by way of Silver City, Boise, Centerville and other outposts. Capital stock was limited to $150,000. This was Lemp's first excursion into leadership in the world of corporate investment. He would serve on many corporate boards throughout the remainder of his life.

The outbreak of the Franco-Prussian War in Europe had a surprisingly large impact on far-off Idaho. On the evening of August 14, the Boise Germans met at the Masonic Hall to raise money for the German sanitary fund and to express sympathy for the German cause in the war with France.[bu] John Lemp was called to the chair, and $162 was raised in a short time. A subscription list was posted at the store of T. Wollstein & Co. so people of all nationalities could contribute. The meeting ended with three cheers for Germany. Most observers of world affairs believed the French army the best in the world and expected them to trounce the upstart Teutons. The imperialistic might generated by this new Germanic entity created by combining the small Germanic states under the blood and iron discipline of militaristic Prussia was not yet understood nor appreciated by world observers. Germany was an adolescent giant about to demonstrate its newly developed strength by delivering a drubbing to the mighty opponent on its western border.

Most events in Idaho were mundane in comparison to European war. Lemp's granary was broken into one Sunday night that fall and seven or eight sacks of barley stolen without the culprit leaving a clue.[bv] In the business directory published in the *Boise Weekly News* listed only two breweries for Boise, Lemp's and the brewery of Misseldt and his new partner Moses Moritz.[bw]

The *Capital Chronicle* announced on the 17th of September under the "Born" heading: "In this city, on the 11th inst., the wife of John

Margarethe Lemp Bach 4 May 1848 to 31 January 1926. Sister of John Lemp, She lived in St. Louis, Missouri. Photo, Idaho State Historical Society

Lemp, of a daughter."[bx] This was Martha Elizabeth, the first Lemp daughter.

Lemp announced he would sell and deliver "that much desired luxury" ice to any part of the city of Boise.[by] He was expanding his sales line.

On September 19, the Turnverein gave another great ball at Slocum's Hall with tickets at $4.00 coin. The invitation Committee included John Lemp.[bz] As if the Germans, and John Lemp in particular, were not busy enough at this time, they all got together to celebrate the downfall of Napoleon (the contemporary one) and Prussia's victory.[ca] Several German-born brewers associated with Idaho then or in the future were combatants in the Franco-Prussian war. Idaho City brewer Alois Riid left his partner John Brodbeck to head to Germany and enlist in its army. He tragically died under bizarre circumstances

Jacob Lemp, 1850 to 5 December 1896. John's brother as a young man. Photo, Idaho State Historical Society.

before he reached his first railroad connection in Nevada. Robert Koeninger, Henry Reiniger and Carl Mallon, future Idaho brewers all, fought for Germany. August Largilliere, future Soda Springs, Idaho, brewer broke the mold and fought for France. When Prussia ultimately won the war with France, Boise's Germans got together, 50 strong, and sat around the table, singing old German songs and drinking Lemp's beer in celebration according to the Statesman.[cb] The Boise City Weekly News reported, albeit a bit exaggerated, that they celebrated with 100 guns and as many kegs. A "brass band played airs of the Fatherland, and many a hearty cheer went up." John Lemp and several others made speeches. They also reported the editor of the rival Statesman had to be "carried home on a shutter in two loads." "Viva la Prussia" was still ringing in the reporter's ears. "Germany" was now a political reality, not a geographic expression.

The Ada County Jockey Club had their annual five-day horse racing event, starting on Monday, 25 October, with $1,250 offered in prizes.[cc] Lemp was among the leading citizens selected for the Grand Jury that November of 1870.[cd] "A better selection could not have been made," according to one local paper. He was to serve on many juries in Boise during the years to come.

On the extended family front, in November of 1870, John was named administrator for the estate of his late father-in-law, William Kohlepp.[ce] Lemp sold a great deal of cattle, hay wagons, and grain from the Kohlepp estate, indicating William had been a successful farmer during his brief tenure in his new home of Idaho.

In late December of 1870, Lemp and former brewery owner John Krall were both stocking their ice houses with solidified water.[cf] The ice was 12 inches thick that first month of winter. Krall made his initial small fortune at Fabulous Florence, Idaho's first bonanza gold camp. Soon after he was in Boise in the brewing and bakery businesses. His earlier life included German birth, learning the miller trade in England, sailing the Seven Seas, and barely escaping being the dinner menu when his becalmed, starving ship was ready to turn to cannibalism.

1871

In 1871, Horace Greeley and others collaborated on a 1,304-page tome, The Great Industries of the United States. Regarding German-American beer, Greeley said: "The stronger kinds of beer, consumed by the great multitude of beer-drinkers, can only have a pernicious influence on health and morals. Its tendency is to heavy sottishness and intellectual paralysis. The average German beer-drinker is so intellectually confused and stupefied that he is said to laugh at a joke only the day after he hears it."[cg] Anti-alcohol and anti-German were the twin tap roots of this philosophy which was embraced by an ever-growing segment of America. Lemp was elected President of the Boise City Turn Verein for a six month term in January 1871.[ch]

Lemp began building a fire proof brick building on Main street in front of the old City Brewery Building during February.[ci] Thomas McHenry began the construction on the building which was to be used as a store. In Boise, the new building was described as "a creditable and substantial structure."[cj] By the end of April of 1871 it was nearly completed and the Messers. Kellogg were prepared to store groceries in a rented portion of the building.[ck] Ownership of local business property was one of Lemp's principal investment strategies. At this same time, Lemp sold all 40 of his cows to banker Henry Greathouse.[cl] Greathouse was selling his ranch near Warm Springs, cattle included, to Messrs. Stabbs and Call.

For community work, Lemp was on the committee that invited Clitus Barbour to make the oration for Boise's Independence Day celebration.[cm] Lemp also led a subscription drive to raise money for the widows and orphans created by the Franco-Prussian War that year. He had not forgotten the Fatherland. He was not indifferent to his new homeland either. Lemp raised relief funds and goods for the Great Chicago Fire victims.[cn]

On June 13, 1871, John filed a government patent on 40 acres of Ada County land under the authority of the cash sale law of 1820.[co] This was apparently his first purchase of federal land, but many were to follow. Eventually, he would own thirteen ranches.

That summer, Lemp's City Brewery Saloon was advertising beer at 25 cents per quart, or 12 1/2 cents per glass, half the price it sold for in its early, gold rush days. The Lemp bartender was "Brother Brown, a fascinating genius" the local newspaper claimed.[cp] Maybe Brown just seemed smart after one had consumed a quantity of his offerings. That September the saloon was closed for repairs.[cq] Lemp's newspaper ad was shortened a bit by 1871. It read: "Boise Brewery and Saloon, Main St. opposite Overland, John Lemp, Proprietor, Keeps on hand the finest and best brewed Lager Beer, Wines, Liquors & Cigars."[cr] The I.O.O.F. held annual elections and made Lemp treasurer again on 14 July.[cs]

On 18 July 1871, Jacob Lemp, age 21, a laborer, arrived in New York from Bremen, Germany, on the Hammunia. This could have been John's brother of that name who made his way Idaho to join the ever-expanding number of extended family there.[ct]

In October of 1871 Lemp placed an advertisement for the wares of his brewery and saloon in the new Tri-Weekly Herald and continued it through that next year.[cu] In February of 1872 the newspaper said he had the best lager and was supplied with " [all] that is wholesome to drink or smoke."[cv]

Richard Adelmann, the man who first gave Boise five cent beer, years later told of his relationship with John Lemp.[cw] As Adelmann remembered the events, Lemp was visiting his sister and brother-in-law, Mr. and Mrs. William H. Jaumann, who were also relatives of Adelmann, in New York in 1872 when they first met.[cx] Adelman had been advised to go west for his health and Lemp's enthusiastic accounts of Boise proved contagious. Both the Jaumanns and Richard Adelmann accompanied Lemp home. They had $6,000 in cash and intended to engage in the grocery business. While this amount of capital would have started a small business in the East, in the West, in Boise especially, a store had "to keep everything from a needle to an anchor" and that meant $40,000 to $60,000. Rather than return home, Adelmann began working for Lemp in the brewery. At this time all drinks, whether beer or whiskey were 25 cents. Lemp reduced the price to 12 1/2 cents just as Adelmann went on his own in the saloon business. Adelmann hoped to encourage beer drinking and discourage whiskey, so he lowered the beer price in his saloon to five cents and started this local deflationary trend.

1872

A U.S. Revenue act in 1872 said anyone who sold malt liquor in quantities over five gallons was a wholesale dealer and must pay a special tax of fifty dollars.[cy] Lemp would be on that list.

Lemp was soon involved with local politics and was among the ten men elected to the Republican county convention in April of 1872.[cz] A public meeting to decide on a Fourth of July celebration for 1872 appointed Lemp—for the second straight year— along with four other men to organize a celebration.

The town was described as "rather dull" but everyone who was "producing anything was having a good year."[da] That year on July 8th, Lemp was also elected councilman of the first ward by a vote of 136 to 104 over his opponent, Mr. Scholl.[db] Lemp's voyage on the local political seas was launched. On August first that same year, the Lemp family also added their second daughter, Augusta Julia Margaret. Possibly her name reflects her birthdate.

That New Years Eve, December 31, 1872, the editor of the Statesman visited various homes in Boise. At Mrs. Lemp's house he found her home with her guests, Mrs. Wolters, Mrs. Scholl (probably the wife of Lemp's political opponent), Mrs. Jaumann (Mr. Lemp's sister), and Mrs. Misseldt (wife of one of the other brewer in Boise) and their "liege lords." The editor exchanged social greetings, had ample refreshments, and then went off to visit elsewhere.[dc] The rival brewers were obviously friendly enough to exchange visits and the Lemps knew how to extend Teutonic hospitality.

1873

The case of People vs. John Lemp was heard by the State Supreme Court on Tuesday 11 February 1873. Lemp was the appelant in the case and he lost. The court affirmed the prior decision of the Justice Court of Boise.

A new Internal Revenue Act of 24 December 1872 was advertised in May of the following year to alert those who owed special taxes.[de] Brewers owed $50 if they brewed under 500 barrels and $100 if over. Wholesale dealers in malt beverages owed $50 and retail owed $20. Hard liquor retailers owed $25. They had to buy special stamps to meet this obligation. Lemp owed for all of these.

Adolphus Busch, St, Louis brewer, having perfected pasteurizing, began bottling beer for large-scale shipment.[df] By 1872 or 1873 the brewery had eighty employees and two stories of automated bottling equipment turning out 40,000 bottles per day. With the railroad reaching the West, competition for John Lemp could arrive from far off places never thought of before.

Lemp continued to sell ice, as many brewers through out the country did, and he advertised its availability in Boise.[dg] Brewers cooled their fermenting rooms with ice so the lager would ferment slowly. They also aged their beer in very cool temperatures. Brewers learned to harvest extra winter ice, maintain a large stock in their ice house, and retail what they did not need. It was a secondary market aimed at a whole different group of consumers.

Far off in Washington, D.C., Congress passed the "Crime of '73," the act to demonetize silver. Gold was afterward the sole monetary standard despite the great increase in U.S. silver production from western areas such as Idaho. The West often viewed this as part of a "gold conspiracy." This view over-dramatizes the situation but shows the issue's importance to westerners. The law and the on-going battle to change it effected Lemp's political attitudes and allegiances, as well as the value of his silver mines.

In local politics, on 14 July 1873, Lemp was elected to another term on the Boise City Council.[dh] Lemp was also a member of the Ada

Martha Elizabeth Lemp 28 May 1849 to 1929. Sister of John Lemp, first husband William H. Jauman, Second husband Albert Wolters. Photo, Idaho State Historical Society

County Jockey Club and he was on the committee of reception for their ball in September of 1873.[di] In November of 1873, Lemp was building a wood frame building with partial brick on the site of a previously burned building.[dj] If he was not busy enough, in November he was impaneled and sworn onto the Territorial Grand Jury.

September of 1873 saw a great nation-wide economic panic or depression caused by railroad speculation, overexpansion in industry, agriculture and commerce. For two years the European demand for American agricultural products had weakened, setting the stage. The immediate cause was when railroad entrepreneur Jay Cooke's banking firm failed, dropping the price of securities. In turn, unemployment rose and national income fell. The national economic depression of 1873 struck America's brewers too. In far off Golden, Colorado, Adolph Coors and his partner Jacob Schueler shrugged off fears and opened their brewing business to supply the beer drinkers of Denver. Their success in John Lemp's former temporary locality was to eventually out-do all others in the Rocky Mountain region. Many German-born brewers, including John Lemp, had paved the way for the success of those that followed. That same year the United States Brewers Association replaced German with English as its official language. Other American organizations related to brewing slowly began to follow this linguistic lead.

Just before Christmas that year the Statesman's reporting crew dropped into Lemp's brewery and and returned a favorable report. They said Lemp employed experienced hands and brewed a good article.[dk]

1874

The year of 1874 proved another exciting one for Lemp. In March, Lemp, along with Governor Curtis, A. Wolters, and D. Henchkel, organized a prospecting company that did some mineral work outside of Boise.[dl]

Lemp was appointed superintendent of the grounds for the 4th of July celebration of 1874.[dm] Just a week after the Glorious Fourth, John was nominated for councilman of the first ward at the Tax Payers Party's mass meeting.[dn] This was a local political party only, as John was a life-long Republican. He was elected on 15 July 1874.[do] In August he was on the commmittee of invitation at the ball to open the new Central Hotel in Boise.[dp]

1874 was the year the Women's Christian Temperance Union was formed. This tiny embryo would grow strong enough to influence Idaho in a few years and create dismay among brewers from coast to coast. Beside working for temperance, they favored laws to restrict child labor and prostitution.

In October of 1874, Mr. Early imported many prize thoroughbred horses from Kentucky to Boise; several of these had been ordered by John Lemp.[dq] That month the Lemp household added two locally bred thoroughbred German-Americans, twins Ida Catherine and Ada Anna were born on 11 October 1874. Ida was named for Idaho Territory and Ada for Ada County. Some reports said these twins were the first twins born in Boise and maybe in the whole of Idaho. There were then six Lemp children.

In November, John's watch was stolen from a jewelry store where it must have been taken for repairs, but a third man brought it back and

George, Martha and John, children of John and Catherine Lemp
Photo, Idaho State Historical Society

explained the thief was drunk when he took it.[dr] Apparently all was forgiven. Diminished capacity proved a successful defense in this case.

With his large and ever-growing family, Lemp needed a big new house. He erected a magnificent dwelling on Grove street that the *Statesman* said might be the finest in the Territory.[ds] George Englehardt and Fred Beckhardt were the carpenters. It had a kitchen, parlor, pantry, and several bedrooms on the ground floor and many more rooms on the second floor, according to the preliminary report in the newspaper. The first description of the house was in December and by the following April work was winding down and there were more details about the structure.[dt] Upon entering, one first saw a hall 7 feet wide that went back 24 feet to the stairs, after which the hall was four feet. The parlor was on the right, facing west and was 16 by 19 feet with gilt wallpaper. The kitchen was 14 by 14 with a four by six pantry. The master bedroom was 14 by 20, and there was a 6 by 10 bath, and three small children's bedrooms, 7 by 8 each on the ground floor. The upstairs was not yet finished by April of 1875 but was to contain six rooms. In the rear was a summer kitchen and wash house that measured 14 by 20. In the entry hall a visitor saw a painting by Jake Welch. The wood work in the hall, the dining room, and all the doors were grained oak. There were also great porches all around on both levels.

John reportedly planted a tree on his house lot in 1868 which was described as magnificent in 1902. The exact dates may be open to question but the fact that Lemp thought and planned ahead was undeniable.

On Christmas day of 1874 Officers were installed for Shoshone Lodge, A F & A. M. (The Masonic Lodge) and Lemp was treasurer.[du] Lemp's future brother-in-law Albert Wolters was elected secretary.

1875

In January 1875 Lemp was elected Treasurer of the Ada Lodge no. 3 of the I.O.O.F. His lodge duties continued.[dv]

The Lemp in-laws, the Samuel Adolph family of Salem, Oregon, lost their five-month-old daughter in late March of 1875 and her death notice was published throughout the state.[dw] Catherine Lemp must have shared her sister's loss.

The South Mountain Brewery

Before Lemp could even think about moving into his new home, he took the stagecoach to the newest, greatest gold camp in Idaho to buy land and begin erecting a brewery. South Mountain was about 20 miles from Jordan Valley, Oregon, and about 25 miles from Silver City, Idaho, in an isolated area. It was touted, as was virtually every other mineral find in the history of the state, as the greatest discovery of the age. If it proved out, and Lemp was the first brewer there, his success would be assured.

When Lemp stopped overnight at Silver City on the first leg of his journey to South Mountain he visited the Owyhee Avalanche office to see their new steam press and to chat with the editor.[dx] The Avalanche had become Idaho's first daily newspaper on 11 October of 1874. The telegraph with its news relaying potential had then reached the town from the railroad stations to the south in Nevada and made real daily national news possible. The editor told his local readers that Lemp was already one of the wealthiest and most substantial citizens of the capital. The stagecoach to Silver City had transported—apparently calmly and peacefully—beside German brewer Lemp, a Chinese, a Negro, a preacher, and a gambler. Lemp reasoned this was a practical test of the civil rights bill that required no court intervention.[dy] Reconstruction in the secessionist South was not yet over and civil rights laws remained hot topics. A week later, the newspaper in Silver City reported Lemp had indeed bought a city lot for his South Mountain brewery building.[dz] Owyhee County records listed that on March second, that Lemp paid $475 to Charles A. Sharing, Frank Pearson, and O. Custar for one log cabin and one lot of thirty feet on Main Street in the townsite of South Mountain.[ea]

With Lemp back home at Boise three days later, the Statesman commented that he looked like he had experienced a rough trip.[eb] The month of March in the Silver City to South Mountain area has deep snow and difficult travel. Modern roads there are often not open until June.

Lemp reported that things were slow at South Mountain but would be lively when the weather permitted mining to start up again. The smelter there, the only one in the state, was inactive because the snow was too deep to bring in coal or wood to keep it fueled. John made several trips to the area that spring to get the business underway. On one occasion he was a late night arrival at the Idaho Hotel in Silver City.[ec] Back at Boise that April, Lemp reported new strikes in South Mountain were occurring all the time and the town was being built better that most mining camps. He expected to have the new brewery in operation by May.[ed]

By late May, a most pleasant surprise delayed Lemp's brewery construction. While excavating for a cellar the workers struck a quartz ledge with valuable gold ore.[ee] Work continued, and by June a listing of the businesses in South Mountain contained "John Lemp brewery & saloon." He was in operation, just a bit behind schedule.[ef] Brother Jacob was John's partner in this business and was probably the on-site manager since John was very busy in Boise.[eg] Jake was born in Germany in 1850, the year his father died.[eh] He was therefore a young man of 24 at this time. John left Germany when Jacob was two years old. They could not have spent much time together before this fraternal reunion in western America.

On the 30th of October 1875, Leonard Spath sold land in South Mountain to John and Jacob Lemp for $600 in coin.[ei] The lot was 30 by 100, fronting on the south side of Johnson street, known as the Boot and Shoe Shop of Spath and Lessman. On the west this lot was bounded by the "vacant lot of John Lemp." The Lemp brothers were consolidating a large piece of property.

The South Mountain mining bubble burst that first year and Lemp did not reopen the brewery in 1876. South Mountain had several small booms and busts in the years to come. Well over 100 years later, the mineral exploration in South Mountain is continued by hardy, optimistic souls, but the isolation and climate will probably never allow a full time community there.

On the 20th of December of 1876, Jacob Lemp sold to the Idaho Mining and Smelting Company for $50 in gold, the "Magnetic Iuso (?) Mine." Previously the claim was known as the "Duilio," and ran 750 feet from the discovery stake.[ej] Apparently Jacob either did some prospecting or purchased a claim from someone he met in South Mountain.

BOISE MAYOR JOHN LEMP

Back in Boise, on July 12 of 1875, Lemp was elected mayor over Charles Himrod by a vote of 80 to 60.[ek] These vote totals show what a small town the territorial capital remained. Lemp's mayoral duties included such things as signing the new ordinance against cattle running at large in Boise City.[el] In November of that year Lemp sold the west half of lot 10, of block 11 to Peter Sonna for $100.[em] That same month a keg of Lemp's beer burst in Fred Dangel's saloon and made the man sitting on it at the time "higher" and wetter than he desired to be.[en]

The first cork-free breakthrough for closing beer bottles was the lightening stopper patented by Charles De Quillfeldt of New York City in 1875.[eo] No Lemp bottles from this era have been located but such developments might have been used.

1876

In February 1876, Lemp bought 40,000 pounds of Lord Gage barley from T.E. Logan.[ep] The newspaper joked that he was partial to the name and was going to brew Lord Gage beer from it. That same month Lemp sold 204 acres near Middleton to Jacob Diehl for $1,500 in coin.[eq] Being Mayor was not enough civic work for John, so he was made treasurer of the Boise City Fire Company in February of 1876.[er] The group was just getting organized at this point and John brought kegs of beer to the meetings to encourage membership and attendance.[es] There was a tradition in German neighborhoods throughout both the old country and the new to entrust brewers with money. Lemp seemed to be the treasurer of every group he joined. "The Hook and Ladder Company" was led by a number of prominent men but citizens of all levels offered their services.[et]

The trust fellow Germans put into their brewers to honestly protect their money was legendary. In Cincinnati, during the 1857 panic, many Germans withdrew their life savings from the bank and gave it to a brewer for safekeeping. One man gave the local brewer the goodly sum of $200 and then awoke from a discomforted sleep wondering if the businessman was as honest as everyone said. After worrying for hours he went to the brewer's house before dawn and banged on the door until admitted. The brewer went to the safe in his library

Augusta Julia Margaret Lemp
1 August 1872 to 10 May 1926
Photo from Idaho State Historical Society

got out the money, threw it at the nervous depositor, and admonished him: "Raus! Put your Gottverdammt gelt in der bank und neffer ask me again!"[eu]

Lemp somehow lost possession of his life insurance policy in April and advertised for it to be returned, no questions asked.[ev] If he got it back, he did not advertise the fact. July 4, 1876 was, of course, the Centennial of the United States and everyone wanted a more elaborate celebration than usual. Already in April, Lemp and two others were on the committee for fireworks, and by early June he was heading up the committee on music too.[ew] At that time he also reported on behalf of the Agricultural Park Association that their grounds were not in proper condition for holding the celebration and it should all be moved to the Turn Verein's grounds.[ex]

In the Centennial races at the Agricultural Park, held before the Glorious Fourth, among the horses going for the trotting purse was "Billy Lemp," John's entry.[ey] Wife Catherine's brother George Kohlepp drove the horse and won the second heat in the sensational time of 2 minutes 58 and 3/4 seconds. After the four heats Billy was second to Vanguard for the day.[ez] On the Glorious Fourth Lizzie Lemp, not quite six years-old, represented "Boise City" on the "Liberty Car," along with a gaggle of girls representing each state, plus "Peace," "Plenty," and the "Goddess of Liberty."[fa] Word was reaching Boise just about this time of the victory of the La Kotah and Cheyenne over the command of Colonel George A. Custer on the Little Big Horn River. The 100th birthday of the nation occurring so near the time of our greatest military defeat of the Indian wars inordinately influenced the thinking and attitudes toward Indians in Boise as it did nation-wide. In each of the next three summers there were Indian wars in Idaho. In the spring of 1876 Lemp entered yet another business venture. He bought 100 shares out of 1,000 total offered for sale, and became one of the eight directors of the First National Bank of Idaho.[fb] This was just the second national bank chartered west of the Rocky Mountains.[fc] The local paper at the time said Lemp was the "Beer King of Idaho," one of the territory's wealthiest citizens, and, of course, the mayor.[fd] The historian of the Idaho banking business wrote that Lemp was the most influential, well known, and colorful of the new directors.[fe] Citizens could and would have faith in the bank with Lemp involved in the ownership. Yet again, a link of trust between Lemp and the money of others was forged. B. M. DuRell, C. W. Moore, David W.

Ida Catherine Lemp 11 October 1874 to1 July 1904,
Ada Anna Lemp 11 October 1874 to 8 June 1959
The first twins born in Boise. Photo Idaho State Historical Society.

Ballard, and William Roberts had formed the bank originally in 1867.[ff]

As the city elections of 10 July 1876 approached, the local newspaper praised the administration of Mayor Lemp and the other councilmen.[fg] Old debts had been paid and many improvements to streets and alleys had been made. John declined to run for mayor again, but stayed in politics and went to the county Republican convention in September.[fh] There he accepted a nomination for county treasurer but in the general election Democrat C. P. Bilderback defeated him.[fi]

In far off St. Louis, Missouri, in 1876 Adolphus Busch began to ship his St. Louis lager beer into the western territories. Busch's beer was pasteurized and could reach its destination in good condition. Railroads were developing refrigerated cars which helped keep beer fresh also. Busch learned of Louis Pasteur's work before it was published and was rightly credited with introducing this monumental development to American brewing. No longer could John Lemp or any western brewer have his local market free of distant eastern competition.

The American brewers erected an exposition building in Philadelphia at the Centennial Exposition that summer. To multitudes of fair-goers they showed off their modern equipment, techniques, and negative opinions about the ever-growing temperance movement.

1877

In January of 1877, Lemp was elected to the office of "C.P." in the I.O.O.F. [Odd Fellows], Encampment no. One of Idaho.[fj] On the homefront, on 7 February, Albert Carl, the Lemp's 7th child, was born.

New city ordinances that were published in the newspaper in 1877 still had the approving signature of John Lemp from his 1875 tour of duty as mayor.[fk] In May, the report on "Billy Lemp," the trotter, was that he was seven years old and looking fine. He was sired by Eph. Maynard and had great endurance and power.[fl] Perhaps the horse was named after the Lemp Brewery of St. Louis.

Lemp of St. Louis had a bottling house including cooper shop and stave yard that took up an entire city block by this time.[fm] It was becoming one of the largest breweries in America.

Stock owner John Lemp remained one of the bank directors, signing off on the report of the financial condition of the First National Bank at about this time.^fn He also donated to the Boise fund for designating a public square and erecting therein a statue of first president George Washington.^fo

Lemp sold $600 worth of hogs that June just as the Nez Perce War started in northern Idaho. The hogs had been fed the spent grain from the brewery, making them almost pure profit. Crushed grains of barley malt remain after the brewing processes have dissolved the fermentable maltose out. The relative protein content is higher than with unprocessed grain and this is an excellent animal food. However, Lemp vowed to get rid of all his hogs and pigeons because the town had grown up around the brewery and the smell was annoying to the new neighbors.^fp However, his vow did not include a time-table for completion.

In June of 1877 the Semi-Weekly Idahoan said Lemp brewed the best beer in the territory and he was receiving orders for it from other counties.^fq Asa Moore purchased a 10 gallon keg of Lemp's beer as a gift for Capt. Hasbrouck's cavalry men as they came into town from a long hot ride.^fr John recognized the efficacy of this idea and the next month he took two kegs to the fort so that the two cavalry companies could have a refreshing draft before they started north in response to

The Lemp home as depicted in Elliot's History of Idaho Territory, 1884.

the Nez Perce War.^fs The troopers cheered John most lustily. The Nez Perce war coupled with the Custer defeat of a year before created a noteworthy level of anti-Native American paranoia in Idaho.

John provided a horse for the volunteers serving under captain Orlando Robbins as did brewer Joe Misseldt. Robbins acknowledged this in a letter to Governor Brayman listing all the services provided for his men.^ft

On the Car of Liberty in the Fourth of July parade that year of 1877 there was Gussie Lemp and Lizzie Lemp among the throng of young girls costumed to represent patriotic icons.^fu The United States of America was 101 years old.

George Kohlepp, Lemp's employee and brother-in-law, ran for sheriff that summer of 1877 but lost to Mr. Paxton. John, after his year of rest from the Boise political battles, was again elected Councilman on 9 July 1877.^fv John, almost simultaneously, was appointed treasurer on the board of the fire commissioners for Boise.^fw This sounds like a titular promotion from just being treasurer of the firemen. John was installed as "second W" of the I.O.O.F. Idaho Encampment No. 1.^fx In other lodge work, Lemp was a delegate to the 10th annual state convention of the A.F. & A.M. Free and Accepted Masons convention in Boise during September, representing the Shoshone Lodge no. 7.^fy

In July, Billy Lemp won $150 as the number one finisher in the trotting races over Seneca and Flora.^fz Lemp's horse was first in all three heats. Lemp's stable at the track, with Bill Young, colored, in charge, had only one horse in it.^ga Lemp was having another horse, "Ribbon," trained in late August but it was not entered that Fall.^gb In October, George Kohlepp again drove Billy Lemp for his brother-in-law in the trotting races and again he took an overall second place.^gc At the third day of the trotting races Lemp entered a new mare named Minnie Clay.^gd She was distanced in the second heat, and ended up second over all, finishing second three times and first in the other two heats. This was the same month the Nez Perce ended their 1600 miles fighting retreat and surrendered in the Bear Paw mountains of Montana.

By September, 1877 Phillip Paul sold out his interest in the Atlanta, Idaho, brewery and went to Boise.^ge Paul began working for brewer

John Lemp, mostly driving a team. That relationship lasted until February of 1885.

John sued J. B. Oldham and had foreclosed on his mortgage in November of 1877.[gf] The following March, the case was reviewed in the District Court and the "Report of Commissioner" confirmed.[gg] Soon the land in question would be Lemp's liquor store. Lemp was elected trustee for the Idaho Agricultural Park Association on the 27th of November.[gh]

At a public meeting in December, a Boise group wanted, among other things, to petition Congress to build a military wagon road from Fort Boise to Fort Lapwai, which would essentially connect the southern and northern halves of the ill-designed Territory of Idaho.[gi] This connection remained less than satisfactory for a century to come as the state struggled to build highway 95 into a ribbon to connect the politically, socially, culturally, and geographically divergent halves of Idaho. The suddenly perceived need for this first road resulted from the recently concluded Nez Perce War. Moving war materials had proved a slow difficult task in Idaho. Ex-mayor John Lemp was on the committee to lobby for the military road. The committee received a response describing what would be involved in each section to make such a road.[gj]

Photo of the Lemp home with family members identified by name. Photo, courtesy of Karl Lemp

1878

In early January of 1878, while his men were cutting the yearly supply of ice, Lemp went visiting to "Dry Creek" with attorney Thomas Cahalan.[gk] At Hull's gulch near Boise they stopped the buggy while Cahalan looked for a way across the ice of the frozen stream. The horse began to kick and plunged forward and Lemp was thrown out of the buggy backwards. The fall was not judged serious but it supposedly set off an attack of gout in the left arm which left John confined to his room. The pain might have been gout, some sort of strain, sprain or other physical damage.

Joseph Misseldt, the main brewing rival to Lemp, could not be found one day in February of 1878. After an extensive search his body was located upside down, fully submerged, in the well at his brewery.[gl] Once in that position, a man of his great girth had no chance to get out. Was it a bizarre accident or a bizarre suicide? Many speculated, no one knew. Misseldt appeared to be doing well on several fronts. Certainly John Lemp and many others of Boise were deeply moved by this sad event.

In March, John Brodbeck of Idaho City bought the Boise brewery owned by Joseph Misseldt's widow, Agatha. He left the high country and began a quarter of a century cross-town rivalry with John Lemp.[gm]

Swiss-born Brodbeck had traveled to Idaho initially with Silver City brewer William Sommercamp; he had been brewing partners at different times with Herman Fischer, Alois Riid and Nicholas Haug. Brodbeck had a thorough background as a brewer and a wealth of connections to many Idaho brewers.

In March of 1878, John Lemp was selected to serve on the U.S. Grand Jury.[gn] He was also on the committee to celebrate the 102nd anniversary of independence, and ended up on the executive committee.[go] In May of that year Lemp refitted his building formerly occupied by Oldham and Taylor into a wholesale liquor store.[gp] It opened in July and was called one of the first such establishments "on the coast."[gq] The definition of "coast" was quite broad at this time. From Boise to the Pacific Ocean is a long trek. Liquor had traditionally been sold at grocery stores, saloons and drug stores. A liquor store was an innovation. Herr Lemp also continued his First National Bank duties and again signed off on the yearly report.[gr]

The Bannock Indian War in southern Idaho and surrounding areas in 1878, just a year after the Nez Perce tragedy, brought out further paranoia in many people in Boise and led them to organize a Home Guard in case of a frontal assault on the city by small, displaced Native American families. The officers and men of this defense outfit had their names published in a local newspaper.[gs] Brewers John Brodbeck, John Krall, and John Lemp were all on the list. Lemp actually used his wholesale house to store rations for the Idaho volunteers during the Bannock War.[gt] He also recieved a large shipment of liquor from Kelton carried by the Conant Brothers at this time.

In June, Herman Hildebrandt and John Mops were working in the bottom of Lemp's newly built 18 by 20, 12 feet high, lager beer cellar when three walls collapsed.[gu] Both miraculously escaped without a scratch. Hildebrandt later became brewery owner. In July, Boise had to have a city council election but "there was really no interest taken in the city election out side of the Marshal's office . . ."[gv] John was again elected to the city council as a Republican with 128 votes, up from the 124 he garnered the year before.[gw] John was on the straight Republican ticket which was opposed by a non-partisan ticket.[gx] Lemp was also secretary for the Ada County Republican Central Committee and, in September, issued his report on the party.[gy]

An article on local horses that summer said Lemp had a planter filly of fine promise, and his well known trotter Billy Lemp was still in fine shape.[gz] In September, just a month before the Fall racing season, a more detailed report from Black's Station said Billy Lemp was in splendid condition and "keeping."[ha] Mr. Black said he had trained the kinks and false steps out of Billy so he could come down squarely to work without breaking. Billy had the fastest single race time of any horse in Idaho the previous year and looked like the favorite for the upcoming races. Billy was a gelding, 15 hands high, a hard bony horse, and his record time was 2:43 3/4.[hb] In October, Lemp entered "Norma" in the race for 3 year-olds and "Billy Lemp" in the trotting races.[hc] The second day drew a crowd due to the nice weather and despite the fact that Billy Lemp was the only local horse competing. [hd] Most observers believed Lemp could not win but would make the other horses work for their victory. With Charley Black driving Billy Lemp took third in the first heat.

The third day's races were particularly exciting.[he] In the first heat, Billy Lemp led in the first turn, King, owned by O. R. Hutchin, crowding him pretty hard, Goldfoil, owned by J. J. Welsh, following him about twenty yards behind until the third turn when he began to gain. Lemp got in the track of King down the stretch and came in first. King's driver claimed a foul and Lemp was put in third place. In the second heat George Kohlepp gave the reigns of Billy Lemp to Charley Black. Lemp led all the way to take the heat. In the third heat Lemp took the lead but Goldfoil got the inside track and could not be caught. The fourth heat Lemp took the lead but was caught by Goldfoil at the very end. For the day, Goldfoil was first and Billy Lemp second.

One thirsty soldier from Fort Boise wandered into Boise City that summer looking for a drink and obnoxiously yelling in a German accent "Yesus Grist! You fellows hat a prewery here somevere; vere you poot him?"[hf] The military continued to recruit frontier troopers right off the immigrant boats in New York. Their English language skills were weak. So called "Dutch humor" was still a mainstay in pre-politically correct times and no doubt the newspaper stretched the trooper's dialectical peculiarity.

Threats of more Indian wars were still in the air and Lemp received a large supply of rations to be used by Idaho volunteers if necessary. He stored these in his wholesale establishment for future needs.[hg] In September Lemp sold an old wooden building used as a Chinese laundry to P. J. Pefly (sic) for him to move off the lot so Lemp would be free to build a new brick, two-story, building to rent to a harness and saddlery establishment.[hh] Lemp also added sidewalks in front of several lots of his downtown property at this time.

In November, Lemp sued Francis Breck for an unknown reason, but the defendant was ordered to pay Lemp $45.12 and to cover court costs.[hi] At the Thanksgiving festival that month, George Kohlepp won the prize for shooting blindfolded with his back to the target. Too bad he had lost the election as sheriff. A lawman no doubt could use that kind of specialized firearm skill.

Lemp had a new ice house ready for its seasonal task as Christmas approached in 1878.[hj] On the evening of Christmas Day a unique, exciting raffel took place at the saloon of Paine & Adelmann and seemed to included dozens of noteworthy Idaho pioneers.^{hk} Some jewelry owned by William Ridenbaugh was left with William B. Morris as collateral on a loan. When it was not redeemed Mr. Morris paid Ridenbaugh about what it was worth and they mutually agreed he could keep it. Ridenbaugh then became the administrator of the Morris' estate upon his death and came up with a scheme to turn the jewelry into cash. One hundred twelve chances were sold for ten dollars each. Chance holders

Albert Carl Lemp. 7 February 1877 to 28 March 1937. Photo, Idaho State Historical Society

threw dice and the highest total score got the first prize, second highest next, and third highest the third share of the jewelry. The three lowest scores took the 4th, 5th, and 6th portions of the prize. John Lemp. Jacob Lemp, R. C. Adelmann, John Brodbeck, Nick Haug, and C. C. Meffert, all one-time brewers, bought chances. Ridenbaugh himself and future historian James Hawley both won parts of the treasure.

Lemp finished 1878 by being elected to "S" in the Masonic Lodge.[hl]

1879

At the early January meeting of the Odd Fellows George Kohlepp was elected L.S.S.C., North Chair.[hm] Early in 1879 Lemp was a surety on the $10,000 bond of J. B. Oldham, Sheriff; the $15,000 bond of Douglas Knox, Assessor; and the $5,000 bond of N. M. Hanthorn, County Auditor.[hn] Lemp was also again made a grand juror that month, and he was actually impaneled in April.[ho] A would-be thief broke the door lever on Lemp's saloon one night in April of 1879, but did not gain entrance.[hp]

On 20 July Sheriff John M. Dauskin gave an indenture to M. G. Luney as a result of a court order of 3 November 1879 resulting from a judgment for J. H. McCarty, John Lemp, John Huntoon, Thomas E. Logan, Peter Sonna, Frank Coffin and Christopher W. Moore against Thomas Elliott. Luney bid at the auction and won the property for $6,818.04.[hq]

Education in Boise

Uncle Jimmy H. Twogood wrote a two part history of education in Boise for the Evening Capital News in March of 1905.[hr] Twogood was there, had a clear memory, and had a most unpretentious interpretation of those events and the motivations behind them. Early Boise schools were private, and noteworthy schoolkeepers were B. F. "Picayune" Smith, and O. H. Purdy who was killed by Indians near Silver City. The first public school was run by Charley May. By 1870 a Mr. Whitson, who had a "smathering of education" was the school master. In 1879 Clinton H. Moore was the principal, "not much of a teacher but good at drawing his salary of $150 per month and loaning it out at 2 per cent per month—a cute Yankee" in Twogood's opinion. In 1878 R. H. Deed, Mounce Bird, and Virgil Lamb were the trustees and "they kind of let the school run itself. To give you a faint idea of how low it had got, the scholars of the Episcopal school called those attending the public school the public 'scrubs'," Twogood recalled.

On the first Monday of September of 1879 a school board election was called with little notice. Dr. J. B. Wright, J. H. Twogood and Charles A. Schnabel were voted in with a grand total of 12 votes cast in the whole election. The elected men didn't even know they were nominated until the election was over. They were finally called together and asked if they would serve. "Well there was Dr. Wright, he was a pharmacist and supposed to know all about Latin and other dead languages, not dead like postoffice matter, for there was no 'cent' in it, like a postmaster taken short in his accounts. Charley Schnable he had a liberal education, could spracum Deutch (sic), and several other languages. He would do. But there was Jimmy, the stick. What did he know? Well he had never been accused of being guilty of knowing anything in particular. Knew about as much as last year's bird's nest. His last "skulin" was in the winter of '42 and '43. State and Monroe streets, Chicago. Schoolmates, J. M. Ballentine, few years afterward a big stock raiser of Boise Valley, and Louis A Kimberly, afterward rear admiral United States navy, both now deceased."

"There was no public school in Chicago until 1845! As a result Jimmy's early education had been sadly neglected, but could stand a physical test in the rule of three, provided the rule would work both ways, and he could speak Chinook as fluently as a native, and make a Kricatat (sic) ashamed of himself on general sounds. And as the board's physical culture was all o.k., they concluded they would wade in and start a real live school that would surprise the natives. How well we succeeded in our feeble efforts, the Boise school of today are an answer to the problem."

"Our first work was to look around for suitable timber for teachers. Luckily we dropped on Professor Giffin, found that he had been dropped from the Episcopal professorship for reasons that we did not stop to inquire into: found him a man of education and in the analysis of words he had no peer in the territory. He was out of a job, so we engaged him for the school term at $75 per month, engaged the best material available for his assistants, and started a real lived school. The children improved under Professor Giffin's tutorship faster than anything that had ever happened in Boise. Children that would only make pot hooks when they commenced at the end of the term could write a good legible hand, everybody was surprised and nothing would seem to satisfy but another term."

"After the term closed the board got together, and the first question asked was what were we going to do about it? The old school house was filled to overflowing and we were hampered about our finances, but Charley Schnabel gallantly came to our rescue and said he would donate his old store building for a school room. If I would move it into the school grounds. All right. So, with the help of Harry Lomkin and my son Merritt, we commenced getting the building ready to move. It stood opposite the Overland, built, I think, in '64, and occupied by Dan Roth, the place is now Al Kohny's clothing store. The building was 24 by 60 feet; July 10, 1880, we raised it; July 11, Merritt's birthday, we sawed the building in two making two 30-foot lengths; 12th, my birthday, got timbers under it, ready to shove out into the street; 13th got it across the street about noon, when a messenger came running up to me and said there was trouble at our house at home. I rushed down, found Dr. John L. Stearns, who said he had just received a present for me, and it was found behind a log in Rocky Bar, and her name was Carrie Chapin."

"We got the building out all o.k. joined it together, built a chimney, put in four windows on the sides, got tables, benches and blackboard, and had it all ready for business at an expense not exceeding $76."

As September first rolled around again another election for the school board was held. This time after great effort at getting out the votes the men were reelected with 15 votes, an increase of three over 1879 being cast. Education had a way to go to become a priority.

The Episcopal school was closed by this point. They needed more room and rented the old Baptist church on the northwest corner of Ninth and Idaho. They covered it with rustic and painted it in exchanging for using it for the term. Miss Wellington took charge and soon her school was filled and all the children that had been going to private schools came to the public school.

While the school board wrestled with building problems and their personnel deficiencies, in April of 1879 John Lemp formed a committee to bring improved education to the Territory by means of a new public school in Boise.[hs] The old school, built in 1868 and located on the corner of 8th and Washington remained in use until the new school, Central, was opened in 1882.[ht] This seems to be a simplified version of those events compared to Mr. Twogood's remarkably detailed memory. Central school had 16 rooms although not all were utilized the first year and the expected cost of $25,000 escalated to $44,000 by completion. The board was criticized by some for erecting a building that was too large and too expensive. However, by 1893 it served 700 students, was overcrowded, and an additional school had to be built. Seven years after Central school was built the builders of the public school, including Lemp, were praised because Boise had taken a high educational position in the whole region because of the facilities their foresight made possible.[hu]

In 1879, Clinton H. Moore was the principal of the Episcopal school. The patrons of the St. Michael Episcopal school choose Lemp as one of the directors of the school in May of 1880.[hv] Lemp's new allegiance to this denomination may be related to this service.

A bill passed by the eleventh territorial legislature and signed by the governor on 4 February 1881 created the Independent School District of Boise City.[hw] The bill listed the district's founders and trustees as C. W. Moore, Charles Himrod, John Lemp, P. J. Pefley, H. B. Eastman, and Richard Z. Johnson, who authored the legislation.[hx]

Non-Education Matters

Among the freight arriving in Boise that May were 27,000 pounds sent from the railroad transfer depot at Kelton, Utah, which included a great amount of goods for Lemp.[hy] In fact, the Conant Brother's load had about 20,000 pounds for Lemp's wholesale liquor house on Main street.[hz] Lemp painted up his saloon in honor of the 50 barrels of choice liquor it received.[ia]

Lemp was on the Committee for "stands," meaning places to sell things at the July 4th celebration that year.[ib] There was to be one bar with exclusive right to sell cigars, one soda stand, and one ice cream and candy stand. The privilege of operating any such stand was to go to the highest bidder.[ic] Sealed bids were to be sent directly to Lemp.

R. C. "Dick" Adelman began advertising his Gem Saloon in the Boise City Republican in May of 1879.[id] He described himself for the next few years as "late with John Lemp." The value of this bit of name dropping was obvious. At the City elections that year brother-in-law George Kohlepp ran for Councilman as a Democrat but lost. One seat was won by brewer, and future father-in-law to Kohlepp, John Brodbeck.[ie]

In August of 1879 a list of the highest tax payers in Ada County was published. Everyone with over $5,000 in assessed valuation was listed. John Lemp with $25,110 in property topped the list.[if] On August 10th an 11 pound son became the eighth child of the Lemp family. "John is the happiest man in town."[ig] William Adam Lemp began what was to prove a very short stay on earth.[ih]

One day in September a fine span of Lemp's draft horses were two miles above town awaiting a load of rock at Buckley's quarry.[ii] Something frightened them and they took off without their driver. They kicked up a ton of dust but kept to the center of the road, crossed two bridges and reached the head of Main street where they were stopped with no injury done to themselves, the wagon, or anyone else. In other horse business, Billy Lemp, the trotter, was again being prepared for the fall harness races and much was expected of him, but he had new owners. John Lemp had sold him to Ed Ryan and Major Taylor.[ij]

John Allen who worked in Lemp's wholesale liquor store financed "old man Emery" so he could prospect in the mountains south of Boise.[ik] Emery found a large load of lead about 8 miles from town. Allen was still tending bar after this, so his share must not have allowed him to enter the leisure class.

Lemp made improvements to his brewery that September of an unspecified nature.[il] The brewery of the distantly related William Lemp of St. Louis was on the list of the ten largest in America by 1879. That October,

John Lemp, no longer owning an entrant, was instead one of three judges at the yearly horse races.[im]

At Lemp's saloon there was a billiard match of note between Mac Short and Joe Edwards for $100.[in] In October, Lemp got 12,000 pounds of assorted articles for his wholesale liquor house.[io] Boise nearly lost its downtown section to a fire that October but the force pumps in the wells of the Statesman and John Brodbeck's brewery, and a shift in the wind enabled the firemen to save the day.[ip]

The Lemp liquor house was visited by the *Statesman* as part of a survey of Boise businesses and they gave a light-hearted account.[iq] The reporter said "we encountered the emaciated and consumptive looking corporosity of our delicate young friend John Allen." Allen was apparently a large man. Allen talked to the reporter about O.P.S. which either meant "old private stock" or "oh please stop." The reporter had a drink and then gazed fondly at all the hogsheads, punchens, barrels and wicker cases. There were also many bottles of Lemp's beer, brewed just up the block. Adjoining the saloon and liquor store was a commodious billiard room. Lemp had another fine saloon on the other side of Main street opposite the stage and express office. For Christmas, Lemp's man, John Allen, served free egg nog at the saloon.[ir]

That same December, Lemp was made treasurer of the I.O.O.F. for the next year, and he continued his long running term as vice-president of the First National Bank.[is] It was also reported that Lemp was seen on horseback for the first time in 40 years.[it] A bit of an exaggeration no doubt. Early the next year Lemp was again serving on the Grand Jury.[iu]

The 1870s ended with John Lemp a prominent Boise businessman successful in many fields.

1880

Abnormally warm temperatures caused ice cutting that winter of 1880 to wait until February and the ice was only four inches thick, but clear and firm by then.[iv] Lemp had several horse teams running ice blocks into his ice house.

In February, 1880, Kate Lemp's brother George Kohlepp married 19 year-old Lena Brodbeck, oldest daughter of John and Sarah Brodbeck.[iw] Brewing rivals Brodbeck and Lemp were forever more linked as extended family.

Nine year-old Lizzie Lemp was dressed as a French newsboy at the annual masquerade ball in February, while Emil, 13, went as a girl.[ix] Lemp donated $10 for relief work in Ireland that same month.[iy] Lemp was a pall bearer for Major S.R. Howlett's funeral later that February.[iz]

In March, Gussie (Augusta Julia Margaret) Lemp was the third best student in the 4th grade at the public school.[ja] In May, she was a member of the group that ceremoniously wound the ribbon around the May pole. Lizzie (Martha Elizabeth) was the scepter bearer at the May Pole festivities. Emil and George Lemp were busy exercising with the Boise Athletic Club.[jb]

John Lemp, Joseph Perrault and James H. Bush were appointed at a meeting of the agricultural park to start a program of horse racing.[jc] The meeting voted to offer $2,500 in purses and to add 35 per cent to any citizen's purse that might be offered.

Lemp bought a horse in May, 1800 that turned out to be stolen.[jd] Two men giving their names as Richard Lowe and John Collins had possession of two horses owned by Mr. Jacob Algenbarger who lived near Middleton. Lemp paid $100 total, some cash and some saloon supplies for a business the men claimed they were going to open by Falk's Store on the Payette. The thieves were lodged in jail and the rightful owner received his horses.

In May, Lemp advertised that he had the choicest lot of liquor and cigars ever at his wholesale store and suggested that saloonkeepers could do better there than ordering outside the local area.[je] Also he ordered several patent refrigerators which looked like cupboards. Before they were installed, the six or seven year old sons of Mr. Boomer and Dr. Smith walked by and saw them on the sidewalk. Young Boomer confided to young Smith that he knew they were "Dutch coffins."[jf] Actually, these devices were being used in breweries all over America to cool the boiling wort before the yeast was added to start fermentation.

The U.S. Census of 1880, taken on the 10th of June, listed Lemp as a 42 year-old brewer, born in Prussia; wife Kate was 30, Amil (sic) 13, George 11, Lizzie 10, Augusta 9, Ida 5, Ada 5, Albert 3, and William 9 months. John's brother Jacob was listed as a brewer who roomed with Topp Consorting, another brewer from Hesse, Germany. They apparently both worked for John Lemp.

Peter Neth, another man from Wurtemberg, Germany, reached Boise on the 26th of May, 1880.[jg] His wanderings in the New World had led him from New York to Nevada, and from mining to the butcher business. He left Nevada pushing through snow drifts seven feet deep but arrived to find ripe cherries on the Boise trees. Here he met brewer Lemp and went to work in his brewery for the next two years. They became friends, and Neth then moved to Middleton to conduct a saloon in partnership with Lemp. By 1920 when he had a biographical sketch published, Neth had become highly successful in the ranching business. This was just one more German who got a profitable start from John Lemp.

On the 1880 U. S. Census, John's sister Julia's family consisted of Charles Leyerzaph, a 38 year-old gunsmith, Julia, 35 and keeping house, Lena 10 at school, Annie 8, Jennie 4 and Lizzie 2. Sister Eliza's family included William Jauman 43, saloonkeeper, Eliza 36, keeping house, daughter Minnie 13 at school, and nephew William Mayer 20, bartender in a saloon.

By 1880, there were 2,272 breweries in the United States. Forty-one states and territories had at least one. New York led with 334, while Georgia, North Carolina and Vermont had only one each. There were ten breweries in the Territory of Idaho that year. Idaho's population had increased to 32,610 by 1880. This was about the number of beer drinkers in an Eastern urban neighborhood, but in Idaho these were spread over hundreds of nearly impassable miles. Idaho had one brewery for every 2,717 people; only Nevada and Montana had lower per capita ratios.[jh] North Carolina in contrast had one brewery for each 1,399,750 people, and six states had no brewery at all.

Hop growing began in Oregon that year, but New York produced over 80% of the American hop crop.[ji] Oregon hops would be much closer for Lemp.

The July 4th parade had a Liberty Car on which rode Lizzie (Martha Elizabeth) Lemp costumed as "Massachusetts," Gussie (Augusta Julia Margaret) as "South Carolina," Ida as "Plenty," and her twin Ada as "Peace."[jj]

John ran for mayor of Boise again but lost to Mr. Bilderbach 176 to 168. Rival brewer Brodbeck was elected to the city council with 203 votes, more than any other man.[jk] Later that month, four Boise families, including Mrs. Lemp and children, took camping gear and went to the Wood River country to get out of Boise's torrid summer heat.[jl] In two weeks they returned.[jm] This was the year the discovery of the great silver-lead loads in the Wood River area started a stampede and transformed south-central Idaho forever.

A Boise reporter who was walking from Placerville to Quartzburg that July was given a ride by a coach containing John Lemp and several other men from the lower country.[jn] I'm not sure what business Lemp had in Boise Basin at that time, nor why a newspaper reporter preferred walking for his transportation.

Lemp sued Peter Olson of Weiser in July. The defendant died but Olson's administrator was judged liable for $498 and costs.[jo] The Boise City Fire Company signed its official organization papers that August.[jp] John's name was among the many others agreeing to become members. He had been involved in the previous fire fighting groups.

Lemp had another story added to the brick building he leased to Calkins and Beachey on the south side of Main.[jq] The Ada Lodge of the Odd Fellows was going to use the fine large additional room there. Lemp also bought the land where John Early's restaurant had set before being destroyed in a large fire.[jr] This 16 by 120 foot strip of land was to have a front and back put on so it could serve as a storeroom between the adjacent buildings. By early November the brickwork on the building was going up.[js]

In September, Lemp was again a delegate to the Republican Territorial convention.[jt] Seven or eight sacks of grain from Lemp's granary were stolen that October.[ju] That same month Messrs. Martin O'Farrell & Brothers were still engaged in laying up the new brick walls between Lemp's and Early's saloons.[jv]

In October 1880 John Streb, Joseph Christian, and William Schweitzer arrived in Boise from Atlanta, Idaho.[jw] They had been inspecting mining property. After an overnight stay, they took the stage to Umatilla as the first leg of a journey to Portland and eventually home to Buffalo, New York. To remind them of their Boise visit and to console them on their journey, they took a keg of Lemp's best with them on the stagecoach.

In November, Mr. and Mrs. George Kohlepp had their first child, George.[jx] John and Catherine Lemp had a new nephew, and John and Sarah Brodbeck had their first grandchild.

John was installed "M. 1st" at the Boise Chapter No. 3 of Royal Arch Masons in late December.[jy]

1881

As the new year of 1881 dawned, Lemp decided on new prices for his whiskeys. Imports (from Kentucky that means) were 12 1/2 cents a drink and non-imported (from Boise) would be sold right out of the barrel.[jz]

In early February, torrential rains and melting snow combined to turn every little Boise area stream into a torrent, and that gave Lemp a chance to prove himself a bit of a hero. Cottonwood Creek, which comes out of the mountains near the military garrison, broke its levee and swept into town, down Sixth Street to Main, and to the Statesman's office.[ka] Many people were stranded and unable to get home. Lemp took a crew into the street and they dammed up the flow and diverted it into the Grove Street Canal. Then his men went to the garrison to help the soldiers restore the levee there. While the flood raged, reporter W. A. Goulder of the Statesman went through the town showing off and jumping over the water at every opportunity. Finally he slipped and went flat into the torrent and was being swept away. With gum boots on and spade in hand, Lemp jumped in and grabbed Goulder's shoulders and pulled him to safety. A dry suit of clothes, a bottle of Lemp's "lite invigorator" and he was good as new, but too embarrassed to write the newspaper report, a job which he left for another. Years later, Goulder wrote a biographical sketch of the man who saved him.

Katherine's mother, Martha E. Kohlepp, died on February 7, 1881, nearly twelve years after her husband's death. She was nearly 68 years old. According to the Statesman, the funeral, conducted by Rev. J. McKean of the Methodist Episcopal church, "drew an unusually large number of persons."[kb] The newspaper said she "had resided long in our midst, and was highly esteemed by those who knew her. The service was read and uttered in so impressive and touching a manner as to deeply affect those present. The bereaved relatives have the sincere sympathy of the entire community."

At the same time John was "suffering from a severe indisposition which confines him to his room."[kc] Stress in the family triggered Lemp's rhumatism.

A petiition presented to the Boise City Council in April requested that the contract giving Thomas Davis the control over the water form Cottonwood Creek be annulled and a new flume built there. Mr. Lemp appeared at the council to ask that his name be removed from the petition.[kd]

"Mr. O. L. Gabner, who suceeds John Allen as clerk and bartender in Mr. Lemp's wholesale and retail liquor establishment is one of the most proficient and gentlemanly men that you will meet in many a day. He has the art of mixing beverages in every conceivable style that may be named and a pleasant word for his many customers."[ke]

Later that spring, Lemp was hauling in brick to add a second story to his wholesale liquor building.[kf] This would make the third two story brick business house Lemp owned on Main Street. By later that month, the bricklayers were at work.[kg]

In May of 1881 was the most dangerous fire that T. P. Woodcock, chief of the volunteer fire department and future son-in-law of brewer John Brodbeck, remembered.[kh] It started in Cole's restaurant at 1:00 a.m. and was not under control until 7:00 a.m. Every able bodied man in Boise assisted at the fire. The only apparatus was the No. 2 Silsby engine and the hook and ladder truck. Water was first taken from the cistern at Eighth and Idaho. They pumped it dry in about an hour and then they took water from the ditch at Grove and Eighth streets.

A large cache of blasting powder was stored in back of F. R. Coffin's store and if not for a timely warning many firemen would have lost their lives. The powder was loaded in wagons by a few daring men and when they pulled away the tires of the heavy wheels of the wagons were so hot one could scarcely hold a hand to them. Every building between Jaumann's saloon and Jacob's store was destroyed except for R. B. Reed's store. Cyrus Jacobs was, among other things, a distiller, and a bucket of his whiskey with a miner's tin cup hanging on the side was passed around until day break when the women of Boise appeared to replace it with hot coffee for the men.

Lemp lost an $800 building in this downtown fire but he was insured for the full amount.[ki] Another report said it was a $1,000 building with $800 covered.[kj] Other men who lost property were John Broadbent, R. C. Adelman, C. B. Humphrey, Mr. Pefferlee, Mr. Lubkin, Charley Young, Neilley & Co., and Al McHendry.

In May, Lemp rehired R. C. "Dick" Adelmann as bartender.[kk] Former bartender A. I. Gaumer left for Wood River to start his own saloon in either Bellevue or Hailey. Lemp and Peter Sonna were the sureties on tax collector S.H. Walker's $15,000 bond.[kl] In June, a fire at Ogden, Utah, burned the transfer depot for the Union and Central Pacific railroads. Lemp was unfortunately among those who thereby lost all their goods that were in transit.[km]

Brother-in-law George Kohlepp in partnership with Joe Stadtmiller started a brewery in Haileyville (later just Hailey) on the Wood River where there was a major mineral strike in progress.[kn] He had learned a lot from John Lemp. Kohlepp's business was to last for a number of years, though Stadtmiller soon left.

At the Idaho Park Association meeting a majority of the stockholders were represented by five men including Lemp. The decided to have fall races, and they set up committees to do the organizing.[ko]

Lemp was elected to the Boise City Council—the first time he'd served since 1877—on 11 July 1881.[kp]

There was a story in the Boise Statesman involving Lemp which was probably an inside joke and a challenge to decipher from a later perspective.[kq] The report said an island in the Boise river 8 miles south of town was known by some Boiseites as St. Helena. John Lemp was governor and commissioner of emigration and would furnish free transportation to those who wished to settle there. It would have an asylum for those with "an eclipse of the right or left optic, a nose the color of a ripe tomato, a head as large as the front wheel of a bicycle, or an inner disgust with themselves." All liquor would be excluded and all baggage checked for contraband. Those that behaved properly would get some of Jimmy Hart's clam chowder on Saturday evenings. The newspaper hoped the island would be well patronized. This must have been what was known as Lemp's Island Ranch.

The Lemp family suffered its first loss that July of 1881. Son William Adam died of Cholera infantum followed by convulsions on the 28th.[kr] He he was only 23 months old.

In late August, John served with Mr. Logan on a committee to receive bids for the liquor bar concession and other retail stalls at the annual fall horse races.[ks] That same week a carpenter named Hall who was working on an awning in front of Lemp's billiard room fell and suffered severe facial injuries.[kt] His recovery was described as doubtful. I did not find a subsequent mention of his demise. The billiard hall was being fixed up because Lemp had four new Monarch billiard tables arriving.[ku] They were mounted on beautifully carved and gilded iron lions and were Brunswick brand. The billiard room was to be ready before the fall races and to be the largest north of Sacramento, eclipsing anything in Portland or Walla Walla.

The baptismal contest for the new billiard tables featured Joshua Davies vs. E. Rivers, lately from Montana, for $100 in a 300 point four ball carom game.[kv] Davies played "wretchedly" and Rivers won with ease. There was talk of a rematch after Davies had a chance to practice.

On the first day of September 1881, Wiliam Bedell shot and killed Frederick Hihn at a house of prostitution in Boise.[kw] Hihn, known as "Dutch Fred" was former Boise City Marshal, and currently a shot-gun messenger for the stage company. After the shooting William C. Austin, lately arrived form Wood River, followed Bedell out and went downtown telling of the events. John Lemp was one of the men who heard Austin, and he later remembered the story very differently than Austin. Austin testfied at the trial that he had never said the things Lemp remembered. Eventually Bedell was convicted and sent to prison for seven years.

Lemp was also erecting a three story—the first in Boise of that height—brick, 31 by 80 building that summer.[kx] By the end of October, the walls were high enough to receive the first story joists. This was in the area that had been burned on the south side of Main. Lemp's building was to be the focus for the whole rebuilding effort and only a lot owned by Mr. Broadbent, the wealthy capitalist, was still vacant.[ky] A local reporter went to Middleton to meet with important business leaders and found Mr. Barte Winn, "agent for our fellow townsman, John Lemp, Esq. . . ."[kz] By mid-December the trim was going up on Lemp's building.[la] Lemp also received a large load of freight at the end of October designed to last his businesses all winter.[lb] He was elected a trustee of the Idaho Agricultural Park Association along with six other men.[lc]

John Lemp, L. F. Cartee and Thomas Davis bought from W. S. Plummer the sole right to use his patented fruit dryer, in the Idaho Territory.[ld] They got it at a low price because the season was over and they would have to wait until the next year's crop. They planned to begin supplying every town in the territory with home-grown and home cured fruit.

The Boise Engine Company—fire department—publicly thanked Lemp, Brodbeck, and several others for their contributions to the group's Thanksgiving dinner.[le] Lemp was also attending City Council meetings as a member.[lf]

The first tenant in Lemp's new building was Idaho State Secretary, Mr. Singiser.[lg] By February, the Governor's office was also in the building.[lh] While Lemp was busy with all these things, he continued his service on the City Council and was rarely absent from a meeting.[li]

Christmas treats were soon in order to end the year of 1881. "That ham at Jimmy Hart's still attracts attention. A committee of five, with John Lemp as chairman, made a critical examination of the ham the other evening, and by counting the wrinkles, which Lemp says is the true test, which he learned in hogology from his neighbor Stout, the ham is just 18 years and 2 months old, Jimmy is going to make a feast on New Year's, when the ham will be served up in grand style to all his friends."[lj]

1882

On January 1 of 1882, Boise saloon owner Andrew Coyle died after an illness.[lk] Coyle was an Irish Catholic and former sailor but when he died he appointed John Lemp and Joseph Perrault his executors and left his money to his sister and his church. This is an indication of the esteem the people of Boise felt for Lemp and the level of trust they were willing to put in him. In late February, Coyle's personal property was sold.[ll] This consisted mostly of liquor and saloon supplies.

Lemp took the position of President of the First National Bank in 1882.[lm] He would retain this post for years to come.

The *Boise Statesman* newspaper was put up for sale that February and for a while a proposed company of Lemp, a Mr. Berry, John Post and others negotiated for the sale.[ln]

This never materialized. Lemp added a large sign over the sidewalk at his wholesale liquor store that month. Lemp bought a mine on Wood River in March of 1892.[lo] The whole story of the mine is in the next chapter. The rest of his life Lemp was involved in mining in the Hailey/Wood River area.

When Lemp went to see his new mine in the Wood River area he told the locals his bank would no longer purchase county certificates of indebtedness. He said: "You are turning them out too fast." Subsequently their value depreciated, and the influence of Lemp's opinion was blamed for the fall in price.[lp]

At the close of the school term that April many students recited speeches in an oratorical recitation. Among the students involved were Lizzie Lemp, her cousin Minnie Jaumann, and Emma Krall, the daughter of former brewer John Krall.[lq] George Lemp, who was in the principal's class, was listed with those who had never been absent or tardy.[lr]

Lemp began brewing with the water from the Eastman water works in May and said it was superior to any well water.[ls] He said he would now make the best beer in the country. There was also a great public interest at this time in getting a proper sewage system in Boise to stop the typhoid and diphtheria epidemics that ravaged from time to time. The favored proposal was a direct underground sewer from Lemp's brewery to the river.[lt]

Historian Max Rudin contends the modern period of American

beer history begins during this Spring of 1882.[lu] When the National League sought to ban beer at baseball games, the teams in cities associated with brewing withdrew and formed the American Association. Derisively labeled the Beer and Whiskey League, they catered to the working class man. They played on Sunday, kept ticket prices low and served beer. The role of beer was defined for many decades to come. " . . . its (beer's) connection to sports and other places men go to escape and bond; its connection to leisure, especially of the American working class; and its implicitly rebellious, nose-thumbing attitude toward the tastes and rules of social "betters" and other authority figures." This may explain the way that John Lemp, undeniably a part of the frontier aristocracy, kept the common touch and his connection with the working class. He made the working man's beverage and thus was the source of that symbol of their rejection of the aristocracy Lemp represented. Lemp could, ironically, be simultaneously the symbol of the working class and the capitalist class.

That May, Lemp's extended family endured a tragedy which eventually had repercussions at John's home too. Lemp's brother-in-law, Hailey brewer George Kohlepp, suffered the loss of his wife and new-born son. Early, overly optimistic, reports said mother and new baby were fine. Both died. John and Sarah Brodbeck, Lena Brodbeck Kohlepp's parents, hurried to the scene but arrived in Hailey just after the funeral of their daughter. At various future times the surviving Kohlepp child, George, would live with John Lemp's family.

James Alonzo Pinney served as mayor in 1882 and Lemp was again a councilman.[lv] In July, Lemp was reported confined to his bed with inflammatory rheumatism.[lw] This was the first mention of a condition that was to plague him for the rest of his life. By late August, John was well enough for a little outdoor recreation. A company of old sports, Lemp, Fred Dangle, Louis Seitzel and Judge Heed, left for a hunting excursion down the Boise River.[lx] Their supplies allegedly included ten gallons of rye whiskey, four kegs of beer, ten bottles of pickles, one loaf of bread, several guns and dogs, and about 100 pounds of salt to catch birds with. Lemp furnished a span of horses and a light wagon, and each man brought his own umbrella. The *Statesman* deadpanned "we can't see what they wanted with so much bread."

By October, Lemp was back at business and was having a fifty foot extension put on his brick store building which was under lease.^{ly} Lemp was involved in a case in the District Court in November, when he sued E. Moudy.^{lz} Moudy was enjoined by presiding judge H. E. Prickett from diverting the surface water of the Middle Slough into irrigation ditches owned by Lemp.^{ma}

Also that November, Lemp was again elected treasurer of the Odd Fellows.^{mb} In December, Lemp advertised that he had 60 acres of redtop clover and alfalfa available for pasturage.^{mc} In early January of 1883, Lemp and all the other ice users and retailers of Boise were putting up another year's crop cut from the pond near the garrison.^{md}

In late February, Lemp made a short trip to nearby Middleton which was reported in the paper.^{me} He seemed well pleased and said he would be down again soon.

A Railroad for Boise?

In the 1850s Congress authorized four surveys to determine the best railroad route to the Pacific. The northern and southern Solons had a dispute about which was the best—by political, not geographic standards—route and the situation deadlocked for that decade. During the Civil War, with no southerners in the halls of Congress, two railroads were authorized to build along a central route. By 1869, Sacramento and Omaha were linked, and indirectly the Atlantic and the Pacific. The rails ran south of Idaho through Nevada and Utah. Idaho and the rest of the Northwest were unsatisfied; they coveted a direct railroad of their own. Railroad developers in the Puget Sound area in the 1870s promised to push for an eastern connection but their financial bubble burst. The Jay Cooke railroad company collapsed in 1873 and that helped start a national depression. No northern intercontinental railroad through Idaho would be built for years.

In 1875, the Utah Northern Railroad put a narrow gauge line 85 miles north from Ogden, Utah into Franklin, a Mormon settlement and probably the first town in Idaho.^{mf} Idaho now had a railroad— of sorts. By that same year the few other Northwest tracks so far included the Northern Pacific which in its infancy ran only a 100 miles in Washington from Kalama to Tacoma, and the Walla Walla and Columbia River Railroad which went, as it name implied, 30

William Adam Lemp, Tombstone in Pioneer Cemetery, Boise, Idaho. 10 August 1879 to 28 July 1881. Photo by the author.

miles from Walla Walla to the great river. Nearly 500 miles of sagebrush separated Franklin and Walla Walla.[mg] To link these was not a direct nor easy undertaking. America was in a headlong, lustful pursuit of railroads almost for their own sake, and Idaho was on the sidelines being a wallflower at the great ball. Soon idle flirtation gave way to tangible possibilities.

A Union Pacific subsidiary, the Oregon Short Line, formed in April of 1881, and began to build tracks from Granger, Wyoming, into Idaho, through the Snake River plain, with the ultimate goal of Huntington, Oregon, and a link with the Oregon Railway & Navigation Company's tracks.[mh] On 25 November 1884, three and one-half years after the work began, the locomotives of each company touched and a second transcontinental railroad was completed. Its task had not been easy, nor its completion timely. Running far behind schedule and approaching a theoretical town —Huntington—that in fact did not even exist yet, marred the achievement. A branch line had been completed along the way, running north to Hailey, Idaho, where the new lead-silver mines needed rail service. The Wood River area had rail service but their state capital did not. The explanation for this anomaly is a curious tale.

Boise's business community knew that the country was in the railroad age and the town must act or be cut off and face extinction. At a railroad meeting held in late November, 1881, Thos. E. Logan, Cy Jacobs and John Lemp were appointed a committee to raise funds to pay the expenses of a proposed survey to show a route into Boise.[mi]

The City Council was concerned throughout 1881 and 1882 with getting a railroad into Boise, and they appropriated money to pay for a survey of the route. Lemp made the motion to that effect which was unanimously carried.[mj] An editorial in the *Statesman* in November of 1881 asked "Will the Railroad come to Boise City?"[mk] They said they knew for sure the Oregon Shortline [OSL] would pass through the Boise valley, and a branch would go to Hailey. They believed that San Francisco could not afford to miss the business of southern Idaho, and Boise must be the ordained connection site.

In January of 1882 a meeting was held in the court rooms in Boise to deal with railroad issues.[ml] A letter from A. L. Robinson, right-of-way agent of the Oregon Short Line addressed to Major J. W. Huston, was read. It said in essence that if Boise would pay $8 to Colonel Wolcott for every mile surveyed in determining a practical route into Boise the railroad company would order the survey made. In less polite terms, a bribe was in order. If the survey proved the route feasible Robinson said "I have little doubt that the road will go through Boise, provided the citizens of Boise secure to the company free of charge, the necessary depot grounds and the right-of-way from the point of divergence to the point of intersection." John Lemp moved that the $8 per mile for the survey be approved for Col. Wolcott. The measure passed unanimously.

With the OSL deal uncertain at best, in May of 1883, the businessmen of Boise organized the Idaho & Oregon Railway Company to try and induce the Oregon Railroad and Navigation Company (O.R.N.) to bring its tracks to Boise.[mm] They feared their earlier overtures to Sidney Dillon's Oregon Short Line (O. S. L.) had been a case of putting all their eggs in one basket. The O. R. N. railroad told them that with similar inducements as their rival had received they could be persuaded to come to Boise. The men capitalized at $5,000,000. Lemp was on the Committee of Organization and of course was listed as an incorporator. A few days later there was an official notice of the incorporation in the *Statesman*.[mn] The name had been altered to include Utah in the title. The express purpose was to run railroad and telegraph lines to Burnt River, Oregon, on the west; north to Horseshoe Bend on the Payette river; east to Atlanta; with a branch line to Idaho City; from there to Ogden, Utah. The press said Lemp and eight other men filed the articles of incorporation, and he was listed also as a trustee.

The promoters had hopes of obtaining an Oregon Pacific-Chicago Northwestern connection with a coastal outlet at Newport, Oregon.[mo]

Eventually the Oregon Short Line did reach the general Boise area, but 15 miles south of town, causing many to fear the town was doomed and a new city would be built by the tracks. The Short Line gave the silly excuse for going further to the south that it believed— or claimed to— that Boise's position in a valley would have created operating problems for through trains.[mp]

Years later the real story of why the railroad missed Boise was told.[mq] In 1926 Boise Mayor Ern G. Eagleson implored the community not to repeat the mistakes of 40 years before. His version of the "Railroad Almost comes to Boise" was about that time the head survey engineer for the Union Pacific system visited Boise and stayed at the Overland Hotel for a week. He told the citizens of Boise that if he was given $10,000 the railroad would go through Boise and its shops and offices would be established there. No assurance was given him that the money would be forthcoming.

The railroad men gave the city a second chance. Later, when the survey engineers were at the Corder place south of Boise, they met with the city council in the Overland Hotel. As the meeting broke up these engineers said they would wait until the following morning for the payment of $25,000 they wanted. The line would not hit Boise without it. The next morning they left town—minus the bribe—, went to Black's Creek and told Mr. Corder then that they were going back a ways and change their surveys. He told them to wait; he would go to Boise and fix things up. He tried but he met with no success either and returned the next day disgusted. The engineers went back to Cleft and surveyed a route that took a 60 degree detour and followed the bench down to Caldwell. The engineers explained they found it impractical to go through Boise because of its low elevation.

Later, a Boise delegation went to Omaha to plead their case, but again in vain. Mayor Eagleson's 1926 recounting said: "Such men as Theo Randall, Hosea Eastman, Milton Kelly, who was editor of the *Statesman*, Corder, Nathan Falk, and a lot of others knew why Boise was left off the survey."

Various local lines shuttled passengers from Caldwell and Kuna for years. Boise blamed Robert Strahorn for their misfortune and hanged him in effigy. How he figured in to the town's refusal to pay a bribe is unclear. It was not until 16 April 1925 that Boise had a through line and a train station.

The OSL completed its line down Indian Creek and reached the new townsite of Alkali Flat on September 6, 1883.[mr] Boise railroad interests thought this tract not worth acquiring but the Idaho and Oregon Land Improvement Company acquired it and established the Alkali Flat townsite. They decked the town with an array of August Christmas trees to impress a train load of investors from Iowa that they were courting. The Boise Board of Trade denounced this "villainous and unprincipled conduct," and called the promoters of the O.L.I.C. "a gang of unprincipled, impecunious and insatiable cormorants . . . who invade our country as do the leprous hordes of China, solely to 'pillage and depart' . . ."[ms] The indirect result of their invasion was to leave Boise without a railroad.

Idaho historian Merle Wells commented that the Alkali Flat syndicate included a man wealthy enough to purchase a U. S. Senate seat the previous decade and another man who became one of Pittsburgh's most illustrious millionaires with a long record of distinguished service as Treasury Department Secretary. He declined to put a name with the descriptions.

Union Pacific President Charles Francis Adams came to Boise on 17 October 1883 to promise that with local support in obtaining a right of way a branch of the railroad up the river to Boise would be completed without delay. The financial panic of 1884 interfered and construction had to be suspended. The Alkali Flat or Kuna station, 15 miles from Boise, remained the closest for the next four years.

In March, 1887, J. A. McGee of the Union Pacific affirmed that plans for a branch road would proceed, and J. A. Hickey of the Oregon Short Line, asked for the OSL to be released so that the Idaho Central, backed by the Union Pacific, could construct the branch road.[mt]

There were however, frequent false alarms about a railroad. In mid-February of 1887, a report said that Charles F. Adams had issued instructions to prepare for the work of bringing a line from Nampa to Boise. "The work will no doubt commence within a few weeks."[mu]

In only three months during the summer of 1887 the branch line, nicknamed "the stub," was completed.[mv] The people of Boise could travel 20 miles to Nampa and connect to the main-line.

The effort to secure a direct railroad into Boise was far from concluded at this point and the subscribers to the fund met to decide their next move after the Union Pacific declined to build from Caldwell to Boise.[mw] The subscribers decided the best course was to hold their land so it could potentially be used as an inducement to some other railroad to come to town. The problem was that the subscribers were now $8,000 short due to interest charges and taxes for three years. Lemp, Sonna, Ridenbaugh and Broadbent individually made up that amount.

An unnamed "subscriber" analyzed the railroad issue in the next issue of the newspaper.[mx] Boise, he felt, had not made proper inducements to the railroad as other towns had, but had smugly and erroneously felt that as the leading city of the territory they could not be left in the cold. In the present circumstances Falk and Lemp had proved the correct advisors when they said to make haste slowly. The Oregon Pacific's new construction seemed to be heading to Boise. This might offer Boise the transportation it craved.

In August, 1888, the question of a railroad for Boise surfaced yet again.[my] President Dickinson of the Idaho Central railway offered to bring the railroad into Boise provided his company was given all the right of way and depot grounds. Forty or so of the subscribers who had acquired that land met to discuss the offer. A proposal was made to reject the offer and then a lively discussion ensued. Mostly the investors feared that if they complied, another railroad would never be able to come to Boise. Lemp was one of the men especially involved in the discussion. Finally, it was decided that the meeting could not legally authorize the trustees to take a specific action.

Three years later Boise still wanted a railroad and the company that owned all the potential rail and station land in Boise formed a corporation with John Lemp as treasurer. The new railroad corporation continued to negotiate and debate whether they should try to link with the Union Pacific or the Oregon Short Line.[mz] The railroad grounds were conveyed from Lemp and the other previous owners to the Boise Railway Company as a formality to give the new corporation control.[na]

BACK TO OTHER BUSINESS 1883

Rival brewer John Brodbeck put a new furnace, malt kiln and boiler in his brewery and was getting pure mountain water from the Eastman water works in April of 1883.[nb] He was making every effort to compete with Lemp.

Lemp received 5,000 pounds of freight—wines and liquors—during May of 1883 via the teams of W. H. Hudson.[nc] Lemp's cash cow businesses obviously continued to produce. A few days later Bob Len, Lemp's beer wagon driver, was thrown from a horse and had his leg broken.[nd] Later that month Lemp took shipment of 1,000 pounds of cigars.[ne]

The R. G. Dun Mercantile Reference Agency of 1883 listed Lemp as a brewery and wholesale liquor dealer in Boise and as a saloon owner in Middleton, Ada County, Idaho. Lemp brothers-in-law William Jaumann was a saloon owner in Boise, and Leyerzaph was a gunsmith.

In June, Lemp had the materials ready to build a large brick building, or block in the parlance of the day, on the southeast corner of Main and Ninth streets.[nf] It was to be 75 feet on Main and 125 on Ninth, two-stories and divided up for stores and offices. There was a need for even more buildings as soon as the arrangements for construction could be made.

John was again elected to the Boise City Council on 9 July 1883.[ng]

In the hot weather of late July, a keg on one of Lemp's beer wagons blew up and allowed beer to squirt in the air.[nh] The frightened horses ran but were soon stopped. This was called a real calamity since the supply of beer for the mid-summer thirsts of the capital city was questionable.

Next that summer, Lemp visited San Francisco where their Chronicle newspaper said he was the richest man in Idaho Territory and worth $10,000,000.[ni] The *Statesman* joked that John "indignantly resented the estimate and turned his back on the would-be flatterers."[nj] Lemp's trip took him through Oregon, California, and Nevada, and then he also visited Hailey in August to see its prospects.[nk] His brother-in-law, George Kohlepp who was still brewing there, showed him around. The local Hailey paper described Lemp as the "heaviest tax payer in the Capital of Idaho." John told the newspaper he was to stay on Wood River a week or ten days.[nl] Hailey, incidentally, became the first city in Idaho with telephone service that year. Before Lemp left he gave an interview to the Hailey newspaper in which he praised Idaho.[nm] He said Idaho surpassed the states he had just visited for a working man to live in. He had not seen any place where the people were doing as good as in Boise. His return to Boise was duly noted in his hometown too.[nn]

As though John was not involved in enough things, he joined the new Boise chapter of the Ancient Order of United Workmen and was made a trustee in the first election of officers.[no] It was described as an organization like the Odd Fellows but it paid its deceased members' heirs $2,000 as a sort of life insurance program. Lemp was also re-elected to the city council in August of 1883.[np]

In October of 1883 Lemp began to advertise out-of-state beer as well as his own product.[nq] He offered Best Wiener Export Beer from San Francisco, California by the barrel or in bottles. This appears to be a major new direction and may indicate Lemp was losing interest in his own brewing business. Pasteurized, bottled beer from many locations was flooding the West. This was an unenvisioned result of the railroad boom.

In November, Lemp was again elected treasurer of the Odd Fellows.[nr] Children Lizzie and George each were on the honor roll at the Boise City school for having one hundred percent in one subject.[ns] A month later Dr. J. C. Leonard moved his dental office to Lemp's new brick building.[nt]

1884

In May, 1884, there was a court case, a civil suit, of United States vs. John Lemp which became a jury trial.[nu] The particulars were not available, but the verdict the next day was for Lemp. Lemp had other good news soon. On 24 June, son Herbert Frederick Lemp, future Mayor of Boise, and the 10th Lemp child, was born.

In July, John began work on a new brewery.[nv] The corner stone was ceremoniously laid in the presence of Lemp, the carpenter, the mason, and the proprietor of the *Statesman* newspaper. In it they put a history of the public school building, the court house, and other public buildings, hoping this would be of interest 100 years later. This was claimed to be the most substantial brick building in the territory. Upon a foundation of large stones was a brick wall 25 1/2 inches thick and 35 feet high. The building was to be 22 by 40 feet. The equipment would be the best available and supply the whole area with beer as good as that from Chicago or St. Louis, Lemp claimed. One report said his sales were up to 1,200 barrels per year by then.[nw]

At this time, Lemp's farm was described as 2,000 acres with rich, sandy, granite soil. He was mostly growing wheat and oats. He also had 1,000 fruit trees, 200 hogs and 250 horses.[nx] *The History of Idaho Territory* published in 1884, authored by Wallace W. Elliot, praised Lemp and listed his wealth of accomplishments achieved in two decades in Boise. "The work of his hands and brain stands out prominent as an example of his ambition and industry, a credit to his manhood, and an example to his followers."

In August of 1884 John C. Ruckdaschel began advertising his saloon, The Casino. He had worked for Lemp periodically over many years.[ny]

A notable event in Idaho brewing history occurred that August of 1884. Colonel William Dewey shot and killed Silver City brewery worker Joseph Koenig in an exchange of gunfire.[nz] Undoubtably Lemp knew mining magnate Dewey, brewery owner William Sommercamp, Koenig's employer, and due to their mutual activity in the Masonic Lodge, had probably met Koenig also. In a nutshell, the men quarreled, Dewey called Koenig anti-German names, and Koenig seethed with resentment. The next day they went together into the cellar below the brewery saloon and a number of shots were fired in a classic western

Lemp liquor store, as shown in Elliot's History of Idaho Territory, 1884. A store to sell just liquor was a novelty in Boise. Lemp was again ahead of his times.

gunfight scenario. Koenig's little son ran over from his house across the street and yelled "don't shoot my papa any more."[oa] Sentiment against Dewey was high but he was a major employer in the area. He was convicted of manslaughter, sent to the penitentiary but he appealed for a new trial. At the second trial, a prostitute came forward to testify that she had seen the event, and Dewey shot in self defense. Credible or not, the jury accepted the testimony. The town needed Dewey and this new testimony gave them a workable excuse for an acquittal. Dewey was a free man.

Eventually William Dewey made many mineral strikes and successful investments, and no one in Idaho ever seemed to be impolite enough to ever again bring up this stain on his record. He died an old rich man.

Idaho's brewers and brewing industry must have endured some painful publicity from this, but in Lemp's case there was no obvious damage done.

In August, George Kohlepp remarried to Miss Elizabeth Garrety, one of the first children of European ancestry born in Idaho.[ob] The newspaper described the bridgroom as a wealthy brewer and brother-in-law of Lemp.

Lemp was, as always, a delegate to the Republican county convention that fall.[oc] He was in the pool of men seeking to be a delegate to the state level convention but was not one of the three actually nominated.[od]

In October, Lemp sued Fred Schaffer, et al. and the defendant was given ten days to answer.[oe] At the yearly Odd Fellows convention John was once again elected Grand Treasurer.[of]

At a meeting of the Boise Board of Trade they made a definite decision to work for a wagon road to Atlanta.[og] Lemp and four other men were made a committee to solicit funds, hire an engineer, and get the survey completed. They hoped to have the road completed early the next season. A year and a half later the road was not done, but Lemp was among those donating money for its completion.[oh] He gave $1,000 which was as large an amount as any individual gave.

Before December, 1886, was up, George Kohlepp made a trip to Boise to lease the Star Gulch mine from brother-in-law John Lemp.[oi] George was bragging that the silver recently assayed 198 ounces to the ton and that was below the average of 300 to 400 ounces.[oj] The miner's optimism and lust after wealth seemed to have had at least a temporary hold on George. Mrs. Kohlepp did not go along on the trip to Boise. George returned just before Christmas to report that Boise weather was worse than Hailey's.[ok]

Meanwhile Lemp's new brewery was progressing and the builders hoped to have the roof on by mid-November.[ol] Just before Christmas John was again sick with rheumatism and confined to his home for several days.[om] It was mid-January of 1885 before he was fully recovered.[on] He said he had been confident all along that he would recover and had even reinsured himself.

An Aside about George Leyerzaph

During the 1880s John Lemp's sister Julia was married to gunsmith Charles Leyerzaph and they were living in Boise. Charles petitioned the court in Boise to probate the will of his late brother George Leyerzaph.[oo] This unremarkable event was the very tiny tip of a most curious iceberg. George's handwritten will was dated 5 June 1884 at Camp Clay, Cape Sabine, Ellsmere (sic) Land. It had been sent to Charles from the Chief Signal Office of the War Department, Washington, D.C. In its totality it said:

> "I George Leyerzaph now serving in the U. S. Army under the name Jacob Bender being of sound mind and health do hereby declare this to be my last will and testament. All my property both real and personal I bequeath to my four brothers, Conrad Leyerzaph, Freidberg near Frankfort on Maine Germany. Ernest Leyerzaph of same place. Carl Leyerzaph of Boise City Idaho Terr. Phillip Leyerzaph Friedberg Germany.
>
> George Leyerzaph, Poh. Gam. Service U.S.A.
>
> Witnesses
> C. B. Henry U.S.A.
> H. L. Gerdiner
> Henry Biederbick"

The probate request from Charles (Carl) Leyerzaph said his brother was owed a sum not to exceed $2,000 from the U.S. Army for services rendered and that money constituted his entire estate. Jacob died on or about the 6th of June 1884, the day after his will was made, at the age of 32. The probate request said his mother Christiana was also still alive at Friedberg near Frankfort on Main, Germany. Judge T. J. Curtis eventually took the testimony of Adolphus Washington Greely on 8 April 1885. Greely was a first lieutenant, 5th Cavalry, United States Army. Greely testified that he knew the deceased from May 1881 to June of 1884 when he died. Greely said he recognized the handwriting and signatures of Leyerzaph and the witnesses but was not actually there to witness the signatures. Greely said that Mr. Henry and Mr. Gariner were dead and that Mr. Biederbick was living in New York. The petition was approved, Charles was required to provide a bond of $3,000 and the will was admitted to probate.

Two questions: what was a German man using a fictitious name, enlisted in the U.S. military, doing dying in the Canadian Arctic in 1884? And how could the army owe an enlisted man $2,000 when standard pay rates were only a couple of hundred dollars per year? The answer begins when the U. S. Army Signal Corps planned the "Lady Franklin Bay Expedition," under Lieutenant Greely to find the North Pole, and then underfunded it at a mere $25,000. A correspondent of the *New York Herald* accompanied the initial days of the voyage but then left their ship *Proteus* with the pilot who had guided it out of the narrows of St. John's, New Foundland, two days before on 8 July 1881.[op] At the first opportunity, he wired his paper to report that Lieutenant Greely's northerly mission's aim was to reach the North Pole, and to rescue the men of the missing Arctic steamer *Jeanette*. In fact, the Greely expedition was primarily to set up a base camp for scientific research. The expedition had three officers, eight noncommissioned officers, twelve enlisted men, two Eskimos, and one civilian photographer.[oq] Charles B. Henry (witness to the will) was reporting on the expedition for the *Chicago Times*, and George Leyerzaph, alias Jacob Bender, was another one of the twelve enlisted men.

In August, they reached Lady Franklin Bay on the eastern shore of Ellesmere Island. Here they set up Fort Conger, named for a Michigan Senator whose support made the expedition possible. The next spring

James Lockwood led a team of eleven men northward following supply depots they had established the summer before and eventually three of the group reached 83 degrees 24 minutes North Latitude, the most northerly point ever visited by civilized man to that point in history. The 1882 relief ship *Neptune* was unable to go further north than Cape Hawks and never reached the expedition. In 1883 the *Proteus* was crushed by ice just north of Smith Sound and thus also failed to resupply the expedition. The situation was growing impossible.

Herbert Frederick Lemp
24 June 1884 to 6 May 1927
Photo, Idaho State Historical Society

In August of 1883, Greely headed his command south. They reached Cape Sabine and set up Camp Clay. Henry Clay, grandson and namesake of the respected Kentucky statesman, had joined the expedition at Disko the first year and the camp was named for him. The original 2000 pounds of canned potatoes plus other supplies had dwindled to only fifty day's supply. Some men ate lichens, shoes of leather, and human flesh the doctor cut from a man who had committed suicide.[or] The cabin they built of stone collapsed and the men took shelter in a tent. They began to die of scurvy, malnutrition and pulmonary problems. On 23 June 1884, seventeen days after Leyerzaph's death, sailors of the *Thetis*, one of three relief ships sent that summer under the command of Winfield Scott Schley, spotted the expedition's camp. Seven were still alive, including Greely, and hospital steward Henry Biederbick (signing witness to the will.) The men were all too weak to stand and one died three days later.[os]

Charles Buck Henry, who signed the will, was shot under orders of Lieutenant Greely for stealing food on June 4th.[ot] Three men with rifles, one of which was loaded with a blank, approached him on the beach, read the commanding officer's order and shot him dead. That was about 1:30 on June 4th. A different version of the story emerged later that only one gun was serviceable and the sergeant with the short straw fired the fatal shot. Bender too had been guilty of stealing the minute shrimp which was the main food source late in the expedition. At 3:45 Private Bender died —"very cowardly," according to expedition member Schneider. Then later that day Dr. Pavy died, his death "hastened by narcotics." Was the will misdated? Some details left out? Or did the execution of Henry take place a day after it was reported? It is implausible that anyone else could have known the names and locations of Bender's (Leyerzaph's) brothers. Therefore I conclude the will was authentic.

On the 7th of June, Greely read the burial service over Pavy and Bender. The bodies were tied up. Three of the strongest men dragged them some distance from the tents. Commander Greely moved into Bender's sleeping bag. Later, Dr. Pavy's and Bender's bodies were placed into an ice crack.

Back in Boise, Lemp's extended family had a curious tale to tell of a relative's adventures in the far north.

1885

Mr. Phillip Paul, former Atlanta, Idaho, brewery owner and Lemp employee, was driving a four-horse team to Lemp's ranch at Middleton one day and traveling with Eugene Borll who was driving a similar team.[ou] Philip had been ill and Lemp advised him not to go, but he went anyway. Eight miles below Boise Eugene looked around and saw Paul's team had stopped. He went back and Paul said he was too sick to go on, fix his blankets and he'd lie down. Before Borll could get the blankets ready Paul was dead. Borll unhitched a horse, left the wagons and corpse in charge of some neighbors and road to Boise for help. Lemp sent a wagon to pick up Paul's body.

Paul was remembered as a native of Germany who had previously worked for A. H. Robie on Dry Creek. He was an excellent teamster and hard working man. His brother had once been in Idaho but was now in Arizona or New Mexico somewhere. Philip Paul, left the fold at the age of 57.

Later that month of April, J. G. Duncan moved his cooper shop to Lemp's brewery.[ov] A brewery needed a steady supply of kegs and barrels of all sizes. John bought mining land in Custer County from John B. Eliot and from S. T. Henderson early in 1885 also.

In April of 1885, John McNamara, well known Boise man was appointed to the Washington, D.C. police force.[ow] He had been at Fort Sumter when the rebels took it and the Civil War began, and later was a first sergeant stationed at Fort Boise. Just before moving east a few months before he had been in the employ of John Lemp. Lemp was also busy with City Council duties at this time.[ox]

John wanted an iron front on the new building he was about to erect on Main Street. He was negotiating with Lawton and Torrence to build it. In a month they were casting 7,000 pounds of plates for the G. & S.M. Co at Banner and also found time to make the front for Lemp's new brick building to be erected adjacent to Pefly's harness shop.[oy]

In June of 1885, John Lemp was part of the Masonic delegation that went to the train station to pickup the body of deceased Judge Prickett and convey it to the Masonic Hall.[oz] The judge was properly buried the next day with Masonic rites.

The Glorious Fourth of July was duly observed in 1885. Joining with a host of young Boise ladies, twins Ada and Ida Lemp were the twin joys Peace and Plenty on the Liberty Car.[pa]

In the summer of 1885, John went to Hailey to look at mining property.[pb] He was described as President of the First National Bank and brother-in-law of County Commissioner Kohlepp.[pc] It was news worthy in Boise when he returned.[pd]

In late September, the billiard tables at Lemp's were moved downstairs in the same building.[pe] Henry Robie and Tom Carder were to run the reconfigured establishment. Robie had learned about a swindler's technique of getting extra change on a purchase and was ready when a couple of disreputable gents were trying the trick in Boise.[pf]

John and a man named Joel M. Jones of eastern Oregon both claimed ownership of a horse in June of 1885.[pg] Finally, the local paper reported, Jones abandoned the dispute and let Lemp have the creature.[ph] This report was premature and the dispute continued. They were in the Supreme Court in March of 1886.[pi] On the calendar for the March 1886 term of the District Court was the case of J. M. Jones vs. John Lemp.[pj]

Lemp was back in the race horse ownership game at this point. His 2-year-old bay, Cleveland, was described as a "pretty a piece of horse flesh as was ever bred in Idaho."[pk] It was sired by Saxey out of thoroughbred mare Vanguard and was being trained by Mr. N. G. Smith.

Mr. Peter Neth of Middleton stopped in Boise one day and reported on the prosperous conditions of his hometown. He cited the example of the large building his employer John Lemp had just completed in Middleton.[pl]

At this same time, rumors out of Weiser City said John was thought be the next Republican candidate for Congress.[pm] *The Statesman* said the Republicans "might go a great deal further and fare worse than with the burly John." This was not to be.

In October, John went to Idaho City accompanied by J. W. Brum for the yearly gathering of the Odd Fellows.[pn] The arrival of the Grand Treasurer from Boise City was properly noted in Idaho City.[po] Back in Boise, attorney T. D. Cahalan moved his office into Lemp's brick building on Main Street.[pp] In November, Lemp was having repairs made to his building on the corner of Main and Ninth streets.[pq] In early December, the Turnverein had another ball.[pr]

1886

Early the next January (1886) one of John's ice wagons bringing in the liquid freeze tipped over, threw the driver over a fence, and the horse ran off with the fore wheels. "No particular damage done," according to the Statesman.[ps] Since it was an election year that was dawning, Lemp quipped the 540 tons of ice he brought in might help keep tempers cool in the Idaho Capital.[pt] It was the largest ice harvest ever in Boise to that time.

Little is known about the daily work in Lemp's brewery. At that time brewery workers throughout the country were joining unions and working for better conditions. For instance, Brewery workers in Chicago negotiate a 64-hour workweek with free beer five times per day but only three glasses each time.[pu]

In March, John took possession of a new stallion out of Oregon purchased for him by James H. Bush.[pv] Lemp also subscribed $1,000 to the building of a road between Boise and Atlanta.[pw] This was a potential market for beer and other goods. Lemp was reportedly the biggest farmer in Ada County that spring.^px He had 750 acres of grain seeded in wheat, oats, rye and barley. Two hundred of those acres were for fall grain.

In April, John bought the one-third interest of John Roberts in the Grand Prize and Crown Point mining locations in the Silver District on North Boise River.^py Mat. Graham had the power of attorney for Roberts and actually concluded the $1,000 deal with Lemp. The quartz showing on the surface was described as immense. Tunnels were being run to see how extensive the veins were. The Idaho City paper felt Lemp had the "capital and faith and push to drive the work of development..."

Lemp and four other men were on the committee to set up the 1886 Fourth of July celebration in Boise.^pz Shortly after this, Lemp went to Wood River to look after his mining interests there.^qa He arrived back in Boise by stage.^qb The next month he suffered serious injuries when a young horse kicked him.^qc John expected no attack from the horse and, at first, did not think himself seriously injured. He walked to his store on Main and then to his house on Grove Street. Late in the night a Dr. Dubois was finally summoned and he diagnosed a dislocated shoulder and broken ribs.^qd John was reported doing well and expected back on the street in a couple of weeks.

In about ten days Lemp was able to be up and about again though sore in the chest and shoulder.^qe The *Statesman* opined that it would take pretty severe injuries to keep John in bed a week.

Lemp's farming activities were very successful again in 1886. He cut 600 acres of grain.^qf Lemp's ice wagons were busy that summer and driver Charles Crouch gave a big chunk to the Republican newspaper staff, winning their praise.^qg In late August, John, along with other area orchardists such as former brewer John Krall, was shipping fruit—apples, pears, plums, peaches and berries—to the mining camps of Idaho and Montana.^qh Lemp also raised over 100 hogs that fed on a field of alfalfa near the city limits.^qi

Brewer Brodbeck built a 32 by 42 one story brick at his brewery for a bottling house, malt house and granary.^qj The competition continued, and bottled beer in Boise as in the rest of America was continuing to gain market share.

Lemp went to the Republican convention as always that September.^qk

In an entirely different business venture, Lemp was an early investor with $2,500 in the new light company in Boise.[ql] John was, of course, one of the directors for the first three months of its existence.

John sent three four-horse teams loaded with bacon and flour for the Elmira Company at Banner, Idaho in early October.[qm] These supplies would see the miners through the coming winter.

The Grand Lodge of the The Odd Fellows (I.O.O.F.) met in Bellevue that Fall. John was there, as always.[qn] Again he was reelected to his perennial job as Grand Treasurer.[qo] Beside lodge work, John must have made many important business connections at these meetings.

In December of 1886, John's brother Jacob had bought "a valuable piece of town property" in Payette and planned to settle down and become a full-fledged citizen of the town. Mr. Joe Miller, former employee of John Lemp, was reported building a brewery in Payette.[qp] Jacob was involved with the brewery, but to what extent I do not know.

LEMP'S CANALS,
20 YEARS OF IRRIGATION LEADERSHIP

The Boise Valley is very dry in terms of precipitation but it has a verdant river flowing through it.[qq] When John Jacob Astor, the once richest man in America, sent the Wilson Price Hunt party through the area in 1811, they followed the river for water to survive. Old Fort Boise, where the Boise river meets the Snake had irrigated farming before 1843 when John C. Fremont suggested they have more of it. The need to feed the miners north in the Boise Basin and South in the Owyhee area led to diversified farming in the area starting in 1863. By the next year, all the easily watered riverside farm land was in use.

Tom Davis built a head gate about a mile and a half above the new city of Boise and in 1863 and 1864 he constructed a good substantial ditch. By the end of 1863 three cooperative canal companies with twenty-one miles of ditches watered the farm land. The Vallisco Water Company incorporated in 1864 and constructed ditches on the north side of the river. An offshoot of this was the Boise Canal Company which incorporated on 8 March 1869. In 1872, Tom Davis' system was sold and became the Jacobs Canal Company. The Ridenbaugh Canal company, founded by William Morris, developed out of two other early canals. The Pioneer Ditch in Middleton, dating from 1864 was renamed the Star in 1870. In 1878, William Morris' heir and nephew William Ridenbaugh took over that canal system.

That October of 1886 Lemp began his long involvement with the Settlers Canal near Meridian.[qr] The canal began on the south side of the Boise River at a point near the head of the government hay reservation, now known as Ann Morrison Park. There were about fifty settlers in its area which required water, and there was room for many more. The saga began on 17 October 1884 when Christian R. Purdum, Adolphus Purdum, and William H. Smith filed for a water right and claimed 50,000 inches of water. It was known as the Settler Ditch from October 30, 1884.[qs] The purpose was to bring irrigation water to the south side of the Boise River and entice settlers to the area. It was started as a cooperative, but few members would meet their labor obligation. One account said one of the original promoters, William H. Smith, was a Methodist minister who converted to Seventh Day Adventist in 1885.[qt] The farmers too joined the new denomination and spent so much time on religious activities that no work got done. The people had had no water and consequently almost no crops, and were in grave shape with winter approaching. Then Lemp became an investor in the canal. Lethargy was doomed.

A report in the *Boise City Republican* in November of 1886 explained the situation.[qu] The ditch was cut into the Boise River about two miles below Boise City and carried out on to the sage plains from there. It was to carry 9,000 inches of water, enough for 200 farmsteads. Some $5,000 of work was done in the previous year but when the farmers saw they were not able to finish in time to save their crops, they relinquished their right to an Eastern company. That company postponed work under one pretext after the other until it was too late for the 1886 crop, then forfeited their right. Now the settlers were doing the work themselves with the aid of "several of our enterprising businessmen in Boise City ... " "Their heads are level; for, besides realizing fair profits upon their investments, they will enhance the value of their business by having the country settled by an agricultural community, which will be tributary to the city." The Eastern company sent word that they now had the capital to finish, but they had lost their chance. One of those level headed Boise businessmen now committed to the ditch project was John Lemp.

Work in the winter of 1886-1887 continued on the irrigation project that was then still being called the Settlers Ditch.[qv] John had six teams working, and daily there were 25 to 35 total teams from all the other stock holders. If they could just get the water to the top of the bluff it would be easy to direct it to all the desired areas, and Boise could have a large fertile addition.

Six years after he became involved, on 31 August 1892 it became "Lemp's Canal." As the Lemp Canal it was credited with helping develop the south side of the river.[qw] One report said the settlers "did not take very kindly to the Lemp enterprise" despite the fact that it succeeded in bring them the water that made agriculture possible.[qx] The men had been living on the bounty earned hunting jack rabbits in some cases before the water arrived. After 15 October 1904 it became the Settler's Irrigation District.

The Settler's Ditch project continued on in 1888. In January the annual meeting of the shareholders was held at the Turn Verein hall and some unnamed capitalists offered to buy the project for cash and push it to completion in time for the 1888 growing season.[qy] The offer was not accepted. In the spring Lemp went out frequently to look at the canal construction.[qz] The *Statesman* said "John does first and talks afterward. A few more men like John Lemp wanted." By the middle of March some of the teams working there left to put in crops but vowed to return when that seasonal work was done.[ra] A week later, 22 extra teams were put to work on the project, and alderman Lemp again went out to examine the work.[rb] In April, he went with engineer Stevenson to Nampa to see if it would be practical to extend it all the way out there.[rc] They thought in all probability it would someday extend to Nampa. Work was progressing nicely, but it was too late for that year's agricultural needs.

In May, the Settler's Ditch was again in the news.[rd] Lemp drew off his teams because he was not getting any help from anyone and he did not think he should have to build it all alone. Work was destined to start and stop from 1884 to 1904 as the boundaries expanded and altered.

In December of 1891 Lemp successfully sued the Settlers Ditch Company, Inc. in District Court.[re] Lemp held a mortgage for $25,317 against the corporation which with costs of $23.10 and attorney fees of $500 then totaled $25,840.10. A sheriffs sale was ordered. Later that same month of December 1891, Lemp filed another suit against the Settlers Ditch Corporation and was awarded $8,521.03 plus $17 in costs.[rf]

Five years later in 1893, Lemp was sued by J. R. Russell for a Settler's Ditch matter.[rg] Russell contended that he was due $450 for the damages sustained to his farm when the ditch was put through it. The amount had been fixed by arbitration. Lemp, as president of the canal , and J.W. Daniels, as secretary, gave Mr. Russell a note in December of 1891 for the money, Russell alleged, and now he wanted to collect.

Lemp's canals had some difficulties with the water users in the Spring of 1900.[rh] Lemp had been charging water users $1.50 per acre but a new law required that the water actually be measured and charged for on a more accurate basis. State Engineer D. W. Ross became the go-between for the settlers with Lemp in regards to their demands for the new system. First Ross met with about 40 settlers at the White Cross school house. They came away convinced that proper measurement would be to their benefit. A settlers committee then met with Ross and Mr. Lemp to discuss the matter. The *Statesman* reported that Lemp would put in the main measuring weirs and the settlers would put in the individual weirs.

Under the old system, there was no incentive to conserve the water. About 54 inches was being applied to each acre when 30 would have been sufficient. Some places the water went to waste while at the end of the lateral canals there was often an insufficient supply. Five thousand acres were being irrigated while the canal theoretically carried enough water for 9,000 acres if it was used judiciously. Nearly all the farmers were prepared to increase their acreage if more water was assured.

Under the new system, the water would be measured at an inch flowing 24 hours which is very close to an acre foot (an acre covered one foot deep in water). The canal carried 180 acre feet per day and they calculated a loss due to evaporation and seepage of 20 per cent. This left 144 acre-feet per day for irrigation. If the rate charged was two cents per unit, the canal owner would reap about $9,000 a season. Currently, Lemp was only taking in $7,500. Using measuring weirs, the farmers would cover the land quickly and then shut the water off without allowing any waste. Another advantage was that use could be planned for more accurately and no one would fail to get what was needed when it was needed.

Lemp published a formal reply to the committee in the *Statesman*.[ri] Lemp stated he would charge two cents per inch per 24 hours, as the committee and Mr. Ross had discussed with him. Also he agreed to have "appliances, boxes, weirs and measuring devices" placed in the canal as the state engineer directed.

The whole deal was not quite as smooth as this would seem, for in July the county commissioners had to issue an order to Lemp to place weirs or measuring devices on the three lateral ditches.[rj] One lateral was for A. M. Wolfkell and others, one for George Dubois and others, and one for William Lewis and others. The commissioners said if the devices were not installed they would install them at Lemp's expense.

The Canal became the Settler's Irrigation District on 15 October 1904 and was still in existence when that century ended. A description by the company in 2001 said the district consisted of 12,322 acres, and got its water from four sources: 2,878 acre feet of storage in Arrowrock Dam, 6,082 acre feet in Anderson Ranch Dam, 10,000 acre feet in Lucky Peak Dam and 9,322 miner's inches of natural flow water rights.[rk] The canal then was 20 miles long with 95 miles of laterals. Deliveries of water were from west of Five Mile Road and south of Usdtick Road to eventually discharge into a Nampa and Meridian Irrigation District drain below Black Cat Road. John Lemp could take credit for being a major force behind irrigation development in the general area around Boise.

On Sunday, November 7 Bernard Louis Lemp, offspring number eleven, entered the John Lemp family.[rl] As the newspaper said Lemp "believes in the commandment, increase and multiply." Yes, indeed.

1887

Lemp was one of several mine owners doing development work in the Sheep Mountain area. John was planning to build a cabin there and take in enough supplies so his miners could work all winter.[rm] In January of 1887, "Beer by the quart at Lemp's saloon" was the extent of John's advertising in the *Boise City Republican*.[rn] This newspaper had a weekly temperance column and he may not have considered them beer-friendly.

In February, 1887, the rumor around Idaho was that Lemp and Nathan Falk were going to visit the Vienna Exposition—the great European world's fair.ʳᵒ Since there were no subsequent reporting on it, I do not believe this trip was made. Also in February, Lemp came out against the proposal for dividing Ada County.ʳᵖ He and several other solid citizens of Boise believed division would create bitter feelings and not produce benefits.

When brother Jacob Lemp moved to Payette and purchased Mrs. Mohr's property, the Boise paper at first attributed the transaction to John.ʳᵠ Jacob was indeed building a brewery and a house, and was about to take a partner.ʳʳ Official records show no Jacob Lemp Brewery in Payette, but there was a W. F. Stirm brewery starting the next year. The 1880 U.S. Census listed Jacob as 30 year-old single man born in Hesse (Germany) of Hessen parents. On 16 January 1887 he married Mary Stirm at Payette, Ada County, Idaho.ʳˢ She was the sister of W. F. Stirm. The intertwined net of Idaho's brewing families continued.

George Kohlepp was in Boise for a few weeks that March, and probably took in the wedding. Primarily he was fixing up his old homestead before returning to Hailey. *The Boise City Republican* commented: "When he has made his fortune on the Galena Belt he will settle down here, and we hope it won't be long, for George is a good citizen."ʳᵗ

In April, the County District court was to meet, as well as the United States Circuit, and District courts.ʳᵘ The U.S. courts were only to dispose of routine business since they had no funds to pay jurors or witnesses. The county court, however, was set to have a jury trial of any cases the grand jury referred to it. Among the twenty-five men picked for the jury pool was good old John Lemp.

John gave the *Statesman*'s editor a bottle of imported Maslas (sic) wine and got a plug from him.ʳᵛ The editor said the wine was pure and highly recommended for medicinal

Bernard Louis Lemp. 8 November 1886 to July 1950 Cemetery, Boise, Idaho. Photo by the author.

purposes, especially for ladies who needed "some kind of relaxant." John's gin, whiskey, and brandies were also recommended. About this same time in April, the local paper carried a detailed article about how much freight was carried into Boise by each merchant and consequently how much a railroad could expect to haul.[rw] Lemp and Brodbeck, rival brewers, were on the list without specific volumes being listed.

In Hailey, where Lemp had mining interests, the electric light plant—first in the state— went into operation. As with telephones, it was leading Idaho into another infrastructure development.

John Lemp filed suit in the district court against Arabella C. Maxon, executrix of the the last will of Hamilton J. G. Maxon, to foreclose a mortgage he held from the late Maxon.[rx] In April 1887, Lemp was awarded the land in question, $2,201.15, and the sheriff was ordered to sell enough of the estate's other land to cover what was owed. Ten shares of stock in the Dry Creek Ditch Company were also surrendered to Lemp.

The citizens of Boise held a meeting to organize for a Fourth of July celebration. The committee, whose names were "a sufficient guarantee that arrangements will be made and Boise will celebrate," were Eastman, Ridenbaugh, Bush, Epstein and John Lemp.[ry]

In May, Lemp suffered a fire that originated in his stable by his brewery.[rz] The alarm went out and soon the hook and ladder company as well as two or three hundred people were there to fight the blaze. There was no chance of saving the tinder-dry hay and straw-filled building, but nearby roofs were wet down, and a favorable breeze helped. A pigeon house, hog pen and several sheds were torn down to stop the spread. Lemp had promised earlier to remove his hogs from town but apparently he had not. The newspaper supposed that a cigar, pipe or match had caused the problem. Lemp's barn contained a quantity of hay and grain and his uninsured loss was about $1,000.[sa] Considering the buildings that might have caught fire, all ended well.

George Kohlepp was sued for divorce in Hailey by his wife Elizabeth G. Kohlepp and lost the case, being ordered to give up half of his real property, pay $100 in attorney fees, and pay $30 twice a year for support of their child.[sb] The plaintiff called eight witnesses and the defense ten, with six more in rebuttal. Elizabeth was given one half of the brewery property which must have been the severest blow to Kohlepp. George then moved back to Boise and began intermittent work for his brother-in-law.

On the Glorious Fourth of July of 1887, Lemp, Peter Sonna and Hosea Eastman were serenaded at five A.M. to kick off the ceremonies.[sc] This was a fitting tribute to men who had done so much for the growth and prosperity of the city, according to the Statesman.

At the end of July, John went to Idaho City to attend the funeral of fellow brewer, Nicholas Haug, who had died after a long illness.[sd] Lemp and John Early went on from there to look at the Sheep Mountain mining district, and the word in Idaho City was that they might build a smelter.[se] In Boise it was anticipated the trip might last two or three weeks. When the men got back to Idaho City, a report said that on the trail one of John's horses had died and one had been stolen.[sf] When Lemp had reached Banner, he learned his saloon in Boise had burned. Perhaps the misfortunes soured him on Sheep Mountain, for he decided not to put up a smelter until a better road was made into the district. When Lemp returned to Boise, he said he had not lost a horse, as reported, and he had not decided what to do about rebuilding after the fire.[sg]

Louise Bernice Lemp.
24 October 1888 to 3 November 1966.
Photo, Idaho State Historical Society

Within a week or so Lemp had decided to build one brick building on the lot the fire in May cleaned off, and another "above Bennett's furniture store."[sh]

As summer closed, Lemp and rival Brodbeck were on the committee to organize a celebration over the completion of the new school.[si] It was to be held at Miller's Grove and Governor Stevenson was president of the day. John was also reelected Grand Treasurer at the Odd Fellows yearly gathering.[sj]

That October, John sold one of his buildings, the one occupied by Shainwald Brothers as a clothing store, to John Broadbent (not the similarly named brewer) for $15,000 cash.[sk]

Late in the month of October, Lemp and wife sold sections of two downtown lots to John R. Broadbent for $12,000.[sl] Another very timely city question arose at this time. The Electric Light Company wanted three dollars per month from the city council for each street light it had newly installed.[sm] Councilman Lemp spoke in favor of this since strangers would need light to get around town at night. When the mayor was absent during this period of time, John, with his vast experience, was the one called to the chair to conduct the city council meetings.[sn]

Lemp and Nathan Falk filed on the claim known as the "Ironclad" on 25 November 1887.[so] This was recorded on 17 March 1892. The next entry in the Mineral Patent record book is for the Concordia being sold by the United States to John Lemp and Nathan Falk on 25 November 1887 and not being recorded until March of 1892.[sp] On the 31 of December Lemp and Nathan Falk also took possession of the Hancock Lode which was not recorded until 17 March of 1892.[sq] A marginal addendum in the deed book shows Kathryn Lemp Langdon to John Lemp on 28 September 1953. The property stayed in the family.

In a published list of assessed valuations for Ada county, John Lemp at $60,880 had more than any other individual and was only behind the Oregon Short Line Railroad in property owned.[sr] N. G. Smith returned to Boise the first week of November to report that Lemp's stallion, Cleveland, had won first money in Oregon at Baker City, and second money at La Grande.[ss]

1888

At the January 5, 1888 City Council meeting, the members, including Lemp, complained about the road between the city and the bridge, and they instructed the road supervisor to fix it.[st]

In January the annual ice harvest of 1888, Lemp brought in 700 tons.[su] By way of comparison, his rival, John Brodbeck, brought in 375 tons. It was the best crop in years. During this year John's mother emigrated from Germany and came to live with him in Boise. Lemp nearly lost his saloon one night when smoke was discovered coming from the sawdust on the floor by the stove.[sv] When the men who first saw it kicked the sawdust away a flame blazed up from beneath the floor. It was extinguished. Had they not taken action the saloon would have been a total loss. Sawdust was commonly put on saloon floors to soak up spills and tobacco juice. In February, John was still deciding what kind of building to place on his lots on Main Street between Eighth and Ninth where the fire the previous summer had been.[sw] He did tell the press that he would build something.

In late January of 1888, Lemp had a horse die.[sx] This proved to be part of a pattern. Lemp had five or six horses sick in late February of 1888 and had lost another one to illness a few months before.[sy] The report was that Dr. Christe was treating them and they were getting well.

In political business, John was at the Republican Central Committee meeting in January and was appointed to a committee of three to report on the Republican vote for delegates to Congress at the last election.[sz] The Republicans, with John, met again in March.[ta]

John made some improvements on his brewery that spring.[tb] The kettle was replaced and some new walls put up. The *Statesman* complained that now John Brodbeck would have to enlarge his brewery to keep pace, and then Lemp again in retaliation. "We want a little of this city left for churches and printing offices, and not have Gambrinus [the mythical inventor of European beer] brooding over the whole valley." John Rost, not to be mistaken for the long lost Charley Ross— was tending bar for Lemp then.[tc] The billiard tables were dissected and rebuilt that April.[td]

John took shipment of half a car load of New York cider that April and one of the barrels burst in being brought from the depot.[te] John decided to add to his real estate and to put up a brick building on the corner opposite Sonna's building.[tf] Lemp also sent two of his young horses to N. G. Smith for exercise and training.[tg]

John C. Ruchdaschel, who tended bar for Lemp, had owned, since 1885, a small turtle that he had found in the rear of John Hailey's residence.[th] At one point he lost the turtle for four months before relocating it under a safe in the saloon. It declined food for an additional two months at that point. Ruchdaschel treated it occassionally to an outing in the gutter in front of the saloon building where it seemed to enjoy itself.

There was a more sinister altercation of note at the brewery one Sunday that spring when a young Mr. E. E. Prosser went after barkeep Rost with a Winchester.[ti] Marshall Isell tried to apprehend the fleeing lad and even fired a warning shot, but Prosser was full of beer and adrenalin and was able to jump a six foot fence. Finally he was caught and scheduled to have his day in court. At the hearing it was said he had a knife and a gun, and he was therefore made to give a $200 bond to keep the peace.[tj] Ironically, the bond was furnished by none other than John Lemp.

A large Barn belonging to Lemp at Middleton burned that month of May.[tk] There was a loss of grain, hay, and a great deal of farm machinery, aggregating about six or seven thousand dollars in value. Lemp's Boise farm did well that year, however. Young son Albert Lemp brought a bucket of ripe strawberries into town on the 15th of May which caused the local paper to brag about the early date.[tl] Late in May, hail stones fell at Lemp's farm—the old Kingsbury ranch—sufficient to cut all the leaves off everything.[tm]

Eleven year-old Albert Lemp suffered a scary event that summer.[tn] He hitched his saddle horse and another to a wagon to see if he would work as part of a team. As Albert came down Main Street some boys ran in front of the wagon, and scared the horse, and he bolted. Albert hung on and managed to steer them toward the hay field in Arnold's addition. He had several near misses running them around the field a while and getting them under control. Albert put some hay on his wagon, and, when they again tried to run away, he headed the wagon back to town. He again checked them before they made much headway. Overall, Albert showed impressive presence of mind and notable maturity for an 11 1/2 year-old in a dangerous situation.

The Glorious Fourth of July of 1888 witnessed Lemp selling 150 gallons of beer, and rival John Brodbeck an equal amount—about 2,500 glasses.[to] This sounds like Boise had returned to the old town-wide binge drinking of colonial holiday tradition.

In August, there was a local Republican convention in Boise to elect delegates to the Territorial convention in Hailey where a candidate for Congress was to be nominated.[tp] Lemp was one of three men on the credentials com-

William Brower Conner
Photo, Idaho State Historical Society

mittee. In early October, he was on the transportation committee for the territorial level meeting.[tq]

One of Lemp's four-horse beer delivery teams ran away one morning while the driver was away looking for a hammer to fix something on the wagon.[tr] It ran through the streets and bent a light pole before coming to a rest. Lemp was reelected to the school board that September, a move the *Statesman* said assured at least two more years of well managed public schools.[ts]

Lemp went to the Odd Fellows convention in early October and then looked over his mining property on Wood River.[tt] He told the citizens of Hailey "Wood River is all right! All you want is a little time and some capital. With time capital will come. I've got $42,000 invested in mines here, and I know it is all right. I'm working a few men now, and will do more work next spring." When he returned to Boise, Lemp said he was much pleased with the trip.[tu]

John soon had another major reason to be pleased. On 24 October Louise Bernice Lemp was born. (The *Statesmen* erroneously said it was a new son.)[tv] Lemp continued to smile and his friends smiled back was the report. This was the 12th Lemp child and she was destined to live 78 years.

The new baby's brother Albert had another problem with a horse and did not come off well.[tw] While riding, the animal fell with him and its weight landed on his leg. It fractured between the knee and ankle and Dr. Girard treated it. Within a month Father John joined new daughter and broken legged son in being confined to his bed at home.[tx] Rheumatism again proved to be the culprit with the senior Lemp. An unnamed caller went to Lemp's home during this time and said Lemp had such *bonhomie* and was attired like a king at ease so that the caller imagined himself in the "presence of a veritable Kaiser Wilhelm."[ty] In a few days John was back on the street.[tz] The newspaper editor recommended that he try Professor North's liniment. By early December, son Albert was up and about again too, but with crutches.[ua] Son Emil spent several days in Mountain Home in late November.[ub]

1889

On January 3 of the new year of 1889, the new Boise Opera House was dedicated with a grand concert, dedicatory address, and grand ball.[uc] Lemp was on the reception committee. Lemp's first business mention of 1889 was when he was rumored to have an $11,000 attachment against the Graham mines.[ud]

In March, John announced he would rebuild on the burned district between Eight and Ninth on Main.[ue] That same month John sued the Idaho Gold and Silver Mining Company, Limited, in District Court.[uf] The demurrer was withdrawn and the judgment entered in accordance with the stipulation filed. Lemp was awarded $10,999.39 and an additional $240.42 in costs.[ug]

A strong wind one April day detached a section of brick from the top of Lemp's billiard hall.[uh] It fell in front of a nearby restaurant but, miraculously, no one was injured. Lemp had a new saloon which was ready for business that same month.[ui] He was then ready to construct his new brick building on the burnt district.[uj] The Boise newspaper said they would commence hauling the stone for the building about the first of May.[uk] The structure was actually to be a row of fireproof buildings between Leyerzaph's building and the Odd Fellows Hall. Two or three "Chinese rookeries" were to be torn down, and the new building was to be three stories.[ul] In June, Lemp was praised for being a genuine builder who had done his fair share of the building up of Boise from the beginning.[um]

In late May, John was one of seven unanimously elected to the committee to have full charge of the Boise 4th of July celebration.[un]

Thomas Cremin and Thomas Finnegan were laying the bricks for Lemp's building and the project was expected to require 3/4 of a million before it was finished. It was 100 feet on the front and 110 feet in length.[uo] It was described as the largest building yet begun in Idaho by the means of one man. In defending the capital, the *Statesman* said "when any city in Idaho will equal Lemp's block it will be time enough to talk of the decadence of Boise City."[up] Near the end of June the walls were nearly high enough for the second floor joists. At that stage it looked like several buildings going up at once, the newspaper said.[uq] It was the most imposing commercial building ever erected in Boise to that date. By mid July, Lemp's new brick building was up to the second story and progressing nicely with only a small crew working.[ur] The newspaper began to speculate whether the building would be for offices or a hotel. Whichever, it would meet the needs of Boise for some time to come, they opined.[us] In September it was finally announced that Lemp's new building would be for merchants on the first floor and the upper two would be a hotel.[ut]

At the Republican caucus in late June, Lemp was again nominated for the city council.[uu] John was also an Ada county delegate at the State Constitutional Convention this year.[uv] This was mentioned in the press throughout the state.[uw] He and J. W. Ballentine were the only two men associated with brewing who were involved in writing the first fundamental law of the new state of Idaho. At the close of the convention they adopted a memorial to Congress asserting the loyalty of the people of Idaho for the past 26 years and offering the opinion that the "present system of territorial government is unrepublican and undemocratic in theory."[ux]

In early July, Major General William H. Jaumann (husband of Martha Elizabeth Lemp, John's sister) organized a picnic of seventeen that went to Robie Gulch for hunting and fishing. In the group were Mrs. John Lemp, her sister-in-law Mrs. Jaumann, Lizzie Lemp, Gussie Lemp, Emil Lemp, and others. They caught 239 trout and shot seven full sized turkeys.[uy]

John sustained the tradition of brewers being fireman and continued as a member of Boise Engine Company no. 1.[uz] In August, one of John's teams was returning from delivering a load of brick to the new building project when a clip on the doubletree broke.[va] The back of the wagon hit the ground, scaring the team which bolted. Tom Kane, the driver, was thrown off, but only slightly cut on the hand. One of the horses was cut badly though.

Mrs. Lemp was mentioned in the local newspaper that year in a thinly disguised ad. She was reported to be the happy possessor of the improved White sewing machine purchased from C. Ellsworth. She was described as a practical sewing machine operator and she pronounced the White king of all brands.[vb] Considering how many clothes her twelve children must have needed, sewing was more than a hobby to Catherine.

Lemp filed suit in District Court in September of 1889 against William F. Bair and Mrs. E. Bair.[vc] Lemp was awarded $299.88. On the September 1889 issue of Bradstreet's Commercial Reports Lemp was listed as wholesale and retail liquors in Boise, and also as a saloon owner in Middleton.[vd]

In October, the brick work was completed on the new building with half a million used. Lemp had another half million for future projects ready to be burned.[ve] The roof was expected to be completed by the end of the first week of October. By mid-November, the first floor was being plastered.[vf] Work was progressing on the second floor but it was still a long way from completion. The east room was to be occupied by J.B. Wright Drug Store and the west room was to be sublet apparently from Hollister, Bishopric & Co. to a new drug firm of Whitehead & Boomer.[vg] The building was listed with the forty-one other new dwellings as one of Boise's greatest accomplishments of 1889.[vh]

Before winter set in Lemp visited his Star mine on Wood River in October. From there, Grand Treasurer Lemp was soon off to Mountain Home for the yearly Odd Fellows meeting which that year included the dedication of the new lodge hall in the town.[vi]

One of Lemp's teams ran away from in front of the brewery that October. Jack Morris, the driver, was not on the wagon at the time but he grabbed a nearby saddle horse and raced after the runaways.

Two wagons were hooked together and when the second one struck a telegraph pole the wagon tongue splintered and disconnected. Morris got in front of the horses at that point and stopped them from continuing on with just the first wagon.[vj] As the newspaper said, "these runaways are exciting but not funny."

In 1889, North Dakota embraced prohibition by amendment to their state constitution. This was the last of the seven states to go dry during that decade. The second great wave of dry sentiment was then out of steam and had to pause to rest and regroup. Eighteen years were to pass before another state opted to try this instant solution to all social evils. Idaho had been little effected by this second wave. The third wave though was biding its time and building strength, and when it came, early in the new century, it would sweep up the Gem state and all of the nation. Lemp, unbeknownst, had a decade and half to continue the beer business as usual.

On Christmas Eve, 24 December 1889, the first wedding among the children of John and Catherine was celebrated.[vk] In the Lemp home, the Reverend David C. Patteg of St. Michael's Episcopal church joined Martha Elizabeth with William Brower Connor in holy wedlock. Connor was described as a successful businessman. Elizabeth, as she was known as an adult, was nineteen. The great Lemp nuclear family nest was one smaller, and the extended family that much larger.

Connor was born at Boyertown, Berks County, Pennsylvania and was the son of Willoughby and Amanda Brower Connor, both of whom were from the Keystone state.[vl] William's father was in the iron business and was superintendent for Gable Iron and Steel Company at Pottstown. The father served in the Civil War and eventually died of wounds he received there. The Family had twelve children. William worked for Marshall Field in Chicago when it was the greatest mercantile concern in the United States and for eight years was in charge of the dress goods department. He left Chicago planning to eventually own his own business and emigrated to Boise. In Boise he was an interested principal in the Hollister, Bishoprick & Co. firm. After seven years, he opened his own exclusive men's furnishing store on Bannock Street.

The 1890s began with the glow of the nuptial joy still fresh in the minds of all the Lemp kith and kin.

END NOTES

a There are more published biographical sketches of Lemp than any other Idaho Brewer, maybe more than any other Idaho pioneer. Some of these are. Hawley, *History of Idaho* (1920) vol. II, p. 214 & p. 844 & p. 18; French, *History of Idaho* (1914) vol. II, p. 596-7; Flenner, *Syringa Blossoms*, (1912) p. 167; *Illustrated History of Idaho*, (1899) p. 499.; *Progressive Men of Southern Idaho*, (1904) p. 70. Elliot, *History of Idaho Territory* (1884) unnumbered page between p. 254 and 255. Hart, *Boiseans at Home*, p. 16.; Wells, *Boise: An Illustrated History* 1982, p. 48. Beal and Wells, *History of Idaho* (1959) *The Weekly Capital*, 23 December 1899, p. 14, c. 4. *The Evening Capital News—Mid-Summer Supplement*, 30 August 1902, p. 11, c. 4-5. "John Lemp: Foundation Builder of Boise, *The Idaho Magazine*, March, 1904, p. 30. W. A. Goulder, How a Penniless German Boy Made It Go in the Early Days of Idaho," *Idaho Daily Statesman*, 15 November 1908, p. 5. MacGregor, *Boise, Idaho, 1882-1910*, p. 101.

b On the Passenger and Immigration Index, there is a John Lemp coming to Allegheny county, Pennsylvania in 1852. This may have been our John Lemp but there were a number of men coming to America during that era with the same name. Genealogy.com.

c Elliot, *History of Idaho Territory*, 1884, lists his birth place as Butzbach, Germany. This is the only mention of this place in all the sources.

d Internet. Niederweisel.

e French, *History of Idaho*, 1914, vol. II, p. 597.

f French, *History of Idaho*, 1914, vol. II, p. 597.

g Peter R. Guetig and Conrad D. Selle, *Louisville Breweries: A History of the Brewing Industry in Louisville, Kentucky, New Albany and Jeffersonville, Indiana* 1995, p. 15.

h Page 88 of *Census Population Schedules*.

i Genealogy,com. from Gary J. Zimmerman and Marion Wolfert, *German Immigrants*, 1986, p. 86.

j Clark was of mostly Irish descent. After teaching school in Missouri in 1859-60, and serving briefly in the Confederate army, he drove a team to South Park, Colorado, where he worked in a mine. In 1863, he was among the first to head for the new mines, and he arrived at Bannack, Montana, after 65 days of travel. While in business in the early days there he rode horseback to Boise to secure several thousand pounds of tobacco which was in short supply in Montana. See Joaquin Miller, *Illustrated History of Montana*, vol. I, Lewis Publishing Co., Chicago, 1894, pp. 364-369. *Idaho Daily Statesman*, 29 October 1911, Section II, p. 3, c. 1-3. See Also William D. Mangam. *TheClarks: An American Phenomenon*. New York: Silver Bow Press, 1941, p. 9-15.

k *Idaho Daily Statesman*, 28 July 1892, p. 8, c. 1-2.

l Mangam, *The Clarks*, p. 13.

m Some sources say the name was West Bannock, which was one of the names given to what was later Idaho City. The sources can be quite confusing.
n *Idaho Daily Statesman*, 4 November 1905, p. 6, c. 4. This was an obituary for Jeff Thompson. Other sources say future brewer Samuel Adolph built the first cabin in Boise.
o Hawley, *History of Idaho*, supplement volume, p. 23.
p Hart, *The Boiseans at Home*, p. 16.
q *Idaho Daily Statesman*, 20 November 1910, Section II, p. 7, c. 1-3. This photo was owned by a Dr. Gillespie of Portland, a former Boise resident. It came to light in 1910. Robert Meinke operated the "City Brewery" in 1864.
r *The Evening Capital News*, Mid-Summer Supplement, 30 August 1902, p. 11, c. 4-5. Of all his biographical sketches, this is the only one with this tidbit.
s *A General Directory and Business Guide of the Principal Towns East of the Cascade Mountains for the Year 1865*. San Francisco: Roman & Co.p. 66-73. Both Collins and Lemp are listed as Boise Brewery, Main, Between Third and Fourth. Lemp retained this name for the brewery.
t *The Evening Capital News*, Mid-Summer Supplement, 30 August 1902, p.11, c. 2.
u *Idaho Tri-Weekly Statesman*, 27 August 1864, p. 4, c. 3.
v Federal Tax Records, 1865-66, University of Idaho Library, Microfilm # 558
w Federal Tax Records, University of Idaho Library Microfilm # 558.
x Federal Tax Records, 1865-66, University of Idaho Library, Microfilm # 558.
y Federal Tax Records, 1865-1866, University of Idaho Library, Microfilm # 558.
z *Idaho Statesman*, 27 October 1866, p. 4, 4.
aa Bill Gulick, *Outlaws of the Pacific Northwest*, pp. 13-27.
ab *Idaho Daily Statesman*, 11 December 1910, Section II, p. 7, c. 1-3. A Felix Collins, likely this same brewery owner, owned a saloon in Leavenworth, Kansas on Cherokee Street back in 1859.
ac *Owyhee Avalanche*, Ruby City, 21 April 1866, p. 2, c. 4.
ad *The Capital Chronicle*, 19 March 1870, p. 3, c. 2.
ae *Idaho Tri-Weekly Statesman*, 2 August 1866, p. 3, c. 2.
af Mittelman, Amy. "The Politics of Alcohol Production: The Liquor Industry and theFederal Government, 1862-1900." Dissertation, Columbia University, 1986, p. 167.
ag *Idaho Tri-Weekly Statesman*, 10 June 1882, p. 3, c. 2. *Idaho Daily Statesman*, 9 June 1912,Section II, p. 3, c. 2. Thirty Years Ago column.
ah Announcement in the *Weekly Statesman*, about the closing of the banking business of the Greathouse Brothers in May of 1871. See *Idaho Weekly Statesman*, May 20, 1871. Internet site, gesswhoto.com.
ai *Idaho Tri-Weekly Statesman*, 31 August 1867, p. 2, c. 3.

aj *Idaho Tri-Weekly Statesman*, 11 July 1868, p. 3, c. 2. Professor James Hurd was still designing buildings in Boise in 1881 when he showed drawings for a new school. *Idaho Daily Statesman*, Hurd's original business was putting flag stone and paving stone in front of businesses.5 March 1911, Section II, p. 7, c. 3. 30 years ago column.

ak *Idaho Tri-Weekly Statesman*, 13 August 1868, p. 1, c. 1. The name Stutzenacker had various spellings. Perhaps this was the whistling Pete of legend from whom some claim Lemp purchased the brewery.

al "Boise, Idaho Elections, January 6, 1868." Internet site. gesswhoto.com.

am *Idaho Tri-Weekly Statesman*, 22 December 1868, p. 2, c. 2.

an *Idaho Tri-Weekly Statesman*, 18 February 1869, p. 1, c. 1.

ao *Idaho Tri-Weekly Statesman*, 16 February 1869, p. 1, c. 4.

ap *Idaho Tri-Weekly Statesman*, 6 October 1868, p. 2, c. 2. These would have included the establishments of John Krall, and others too small or transient to have been etched in history.

aq Ronnenberg, *Beer and Brewing in the Inland Northwest*, p. 198.

ar Salem, *Beer, Its History and Economic Value*, p. 200.

as *Idaho Tri-Weekly Statesman*, 10 September 1870, p. 3, c. 3. On the 1870 U. S. Census the family —misspelled "Kehlepp," consisted of mother Martha, Henry, and "Scortz." All living in Boise Valley.

at Mittelman, Amy. "The Politics of Alcohol Production: The Liquor Industry and the Federal Government, 1862-1900." Dissertation, Columbia University, 1986, p. 176.

au Hawley, *History of Idaho*, 1920, supplement volume, p. 24.

av Catherine's obituary said the family came west in 1865 with a freighter's outfit. See *Idaho Dailey Statesman*, 8 January 1908, p. 5, c. 3.

aw Various sources give the wedding date as 1865 which is erroneous. *Idaho Tri-WeeklyStatesman*, 8 May 1866, p. 3, c. 2. Catherine was born 20 November 1850.

ax *Idaho Tri-Weekly Statesman*, 28 November 1868, p. 3, c. 3.

ay *Idaho Tri-Weekly Statesman*, 11 January 1870, p. 3, c. 2. *The Capital Chronicle*, 8 January 1870, p. 4, c. 1.

az *Illustrated History of Idaho*, 1899, p. 499.

ba *Capital Chronicle*, Boise, 2 March 1870, p. 2, c. 2.

bb *Idaho Daily Statesman*, 8 January 1911, Section II, p. 6, c. 4. Forty years ago column.

bc *Idaho Daily Statesman*, 4 April 1907, p. 2, c. 4.

bd *Idaho Daily Statesman*, 7 April 1907, p. 10, c. 2 & 3.

be *Idaho Tri-Weekly Statesman*, 23 February 1869, p. 2, c. 3.

bf *Idaho Tri-Weekly Statesman*, 23 February 1869, p. 3, c. 3.

bg *Idaho Tri-Weekly Statesman*, 11 March 1869, p. 1, c. 2.

bh *Idaho Tri-Weekly Statesman*, 6 January 1870, p. 3, c. 1.

bi *The Capital Chronicle,* 8 January 1870, 2. 4, c. 2
bj *The Capital Chronicle*, 30 April 1870, p. 4, c. 3.
bk U.S. Census, 1870, p. 49, text.
bl Arthur Hart, *Chinatown: Boise, Idaho, 1870-1970*. Historical Idaho, Inc., n.d., p. 57.
bm *Idaho World,* Idaho City, 17 March 1870.
bn *Idaho Tri-Weekly Statesman*, 2 June 1870, p. 4, c. 1 & 2.
bo *The Capital Chronicle*, Boise, 8 June 1870, p. 3, c. 2, and 15 June 1870, p. 3, c. 1.
bp *Idaho Tri-Weekly Statesman*, 13 September 1870, p. 2, c. 4.
bq *Idaho Daily Statesman*, 18 September 1910, Section II, p. 6, c. 2 & 3. Forty years ago column.
br *Semi-Weekly News*, Boise, 2 July 1870, p. 4, c. 2.
bs *The Capital Chronicle*, 21 July 1870, p. 3, c. 1.
bt *Boise City Weekly News*, 24 September 1870, p. 2, c. 5. September 18, 1910, Section II, p. 6, c. 4. Forty years ago column.
bu *Idaho Daily Statesman*, 14 August 1910, Sec. II, p. 2, c. 3. Forty years ago column.
The Capital Chronicle, 17 August 1870, p. 3, c. 1.
bv *Idaho Daily Statesman*, 18 September 1910, Section II, p. 6, c. 1. Forty Years ago column.
bw *Boise City Weekly News*, 15 October 1870, p. 3, c. 3. Mortiz had owned clothing stores and instructed the Turnverein in gymnastic exercises.
bx *Boise City Weekly News*, 17 September 1870, p. 2, c. 6.
by *The Boise City Weekly News*, 17 September 1870, p. 4, c. 5.
bz *The Capital Chronicle*, 14 September 1870, p. 3, c. 3.
ca *The Boise City Weekly News*, 17 September 1870, p. 3, c. 2.
cb *Idaho Daily Statesman*, 5 February 1911, Section II, p. 8, c. 3. Forty years ago column.
cc *The Boise City Weekly News*, 24 September 1870, p. 3, c. 5.
cd *Boise City Weekly News*, 12 November 1870, p. 3, c. 2.
ce *Idaho Tri-Weekly Statesman*, 19 November 1870, p. 2, c. 2.
cf *Idaho Tri-Weekly Statesman*, 29 December 1870, p. 3, c. 2. *Idaho Daily Statesman*, 25 December 1910, Section II, p. 6, c. 1. Forty years ago column.
cg Will Anderson, *Beer, USA*, 1986, p. 10
ch *Idaho Democrat* Boise, 11 January 1871, p. 3, c. 1. *Idaho Tri-Weekly Statesman*, 12 January 1871, p. 3, c. 2.
ci *Idaho World,* Idaho City, 9 February 1871, p. 3, c. 2. *Idaho Daily Statesman*, 5 March 1911, Section II, p. 7, c. 4. *Idaho Democrat*, Boise, 4 March 1871, p. 3, c. 2.
cj *Idaho Tri-Weekly Statesman,* 11 April 1871, p. 3, c. 2.

ck *Idaho Tri-Weekly Statesman*, 29 April 1871, p. 3, c. 3. *Idaho Daily Statesman*, 23 April 1911,Section II, p. 5, c. 4. Forty Years Ago column.

cl *Idaho Democrat*, Boise, 4 March 1871, p. 3, c. 2.

cm *Idaho Tri-Weekly Statesman*, 17 June 1871, p. 3, c. 1.

cn Arthur Hart, "Lemp Helped Raise Funds," *The Idaho Statesman*, 8 January 1973, p. 11, c. 1-4.

co Bureau of Land Management. Land Patent Records. Internet. Accession/Serial #IDIDAA 036344. Document # 33. Description was Aliquot Parts NWSE, Section 19, Township 3-N, Range 3-E.

cp *Idaho Tri-Weekly Statesman*, 11 July 1871, p. 1, c. 1.

cq *Idaho Tri-Weekly Statesman*, 2 September 1871, p. 3, c. 2.

cr *The Idaho Herald*, Boise, 15 March 1872, p. 4, c. 3.

cs *Idaho Tri-Weekly Statesman*, 18 July 1871, p. 3, c. 2.

ct Genealogy.com. International and Passenger Records.

cu *Tri-Weekly Herald*, Boise, 8 November 1871, p. 3, c. 4.

cv *Tri-Weekly Herald*, 2 February 1872, p. 2, c. 3.

cw *Idaho Daily Statesman*, 5 June 1910, Section II, p. 5, c. 1-2. This was the weekly historical column which featured pioneer biographies and reprints of old news.

cx William Jaumann was on the New York City Directory of 1869: "Liquors, 49 Bleecker, home 54 Bleecker." Ancestry.com.

cy Mittelman, Amy. "The Politics of Alcohol Production: The Liquor Industry and the Federal Government, 1862-1900." Dissertation, Columbia University, 1986, p. 177.

cz *Idaho Tri-Weekly Statesman*, 23 April 1872, p. 2, c. 2.

da *Idaho Daily Statesman*, 9 June 1912, Section II, p. 3, c. 3. Forty Years Ago Column.

db *Idaho Tri-Weekly Statesman*, 11 July 1872, p. 3, c. 1. See also

dc *Idaho Tri-Weekly Statesman*, 4 January 1873, p. 3, c.1-2.

dd Minutes of the Idaho State Supreme Court, Microfilm #128, p.45-46 of original.

de *Idaho Signal*, Lewiston, 17 May 1873,

df Bull, Friedrich and Gottschalk, *American Breweries II*, 1995, p. 4. Appel, "The Midwestern Brewery Before Prohibition: Development of an American Industrial Building Type," Dissertation, University of Illinois, 1990, p. 40.

dg *Idaho Tri-Weekly Statesman*, 16 September 1873, p. 3, c. 4. See Ronnenberg, "Idaho on the Rocks: The Ice Business in the Gem State," *Idaho Yesterdays*, Winter 1999, p. 2.

dh "Boise City Elections, 1867-1885," Internet site. gesswhoto.com.

di *Idaho Tri-Weekly Statesman*, 20 September 1873, p. 2, c. 4.

dj *Idaho Tri-Weekly Statesman*, 8 November 1873. This area of that issue of the newspaper is illegible and the information here is a best guess at transcription.

dk *Idaho Tri-Weekly Statesman*, 23 December 1873, p. 2, c. 5.
dl *Idaho Tri-Weekly Statesman*, 24 March 1874, p. 1, c. 3.
dm *Idaho Tri-Weekly Statesman*, 23 June 1874, p. 3, c. 1.
dn *Idaho Tri-Weekly Statesman*, 11 July 1874, p. 2, c. 4.
do "Boise City Elections, 1867-1885," Internet site. gesswhoto.com.
dp *Idaho Tri-Weekly Statesman*, 8 August 1874, p. 2, c. 3.
dq *Idaho Tri-Weekly Statesman*, 13 October 1874, p. 2, c. 3.
dr *Idaho Tri-Weekly Statesman*, 17 November 1874, p. 3, c. 1.
ds *Idaho Tri-Weekly Statesman*, 22 December 1874, p. 3, c. 1.
dt *Idaho Tri-Weekly Statesman*, 20 April 1875, p. 3, c. 2.
du *Idaho Tri-Weekly Statesman*, 2 January 1875, p. 3, c. 2.
dv *Idaho Tri-Weekly Statesman*, 5 January 1875, p. 3, c. 1.
dw *Morning Oregonian*, Portland, 1 April 1875, p. 2, c. 2.
dx *Owyhee Avalanche*, Silver City, Idaho, 27 February 1875, p. 3, c. 2. Silver City in the late Twentieth Century and beyond was the most celebrated ghost town in Idaho.
dy *Idaho Tri-Weekly Statesman*, 11 March 1875, p. 3, c. 1.
dz *Owyhee Avalanche*, Silver City, Idaho 6 March 1875, p. 1, c. 3.
ea Owyhee County Deeds, Idaho State Historical Society, Owyhee County Judicial Records, Microfilm Reel 4, page 156 of original book. Handwritten deed is difficult to read and to be sure of the spellings of the names.
eb *Idaho Tri-Weekly Statesman*, 9 March 1875, p. 3, c. 1.
ec *Owyhee Avalanche*, 10 April 1875, p. 1, c. 3.
ed *Idaho Tri-Weekly Statesman*, 6 April 1875, p. 3, c. 1. French, *History of Idaho*, (1914), vol. 2, p. 596. Of the nine short biographical sketches of Lemp about half mention his sojourn as a brewer in South Mountain, although some have this happening before he brewed in Boise, which is preposterous.
ee *Idaho Tri-Weekly Statesman,* 27 May 1875, p. 3, c. 1.
ef *Idaho Tri-Weekly statesman*, 19 June 1875, p. 2, c. 4.
eg Ronnenberg, *Beer and Brewing in the Inland Northwest*, p. 186.
eh Idaho State Historical Society Photo file. They incorrectly listed his death as 1896.
ei Owyhee County Deeds, Idaho State Historical Society, Owyhee County Judicial Records, Microfilm Reel 4, page 518 of original book. Handwritten deed is difficult to read and to be sure of the spellings of the names.
ej Owyhee County Deed, Idaho State Historical Society, Owyhee County Judicial Records, Microfilm Reel 4, page 781 of original book. Handwritten deed is difficult to read and to be sure of the spellings of the names.
ek *Idaho Tri-Weekly Statesman*, 15 July 1875, p. 3, c. 1. "Boise City Elections, 1867-1885," Internet Site. gesswhoto.com.
el *Idaho Tri-Weekly Statesman*, 11 September 1875, p. 3, c. 2.

em *Idaho Tri-Weekly Statesman*, 23 November 1875, p. 3, c. 2.
en *Idaho Tri-Weekly Statesman*, 23 October 1875, p. 3, c. 4. eo Morris and Johnson, *Richmond Beers*, 2nd ed., 2000, pp.100.
ep *Idaho Tri-Weekly Statesman*, 1 February 1876, p. 3, c. 1.
eq *Idaho Tri-Weekly Statesman*, 15 February 1876, p. 3, c. 3.
er *Idaho Tri-Weekly Statesman*, 17 February 1876, p. 3, c. 3.
es Arthur Hart, "Idaho Yesterdays: Lemp Helped Raise Funds," *The Idaho Statesman*, 8 January 1973, p. 11, c. 1-4.
et MacGregor, *Boise, Idaho, 1882-1910*, p. 147.
eu Richard O'Connor, *The German Americans: An Informal History*. (Little Brown and Co. 1968), p. 296
ev *Idaho Tri-Weekly Statesman*, 19 April 1876, p. 3, c. 4.
ew *Idaho Tri-Weekly Statesman*, 15 April 1876, p. 3, c. 2. 3 June 1876, p. 3, c. 2.
ex *Idaho Tri-Weekly Statesman*, 3 June 1876, p. 3, c. 2.
ey *Idaho Tri-Weekly Statesman*, 24 June 1876, p. 3, c. 2.
ez *Idaho Tri-Weekly Statesman*, 8 July 1876, p. 3, c. 2.
fa *Idaho Tri-Weekly Statesman*, 24 June 1876, p. 3, c. 1.
fb Anderson, *Frontier Bankers*, p. 25.
fc *Progressive Men of Southern Idaho* 1904, p. 70
fd *Idaho Tri-Weekly Statesman*, 11 April 1876, p. 2, c. 1.
fe Anderson, *Frontier Bankers*, p. 26.
ff MacGregor, *Boise, Idaho, 1882-1910*, pp. 114-115.
fg *Idaho Tri-Weekly Statesman*, 29 June 1876, p. 3, c. 3.
fh *Idaho Tri-Weekly Statesman*, 14 September 1876, p. 3,c. 1.
fi *Idaho Tri-Weekly Statesman*, 9 November 1876, p. 3, c. 2.
fj *Idaho Tri-Weekly Statesman*, 25 June 1877, p. 3, c. 1.
fk *The Semi-Weekly Idahoan*, Boise, 18 May 1877, p. 3, c. 2. 6 June 1877, p. 3, c. 3. 30 June 1877, p. 3, c. 3. p.2, c. 3.
fl *Idaho Tri-Weekly Statesman*, 5 May 1877, p. 3, c. 2.
fm Appel, "The Midwestern Brewery Before Prohibition: Development of an American Industrial Building Type," Dissertation, University of Illinois, 1990, p. 225.
fn *Idaho Tri-Weekly Statesman*, 5 May 1877, p. 3, c. 5.
fo *Idaho Tri-Weekly Statesman*, 2 June 1877, p. 3, c. 2.
fp *Idaho Tri-Weekly Statesman*, 16 June 1877, p. 3, c. 2.
fq *The Semi-Weekly Idahoan*, Boise, 15 June 1877, p. 3, c. 1.
fr *The Semi-Weekly Idahoan*, Boise, 20 July 1877, p. 3, c. 1.
fs *The Semi-Weekly Idahoan*, Boise, 25 July 1877, p. 3, c. 1.

ft "Nez Perce War Letters," Orlando Robbins to M. Brayman, July 7, 1877. *Fifteenth Biennial Report of the Board of Trustees of the State Historical Society of Idaho, 1935-36,* pp. 109-111.
fu *The Semi-Weekly Idahoan,* Boise, 20 June 1877, p. 3, c. 1
fv "Boise City Elections, 1867-1885," Internet Site. gesswhoto.com.
fw *The Semi-Weekly Idahoan,* Boise, 25 July 1877, p. 3, c. 3.
fx *The Semi-Weekly Idahoan,* Boise, 25 July 1877, p. 3, c. 3.
fy *Idaho Tri-Weekly Statesman,* 13 September 1877, p. 3, c. 4.
fz *Idaho Tri-Weekly Statesman,* 7 July 1877, p. 3, c. 2.
ga *Idaho Tri-Weekly Statesman,* 13 October 1877, p. 3, c. 1.
gb *Idaho Tri-Weekly Statesman,* 28 August 1877, p. 3, c. 1.
gc *Idaho Tri-Weekly Statesman,* 18 October 1877, p. 3, c. 1.
   Idaho Tri-Weekly Statesman, 20 October 1877, p. 3, c. 2.
gd *The Semi-Weekly Idahoan,* Boise, 19 October 1877, p. 3, c. 3.
ge *Idaho Tri-Weekly Statesman,* 18 September 1877, p. 3, c. 1.
gf *Idaho Tri-Weekly Statesman,* 15 November 1877, p. 3, c. 2.
gg *Idaho Tri-Weekly Statesman,* 14 March 1878, p. 3, c. 1.
gh *Idaho Tri-Weekly Statesman,* 29 November 1877, p. 3, c. 1.
gi *Idaho Tri-Weekly Statesman,* 13 December 1877, p. 3, c. 3.
gj *Idaho Tri-Weekly Statesman,* 22 December 1877, p. 3, c. 2.
gk *Idaho Tri-Weekly Statesman,* 8 January 1878, p. 3, c. 1 & c. 2.
gl *Idaho Tri-Weekly Statesman,* 7 February 1878, p. 3, c. 1 & 3. *Idaho World,* Idaho City, 8 February 1878, p. 3, c. 2
gm *Idaho Tri-Weekly Statesman,* 26 March 1878, p. 3, c. 2.
gn *Idaho Tri-Weekly Statesman,* 12 March 1878, p. 2, c. 2.
go *Idaho Tri-Weekly Statesman,* 23 May 1878, p. 3, c. 2. 28 May 1878, p. 3, c. 2.
gp *Idaho Tri-Weekly Statesman,* 23 May 1878, p. 3, c. 1.
gq *Idaho Tri-Weekly Statesman,* 13 July 1878, p. 3, c. 3.
gr *Idaho Tri-Weekly Statesman,* 23 May 1878, p. 3, c. 4.
gs *The Semi-Weekly Idahoan,* Boise, 9 June 1878, p. 3, c. 2.
gt *Idaho Tri-Weekly Statesman,* 20 August 1878, p. 3, c. 1.
gu *Idaho Tri-Weekly Statesman,* 15 June 1878, p. 3, c. 1.
gv *Idaho Tri-Weekly Statesman,* 9 July 1878, p. 3, c. 5.
gw *Idaho Tri-Weekly Statesman,* 11 July 1878, p. 3, c. 3.
gx *Idaho Tri-Weekly Statesman,* 9 July 1878, p.3, c. 5.
gy *Idaho Tri-Weekly Statesman,* 12 September 1878, p. 3, c. 1.
gz *Idaho Tri-Weekly Statesman,* 13 July 1878, p. 3, c. 4.
ha *Idaho Tri-Weekly Statesman,* 12 September 1878, p.3, c. 4.
hb *Idaho Tri-Weekly Statesman,* 5 October 1878, p. 3, c. 2.

hc *Idaho Tri-Weekly Statesman*, 15 October1878, p. 3, c. 2. 16 October 1878, p. 3, c. 2. 17 Oct 1878, p. 3, c. 2.

hd *Idaho Tri-Weekly Statesman*, 19 October 1878, p. 3, c. 2 & 3.

he *Idaho Tri-Weekly Statesman*, 22 October 1878, p. 3, c. 3 & 4.

hf *Idaho Tri-Weekly Statesman*, 8 August 1878, p. 3, c. 1.

hg *Idaho Tri-Weekly Statesman*, 20 August 1878, p. 3, c. 1.

hh *Idaho Tri-Weekly Statesman*, 5 September 1878, p. 3, c. 1. 30 August 1908, Section II, p. 5,c.1-2. Thirty years ago column.

hi *Idaho Tri-Weekly Statesman*, 12 November 1878, p. 3, c. 3. 14 November 1878, p. 3, c. 2. Breck's first name is sometimes Frances.

hj *Idaho Tri-Weekly Statesman*, 21 December 1878, p. 3, c. 1. *Idaho Daily Statesman* 20 December 1908, Section II, p. 5, c. 2. Thirty Years Ago column.

hk *Idaho Tri-Weekly Statesman*, 28 December 1878, p. 3, c. 2.

hl *Idaho Tri-Weekly Statesman*, 31 December 1878, p. 3, c. 1.

hm *Idaho Tri-Weekly Statesman,* 9 January 1879, p. 3, c. 1.

hn *Idaho Tri-Weekly Statesman*, 9 January 1879, p. 3, c. 2.

ho *Idaho Tri-Weekly Statesman*, 29 April 1879, p. 3, c. 2. 29 April 1879, p. 3, c. 2.

hp *Idaho Tri-Weekly Statesman*, 17 April 1879, p. 3, c.1.

hq Boise County Judicial Records, Idaho State Historical Society, Microfilm Records, Reel # 16, p. 91-93.

hr *Evening Capital News,* 18 March 1905, p. 4, c. 2-5. 25 March 1905, p. 8, c.1-3. All thequotes in the following paragraphs about schools are from Twogood's article.

hs *Idaho Tri-Weekly Statesman*, 17 April 1879, p. 3, c. 2.

ht "History of the Boise School District," Independent School district of Boise City.Internet site. www.sd01.k12.id.us/administration/dist1st.html.

hu *Idaho Tri-Weekly Statesman*, 31 August 1886, p. 2, c. 1.

hv *Idaho Daily Statesman*, 15 May 1910, Section II, p. 5, c. 1, Thirty Years Ago column.

hw "History of the Boise School District," Independent School district of Boise City.Internet site. www.sd01.k12.id.us/administration/dist1st.html.

hx MacGregor, *Boise, Idaho, 1882-1910*, p. 159.

hy *Idaho Tri-Weekly Statesman*, 6 May 1879, p. 3, c. 1.

hz *Idaho Tri-Weekly Statesman*, 10 May 1879, p. 3, c. 1.

ia *Idaho Tri-Weekly Statesman,* 13 May 1879, p. 3, c. 1.

ib *Idaho Tri-Weekly Statesman*, 17 June 1879, p. 3, c. 5.

ic *Idaho Tri-Weekly Statesman*, 24 June 1879, p. 3, c. 3.

id *Boise City Republican*, 16 August 1884, 3, c. 4.

ie *Idaho Tri-Weekly Statesman*, 15 July 1879, p. 3, c. 3.

if *Idaho Tri-Weekly Statesman*, 2 August 1879, p. 3, c. 2.

ig *Idaho Tri-Weekly Statesman*, 12 August 1879,p. 3, c. 2.

ih *Idaho Tri-Weekly Statesman*, 12 August 1879, p. 3, c. 2. He was born on the 10th according to his tombstone.
ii *Idaho Tri-Weekly Statesman*, 4 September 1879, p. 3, c. 1.
ij *Idaho Tri-Weekly Statesman*, 13 September 1879, p. 3, c. 3.
ik *Idaho Tri-Weekly Statesman*, 16 September 1879, p. 3, c. 1. This was probably the Mr. Emery who had owned a freighting business in the early days.
il *Idaho Tri-Weekly Statesman*, 9 September 1879, p. 3, c. 1
im *Idaho Tri-Weekly Statesman*, 11 October 1879, p. 3, c. 3.
in *Idaho Tri-Weekly Statesman*, 18 October 1879, p. 3, c. 1.
io *Idaho Tri-Weekly Statesman*, 23 October 1879, p. 3, c. 1.
ip *Idaho Tri-Weekly Statesman*, 28 October 1879, p. 3, c. 2.
iq *Idaho Tri-Weekly Statesman*, 18 December 1879, p. 3, c. 2.
ir *Idaho Tri-Weekly Statesman*, 25 December 1879, p. 3, c. 4.
is *Idaho Tri-Weekly Statesman*, 25 December 1879, p. 3, c. 1, p. 3, c. 2.
it *Idaho Daily Statesman*, 26 December 1909, Section II, p. 2, c. 4. Thirty Years ago column.
iu *Idaho Tri-Weekly Statesman*, 8 January 1880, p. 3, c. 2.
iv *Idaho Tri-Weekly Statesman*, 3 February 1880, p. 3, c. 1.
iw *Idaho World*, Idaho City, 13 February 1880, p. 3, c. 1. The *1850 to 1951 Idaho Marriage Index* (Family Tree Maker, CD-ROM) gives the wedding date as 30 January.
ix *Idaho Tri-Weekly Statesman*, 12 February 1880, p. 3, c. 2.
iy *Idaho Tri-Weekly Statesman*, 14 February 1880, p. 3, c. 2.
iz *Idaho Tri-Weekly Statesman*, 24 February 1880, p. 3, c. 1.
ja *Idaho Tri-Weekly Statesman*, 2 March 1880, p. 3, c. 2.
jb *Idaho Tri-Weekly Statesman*, 20 May 1880, p. 3, c. 1. *Idaho Daily Statesman*, 15 May 1910, Section II, p. 5, c. 1. Thirty Years Ago column.
jc *Idaho Daily Statesman*, 24 April 1910, Section II, p. 5, c. 3, Thirty years ago column.
jd *Idaho Tri-Weekly Statesman*, 18 May 1880, p. 3, c. 3.
je *Idaho Tri-Weekly Statesman*, 4 May 1880, p. 3, c. 1.
jf *Idaho Tri-Weekly Statesman*, 29 June 1880, p. 3, c. 1.
jg James H. Hawley, *History of Idaho, The Gem of the Mountains*, vol. 2, Ths was a biographical sketch.
jh Charles Edwin Dick, "A Geographical Analysis of the Development of the Brewing Industry in Minnesota," Dissertation, University of Minnesota, 1981, p.46-47.
ji Tomlan, Michael A. *Tinged with Gold: Hop Culture in the United States*. Athens: University of Georgia Press, 1992, p. 22.
jj *Idaho Tri-Weekly Statesman*, 6 July 1880, p. 3, c.2. *Idaho Daily Statesman*, 3 July 1910, Section II, p. 8, c. 1. Thirty Years Ago column.

jk *Idaho Tri-Weekly Statesman*, 13 July 1880, p. 3, c. 1.
jl *Idaho Tri-Weekly Statesman*, 20 July 1880, p. 3, c. 1.
jm *Idaho Tri-Weekly Statesman*, 3 August 1880, p. 3, c. 1.
jn *Idaho Tri-Weekly Statesman*, 17 August 1880, p. 3, c. 2.
jo *Idaho Tri-Weekly Statesman*, 15 July 1880, p. 3, c. 2.
jp *Idaho Daily Statesman*, 23 June 1902, p. 3, c. 2.
jq *Idaho Tri-Weekly Statesman*, 9 September 1880, p. 3, c. 2. *Idaho Daily Statesman*, 4 September 1910, Section II, p. 5, c. 7. Thirty Years Ago column.
r   *Idaho Tri-Weekly Statesman*, 9 October 1880, p. 3, c. 1.
js *Idaho Tri-Weekly Statesman*, 2 November 1880, p. 3, c. 1.
jt *Idaho Tri-Weekly Statesman*, 18 September 1880, p. 3, c. 2.
ju *Yankee Fork Herald*, Bonanza, 2 October 1880, p. 2, c. 1.
v   *Idaho Daily Statesman*, 23 October 1910, Section II, p. 6, c. 2. Thirty Years Ago column.
jw *Idaho Daily Statesman*, 16 October 1910, Section II, P. 7, c. 1. Thirty Years Ago column.
jx *Idaho Tri-Weekly Statesman*, 20 November 1880, p. 3, c. 2.
jy *Idaho Tri-Weekly Statesman*, 28 December 1880, p. 3, c. 2.
jz *Idaho Tri-Weekly Statesman*, 4 January 1881, p. 3, c. 1.
ka *Idaho Tri-Weekly Statesman*, 3 February 1881, p. 3, c. 1 & 2. *Idaho Daily Statesman*, 29 January 1911, Section II, p. 7, c. 1-3. Thirty Years Ago column. Many years later Goulder wrote a brief biographical sketch of Lemp from memory.
kb *Idaho Tri-Weekly Statesman*, 10 February 1881, p. 3, c. 1. They spelled her name Kohlhepp and gave no first name nor survivors. The obituary is vague enough to cause one to wonder if the reporter even attended the funeral.
kc *Idaho Tri-Weekly Statesman*, 10 February 1881, p. 3, c. 1.
kd *Idaho Tri-Weekly Statesman*, 9 April 1881 , p. 3, c. 2.
ke *Idaho Tri-Weekly Statesman*, 16 April 1881 , p. 3, c. 2.
kf *Idaho Tri-Weekly Statesman*, 19 March 1881, p. 3, c. 1. *Idaho Daily Statesman*, 12 March 1911, p. 5, c. 4. (30 Years ago section.)
kg *Idaho Tri-Weekly Statesman*, 24 March 1881, p. 3, c. 2.
kh *Idaho Daily Statesman*, 15 October 1911, Section II, p. 1, c. 1-7.
ki *Idaho Tri-Weekly Statesman*, 17 May 1881, p. 3, c. 1. *Idaho World*, Idaho City, 20 May 1881, p. 3, c.2. *Idaho Daily Statesman*, 14 May 1911, Section II, p. 5, c. 1-3. Thirty Years Ago column.
kj *Boise City Republican*, 21 May 1881, p. 1, c. 2.
kk *Idaho Tri-Weekly Statesman*, 31 May 1881, p. 3, c. 1.
kl *Idaho Tri-Weekly Statesman*, 6 June 1881, p. 3, c. 2.
km *Idaho Tri-Weekly Statesman*, 14 June 1881, p. 3, c. 1.

kn *Idaho World*, Idaho City, 7 June 1881, p. 3, c. 1. *Wood River Times* (Weekly) Hailey, 6 July 1881, p. 3, c. 1.
ko Idaho Tri-Weekly Statesman, 7 July 1881, p. 3, c. 2
kp "Boise City Elections, 1867-1885," Internet Site, gesswhoto.com.
kq *Idaho Tri-Weekly Statesman*, 26 July 1881, p. 3, c. 1. *Idaho Daily Statesman*, 23 July 1911, Section II, p. 3, c. 1-4. Thirty Years Ago column.
kr *Idaho Tri-Weekly Statesman*, 30 July 1881, p. 3, c. 1. The newspaper gave his name as William Charles Lemp. His tombstone in Pioneer Cemetery in Boise says William A., son of John and Kate, and gives his birth and death dates.
ks *Idaho Tri-Weekly Statesman*, 23 August 1881, p. 3, c. 1.
kt *Idaho Tri-Weekly Statesman*, 27 August 1881, p. 3, c. 1.
ku *Idaho Tri-Weekly Statesman*, 30 August 1881, p. 3, c. 1.
kv *Idaho Tri-Weekly Statesman*, 13 September 1881, p. 3, c.1. *Idaho Daily Statesman*, 3 September 1911, p. 3, c. 1. Thirty Years Ago column.
kw *Idaho Tri-Weekly Statesman*, 3 September 1881, p. 3, c.1-5. 17 December p. 3, c. 1-5. 20 December 1881, p. 3, c. 1-5. 27 December 1881,p. 3, c. 1.
kx *Idaho Tri-Weekly Statesman*, 22 October 1881, p. 3, c. 1.
ky *Idaho Tri-Weekly Statesman*, 8 November 1881, p. 3, c. 1.
kz *Idaho Tri-Weekly Statesman*, 12 November 1881, p. 2, c. 2.
la *Idaho Tri-Weekly Statesman*, 15 December 1881, p. 3, c. 1.
lb *Idaho Tri-Weekly Statesman*, 27 October 1881, p. 3, c. 2.
lc *Idaho Tri-Weekly Statesman*, 29 November 1881, p. 3, c. 1.
ld *Idaho Daily Statesman*, 12 November 1911, Section II, p. 3, c. 1. 30 Years Ago Column.
le *Tri-Weekly Statesman*, 26 November 1881, p. 3, c. 1.
lf *Tri-Weekly Statesman*, 26 November 1881, p. 3, c. 2.
lg *Idaho Tri-Weekly Statesman*, 29 December 1881, p. 3, c. 1.
lh *Idaho Tri-Weekly Statesman*, 28 February 1882, p. 3, c.1.
li *Idaho Tri-Weekly Statesman*, 6 December 1881, p. 3, c. 2.
lj *Idaho Tri-Weekly Statesman*, 24 December 1881, p. 3, c. 4.
lk *Idaho Tri-Weekly Statesman*, 3 January 1882, p. 3, c. 1.
ll *Idaho Tri-Weekly Statesman*, 25 February 1882, p. 3, c. 1 & c. 3.
lm *Idaho Tri-Weekly Statesman*, 9 February 1882, p. 2, c. 3. This was the first bank ad I found that listed Lemp as President. See also Anderson, *Frontier Bankers*, p. 6. Lemp stayed as President for 7 years.
ln *Idaho World*, Idaho City, 14 February 1882, p. 3, c. 1.
lo *Idaho Tri-Weekly Statesman*, 10 March 1882, p. 3, c. 1. *Ketchum Keystone* , 13 April 1882, p. 1, c. 3.
lp *Wood River Times*, Hailey, 14 October 1882, p. 4, c. 1.
lq *Idaho Tri-Weekly Statesman*, 15 April 1882, p. 3, c. 1.
lr *Idaho Tri-Weekly Statesman*, 20 April 1882, p. 3, c. 1.

ls *Idaho Tri-Weekly Statesman,* 4 May 1882, p. 3, c. 2.
lt *Idaho Tri-Weekly Statesman,* 9 May 1882, p. 3, c. 2.
u   Max Rudin, "Beer and America," *American Heritage,* June/July 2002, p. 28.
lv MacGregor, *Boise, Idaho, 1882-1910,* p. 142.
lw *Idaho Tri-Weekly Statesman,* 22 July 1882, p. 3, c. 1.
lx *Idaho Daily Statesman,* 1 September 1912, Section I, p. 4, c. 4. Thirty Years Ago column.
ly *Idaho Tri-Weekly Statesman,* 7 October 1882, p. 1, c. 5.
lz *Idaho Tri-Weekly Statesman,* 21 November 1882, p. 3, c. 2.
ma Ada County Court Records, Microfilmed Judgment Books, Idaho State Historical Society.
mb *Idaho Tri-Weekly Statesman,* 28 November 1882, p. 3, c. 2-4.
mc *Idaho Tri-Weekly Statesman,* 14 December 1882, p. 3, c. 5.
md *Idaho Tri-Weekly Statesman,* 6 January 1883, p. 3, c. 1.
me *Idaho Tri-Weekly Statesman,* 6 March 1883, p. 2, c. 3.
mf Carlos Schwantes, *Railroad Signatures Across the Pacific Northwest,* p. 38.
mg Carlos Schwantes, *Railroad Signatures Across the Pacific Northwest,* p. 38. There were also a number of short portage railroads to get passengers and freight around river obstacles.
mh Carlos Schwantes, *Railroad Signatures,* p. 68.
mi *Idaho Tri-Weekly Statesman,* 1 December 1881, p. 3, c. 2.
mj *Idaho Tri-Weekly Statesman,* 31 January 1882, p. 3, c. 2.
mk *The Idaho Statesman,* 19 November 1911, p. 3, c. 4. Thirty Years Ago column.
ml *Idaho Daily Statesman,* 21 January 1912, Section II, p. 3, c. 3. Thirty Years Ago Column.
mm *Idaho Tri-Weekly Statesman,* 3 May 1883, p. 3, c. 2.
mn *Idaho Tri-Weekly Statesman,* 19 May 1883, p. 3, c. 2.
mo Merle Wells, *Boise, An Illustrated History,* p. 47.
mp Schwantes, *Railroad Signatures,* p. 229.
mq *Idaho Statesman,* 31 January 1926, 3, c. 3. Headline: "Mayor Explains Boise's 'Mistake' Forty Years Ago."
mr Wells, *Boise, An Illustrated History,* p. 47.
ms Wells, *Boise, An Illustrated History,* p. 48.
mt MacGregor, *Boise, Idaho, 1882-1910,* p. 42.
mu *Boise City Republican,* 12 February 1887, p. 1, c. 5.
mv MacGregor, *Boise, Idaho, 1882-1910,* p. 42.
mw *Idaho Tri-Weekly Statesman,* 15 November 1887, p. 3, c. 2.
mx *Idaho Tri-Weekly Statesman,* 17 November 1887, p. 3, c. 3.
my *Idaho Daily Statesman,* 8 August 1888, p. 3, c. 2.
mz *Idaho Daily Statesman,* 28 March 1890, p. 3, c. 2.

na *Idaho Daily Statesman*, 20 April 1890, p. 3, c. 3.
nb *Idaho Tri-Weekly Statesman*, 7 April 1883, p. 3, c. 1.
nc *Idaho Tri-Weekly Statesman*, 15 May 1883, p. 3, c.1-2.
nd *Idaho Tri-Weekly Statesman*, 15 May 1883, p. 3, c. 2.
ne *Idaho Tri-Weekly Statesman*, 24 May 1883, p. 3, c. 3.
nf *Idaho Tri-Weekly Statesman*, 9 June 1883, p. 3, c. 2.
ng "Boise City Elections, 1867 to 1885," Inter net Site. gesswhoto.com.
nh *Idaho Tri-Weekly Statesman*, 31 July 1883, p. 3, c. 1.
ni *Idaho Tri-Weekly Statesman*, 4 August 1883, p. 3, c.1.
nj *Idaho Tri-Weekly Statesman*, 11 August 1883, p. 3, c. 2.
nk *Wood River News Miner*, Daily, Hailey, 7 August 1883, p. 3, c. 2
nl *Wood River Times*, Hailey, 8 August 1883, p. 3, c. 5.
nm *Wood River Times*, Hailey, 22 August 1883, p. 3, c. 4.
nn *Idaho Tri-Weekly Statesman*, 14 August 1883, p. 3, c.1.
no *Idaho Tri-Weekly Statesman*, 23 October 1883, p. 3, c. 3.
np *Idaho Tri-Weekly Statesman*, 25 August 1883,p. 3, c. 1.
nq *Idaho Tri-Weekly Statesman*, 18 October 1883, p. 3, c. 5.
nr *Idaho Tri-Weekly Statesman*, 20 November 1883, p. 3, c. 1.
ns *Idaho Tri-Weekly Statesman*, 1 January 1884, p. 3, c. 3.
nt *Idaho Tri-Weekly Statesman*, 9 February 1884, p. 3, c. 1.
nu *Idaho Tri-Weekly Statesman* , 1 May 1884, p. 3, c. 2.
nv *Idaho Tri-Weekly Statesman*, 19 July 1884, p. 3, c. 1.
nw Elliot, *History of Idaho Territory*, 1884, p. unnumbered between p. 254 and 255.
nx Elliot, *History of Idaho Territory*, 1884, p. unnumbered between p. 254 and 255.
ny *Bose City Republican*, 16 August 1884, p. 3, c. 5.
nz The definitive history of this event awaits publication. The Silver City and Boise newspapers give some information and the court decision is in *Idaho Reports*.
oa *Ketchum Keystone*, 8 August 1884, p. 3, c. 1.
ob *Wood River News Miner* (Daily) , 19 August 1884, p. 3, c. 5. *Wood River Times* (Weekly), 20 August 1884, p. 3, c. 5. She was born in Oro Fino in 1862.
oc *Idaho Tri-Weekly Statesman*, 4 September 1884, p. 3, c. 1.
od *Idaho Tri-Weekly Statesman*, 9 September 1884, p. 3, c. 3.
oe *Idaho Tri-Weekly Statesman*, 11 October 1884, p. 4, c. 1.
of *Idaho Tri-Weekly Statesman*, 16 October 1884, p. 3, c. 3.
og *Idaho Tri-Weekly Statesman*, 21 October 1884, p. 3, c. 2.
oh *Idaho Tri-Weekly Statesman*, 4 March 1886, p. 3, c. 2.
oi *Wood River Times* (Weekly) Hailey, Idaho, 17 December 1884, p. 3, c. 6. 31 December 1884, p. 1, c. 5. *Boise City Republican*, 20 December 1884, p. 1, c. 1.

oj *Idaho Tri-Weekly Statesman*, 17 March 1885, p. 1, c. 5.
ok *Wood River News Miner* (Daily) Hailey, Idaho, 21 December 1884, p. 3, c. 4.
ol *Idaho Tri-Weekly Statesman*, 4 November 1884, p. 3, c. 1.
om *Idaho Tri-Weekly Statesman*, 23 December 1884, p. 3, c. 1. *Boise City Republican*, 20 December 1884, p. 1, c. 1.
on *Idaho Tri-Weekly Statesman*, 15 January 1885, p. 3, c. 1.
oo Photocopy of the will and probate records, Probate Court, Ada County, Idaho.
op Guttridge, Leonard F. *Ghosts of Cape Sabine: The Harrowing True Story of the Greely Expedition*, G. P. Putnam's Sons, 2000. Internet: nytimes.com/books/first/g/guttridge-ghosts.html.
oq James Booth Lockwood (1852-1884). Internet. freespace.virgin.net/peter.Lockwood/james-booth.htm.
or Internet. http//21623935120. Ellesmere Island, Translated from French.
os Published accounts of this expedition include: Leonard F. Guttridge, *Ghosts of Cape Sabine*. David Brainard, *The White World*. David Brainard, *Six Came Back*. Charles Lanman, *Farthest North*. A. W. Greely, *Report on the Proceedings of the United States Expedition to Lady Franklin Bay*. A. W. Greely, *Three Years of Arctic Service*. Winfield S. Schley, *The Rescue of Greely*.
ot Guttridge, *Ghosts of Cape Sabine*, p. 271-272. The ensuring paragraphs are from Guttridge's account.
ou *Idaho Tri-Weekly Statesman*, 14 February 1885, p. 3, c. 3. This was as close to an obituary as he received.
ov *Boise City Republican*, 28 February 1885, p. 1, c. 1.
ow *Boise City Republican*, 11 April 1885, p. 1, c. 2.
ox *Boise City Republican*, 11 April 1885, p. 1, c. 3.
oy *Boise City Republican*, 23 May 1885, p. 1, c. 1. 27 June 1885, p. 1, c. 1.
oz *Idaho Tri-Weekly Statesman*, 18 June 1885, p. 3, c. 1.
pa *Boise City Republican*, 4 July 1885, p. 1, c. 2. 11 July 1885, p. 1, c. 2.
pb *Boise City Republican*, 1 August 1885, p. 1, c. 1.
pc *Wood River Times*, Weekly, 29 July 1885, p. 2, c. 4.
pd *Idaho Tri-Weekly Statesman*, 4 August 1885, p. 3, c.1.
pe *Idaho Tri-Weekly Statesman*, 29 September 1885, p. 3, c. 1.
pf *Idaho Tri-Weekly Statesman*, 12 May 1885, p. 3, c. 3.
pg *Idaho Tri-Weekly Statesman*, 30 June 1885, p. 3, c. 1.
ph *Idaho Tri-Weekly Statesman*, 23 June 1885, p. 3, c. 1.
pi *Idaho Tri-Weekly Statesman*, 13 March 1886, p. 3, c. 2.
pj *Boise City Republican*, 20 March 1886, p. 1, c. 5.
pk *Idaho Tri-Weekly Statesman*, 25 June 1885, p. 3, c. 2-3.
pl *Idaho Tri-Weekly Statesman* 19 September 1885, p. 3, c. 1.
pm *Idaho Tri-Weekly Statesman*, 6 October 1885, p. 3, c. 1.

John Lemp • The Beer Baron of Boise   111

pn *Idaho Tri-Weekly Statesman*, 13 October 1885, p. 3, c. 2. *Boise City Republican*, 17 October 1885, p. 1, c. 1.
po *Boise City Republican*, 17 October 1885, p. 1, c. 4.
pp *Boise City Republican*, 24 October 1885, p. 1, c. 1.
pq *Boise City Republican*, 21 November 1885, p. 1, c.1.
pr *Boise City Republican*, 28 November 1885, p. 1, c. 1.
ps *Idaho Tri-Weekly Statesman*, 16 January 1886, p. 3, c. 3.
pt *Idaho Tri-Weekly Statesman*, 19 January 1886, p. 3, c. 1.
pu Skilnik, Bob. *The History of Beer and Brewing in Chicago, 1833-1978*. St. Paul: Pogo Press, 1999, p. 51.
pv *Idaho Tri-Weekly Statesman*, 2 March 1886, p. 3, c. 1.
pw *Boise City Republican*, 6 March 1886, p. 1, c. 4.
px *Idaho Tri-Weekly Statesman*, 8 April 1886, p. 3, c. 1.
py *Idaho World*, Idaho City, 13 April 1886, p. 3, c. 2. *Idaho Democrat*, 14 April, 1886, p. 2, c. 3.
pz *Idaho Tri-Weekly Statesman*, 18 May 1886, p. 3, c. 3.
qa *Idaho Tri-Weekly Statesman*, 25 May 1886, p. 3, c. 1.
qb *Idaho Tri-Weekly Statesman*, 27 May 1886, p. 3, c. 1.
qc *Idaho Tri-Weekly Statesman*, 24 June 1886, p. 3, c. 2.
qd *Boise City Republican*, 26 June 1886, p. 1, c. 1.
qe *Idaho Tri-Weekly Statesman*, 3 July 1886, p. 3, c. 1.
qf *Idaho Tri-Weekly Statesman*, 6 July 1886, p. 3, c. 1.
qg *Boise City Republican*, 17 July 1886, p. 1, c. 1.
qh *Idaho Tri-Weekly Statesman*, 28 August 1886, p. 3, c. 3.
qi *Idaho Tri-Weekly Statesman*, 17 August 1886, p. 3, c. 3.
qj *Idaho Tri-Weekly Statesman*, 14 August 1886, p. 3, c. 2.
qk *Idaho Tri-Weekly Statesman*, 11 September 1886, p. 3, c. 1.
ql *Idaho Tri-Weekly Statesman*, 5 October 1886, p. 3, c. 2.
qm *Boise City Republican*, 9 October 1886, p. 1, c. 1.
qn *Idaho Tri-Weekly Statesman*, 19 October 1886, p. 3, c. 1.
qo *Idaho Tri-Weekly Statesman*, 23 October 1886, p. 3, c. 2.
qp *Boise City Republican*, 11 December 1886, p. 4, c. 2.
qq Treasure Valley Hydrology. History of Water Development. Internet. derived from Idaho State Historical Society Reference Series #171.
qr *Idaho Tri-Weekly Statesman*, 26 October 1886, p. 3, c. 2.
qs Settler's Irrigation District, History, Internet Site.
qt "Settlers Canal (Lemp Canal)," *Idaho State Historical Society Reference Series*, number 531, 1974, p. 1.
qu *Boise City Republican*, 20 November 1886, p. 1, c. 1.
qv *Idaho Tri-Weekly Statesman*, 15 January 1887, p. 3, c. 2.

qw Annie Laurie Bird, *Boise: The Peace Valley*. Caldwell: Caxton Press, 1934, p. 276-277.

qx French, *History of Idaho*, vol II, 1914, p. 364. In the biographical sketch of George Parkin.

qy *Idaho Daily Statesman*, 24 January 1888, p. 3, c. 3.

qz *Idaho Daily Statesman*, 14 March 1888, p. 3, c. 1.

ra *Idaho Daily Statesman*, 15 March 1888, p. 3, c. 1.

rb *Idaho Daily Statesman*, 21 March 1888, p. 3, c. 1.

rc *Idaho Daily Statesman*, 26 April 1888, p. 3, c. 1.

rd *Idaho Daily Statesman*, 2 May 1888, p. 3, c. 1.

re Ada County Court Records, Microfilmed Judgment Books, Idaho State Historical Society.

rf Ada County Court Records, Microfilmed Judgment Books, Idaho State Historical Society.

rg *Idaho Daily Statesman*, 29 March 1893, p. 5, c. 1.

rh *Idaho Daily Statesman*, 21 March 1900, p. 6, c. 1.

ri *Idaho Daily Statesman*, 22 March 1900, p. 4, c. 3.

rj *Idaho Daily Statesman*, 20 July 1900, p. 4, c. 3.

rk Settlers Irrigation District. Internet site.

rl *Idaho Tri-Weekly Statesman*, 11 November 1886, p. 3, c. 2. *Boise City Republican*, 13 November 1886, p. 1, c. 1. Some sources say he was born on the 8th.

rm *Idaho Tri-Weekly Statesman*, 2 November 1886, p. 3, c. 3.

rn *Boise City Republican*, 29 January 1887, p. 1, c. 1.

ro *Owyhee Avalanche*, 15 February 1887, p. 3, c. 1. The Falk brothers and their families were Jewish; a fact which speaks to the lack of ethnic strife on the Idaho frontier. His son's bris was mentioned in the *Statesman*, 15 August 1895, p. 6, c. 4.

rp *Wood River Times*, Hailey, Weekly, 16 February 1887, p. 3, c. 5.

rq *Idaho Tri-Weekly Statesman*, 4 January 1887, p. 3, c. 1

rr *Idaho Tri-Weekly Statesman*, 13 January 1887, p. 3, c. 1.

rs Idaho State Historical Society, Manuscript File 178, The John Lemp Family. *1850 to 1951 Marriage Index*, Family Tree Maker, CD-ROM.

rt *Boise City Republican*, 2 April 1887, p. 1, c. 3.

ru *Idaho Tri-Weekly Statesman*, 2 April 1887, p. 1, c. 5.

rv *Idaho Tri-Weekly Statesman*, 9 April 1887, p. 3, c.1.

rw *Idaho Tri-Weekly Statesman*, 7 April 1887, p. 1, c. 4.

rx Ada County court Records, Microfilmed Judgment Books, Idaho State Historical Society.

ry *Boise City Republican*, 26 May 1887, p. 1, c. 2.

rz *Idaho Tri-Weekly Statesman*, 28 May 1887, p. 3, c. 3.

sa *Boise City Republican*, 26 May 1887, p. 1, c. 2.
sb *Wood River Times*, 20 July 1887, p. 3, c. 4 Blaine County Judicial Records, Idaho State Historical Society, Microfilm reel 34, original pages, 248, 251,255-256.
sc *Idaho Tri-Weekly Statesman*, 5 July 1887, p. 3, c. 1.
sd *Idaho World*, Idaho City, 29 July 1887, p. 1, c. 2.
se *Idaho Tri-Weekly Statesman*, 30 July 1887, p. 3, c. 2. *Idaho World*, Idaho City, 2 August 1887, p. 1, c. 3.
sf *Idaho World*, Idaho City, 16 August 1887, p. 1, c. 3.
sg *Idaho Tri-Weekly Statesman*, 16 August 1887, p. 3, c. 3.
sh *Idaho Tri-Weekly Statesman*, 27 August 1887, p. 3, c. 1.
si *Idaho Tri-Weekly Statesman*, 1 September 1887, p. 3, c. 1.
sj *Idaho World*, Idaho City, 18 October 1887, p. 1, c. 2. *The Elmore Bulletin*, 19 October 1889, p. 3, c. 3.
sk *Idaho Tri-Weekly Statesman*, 29 October 1887, p. 3, c. 1.
sl *Idaho Tri-Weekly Statesman*, 3 November 1887, p. 3, c. 2.
sm *Idaho Tri-Weekly Statesman*, 5 November 1887, p. 3, c. 2.
sn *Idaho Daily Statesman*, 4 February 1888, p. 3, c. 2.
so Blaine County Judicial Records, Idaho State Historical Society, microfilm reel 31, original book, pages 527-529.
sp Blaine County Judicial Records, Idaho State Historical Society, microfilm reel 31, original book, pages 530-532.
sq Blaine County Judicial Records, Idaho State Historical Society, microfilm reel 31, original book, pages 533-536.
sr *Idaho Tri-Weekly Statesman*, 29 November 1887, p. 3, c. 2.
ss *Idaho Tri-Weekly Statesman*, 8 November 1887, p. 3, c. 2.
st *Idaho Tri-Weekly Statesman*, 7 January 1888, p. 3, c. 2. "J. Lemp" was also paid $20.18 as part of the city expenditures that night.
su *Idaho Daily Statesman*, 11 January 1888, p. 3, c. 1.
sv *Idaho Daily Statesman*, 12 January 1888, p. 3, c. 2.
sw *Idaho Daily Statesman*, 17 February 1888, p. 3, c. 1.
sx *Idaho Daily Statesman*, 26 January 1888, p. 3, c. 1.
sy *Idaho Daily Statesman*, 28 February 1888, p. 3, c. 1.
sz *Idaho Daily Statesman*, 29 January 1888, p. 3, c. 2.
ta *Idaho Daily Statesman*, 10 March 1888, p. 3, c. 2.
tb *Idaho Daily Statesman*, 13 April 1888, p. 3, c. 1.
tc *Idaho Daily Statesman*, 17 April 1888, p. 3, c. 1. The newspaper spelled his name "Ross."
td *Idaho Daily Statesman*, 14 April 1888, p. 3, c. 1.
te *Idaho Daily Statesman*, 18 April 1888, p. 3, c. 1.
tf *Idaho Daily Statesman*, 28 April 1888, p. 3, c. 1.

tg *Idaho Daily Statesman*, 5 April 1888, p. 3, c. 1.
th *Idaho Daily Statesman*, 12 April 1888, p. 3, c. 1.
ti *Idaho Daily Statesman*, 8 May 1888, p. 3, c. 1.
tj *Idaho Daily Statesman* 12 May 1888, p. 3, c. 1.
tk *Idaho Daily Statesman*, 9 May 1888, p. 3, c. 1.
tl *Idaho Daily Statesman*, 16 May 1888, p. 3, c. 1.
tm *Idaho Daily Statesman*, 29 May 1888, p. 3, c. 1.
tn *Idaho Daily Statesman*, 29 June 1888, p. 3, c. 1.
to *Idaho Democrat*, Boise, 11 July 1888, p. 3 c. 2.
tp *Idaho Daily Statesman*, 12 August 1888, p. 3, c. 1.
tq *Idaho Daily Statesman*, 5 October 1888, p. 3, c. 2.
tr *Idaho Daily Statesman*, 2 September 1888, p. 3, c. 1.
ts *Idaho Daily Statesman*, 4 September 1888, p. 3, c. 1.
tt *Wood River Times*, Hailey, Weekly, 17 October 1888, p. 4, c. 2.
tu *Idaho Daily Statesman*, 18 October 1888, p. 3, c. 1.
tv *Idaho Daily Statesman*, 25 October 1888, p. 3, c. 3.
tw *Idaho Daily Statesman*, 27 October 1888, p. 3, c. 3.
tx *Idaho Daily Statesman*, 18 November 1888, p. 3, c. 1.
ty *Idaho Daily Statesman*, 22 November 1888, p. 3, c. 1.
tz *Idaho Daily Statesman*, 20 November 1888, p. 3, c. 1.
ua *Idaho Daily Statesman*, 6 December 1888, p. 3, c. 1.
ub *The Mountain Home Bulletin*, 1 December 1888, p. 3, c. 3.
uc *Idaho Daily Statesman*, 26 December 1888, p. 3, c. 3. 8 January 1889, p. 3, c. 3.
ud *Idaho Daily Statesman*, 16 January 1889, p. 3, c. 1.
ue *Idaho Daily Statesman*, 9 March 1889, p. 3, c. 1.
uf *Idaho Daily Statesman*, 28 March 1889, p. 3, c. 2.
ug Ada County Court Records, Microfilmed Judgment Books, Idaho State Historical Society.
uh *Idaho Daily Statesman*, 23 April 1889, p. 3, c. 1.
ui *Idaho Daily Statesman*, 24 April 1889, p. 3,,c. 1.
uj *Idaho Daily Statesman*, 27 April 1889, p. 3, c. 1.
uk *Idaho Daily Statesman*, 30 April 1889, p. 3, c. 1.
ul *Idaho World*, Idaho City, 30 April 1889, p. 1, c. 3.
um *Idaho Daily Statesman*, 7 June 1889, p. 3, c. 1.
un *Idaho Daily Statesman*, 28 May 1889, p. 3, c. 1.
uo *Idaho Daily Statesman*, 12 June 1889, p. 4, c. 1.
up *Idaho Daily Statesman*, 26 June 1889, p. 2, c. 3.
uq *Idaho Daily Statesman*, 26 June 1889, p. 3, c. 1.
ur *Idaho Daily Statesman*, 19 July 1889, p. 3, c. 1.

us *Idaho Daily Statesman*, 30 July 1889, p. 3, c. 1.
ut *Idaho Daily Statesman*, 20 September 1889, p. 4, c.1.
uu *Idaho Daily Statesman*, 30 June 1889, p. 3, c. 2.
uv Defenbach, *Idaho the Place*, vol. I, p. 441. *The Idaho Scimitar*, 2 November 1907, p. 9, c. 1.
uw *The Elmore Bulletin*, Elmore County, Idaho, 22 June 1889, p. 2, c. 1.
ux Hawley, *History of Idaho the Gem of the Mountains*, vol. I, p. 200.
uy *Idaho Daily Statesman*, 9 July 1889, p. 3, c. 2.
uz *Idaho Daily Statesman*, 3 April 1889, p. 3, c. 1.
va *Idaho Daily Statesman*, 14 August 1889, p. 3, c. 1.
vb *Idaho Daily Statesman*, 19 September 1889, p. 3, c. 2.
vc Ada County Court Records, Microfilmed Judgments Books, Idaho State Historical Society.
vd "Bradstreet's Commercial Reports," vol. 87, September 1889, pp. Idaho 1, 3. .
ve *Idaho Daily Statesman*, 3 October 1889, p. 3, c. 4.
vf *Idaho Daily Statesman*, 20 November 1889, p. 3, c. 1 & 2.
vg *Idaho Daily Statesman*, 12 November 1889, p. 3, c. 2.
vh *Idaho Daily Statesman*, 29 December 1889, p. 2, c. 2.
vi *Idaho Daily Statesman*, 26 October 1889, p. 3, c. 1.
vj *Idaho Daily Statesman*, 17 October 1887, p. 3, c. 2.
vk *Idaho Daily Statesman*, 25 December 1889, p. 3, c. 1. Record of Marriage Certificate, Ada County Judicial Records, Idaho State Historical Society, Microfilm reel 87. Witnesses were John and Catherine Lemp.
vl French, *History of Idaho*, Vol. II, pp. 595-596.

Part II

1890 to 1900

PREDICTABLY, IN EARLY JANUARY OF 1890 Boise's ice sellers began the annual ice harvest. The ice was seven inches thick that year and brewers Lemp and Brodbeck were the chief harvesters as always.[a] Boise had two breweries, Idaho had thirty-two, and the United States total was 1,928 as the decade began. Another annual January event was the election of officers for the Idaho First National Bank—Lemp was again named to the board of directors.[b]

In February, John was reportedly offered $400 per acre for eighty-seven acres at the foot of Hill Road in the Boise City limits.[c] He declined to sell, but the offer was presented as proof of increasing land values in the city.

Colorado brewer Adolph Coors became a millionaire in 1890. Brewing was leaving the small scale and become a business giant all over America including the mountain West. This was close to the peak for small breweries in America. Business consolidation and ever larger brewing plants, assisted by pasteurization and refrigerated railroad cars, and powered by Eastern and even European capital, were to be the major themes of the next two decades in the brewing industry.

Congress altered the Internal Revenue Act in 1890 so that beer could be piped from storage cellar to bottling house instead of being barreled and hauled over a public road.[d] This facilitated bottling and helped that segment of the industry to grow.

As the studding and lathing of Lemp's new building progressed,

Lemp was still very closed-mouthed about its future. The *Statesman* asked him if it was to be made into offices, he replied tersely "We can't tell yet, what we will do."[e]

The Boise Central Railway Company decided to incorporate with the individual owners who were previously subscribers to the Boise branch railroad lands and town property. The owners debated the incorporation issue at three sessions of three or four hours each and then 97 percent voted in favor. John Lemp was named the corporation treasurer and as such was on the board of directors.[f] In a few days the incorporation papers were filed. Their stated purpose was to build a railroad from the Snake River to a point two miles north of Boise.[g]

A collection was taken for the stricken people of Camas Prairie in March of 1890. Lemp, as did competitor Brodbeck, gave five dollars.[h] Boise's total was $166.50 for the snow and grasshopper plagued settlers. Lemp had given an option to an unnamed man to build a brick building on the corner of Ninth and Main which was to expire on the first of May without being taken up.[i]

Lemp's other on-going project was his new business building, for which he had a large pile of lath, for use by the plasterers, stacked in front of the site indicating the work was progressing.[j] A Mr. Hemmel showed up in Boise in April looking for a house for his family. He had had a sign in Lemp's unfinished building for months stating that he would open his new store there the first day of March.[k] He was a bit late. In June, Lemp had more bricks ready to fire as soon as the price he could ask for them was favorable.[l] As the new building was ready to begin its productive life, the old wooden awning in front of Lemp's wholesale liquor house had to come down because of advanced age. "Thus another mark of civilization of the past will have passed out of existence," was the Statesman's tender of condolence.[m] By August it was down with a new and more substantial replacement in the planning stage.[n]

John Lemp filed suit in District court against Henry Riggs in March of 1890 to foreclose on Riggs mortgage.[o] A sheriff's sale was ordered by Judge James H. Beatty, and Lemp was basically to receive $1,590.

In April, the Pioneer group, which admitted everyone who had come to Boise before 1866, met and had their group portrait taken in front of the Dobe Pioneer Building.[p] On the roster was John Lemp's 1863 arrival.

The June, 1890, Turn Verein picnic was memorable. The whole group of 45 or 50 went to Lemp's Gulch on John Lemp's ranch two miles north of Boise to "enjoy themselves as only Germans can."[q] The women loaded 54 feet of tables with "all the toothsome vivands imaginable." After dinner was a display of some of the exercises the Turners were promoting. Next came football, followed by several rounds of boxing in which 52 year-old John Lemp got away with first blood and the victory belt: an impressive feat for a middle aged man. Then came firearms. Miss Mattie Kohlepp was second in girls shooting, and Emil Lemp a close second in the boys shooting contest. Brewer Lemp also was awarded an honorable mention in shooting. The extended family had garnered an impressive set of honors. The club finished the day with singing.

A former soldier, and current Lemp saloon employee, named Roy kept three bears of different ages in the back of the saloon as a hobby.[r] They entertained customers and probably discouraged prowlers too. In July, the bears were displayed on the street to delight a crowd of children.[s] Roy also drove one of Lemp's beer wagons, and the city marshal consulted him about which bridges and culverts were dangerous.[t]

Boise still lacked a public park in 1890 and the deprivation was more and more viewed as an inappropriate shortcoming for a modern state capital. The Boise Agricultural grounds—150 acres adjoining the town on the west—with its racetrack was mostly (about 3/4) owned by Lemp and Judge Kelly, and was a perfect spot for a park. Lemp refused to sell it to a private citizen; he would only sell it to the city. He and Kelly agreed to sell it for $100 per share, which would be a cost to the city of about $15,000 or half of its alleged market value.[u]

John took on another building project when he decided to add a story to his brick building on Main Street that was occupied by Mr. Frank Nourse and the I.O.O.F.[v] The third story would make the building uniform with the new three-story structure beside it.

On July second of 1890, John Lemp and Nathan Falk were joint patentees on two pieces of mineral property in Blaine county.[w] One was known as the Ironclad and contained 18.1 acres, and the other was the Concordia and was 20.661 acres. The claims were made under the Mineral Patent-Lode Act of 1866. This was two days before Idaho became a state. On the Fourth of July that year, Idaho celebrated its first day as a state in the Union. It was entering the Union with the constitution which John Lemp had signed the summer before.

At the meeting of the local Republican club everyone wrote down twenty names of individuals they would like to see on the primary ticket. John Lemp was the only name to appear on all 61 ballots.[x] When the final list of twenty was presented to the *Statesman*, Lemp's name was on top. When the Republicans met again on the 13th of August, Lemp was put on the committee of five to consider permanent organization and order of business.[y]

John was considered for the Republican nomination for state treasurer that summer but Frank Coffin was finally nominated instead. The Hailey newspaper said that was because Lemp was a mugwump and this was not a mugwump year. The Republican State Committee Chairman, Joseph Pinkham, wrote them to say that Lemp was not a mugwump and as far as he knows had never before been accused of being one. Lemp was a most pronounced straight out and out Republican, according to Pinkham, and was not questioned in Boise or the county.[z] Originally Mugwumps were Republicans that would not support Blaine for president and instead went to Cleveland in 1884. The term carried over for a decade or so. Mugwumps were thus considered disloyal by the party bosses.

After the convention, Lemp made a trip through the towns of Boise Basin.[aa] Back at Boise City, the new third story on his building was going up fast, and the new building was now officially announced to be a hotel. The carpenters were rapidly finishing the interior.[ab] In early October, a load of dimensional timber was received for that interior work at the hotel.[ac] Also in early October, one of Lemp's teams suffered yet another runaway. This time one horse was killed.[ad] A.L. Swingle who worked on Lemp's ranch discovered a human body on Eagle Island in the Boise river about nine miles from Boise.[ae] There were just small portions of skin on the skeleton, but the clothes were there. An inquest produced the verdict of "found drowned, name unknown." He was buried in the potters' field in Boise.

The list of attendees at the Grand Ball of the Odd Fellows that fall included many names prominent in Idaho brewing. Of course, at the top the list were Mr. and Mrs. John Lemp.[af] John had no trouble in

1890 being elected Grand Treasurer of the I.O.O.F. again, as for so many previous years.[ag]

In November, a new floor was put down in John's wholesale liquor store.[ah] At the same time his new hotel with its "hundreds" of rooms was almost ready for guests.[ai] In late November, some details about the hotel finally emerged. It was to be called the Capitol and to be run by J. H. Butler.[aj] There would be forty to fifty rooms ready by the 8th or 10th of December, and forty-five of the rooms had already been reserved. The furniture would be the best and Butler said his "table" (cuisine) would be his best advertisement. The bar, billiard, and reading rooms and office would all be on the first floor. A formal opening was planned for about New Years Day. Butler made a personal trip back to his former home in Butte, Montana, but then returned to hurry the laying of carpets in the hotel.[ak]

One of the last events in 1890 to involve the brewery was when the hook and ladder company used the building to test their new truck and apparatus. After trying the new ladders, they loaded everything back on the truck (more like a hand cart than a modern truck) and ran around the block with it. Then they came back, set up the ladders, and had a man on top the four-story brewery in one and three-quarters minutes.[al]

At the city council meeting early in January of 1891 there was a heated exchange when Mr. James A. Bogart wanted a mayor's deed to some land north of town. Councilman Lemp remarked about who, in his estimation, had the true ownership of the land, and derided the tactics of Bogart "the tenderfoot real estate jumper." The mayor added that Bogart had no right to be granted a deed, and perhaps the city had a claim to the property in question. Lemp moved that Bogart's petition for the deed be rejected and it was.[am]

Also at the January 10th meeting, the council discussed selling the old fire department hook and ladder truck to the City of Caldwell which had expressed interest.[an] Councilman Lemp explained he had attended a fire department meeting, and suggested the council sell the truck and use the money for new hose and a hose cart. The fireworks for the previous Fourth of July was the next topic. They had arrived too late for the celebration and had been sold. Lemp, the master of accounting and fiscal responsibility, asked "who has the money?"

The council then discussed the cost of fire plugs. Toward the end of the meeting Lemp moved, and the council approved, a motion to have the electric company put in two lights on Ninth street. As a city councilman, Lemp was certainly a solon with mundane local politics.

In February 1891, Lemp was still advertising exported "Wiener Beer" from San Francisco by bottle or barrel, as well as homemade beer from Boise.[ao] Lemp's brother-in-law Charles Leyerzaph was listed on the Boise City directory of 1891 as a soda water manufacturer with property at 1324 Tenth street. He originally had been a gunsmith. Brewing and soda manufacturing share an interest in bottling equipment, technique, and personnel.

The Boise City Board of Trade raised $10,000 that February to entice a Mr. McIntyre to come to Boise and open a woolen mill. Among the subscribers who put up the $10,000 was John Lemp who personally pledged $1,000.[ap] In April, John put up another $500 for a fund to advertise the advantages of Boise City and surrounding territory.[aq] Also in April, Lemp was on the committee that met with officials of the Union Pacific to complain about the lack of a sufficient number of trains on their new schedule.[ar] Mr. Morris of the railroad agreed to the committee's request for more runs.

On May 4, 1891 John filed a patent on a whole section, 640 acres, of Canyon County land under the Desert Land Act of 1877.[as] Lemp seemed to be able to anticipate which lands would eventually get irrigation water and become valuable.

As the spring season of farm work began in southern Idaho, John gave some advice on fence building to the populous.[at] He offered that charring the ends was the best way to preserve posts that he had found, and the post should be cut initially when the sap was up.

In June, a public meeting was held to get organized for the Fourth of July celebration. When America's 115th birthday arrived the bands played, Lemp and several others made patriotic speeches.[au] John's endless series of constructions went on as he added a stairway to his wholesale liquor house so the second floor could be used in the business.[av]

Mr. and Mrs. Lemp gave a dinner party for two nieces of Captain William H. Jaumann who were visiting him.aw Mrs. Jaumann was John Lemp's sister Martha Elizabeth (Elise). In other instances,

Jaumann was referred to as Major General, which was at best an honorary title.

On August 22, the Boise Electric Street Railway commenced operation. As a director of the company, John could justly feel a part of this development.

John was given permission in August by the city council to erect a three-story brick building on Main between Eight and Ninth.[ax] He was also getting architectural iron columns made for the new bank building which was being located between the Idaho Saddlery Company and the brewery saloon.[ay] Only two weeks later the new bank building was reportedly constructed up to the second story.[az]

John suffered a burglary at his house that summer. Someone broke in and took some of his clothes which had a gold watch and chain, and cash of $70 to $80 in them. Officer Sam Howrie tracked the burglar to Thomas Davis' field where the clothes were found minus the valuables. The police said they had suspicions about the identity of the culprit.[ba] I have found no evidence that those suspicions led to a recovery or an arrest.

The Bitter Election of 1891

The first really nasty, vindictive, political battle in Boise history, and the first time the *Statesman*, after years of gushing praise for his every move, found grave fault with John Lemp was in the summer of 1891. There was no inkling of the problem when, on the first of July, the *Statesman* reported on the Republican nominees for the city council.[bb] "Old Reliable" John Lemp got more votes from the Republican caucus than any other candidate. William E. Borah, the future famous U.S. Senator, was made city attorney nominee.[bc] Messers. Lemp and Collister were described as present councilmen who would be certain to succeed themselves as they are "both permanently and substantially identified with every interest of the city, and both have rendered good service, which voters will be certain to remember at the polls."[bd] The next day the newspaper's opinion turned upside down.

Lemp had declined the Republican nomination, so he could run with a newly formed party. The *Statesman*, a Republican newspaper, was plainly angered.[be] The editor said that since Lemp had exercised his personal privilege of declining, the Republicans needed to find "some really reliable and loyal Republican" to fill his place on the ticket. He was not "Old Reliable" anymore. Lemp, the editor went on, had received many honors from the Republicans but now he chose to weaken them at the polls. "This course of Mr. John Lemp gives proof of a nature so ungrateful . . . it can only be accounted for on the grounds of protracted inebriety." The editor continued that if Lemp had just declined "on the grounds that conscious of his recognized habits and infirmities he recognized the duty he owes himself of retiring from public life," that would have been acceptable, but as a recognized Republican he had no right to desert his party and go over to the enemy.

The *Evening Citizen* printed the words of the *Statesman* in side by side columns to show their "deadly parallel" and "Glaring inconsistency."[bf] They editorialized: "How inconsistent is this! One day the 'old reliable,' the next day the inebriate. One day the able and favored one, the next the despised victim of unfortunate habits and infirmities. And this to be said in Boise City of honored and respected John Lemp, the substantial and progressive citizen, the man whom nearly everyone says does more for the city than any other man in it, whose children have been born and raised here, whose wealth had been acquired here by hard work and industry, whose property has been accumulated by his own hands and not wedded at the alter. Is this vile attack to be made on such a man and go unpunished? No! a thousand times, no! The people at the polls will strongly repudiate the utterances of a vile combine of backbiters, calumniators and character assassins who's principal occupation, aside of reveling in the Arid club, is to cowardly attack the character of staunch honest citizens, bring tears to the eyes of their wives and daughters and insult the dignity and good name of the community in which they are temporarily allowed to abide."

According to the *Evening Citizen*, "it appeared better for the city to eschew politics and to unite the two great parties in a citizen's movement. It had been common talk for some weeks in favor of a citizen's ticket to be composed of all the very best material, regardless of political affiliation and this the *Statesman* opposed, urging a straight party fight."[bg] A fusion meeting of Democrats and Republicans was held to nominate a ticket. This was Lemp's new "party," and he and his brother-in-law William Jaumann were among the 10 Republicans listed as being at the meeting. The *Statesman*'s editor referred to it as "the little fusion game manipulated by the Democrats and certain miscalled Republicans" which produced a city ticket "born of political trickery and representative of nothing but the inordinate desire of certain men for political office . . ."[bh] The ticket which came from this meeting had James A. Pinney for mayor, and Lemp heading the list for councilmen, and there were 13 Republicans and 13 Democrats on the 26 man ticket.

The Republicans revamped their ticket minus the name of Lemp. The *Statesman* said "many people have expressed a desire to see a Republican ticket in Boise without the name of John Lemp on it. This very large and eminently respectable class of citizens now have the opportunity of realizing their wishes."[bi] The fusion group had a mass meeting to confirm the nominations they had decided on. The *Statesman* said the orators were "chiefly confined to elegiums on the lamented John Lemp and the damning of the Statesman which was blamed for the sad fate of Lemp . . ."[bj] Specifically, Mayor-nominee Pinney spoke and said he "cared not what a cowardly newspaper had said about him, but he did care for the attack on his friend, John Lemp. He wanted the people to put John Lemp in the council head and shoulders above everybody else when the election came off."[bk]

The *Evening Citizen* was in steadfast agreement. "It is folly to think for a moment that the taxpayers will throw over such a man as John Lemp, one of our most substantial taxpaying citizens. That he and the rest of the Citizen's ticket will be elected is as certain as the sun will rise and set on election day. With John Lemp in the council the people will always have a friend, an honest friend, who will stand between the taxpayers and the gang of schemers and monopolists who are ever ready to bleed a municipality of their hard-earned money. He is the friend of the poor man, and many a one there is who can testify to many an act of kindness rendered by John Lemp. He was needed in days gone bye, is needed now in all times of necessity, and the people cannot afford to do without his services."[bl]

As the election approached new issues arose. The *Evening Citizen* deflected allegations that the Citizens ticket would impose a heavy tax to construct sidewalks to the hot springs, to grade down the street on which the street railway would be built to the river, and to fill in the swamp through which the railroad would have to be laid.[bm] "This stuff is worse than moonshine. In the first place it is malicious slander upon the personnel of the citizens' ticket....This, if possible, is a dirtier fling than the vile drivel that appeared a few days ago in the Statesman against the good name of John Lemp."

John Lemp placed a beer ad in this new newspaper (for Wiener Beer and Home-made beer), and a simple "vote for John Lemp" message.[bn]

The election results showed 375 votes for Lemp, 53 more than for William Bryon who had the second most votes for councilman.[bo] The fusion ticket had swept the day. The *Statesman* sought to explain itself and perhaps scab over a few of the wounds it had inflicted in its futile partisan effort. Lemp had, after all, run ads in virtually every issue of that newspaper for 23 years. The editor said the paper had been Republican all its long years and had never had to apologize for that fact.[bp] He was just defending his party. With the election over, Lemp could return some of his attention to business and brewing.

Street graders in July dug away at the embankment in front of the brewery and used the dirt to fill low places at the crossing of Main and Fourth.[bq] There was a new high license law for Idaho liquor sellers in 1891, which meant the costs of a license to sell liquor went way up. Lemp bought licenses for his three establishments.[br] This was one of the various "temperance" concepts enacted on the march to national prohibition. The thought was that the high price of a liquor license would limit the number of saloons and that magically would limit the total alcohol consumption of the populous.

Ten men invested $500 each to build a foundry promoted by Captain Charles Baxter in 1891. It was at the east end of Warm Springs Avenue near the hot spring development. By 1909 it had ten to twenty workmen and made boilers, pumps, pulleys, hangers, castings and engines of all kinds. The initial investors were C. W. Moore, R. Z. Johnson, W. H. Ridenbaugh, J. B. Broadbent, A. R. Andola, Nathan Falk, John Krall, H. G. Wilson, Thomas Davis, and John Lemp.[bs] In 1890, investors had drilled in the area and struck a copious flow of hot water as they had hoped and expected. The water was eventually used to heat homes, and to provide water for the Natorium, an enormous indoor pool, and, indirectly, to create a boom in real estate in that area of the city.

Lemp bought a 8,105 pound "refrigerator," which had a freight charge alone of $185.00, for his wholesale house on Main. It was from the Brunswick-Balke-Callender Company of Chicago.[bt] Mechanical refrigeration as making great inroads into industry during this period. Lemp's purchase may have been related to the fact that his ice house was completely emptied by mid-September. He was then getting ice out of the brick elevator nearby where excess ice harvest had been stored.[bu]

In District Court Proceedings in Idaho City, John Lemp sued the Idaho Gold and Silver Mines Limited.[bv] There were three days of motions and legal wrangling before the decision was reached. On September 15th Lemp won. The company had to turn over fifty tons of ore, pay court costs of $59.40, but pay only one cent in damages to Lemp.

On Lemp's ranch near Middleton, Henry Kohlepp, the operator and Lemp's brother-in-law, came upon a lady in men's clothes who had shot 53 ducks despite a "no shooting" sign. He came up cussing before he recognized her gender.[bw] When he figured out the situation, he left her to her sport.

The Boise Rapid Transit Company elected their officers in October which again included Lemp as a trustee. They intended to extend the line to the new Union Pacific depot when it was finished.[bx]

Lemp went to Ketchum to check on his mines on Sheep Mountain and was joined there by his partner, John Early, in September of 1891.[by] In that district Lemp also owned the Alta-Johnson mine which had a tunnel over 200 feet to tap its principal body of ore. Lemp was going to work that mine all winter.[bz] Lemp and Early traveled together to the mines, but, after a day or two, Lemp had an attack of rheumatism in one leg. Word of this reached Boise. He went on in pain and completed the business. When he got back to Ketchum he wired his wife that he was better. Catherine went to Ketchum to tend to her husband anyway. Seven months later Catherine gave birth to their 13th and last child. There were rumors that John's condition was dangerous but it was not true.[ca] Lemp and wife arrived in Boise in a couple of days but John was infirmed enough that he had great trouble getting out of the carriage that hauled him from the train depot.[cb]

October was the month for bonds to be filed for those wanting county liquor licenses. Lemp was either an applicant or a surety on five of these.[cc] While that was happening, Lemp's new bank building was being plastered by the workmen.[cd] One of John's fine bulls was struck by the Idaho Central train and died of the injuries. "The train was not materially damaged," according to the Statesman, which I am sure was a great relief to Lemp and the ghost of his bull.[ce]

The Grand Lodge and Grand Encampment of the I.O.O.F. met in Moscow in early October and Lemp somehow found the time to make the long, indirect journey north.[cf] At the meeting the Odd Fellows decided to build an orphanage in Idaho. Eagle Rock (Idaho Falls) offered $10,000 cash, $10,000 worth of property and free building stone if it was located there. Boise wanted the site too but did not match the amount of the offer. After the yearly meeting, Lemp said that if the Eagle Rock offer was legitimate it would be accepted. Incidentally, Lemp was made Grand Treasurer again at the meeting.[cg] Later, Lemp went to Eagle Rock and confirmed their offer for the orphanage.[ch]

Lemp was one of the original stock holders in a new corporation designed to promote mining throughout the state at this time.[ci] Governor Willey, former brewer John Krall, and many other recognizable names were also founders of the company.

At the city council that December of 1891 there was a great discussion as to whether to revoke the license of the Star Variety Theater held by Mr. Augustine. After Councilman Dangel attacked it, Lemp came to its defense. Lemp said there was no evidence to show it was not respectable and he did not believe in acting too quickly. There was also a "Sunday Law" proposal at the same meeting. Lemp protested a section of that law which forbade music in saloons on Sunday; he said it "trenched upon the decent rights of American citizens." There was also a provision to forbid females from singing or playing a musical instrument, and also forbid women just to remain about a saloon or any adjacent room or building. Again Lemp grew indignant. Finally the part about females remaining around a saloon was dropped.[cj] I think this gives some insight into the personal philosophies of John Lemp. He highly valued personal liberty.

Before the year of 1891 was ended, the Boise City Council considered a move to abandon Sun time. Prior to that date Boise hotels had two clocks for visitors: one with railroad time, based on their new time zone concept, and one with Sun time, calibrated from the exact time of high noon in Boise. The sun time clocks were 45 minutes behind the railroad time clocks. The Statesman said "every time a stranger notices the disparity of forty-five minutes between the two times pieces he either thinks his vision has become distorted or that the clocks are running a race."[ck] The newspaper called this dated two-clock practice "moss-backed" and councilman Lemp said Boise was nearly as far behind the times as Las Vegas, New Mexico, where the citizens enjoy four or five "times." The council agreed to pass the ordinance at the next meeting. Boise is on the western border of the Mountain time zone and has both late sunrise and sunset. Throughout the Twentieth Century Northern Idaho was in the Pacific Time Zone, and Southern Idaho in Mountain Time Zone which predicatably caused confusions.

1892

The William J. Lemp Brewing Company of St. Louis had 46 beer depots around the U. S. A. in 1892, including one at Shoshone and one at Boise City, Idaho.[cl] 1892 was to prove a monumentally difficult year for Idaho. On January 16, all the important Coeur d'Alene mines shut down due to high freight rates and low silver prices. Before the year was out the mill at Gem was dynamited and martial law was imposed in the Coeur d'Alenes. The wholesale rounding up of miners without trial left a deep hatred and desire for revenge in the union men

Marie Anna Lemp. 5 March 1892 to 6 January 1896. Thirteenth child of John and Cathrine.
Photo, Idaho State Historical Society

that continued to resurface for decades to come. Idaho would suffer in unexpected ways. The low price of silver certainly effected the value and productivity of Lemp's mines in the Wood River area. It was also time for the annual Boise ice harvest in early January.[cm]

A committee to push for a railroad from Boise to Butte met in early 1892. Mr. O. L. Miller was the promoter and he had maps and statistics to indicate the proposal was sound. Lemp was among the capitalists at the meeting.[cn] In March, Lemp announced at a meeting of the Boise Board of Trade that Mr. Miller was then in Chicago and having some luck in interesting mid-western capitalists in the project.[co]

John filed a patent on 166.28 acres of Boise County land on January 30, 1892 under the cash entry law of 1820.[cp]

During March of 1892, John Lemp and John Krall were the most prominent of many prominent Boise citizens who filed mining claims on Shaw's Mountain just north of Boise. Some expected $10,000,000 in gold to be coming into Boise.[cq] This was a typically exaggerated expectation such as accompanied every speck of gold ever found in Idaho.

On 5 March 1892, daughter Marie Anna, the 13th and last Lemp child, was born.[cr] Catherine was 41 and John was 53. It was 25 years and 2 months since their first offspring John Emil was born. Sadly, Little Marie was fated to have a very short lifespan. On 6 January 1896, Marie Anna Lemp, not quite four years old, died at her home.[cs] She had suffered from scarlet fever for several days. She was buried in the Masonic cemetery. This was the third child John and Catherine had lost. The *Statesman*, rather than offering condolences, carried a report that there were a lot of complaints about the way the quarantine was handled. Some said the other children played in the streets nearby and adults frequently visited and then mingled outside with others. Marshal Rube Robbins courteously explained the child was quarantined in one upper room and notices were posted as soon as the nature of the disease was known.[ct] The physician in charge had reassured the Marshal that the quarantine was effective.

A mass meeting was held in Boise that March of 1892 to not only organize a first state fair for Idaho, but to prepare to hold the initial event in the Fall of that very year. John Lemp moved that a committee be formed at once to organize it because "talking does no good, what we want is hard work."[cu] Lemp was one of the committee members selected for the attempt to raise $50,000. He solicited stock subscriptions in Middleton.[cv]

The Boise city council was having disagreements with the light company over the cost of street lights at this time. At a council meeting, Lemp declared that it would be a step backward to put the lights out; "to talk of a city like Boise putting out its lights in this age of the world sounds like nonsense."[cw] It was finally all resolved.

Lemp sued W. B. Biggerstaff in March of 1892 for failure to pay a loan or mortgage.[cx] Biggerstaff failed to appear, and Lemp was awarded $1250.14 in gold coin, with costs of $48.30 also falling on Biggerstaff.

John was one of the pall bearers for Mrs. Lois Kelly, wife of Judge Milton Kelly, that March of 1892.[cy] Lemp had done a great deal of business through the years with the Kelly family.

Boise was in need of additional water at this time and one suggestion was to buy the ditch belonging to Joseph Perrault. Lemp suggested instead that they build a ditch using convict labor, and that it have enough fall to furnish power for an electric light plant. They awaited further investigation before making a decision.[cz]

The Boise Water Works Company which had been founded in June of 1890, and the Artesian Water and Land Improvement Company, formed about the same time, merged in 1892.[da] A new water company was formed called the Artesian Hot and Cold Water Company, among the directors of the new company was John Lemp.[db] The Company published their rules, regulations and rates in March of 1892.[dc] Breweries—only Lemp and Brodbeck were in that business at the time—were charged seven dollars a month for water plus $2.00 for the first "closet" (toilet), $1.00 for each additional closet, 50 cents for the first urinal, and 25 cents for each additional urinal. Urinals had to have self-closing faucets.

Architects Campbell and Hodgson were making plans for numerous new homes and improvements in Boise that March. One of their customers, John Lemp, ordered a $1,500 new front on one of his buildings.[dd]

THE STAR MINE, HAILEY, IDAHO

The ownership of mining property in this area involved members of Lemp's circle of friends for some years before Lemp himself joined. For instance, Albert Wolters, David Falk and E. J. Chase bought the "Centre" mine from Solon Burgess on 27 November 1880 for ten dollars.[de]

The "Star Quartz Lode" was filed on and thus effectively purchased from the United States on 15 May 1882 by Albert Wolters, David Falk and Eben S. Chase.[df] Another very similar filing for the "Star Quartz Lode" is the next item in the Patent Deed book. Lemp bought an interest in another mine on Wood River in March of 1882.[dg] The rest of his life Lemp was involved in mining in the Hailey/Wood River area. Unfortunately, copies of deeds and newspaper clippings give more of an outline than a detailed account of the mine ownership. The details were very complicated.

In April of 1884, David Falk sold to John Lemp and his own brother Nathan Falk, for $1,000, his interest in the Star Quartz Lode.[dh] This may explain why newspaper sources are often inconsistent as to which Falk brother is involved with ownership of the mine. At virtually the same time Albert Wolters sold his interest in the Star to Nathan Falk and John Lemp.[di] This included the "Washington, "Ohio," and "Sun Rise" mines also. John and Nathan owned the majority of the mine after this.

Before December, 1886, was over, George Kohlepp made a trip to Boise to lease the Star Gulch mine from brother-in-law John Lemp.[dj] George was bragging that the silver recently assayed 198 ounces to the ton and that was below the average of 300 to 400 ounces.[dk] The miner's optimism and lust after wealth seemed to have had at least a temporary hold on George. George did not hold the lease for a long time.

Before winter set in 1889, Lemp visited his Star mine on Wood River. The former United States Assayer at Boise, Albert Wolters, was running the operation for Lemp and his partners at this time. The mine was said to be developing well and had a magnificent body of ore.[dl] Wolters, with whom Lemp was to have many business and family dealings, had recently been in court due to his personal insolvency.[dm]

In early April,1892, Lemp again went to the Star mine near Hailey to see how work was progressing. One vein was exposed which was six feet wide and had about 22 inches of first class ore, including 12 inches of solid Galena (Silver-Lead). It had been exposed for a distance of 70 or 80 feet. Lemp told the *Hailey Times* he had been mining there since 1880 and would like to make some money but would reinvest it locally, "not take it away and spend [it] elsewhere."[dn] He, and 1/4 or 1/3 owner Nathan Falk, planned to return in a month. Brothers Nathan and David Falk both seem to have been owners with Lemp at this point.[do] While in Hailey, Lemp talked to the Odd Fellows about the lodge home to be built in Idaho Falls.[dp] M. B. Gwinn of Caldwell accompanied Lemp on the Odd Fellows business in the Wood River area.[dq] Lemp had visited so often he was well acquainted with the area.

In October, 1892, Lemp and the Falk brothers sold their Star group of mines to a syndicate from Salt Lake for $112,200. Arthur Stayuer acted for the Salt Lake men and Elias Morris and Jesse Wolf of the company were also in Boise to close the deal. The Star group consisted of three of the best paying mines in the Wood River country, and the new owners would use the best machinery to work the property vigorously, they said.[dr] Lemp and the Falk Brothers took a mortgage on the property.

Late in November, 1892, John made yet another trip to Wood River to check on either the Star group of mines which had supposedly been sold or other mining property of his. He left Hailey in time to have his Thanksgiving turkey at home in Boise.[ds]

A month later, the miners at the Star mine in Hailey went on strike under rumors that the company was two months behind on wages.[dt] Lemp and Falk had not been completely paid on the mortgage they held on the property. He made several trips there during that year to check on matters. For instance, in early May of 1893, Lemp arrived by stage in Hailey. He was on mining business as was so often the case.[du]

In September, 1893, a major strike at the Star mine, or mineral location, in Hailey was announced.[dv] The next month, John Lemp again went to Hailey to look after his mining interests.[dw] He was still holding paper on the Star mine. He and David Falk left Hailey after a few days, vowing humorously to come back in the spring, if alive, or sooner if silver went to $1.29 an ounce.[dx]

The Star mine was in the news again in November of 1893. A. E.

Nichols of Salt Lake City, a heavy investor went to Hailey and paid off the workers and shut down the mine while looking for a new manager.[dy] The mine was still considered the best on Wood River.

The next year, April, 1894, the Hailey newspaper said Lemp and Falk considered themselves released from all interest in the Star group of mines. Lemp was then in the East but would again visit Hailey when he returned.[dz]

In the list of Judgments in the Judicial Records of Blaine County for 22 June 1894 John Lemp is listed as debtor ten times to ten different men for $2,814.66 each and then this is all crossed out.[ea] The ten men are the same as the group that had an interest in the purchase of the Star mine. This problem was resolved, and the purchase went through. A deed dated 25 July 1894 conveyed the Star Mining Claim and the Center (sic) claim from John and Catherine Lemp, and Nathan and Rosa Falk to Isaac Brockbank et al. for the sum of $40,000. Rosa Falk signed and was notarized in Ada County, while Catherine Lemp signed and was notarized in Salt Lake City.[eb] At the same time John and Catherine sold their Vanderbilt mining claim in the Mineral Hill Mining District to the same group headed by Brockbank for $2,000.[ec]

In late February, 1896, a report from Hailey said the Star mine, now renamed the Vanderbilt, was working with about twelve men employed. In mid-April, Isaac Jennings and Elias Morris of Salt Lake were reported talking to Lemp and his partners about getting the mine back. According to the *Statesman* the Salt Lake men had defaulted on a payment and gave it up. It was not quite so simple. In October of 1896 John Lemp and David Falk filed a suit to foreclose their mortgage on the Star group of mines.[ed] The unhappy sale had drug on for years by this time without ever being closed.

In Decmber, 1896, two Salt Lake men came to Boise to consult with Lemp and the other owners about the Star mine in Hailey.[ee] The mine was reported doing well and finding good ore but a deferred payment—one that was apparently difficult for the new owners to secure—was still due to Lemp and the others. On the 7th of December Thomas A. Starrh and Wife sold their 1/10 interest in the mine to the other partners, the Vanderbilt mining company of Salt Lake.[ef]

In August of 1897, Lemp and Falk again made the trip to Hailey to look after Star mine matters. A week later was a sheriff's sale for the mine apparently due to the owners insolvency. Lemp and Falk bid $45,000, which covered the amount of the judgment and the costs.[eg] They again owned the mine outright. The next February, 1898, the sheriff's deeds were filed for the record. They conveyed two-thirds of the group to John Lemp in satisfaction of his judgment for $29,843.50, and the other one-third to Nathan Falk in satisfaction of his judgment for $14,921.75.[eh] The owners immediately gave a three year lease to six men from Hailey.[ei] These men intended to tunnel about 1,000 feet and then go upward 100 to 150 feet to drain the present tunnel. Other men leased the upper workings, and the owners had the option of redeeming the property.

In February of 1898, Frank C. Mandell filed a proof of labor upon the Vanderbilt lode (formerly The Star) claim owned by Lemp.[ej] What he hoped to accomplish was not clear.

In October of 1899, Falk and Lemp gave a twelve month extension to their leases on the Star group of mines. The men leasing the mine were Ben R. Gray, William Gibbons, C.W. Pinney, A. G. Viggett, and W.C. Martin of Hailey.[ek] Lemp went to Hailey to conduct this business and complained of feeling poorly when he got there. He told the press there: "I always liked this country. I've heard some people complain of it, but I never did. I have made money here, and expect to make more."[el]

That November of 1899, John took another trip to Hailey to see about the Star group of mines. They were working three shifts and expected to take out a lot of money before Christmas.[em] For several years the Star mine stayed out of the news. First thing in May, 1892, Lemp and Nathan Falk went to Hailey to again look over the Star mine.[en]

In December of 1903, son Albert C. Lemp was noted as a visitor to Hailey.[eo] He was attending to business at his father's Star mine.[ep] He returned to Boise in a few days.[eq]

According to a magazine article in 1904, Lemp still owned the Star mines and was hoping to produce Galena ore there.[er] The magazine said he still had a keen mind and was ready to "take occasion by the beard" as when he was in his prime. In early August of 1904, Lemp made his usual pilgrimage to Hailey to look after the Star mine of which he was half owner.[es] He wanted to add to the work force there. John was back in Hailey to look at the progress of the work on the Star group of mines in Colorado gulch in early September.[et] He deeded over his undivided 1/3 interest in the Louisa Lode, Ohio Lode, and Sunrise Lode in the Warm Springs Creek Mining District of Blaine County to the Boulder Consolidated Mining Company, Ltd. of Boise for one dollar.[eu] M. W. Wood was listed as the trustee for the company. This new company probably included Lemp and this was a legal formality to change ownership. In October, Leo J. and Rosa Falk, co-executors of the will of Nathan Falk, also signed over the Falk stock to the new company for one dollar.[ev] Also in August 1904, Charles Sonnleitner, former brewery operator in Hailey, and the current foreman at the Star mine of Lemp and Falk, announced that they had struck concentrating ore in the sixth level, on the north vein in entirely new ground.[ew] It was four feet across the face of the tunnel and three inches wide. He believed they were on the verge of uncovering new ore that would eclipse all the previous discoveries. The owners had done much dead work the past year and allowed other ore finds to remain in place while the dead work continued. Sonnleitner had also been the Star mine foreman briefly back in 1893 before he leased John Hendel's brewery in Hailey.

John Lemp, accompanied by soon-to-be brother-in-law Albert Wolters, hurried to Hailey to see the most recent ore discovery in 1905.[ex] The Hailey and Boise newspapers noted Lemp's departure.[ey] Lemp did not make another inspection trip to the Star mine in September, but Leo J. Falk went as a representative of the Nathan Falk estate.[ez] The Lemp family retained ownership of the mine for at least the next fifty years.

OTHER BUSINESS, 1892

Colonel John A. Torrence, deputy collector of the Internal Revenue, left Boise surreptitiously in April with several hundred dollars from the public treasury. This would not be of note except the three bondsmen for him were John Lemp, brewer John Brodbeck, and John Early.[fa]

Lemp's brother-in-law, George Kohlepp married his third wife, Sarah M. Beck in Ada County on 13 April 1892.[fb] Also in late April, Lemp was among those making the short journey to Caldwell for the Ada County Republican convention.[fc] Apparently being on the fusion ticket for Boise councilman had not caused them to kick old John out of the party.

On John's 54th birthday the Germania Singing Society, of which he was a member, serenaded him. They met at 8:00 p.m. and went to the Lemp residence for hours of music, speechmaking and feasting. The First Regiment band considered Lemp a special friend because he had donated liberally toward the purchase of their instruments.[fd]

The Boise city water problems continued. Lemp went to talk with Joseph Perrault who offered to supply the city with water for $2,500 a year. An alternate offer was for the city to buy the ditch for $54,000 which the city would pay for with twenty year, six percent bonds. The city would also have to buy a pump to raise the water into a 250 foot high reservoir to supply necessary pressure. The council finally decided to have Lemp confer further with Perrault and then report back.[fe] A month or so later, Lemp reported that Perrault would furnish water for a lowered rate of $1,800 a year and the city, satisfied with that amount, drew up a contract.[ff]

A special report to *The Standard* in Ogden, Utah at the end of May said that John Lemp had good prospects on Sheep Mountain and "he is pulling hard for the erection of concentrating works in that vicinity, and with his usual partinacity (sic) thoroughly enlisted in the cause, he will no doubt succeed."[fg]

In June, son Albert, 15 years-old, returned for the summer from college. A week or two before, son Emil Lemp returned to Boise from the east where he had been selling a band of Idaho horses. He had sold all the animals but the price was very low.[fh] Apparently he went to Illinois on at least part of the trip and did not spend all his time with horses. On 1 November, just two months before his 26th birthday, John Emil was back in Alton, Illinois, for his wedding to Caroline (Carrie) A. Zeltmann.[fi] They then moved to Boise to make their new home. Caroline, according to Lemp family tradition, was also distantly related to Margaret Bach, John Lemp's sister who lived in St. Louis.

Late in July, the corner stone for the new Odd Fellows home in Idaho Falls was laid. Lemp was listed among the prominent men to attend the banquet honoring the event.[fj] He had certainly worked hard to see the project to fruition.

The Lemp-Pence War

One day a group of six or eight armed men appeared at a dwelling being built in Boise by J. C. Pence and proceeded to tear it down, up to and including putting the foundation stones in the street with the rest of the debris. Pence appeared while this was happening and he was allegedly held at bay with a drawn revolver.[fk] The small strip of land where the confrontation took place was part of the Lemp addition near the Bruniback addition. Lemp and Pence had disputed the ownership of the land for years and Pence unilaterally decided to build on it without permission from Lemp.

Each of the men put statements about his side of the dispute in the newspaper. Pence said the land in question had been government land. On 20 December 1891, Pence tried to file on the land at the U.S. land office. His efforts were rejected on the grounds that it was not government land but was part of lot five of a surveyed township. Pence had then appealed to the land commissioner in Washington, D.C. who ruled in his favor. Lemp took an appeal to the Secretary of the Interior but it was again decided in Pence's favor. Pence said "I considered I had a right to the land, and commenced erecting a house on it. Thursday morning last a gang of Lemp's hired men came to the place armed with shot-guns, revolvers and several kegs of beer. They tore down the house and pitched it into the middle of the road, and when I protested a pistol was thrust in my face and I was ordered off the premises. If I was not entitled to the land, I could have been dispossessed without the use of threats backed up by firearms in the hands of a half-drunken mob."[fl]

Naturally, Lemp's version differed. He said the one-acre lot in question was a part of a tract located by Dr. Holton in 1863, and patented by the doctor in 1871. It was not platted in the United States land office, but two years before Lemp had discovered that the land was recorded in the Surveyor General's office. Dr. Holton sold the land to Thomas Cahalan and he, in turn, sold it to Lemp. On August 1, while Lemp was in Wood River, Pence squatted on the land and began building a house. When Lemp returned to Boise, he asked Pence to quit the premises and offered to pay him something to prevent further quarreling over the matter.

Pence refused the offer, so Lemp ordered his men to remove the house. "Most of the men were armed, and Mr. Pence, when he appeared on the scene, was admonished to keep back, although no one drew a weapon upon him," according to Lemp's version.[fm] Lemp did not claim to be an eye witness.

Joseph Pence swore out warrants charging "procuring and inciting another to use force and violence in entering upon and detaining the possessions of another." Those served and arrested were John Lemp, John's son George, brother-in-law George Kohlepp, employees William Reynolds, William Breen, John Meyers, Charles Crouch, Thomas Shevilin and "others." Peter Jensen was not in the city or he would have been arrested too. Those "arrested" were not put in jail or required to give bail. They were to appear before Judge Ryal at 10 o'clock. District Attorney Hayes said he would vigorously prosecute, but Lemp's lawyer George Stewart, of Stewart and Borah, said Pence should be worried because they had complained to the law too.[fn]

At the first hearing, Attorney Stewart entered a demurrer to the complaint upon the grounds that there was no destruction of property. Judge Ryal overruled him and Stewart excepted. Trial was set for 19 September. After the court adjourned Pence asked that the defendants be placed under bonds. The District attorney so asked the judge but was refused by the court. Pence said if he lost the case here he would go on to federal court. The *Statesman* said prospects for a long legal fight were excellent.[fo] That was a sage prediction.

On the 19th of September the case went to court A six man jury of Messers. Van Dorn, Leeds, Ellis, Kent, Jones and Hammell was sworn in. Among other witnesses for the prosecution, was Mr. Pence. He testified that several men drew revolvers on him. Another witness testified that Lemp told him he sent men to demolish Pence's property.[fp]

The defense then sought to introduce testimony that Lemp had possession of the land for years and had, acting in good faith, greatly improved it. The prosecution objected saying this had no bearing on the case. After much argument and many citations, Judge Ryal adjourned court so that he could research the question.

The next day every seat in court was occupied as Judge Ryal decided to admit the testimony showing Lemp's prior possession of the land in question. As the Statesman said this "knocked the case of the prosecution into a cocked hat." Several witnesses confirmed that Lemp had possession of the land for the six years since 1886, had improved it, and paid taxes on it. Lemp testified that it was with the advice of attorney's R. Z. Johnson and George H. Stewart that he hired George Kohlepp and others to perform the demolition. The jury deliberated 15 minutes before ruling not guilty. Lemp walked out of the court room "with a satisfied expression on his good-natured face, . . . amid the congratulations of his friends."[fq]

The next day the prosecution proceeded against Lemp's workers, William Reynolds, George Lemp, Frank Cobb, William Andricks, John Meyers, Peter Jensen, Charles Crouch, Thomas Shevilin, William Breen, George Kohlepp, J. Brink, and J. J. Kane.[fr] The judge took the case under advisement for a few days before deciding they could not be charged since the one who ordered their action had already been found not guilty.

Despite appearances, the issue was not settled at all. Both Lemp and Pence tried to file on the land at the United States land office the next day. Pence wanted to file a homestead, and Lemp wanted a soldier's additional homestead entry. Both were turned away.[fs] The land had been added to the official plot of township three and would not be subject to entry until 22 October. Lemp would have the privilege of filing first at that time, but "that day will be the most exciting Register Kingsley has witnessed during his official career," forecasted the Statesman. The registrar also gave each man a circular that said the land was now platted and it would be handled in accordance with the rules and regulations of the Department of the Interior.

Soon Pence announced he would sue Lemp for heavy damages.[ft] Two months later a suit was filed asking $348.32 damages for the destruction of his house and $10 per month rent from Lemp for holding Pence's property. Jackson and Richards were representing Pence.[fu] The battle entered its next phase in February of 1894.

Back to Non-War Matters

At the annual meeting of the stockholders of the Boise Rapid Transit Company, financial affairs were found to be better than anticipated.[fv] The board, including John Lemp, was selected for the next year. They intended to issue bonds for improvements and extensions. In mid-September the billiard hall on the second floor of Lemp's liquor wholesale house was opened. It had three billiard and two pool tables and had electric lights. The ads mentioned St. Louis beer (without mentioning the brand) at five cents per glass as well as the local product. "Free lunch at all times" was available there too.[fw]

Lemp bought the Boise River ranch of Pat Boyle at public auction for $1,375. It was considered a bargain for the 160 acres, mostly under cultivation.[fx] Lemp had the cash reserves to take advantage of these kinds of opportunities. The Odd Fellows met that year in Pocatello, and Lemp was again a Boise delegate to both the Grand Encampment and the Grand Lodge.[fy] At the Grand Lodge meeting that year Lemp was reelected treasurer by acclamation.[fz] The report said "Mr. Lemp is one of the most popular and influndential members of the order."[ga] The members then made a quick trip to Idaho Falls to see how the new orphanage building was progressing.[gb]

Between 1890 and 1900 Boise experienced enormous expansion. Over ten new additions were added to the city limits.[gc] The Lemp addition, an 80 acre tract north of Boise, was platted and placed on the market by W. E. Pierce and Co. that fall.[gd] It was bounded by Eastman, Resseguie, Harrison Boulevard and 13th streets. The electric street cars which came into service in 1891 made Lemp's and other additions practical for those who worked downtown. Lots in the addition were destined to be sold for decades to come. The 1893 Boise City Directory carried an advertisement that read: "Buy in Lemp Addition/It Beats Them All/Only Two Blocks from the Car Line. Lots 122 to 130 feet deep."[ge] Walter E. Pierce handled the sales in the addition for Lemp.

Albert Wolters bought a city lot in Hailey from Samuel and Mary Boone in October of 1892.[gf]

On November 12, 1892, George W. Kohlepp borrowed $1,000 from John Lemp at 6% interest and signed a note for that amount. This matter would become public knowledge a few years later

Later in November, Lemp sued Albert Fritsch in District court to recover money owed.[gg Fritsch failed to appear] and Lemp was awarded $125 with $18.85 costs.

At the end of 1892 the *Statesman* indulged in a typical end of the year flurry of self-congratulations for the yearly physical improvements to the capital city. They praised the Artesian Hot and Cold Water Company and mentioned Lemp as a director; they also mentioned the new Lemp housing addition to the city.[gh] The plat of that addition was finally completed in early February. It was described as 40 acres, west of Thirteenth street, opposite the Resseguie addition.[gi]

1892 was the year of a seemingly insignificant patent being awarded to a Baltimore machinist named William Painter. His "crown top" was the long sought solution to closing beer and pop bottles efficiently. Eventually his invention made all the various wired cork and ceramic stopper devices obsolete, and the giant brewers of the East had yet another technological ally in their effort to flood the western markets with their beer.

John Lemp's saloon bond was approved, along with those of many other saloonists, at the January meeting of the County Commissioners.[gj] At the first meeting of the Boise Board of Trade of 1893 Lemp was present and spoke against a measure to raise the membership fee from $25 to $50 per year. The proposal was defeated.[gk]

The ice cutting season that year began the third week of January. The Boise Ice and Commission company was filling a large number of houses. Numerous individuals and businesses were cutting their own supply. Brodbeck was not going to retail ice and only wanted 200 or 250 tons for his brewery. Lemp was going to cut his supply from Ridenbaugh's pond, but wanted to examine the ice before deciding how much to cut. The teamsters, who hauled the harvest from pond to ice house, were getting 70 cents a load but went on strike for $1.[gl] They lost and went back to work.

In March of 1893, A. Roderick Grant, representing the O.W.R. Manufacturing Company of Portland, was in Boise on business. He was described as the vice-president of the company.[gm] I suspect Mr. Grant met the Lemp family while in Boise, as this was the future husband of Augusta Julia Margaret Lemp.

At this stage of his life Lemp seemed far removed from the daily concerns of the saloon business, but occasional events would bring that association back to mind. In March of 1893, Dudley Hedden got in a row at Lemp's saloon on Main and Ninth.[gn] The bartender hit him over the head with a poker and cut his scalp. Hedden then went out in the street, drew a "murderous looking knife" and defied the world. Police officers gathered him in and he spent a night in jail before being fined $25 by Magistrate Randall. Again Lemp's name became associated with violent, alcohol related events.

Simultaneously Lemp was again made one of the directors of the Boise Central Railway Company.[go] He was also made a member of the Third District grand jury, a civic responsibility which he had first shouldered a quarter of a century earlier.[gp]

Miss Gussie Lemp sang at the benefit to raise money for the free kindergarten that March of 1893.[gq] She was following the family tradition of charitable work and support for education. That same month intense advertising began to sell lots in the Lemp Addition, an area for new house construction. These were described as "level, healthy, high and dry, 122 to 130 feet deep," and W.E. Pierce & Co. were selling them for $150.00 to $375.00.[gr]

Lemp was still on the city council that year. The big concern on that front was for the spring flood on Cottonwood Creek and the damage it was causing to a new flume which had cost $9,000.[gs]

In April of 1893, Lemp was particularly active in filing mineral claims. On April 5 he and Edson Bishop, Edward Brisbin and Nathan Falk filed on 13.361 acres in Blaine County known as the Louisa under the Mineral Patent-Lode law of 1866.[gt] The same day Lemp and B. B. Eldred, Nathan Falk, and W. H. Savidge filed a patent on 15.588 acres known as the Sunrise in Blaine County under the same mineral law.[gu] From the description these appear to be beside each other.

A difficult political question at the time involved the creation of Canyon County out of part of Ada County. Lemp was among the local businessmen informally discussing the matter and his opinion was sought, as always.[gv] Some felt the valuation placed on the court house was incorrect and Canyon County needed to pay more if the split came. There was no quick or obvious solution to the problem.

On April 24, John Lemp, B. B. Eldred, W. H. Savidge and Nathan Falk filed a patent on a mineral claim of 20.207 acres in Blaine County known as the Ohio.[gw] This was the third claim Lemp was involved with that month, and was very near to the other two.

Mrs. Lemp got one of her few mentions in the newspaper when she attended a luncheon given for Mrs. A. Wolters.[gx] Mrs. Wolters was back in the city after eight years and many friends gathered at Mrs. Jauman's to reminisce. About the same time, friends threw a party to celebrate John Lemp's 55th birthday.[gy] A few days later a historical article about the Odd Fellows mentioned that Lemp was one of the original nine members of Idaho Encampment No. 1 in 1876, a branch of the lodge which only third degree members were permitted to join.[gz]

In business matters in April, 1893, Lemp extended the $100,000 bond on the Settlers ditch for six months.[ha] The bond holders were all residents of Boise, and the bond had begun the previous September.

Three men tried to rob the safe in Lemp's saloon late in May.[hb] Bartender Ruchdaschel stepped out the back door for a moment, and with no one supposedly watching, one of the three men opened the unlocked large door of the safe. One of the men watched the front door of the saloon and extorted his friend to get a move on with the safe. Unfortunately for the would be robbers, Constable N. G. Smith was surreptitiously watching them through a latticed screen. The third man said he could get the drawer out and he tried to take over on the safe. Then they heard the steps of the bartender returning and they stepped to the door and looked around unconcernedly. When the Constable told the bartender what had happened the men said they were only fooling. They were put in jail until officials could reach a decision about prosecuting them.

Mrs. Lemp was one of three Boise women who sent snowballs and other flowers to the Idaho state building at the World's Fair in Chicago that June.[hc] The only western brewer to win a medal at that fair was Adolph Coors of Golden, Colorado. At the fair, Bartholomay Brewing Company of Buffalo installed a four-foot-square working model of the interior of their brewery complete with ice machine and mash tub.[hd] Pabst Brewing put up a gold-platted 13 foot-square model of their Milwaukee brewery.

June was also the month for Baseball. Two impromptu teams were organized to play on the Glorious Fourth.[he] The Fats had to weigh over 200 pounds and know nothing about how to play, while the Leans had to be under 140 and likewise know nothing. Apparently anyone in the 60 pound gap could only gawk at the game. The *Statesman* predicted the "most unscientific game ever played." Holding down the defense at the keystone slot for the Fats was none other than 55 year-old John Lemp.

John had to renew his two saloon bonds for licenses that July. Fred Dangel and George Gumbert were the sureties on his bonds, while Lemp signed for the bond of J. B. Elliot of Boise.[hf] Lemp and partner Nathan Falk filed a mineral patent on 15.9 acres in Blaine county called the Centre on July 15, 1893.[hg] This was Lemp's forth mining claim patent of 1893.

In August, Mrs. Lemp and daughters Ada and Marie went to cool, high, Hailey to wait out the dog days of Summer. They stayed at the Alturas Hotel.[hh] A week later they were off to Ketchum which is a very short trip from Hailey and John came up to vacation with his family.[hi] At the end of August they returned to the hot lowlands of Boise.[hj] While John was in Ketchum he was elected treasurer of the newly formed State Bimetallic League.[hk] This group wanted American money based on the value of silver as well as gold which would have been a great boon to Idaho mining. This was one of the great issues of the day. Eventually this led to Presidential candidate William Jennings Bryan's famous "Cross of Gold" speech in which he pleaded, in overblown rhetoric, that we not "crucify mankind on a cross of gold."

In August, one of John's barkeepers, W. A. Mayer, left for New York to visit his father.[hl] Mayer had been in Boise fifteen years and had not visited home for ten.

In September, Lemp was listed as having $104,885 in assessed valuation in Ada County.[hm] John Broadbent was the only person with more—about $29,000 more.

Lemp was a member of the school board in 1893. John voted with the majority to provide free text books in keeping with recently passed state law.[hn] This was the big educational issue of the day and another step toward providing totally free public education. The so-called Barefoot Schoolboy Law passed in neighboring Washington state had led the way toward free schooling in the Pacific Northwest.

THE SAMUEL ADOLPH FAMILY OF SALEM, OREGON

The Lemp family received tragic news in late September from Salem, Oregon. Brother-in-law and former business partner Samuel Adolph had been killed in a buggy accident. Catherine left at once to be with her sister during the funeral. On the 17th of September 1893 Adolph had been thrown from a horse buggy and killed in Salem.[ho] About four in the afternoon he hitched up a pet yearling colt and started for a drive with his young son, Joseph.[hp] He had scarcely gotten away from the house when the inexperienced young animal took freight and overthrew the buggy. Joseph jumped and saved his life, but Samuel was not so lucky. His right leg was broken in two places, his right arm was also broken and badly lacerated, and his head was lacerated. Doctors Smith and Reynolds were called, but all they could do was make him comfortable. He was conscious until midnight, then took a short nap, and the death struggle began.

Adolph was described as 59, born in Prussia and had been in Salem since 1866. His previous business experience in Portland and Boise was noted. The newspaper said he was successful at everything and he left a good fortune for his wife and six children.

Adolph's daughter Eva was visiting in Chicago and hurried home for her father's funeral.[hq] Samuel had been a Mason, and was Jewish. The first plan was to take his remains to Portland for burial in the Jewish cemetery. He was described as a man of genial disposition, openhanded to the needy, and he enjoyed an extensive circle of admiring friends.

The family finally decided to postpone the funeral until Sunday the 24th of September to allow the relatives to gather. Plans were changed and the funeral was performed by the Masonic order at the graveside and he was buried in City View cemetery.[hr] Friends gathered at the home at 2:00 p.m. and special street cars took them to the cemetery. The funeral was largely attended with seven horse-drawn cars and 75 buggies going to the cemetery.[hs] The Masonic rites were observed in a most impressive manner. Catherine Lemp left for her Boise home on Tuesday.[ht]

The Adolph legacy remains in Salem in to the Twenty First Century. The Adolph home at 25th and State is on the list of historic homes for public viewing.[hu] Joseph and Lilly Adolph owned the Durbin building in the 1920s, which is also a historical landmark.[hv] Joseph, born in 1882, had purchased an interest in one of the Durbin buildings as early as 1911. His brother Samuel Adolph, Jr. joined him in the Adolph Brothers business there—a cigar, soft drinks and billiard establishment.

BACK TO BOISE

While in Hailey on mining business, John was not able to defend a suit against the Odd Fellows Home in Idaho Falls filed by Charles Carson & Co. Lemp was one of the three trustees, none of whom were close enough to get to court.[hw] In early November, however, all three managed to get to Idaho Falls. They visited the home and then left the same day.[hx]

October began with John again elected to the executive Committee of the Boise Rapid Transit Company.[hy] John also got his three county liquor licenses that October.[hz] John was elected president of the Turn Verein that month too.[ia] Again that month, for the umpteenth time, Lemp was elected Grand Treasurer of the Grand Lodge of the Odd Fellows.[ib] Lemp was also elected a trustee of the Odd Fellows home in Idaho Falls.[ic] Quite a month for any executive.

In November, there was talk of a suit by the Odd Fellows against the city of Idaho Falls if they did not fulfill the promises made when they were selected as the home site.[id] In early November it was announced that H.M. Stewart of Ketchum, landlord of the Ketchum Hot Springs, was going to lease Lemp's Capitol Hotel beginning on November 15, but Lemp would run it himself until then.[ie]

John Lemp filed suit against James H. Butler in District Court in December of 1893.[if] Butler failed to appear and was ordered to pay $153 plus $241.55 in costs. Most of these small suits involved saloon owners who failed to pay Lemp for the beer and other supplies they purchased.

Boise held a large charity ball during the holiday season of 1893. John and his daughter, eighteen year-old Ida, attended.[ig]

1893 saw the first use of the brand name Rainier by the Seattle Brewing and Malting Co. This brand name was to be a regional powerhouse—successfully marketing from Seattle to Boise and beyond—for over a century to come. Also that year the Anti-Saloon League was formed in Ohio. Its well-finance, rough and tumble techniques proved the most effective of any organization in strong-arming America into making Prohibition the law.

On February 21 1894, John Emil Lemp became a first-time father, and John and Catherine Lemp became grandparents for the first time.[ih] John Frederick Lemp entered the world. That same month

Ida and her mother made the society pages when they attended a reception.[ii]

John Frederick fell into one of his grandfather's irrigation ditches when he was just a toddler. The family dog, Sultan, rescued him.[ij]

THE LEMP-PENCE WAR: ROUND TWO

Pence was not merely locked in enmity against Lemp, he was also fighting the City of Boise in the venue of the land office.[ik] Pence claimed the election, held under the act of 1885, that added Arnold, Hyde Park, Resseguie, Andola and several other additions to the city was invalid. His tract of land was included in that addition. If this was invalid, the residents could not be compelled to pay further city taxes and previously paid taxes might have to be returned. The newspaper said this was so important that it might go to the state Supreme Court. Next, City Attorney Tipton came up with an 1887 act of the state legislature that fixed the boundaries of the city to include all the land annexed in 1885, which had been admittedly, added improperly.[il] This blow staggered Pence's' attorneys and the case went back to the land office officials.

Pence's suit against Lemp for damages from tearing down his house was heard in the Third District Court in late March of 1894.[im] On the first day, the plaintiff objected when the defense attempted, while cross-examining Pence, to establish that Lemp had prior possession.[in] Judge Nugent took the matter under advisement, and the case was continued to the next day. The case drug on. The defense made no effort to deny that Pence's house was torn down under orders from Mr. Lemp.[io] Their claim was that Lemp owned the land and Pence had no right to build there.

Meanwhile Lemp was sworn in to serve as a grand juror.[ip] He needed to be in court on his matter with Pence, and his absence disrupted the grand jury's work. Foreman George A. Chapman said they lost most of a week's work because of the Lemp-Pence lawsuit.[iq]

On March 28, the Jury found the defendant Lemp not guilty, and Pence was required to pay $207.65 in costs.[ir] Pence then took his appeal to the state Supreme Court.[is] In late November of 1895 the motion to dismiss the appeal was argued by J.H. Hawley for Pence and George H. Stewart for Lemp. The court took it under advisement.

In about 10 days they rendered their decision.it The court did not hear the case on its merits but rather allowed the motion for dismissal. They said the grounds for their decision were numerous, "in fact, there seems to have been, either through negligence or misapprehension, a complete abnegation in the taking of this appeal, not only of the rules of the court, but of the provisions of the statute." Judge E. Nugent had allowed for a new trial but the higher court said "what was intended to be settled by the . . . district judge, God and himself may know, but neither have, either by endowing us with retrospective vision or enlightening us through the record, given this court any basis for an opinion therein." Motion to dismiss was allowed with costs. At last the matter was settled—or was it? [iu]

In February of 1897, the *Statesman* really did contain the final word on the subject. The Lemp-Pence lot was at last disposed of by the Department of the Interior. The commissioner of the general land office authorized the Boise land office " that entry of lot 10 in section B, township 8 north and range 2 east, be made by this city as an additional townsite."[iv]

OTHER BUSINESS

During the spring of 1894 Lemp ran half-page ads in the *Statesman* saying that Boise had a first-class hotel at last. John Lemp was undertaking the management of his new Capitol Hotel, "and his name is sufficient guarantee that the service and equipment will be first class in every respect."[iw]

Later ads called attention to the 120 large and airy rooms, bathrooms with hot and cold water on each floor, electric lights and call bells.[ix] This management position of Lemp's was apparently not too labor intensive, because he went to Omaha to sell his cattle in April and then went on an extended tour through eastern and southern states.[iy] The Capitol Hotel will always have a role in American literary history. Owen Wister wrote much of his famed novel, *The Virginian*, while staying at the hotel. The western novel has been filmed several times and was the basis of a television series in the 1950s.

R. L. Sabin filed suit against John Lemp and John Early in District Court in March of 1894.[iz] The plaintiff never appeared nor presented evidence and he was therefore required to pay $6.75 in costs to

Know all men by these presents: That we, John Lemp and Catharine Lemp, his wife, of Boise City, Ada Co., Idaho, are the owners in fee simple of the following described Real Estate, situated in said Co. of Ada and State of Idaho, to wit: Being all of that portion of U.S. Lot No. 5 of Sec. 3, T. 3 N, R. 2 E. of Boise Meridian (as shown upon the official plat of said Township) which lies above or North of Resseguie St., extended West of 13th St., as the same appears upon the plat of Resseguie Addition to Boise City, Idaho, now on file in the Recorder's Office for Ada Co. aforesaid, including Northwest Corner of Townsite above said Resseguie St.

And we do certify that we have this day platted said lands and we do hereby lay out and plat said land as "Lemps Addition to Boise City, Idaho," as shown by this plat covering said described piece or parcel of land; and we do hereby dedicate to the use of the public forever all the streets and alleys as shown on said Plat.

In witness whereof we have hereunto set our hands and seals this 28th day of February, A.D. 1893.

Witnesses:
John M. Haines
Geo. H. Stewart

John Lemp (seal)
Catharine Lemp (seal)

State of Idaho,
County of Ada

On this 28th day of February, in the year A.D. 1893, before me, John M. Haines, a Notary Public in and for said Ada Co., personally appeared John Lemp, known to me to be the person whose name is subscribed to the foregoing instrument, and acknowledged to me that he executed the same. And this 28th day of February in the year A.D. 1893, before me, the officer above described, personally appeared Catharine Lemp, known to me to be the person whose name is subscribed to the foregoing instrument, described as a married woman; and upon an examination separate and apart from her husband, I made known to her the contents of this instrument; and thereupon she acknowledged to me that she voluntarily executed the same, and that she does not wish to retract such execution.

In witness whereof I have hereunto set my hand and affixed my Notarial Seal, the day and year first above written.

John M. Haines
Notary Public in and for
Ada Co., Idaho.
(SEAL)

Filed in the office of the Recorder of Ada Co., Idaho, March 17, 1893, at 1:30 o'clock, P.M.
Herman G. King,
Recorder.
(seal)

W. E. Pierce & Co., Exclusive Agents,
Boise, Idaho.

Plat of the Lemp addition to Boise. Provided by Dan Lute.

Lemp and Early. Lemp and Early co-owned a mine and this must have involved it.

Lemp published an open letter to his life insurance company which was surely an advertisement they solicited.[ja] He thanked them for the recent check for almost $12,000 and said he had had his family protected for 10 years and was now getting back everything he had paid plus $2,000. He recommended the insurance company to all his friends.

In all this swirl of activity John never forgot the brewery.[jb] He placed an ad for the April season's bock beer which explained how special it was, and that he still had lager for those who found bock too much. Bock was a dark, heavy German brew, traditionally released each spring on Easter to celebrate the end of the self-denial of the Lenten season.

Mr. and Mrs. Lemp and their daughters attended the grand ceremonies and banquet of the Knights Templar early that May.[jc] That month John was again elected a director of the Artesian Hot and Cold Water Company.[jd]

One of the very few strong denunciations of John Lemp was issued by the Caldwell Tribune in May of 1894, Under the headline of "The Land Grabber," they denounced his acquisition of government land. "Among the obstacles to the progress of this section of Idaho at the present time is the prevalence of the land grabber. Thousands and thousands of acres of land are lying idle in Canyon county and destined to so remain for years on account of his nefarious practices. Lands have been proven upon and are in the process of proof where there never was a serious purpose of complying with law and only the most shallow pretenses have been made. JOHN LEMP of Boise City, holds in the neighborhood of 3,000 acres and continues to make fresh entries for the benefit of his dowerless (sic) wife. Go where you will and patents are issued or are about to be issued on desert and timber culture entries which are frauds upon their face. Sixteen year old boys are said to make homestead proof for the benefit of concealed land grabbers and as soon as title is acquired the land is abandoned to coyotes and jackrabbits. Desert proofs are made in cases where it is well known that the water which served to make the proof was never within ten miles of the entry. Ten acres of ground are broken, a few dried cottonwood slips stuck into the ground, a half bushel of seed scattered about and 160 acres of land acquired under a law designed to promote timber culture in the arid regions. If it were only a matter of robbing deserving people of opportunities to make homes for themselves and families, it might not be so serious, but it is retarding growth and prosperity of the country. It is a matter that comes right home to every man who is trying to develop and subdue these western wilds. We can't just now recall anything that the Cleveland administration has done to win the respect and admiration of the people, therefore suggest that here is an opportunity which it can not afford to overlook. Here is a chance to signalize itself by at least an act of justice and humanity. The commission of the General Land office is respectfully urged to send a special inspector and one who can't wiggle his fingers beneath his coat tails."[je]

No other public support for this position was found.

A big issue in Boise that summer involved whether the city should pay the water company for the water needed to fight fires. For a newspaper survey of citizens, Lemp opined: "I do not wish to interfere with the business of the city council but I think the water company should be remunerated."[jf]

In July of 1894, Ex-Postmaster E. R. Leonard skedaddled out of Boise with the post office accounts showing a $7,600 shortage.[jg] Lemp was one of two bondsmen for Leonard whose family said they would make up every penny and neither bondsman would have to pay.

That same month, Mrs. Lemp and daughter Ida went to Salt Lake City for a visit.[jh] This is why she had to sign the Star mine sale documents from there. They returned in late August.[ji] In September, John's term on the school board was completed.[jj] The September, 1894, R. G. Dun, Mercantile Agency Reference Book listed John Lemp as brewery, hotel, saloon owner in Boise.

That fall, William A. Clark, described as a wealthy Montana mining man, was in Idaho looking at copper mines near Houston, where he already owned property.[jk] He was also looking at a mine at Hailey with a view toward purchasing it. This was Lemp's companion on the trail to Idaho 31 years before, when neither was wealthy nor famous. Clark had a number of mining related dealings in Idaho.

Lemp was again elected a director of the Boise Rapid Transit

Company that fall.^jl Lemp also renewed his bonds for five Boise liquor licenses.^jm James Collins, who lived in the Resseguie addition, was charged with stealing 25 of Lemp's hogs.^jn One ear had Lemp's mark and the other was freshly cut. Collins claimed he got the hogs in Weiser. Judge Ryals took the matter under advisement.

In December of 1894, John appeared before the Boise City Council to ask for a rebate of $28.50 for money paid for stock impound when his animals wandered into Boise.^jo The council took no action. A few days later when they met, councilman Falk moved that they return half the money to Lemp and several other men, but councilman Sweet objected and Falk's motion lost.^jp

Late in February of 1895, John Lemp attended the first meeting of the Historical Society of Idaho Pioneers held since September of 1887. ^jq Members consisted of those people and their descendants who came to Idaho before July 4, 1865. After that first meeting the organization had done nothing for the ensuing eight years.

THE DEATH OF JOHN EMIL LEMP

In February, Boise held a giant ball to honor the annual meeting of the state legislature. Mrs. John Lemp's gown was black silk and jet; Mrs. Emil Lemp wore red silk and roses; Gussie Lemp had a gown of lavender bengaline with lavender velvet trimmings; her sister Ida wore blue silk trimmed in thread lace.^jr This may have been Emil's last public appearance.

John Emil Lemp, oldest child of John and Catherine, died of pneumonia in Boise on 9 March 1895. He was at his father's house and was only ill a short time. He was 28 and left a wife and a year-old son.^js The *Statesman* described him as "impulsive and public spirited." This was the second loss of a child for John and Catherine. The family still believes he died from drinking bad water from a mountain stream.^jt The funeral was at the Grove Street family residence and his lodge, the Ancient Order of United Workmen, attended in a large group.^ju The Reverend Charles E. Deuel of the Episcopal church officiated at the Lemp house and the A.O.U.W. conducted the ritual at the grave.

Lemp family legend said that John Emil's wife Caroline was afraid of the Indians that camped in the Lemp backyard on Grove Street in Boise and kept a revolver for protection. During World War One, while living in Illinois, she still kept that revolver—which the family still owns—near her for protection while her son, John Frederick, Sr. was away in the war.[jv]

The Workmen lodge [Ancient Order of United Workmen] put a resolution of condolence in the *Statesman*: "Whereas it has pleased the Supreme Grand Master Workman on high to take from our midst our beloved brother John Emil Lemp. Resolved that in the death of brother Lemp, Idaho Lodge No. 5, A.O.U.W., has lost a true and faithful member, his wife and child a kind and devoted husband and father, his parents, sisters and brothers a noble and affectionate son and brother."

"Resolved that our heartfelt sympathy is extended to these afflicted relatives.

Resolved that the lodge paraphernalia be draped in mourning for a period of 30 days and that a copy of these resolutions be transmitted to the family of our late brother and a copy be published in the *Rocky Mountain Workman* and in the daily papers of this city. I. S. Weiler, D. D. Williams, August J. Moritz."[jw]

In June, Mrs. Caroline A. Lemp, Emil's widow, placed an ad in the Statesman that she had received a check for $5,056.25 from the New York Life Insurance Company.[jx] She went on to say that his sudden death meant his financial affairs were in need of attention except for the life insurance which the company handled promptly. That November she went back to Alton, Illinois to visit her relatives.[jy] She and her son then remained in the Mid-West.

It was over a month before any mourning Lemps ventured back on to the Boise social scene. Albert attended a Chocolitaire social in late April.[jz] John renewed his three saloon licenses about this same time.[ka] He also advertised his bock beer heavily. "A genuine Boise product manufactured from home grown materials and matured in the great casks will be turned loose on April 27th."[kb] He said it was not only Idaho's best product but "it seeks its peer in the United States." Lemp had not completely forgotten his brewery.

That March, George Shrader was hauled back to Boise from Caldwell by Sheriff Moseley.[kc] He was a former soldier at the Boise barracks but had been in John Lemp's employment when he went south—literally— with $53 and a gold watch belonging to his roommate. Yet another bartender gone wrong.

The Boise Central held their annual meeting with the major concern to petition the Union Pacific to build another railroad siding between Ninth and Fifth streets.[kd] John Lemp was reelected a director at the meeting.

While the news of Lemp's brewery seemed slight in this period, others were noticing the beer consumption of Boise. The *Statesman* said beer was consumed from bottle and growler by all grades of the social scale.[ke] S. T. Wiedeneck of the Minneapolis Brewing Association was in Boise on his own volition to check on the city's potential to have another brewery. Nothing else came of this, apparently.

In June, the local Republicans nominated 16 men for eight spots as state convention delegates. Among those nominated were John Lemp, and John Brodbeck.[kf] Lemp was selected. The Republican convention also nominated George H. Stewart for Boise Mayor.[kg]

In late summer of 1895, the social scene in Boise, as reported in the newspaper, always included "Miss Lemp;" this was Augusta.[kh]

Lemp was advertising his beer as : "Honest Beer! Aged Seven Months. The Lager Beer I am now selling is beyond question a perfectly pure and delicious beverage—everything is done to make the finest Beer that good brewing age and the best materials will produce. Remember that Lemp's Beer has Idaho Hops and Barley in it, and in fact is a home production, and when you buy it you get the very

The revolver owned by John Emil Lemp.
Photo, from Karl Lemp

best, and the money you spend for it helps to employ Idaho labor. Family trade supplied with Beer in bottles that are properly corked, and at a lower price than eastern Beer. JOHN LEMP, Main street."[ki] This appeal to home pride and home industry was repeated by many small, local brewers in Idaho. The railroads were bringing in every more competing brands from the East and the West Coast. The many icehouses built by brewing companies near the railroads attest to the increased competition.

By 1895 Americans were consuming 33.6 million barrels of beer per year, five times the 6.3 million of 1869. Beer consumption had increased three times faster than the population in that quarter century. Consumption of hard liquor dropped enormously during the same period.

In September, John was again elected a director and member of the executive committee of the Rapid Transit Company.[kj] That same month William Jaumann, prominent businessman and husband of John Lemp's sister, Martha Elizabeth, suffered a severe stroke of paralysis.[kk] John and this brother-in-law were involved in many lodges and business dealings together. Jauman had just returned from a trip to California and his health seemed improved before the attack.[kl] Death came to him a little over a week later on the 7th of October.

Jaumann had an interesting life in his own right even if he never brewed a pint of lager.[km] He came to the States just before the Civil War and enlisted in the Twentieth New York Volunteers when that conflict started. He fought at Big Bethel, Chickahominy to Harrison's Landing, South Mountain, and Antietam. At the latter he was severely wounded. The surgeons were about to amputate his leg when he pulled a gun and refused to allow it. After the war he went west—on two legs—arriving in Boise in 1872. He was one of the organizers of the Turn Verein, and the first hook and ladder company. He was a member of the Phil Sheridan Post No. 4 of the G.A.R. (Grand Army of the Republic), a Mason and a member of the A.O.U.W. At his grave, the Masons read their ceremony and then the Zouaves, a colorfully garbed military unit famous for their Civil War service, fired three volleys over the grave.

Jaumann had been the president of the A.O.U.W. (Ancient Order of United Workmen) back in 1885.[kn] The will of William H. Jauman (sic), dated 10 April 1891, gave his niece Minnie Lusk, wife of James Lusk, one city lot.[ko] Everything else went to his wife "Elise." His attorney had been William E. Borah. Jaumann owned a great deal of property, and shares in the Light Company and Rapid Transit Company.

It was March of 1897 when Mrs. Jaumann filed her final accounts on the estate and was left with $13, 740.[kp] This was a large amount those days.

In October, Lemp attended another meeting about getting a railroad to Butte.[kq] The locals offered a $150,000 bonus to entice someone to get the project underway.

On 11 October 1895, daughter Ada Anna Lemp married Edwin G. Hurt. It was not a big affair due to the mourning in the extended family. Reverend J. W. Huston married them at the Methodist parsonage.[kr] Hurt was a local man trained in business.

Late that month, Lemp and several other liquor men petitioned the city to return some of their license fees which had been inaccurately calculated.[ks] They returned $25 to Lemp. In other government business John, probably through the Capitol Hotel, was supplying meals to jurors in Boise. In October, for instance, he was paid $91.00 for the meals provided that month.

In November of 1895, Lemp was still advertising himself as the proprietor of the Capitol Hotel and its 120 rooms.[kt] John offered

The Samuel Adolph home, Salem Oregon, in the early 21st Century.
Photo by the author

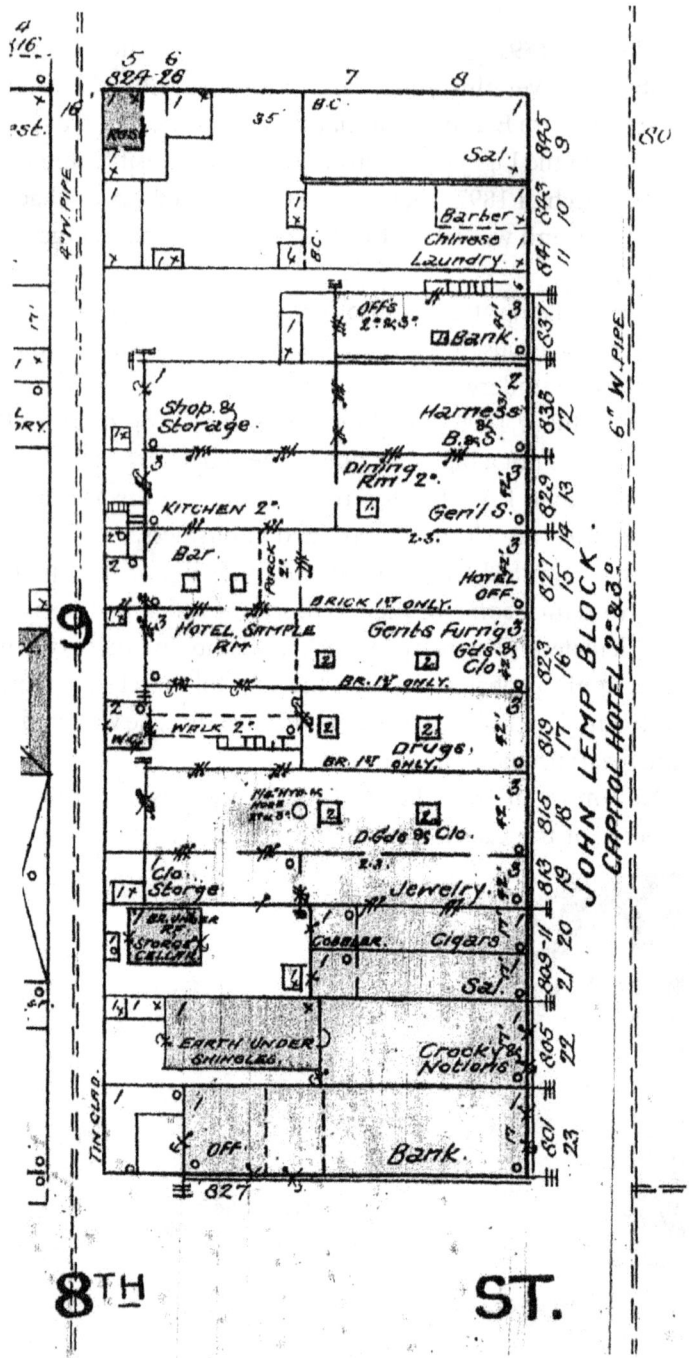

1893 fire insurance map showed the Capitol Hotel.

lots 3 and 6 of the south half of block 33 to the government for a proposed federal building for $10,100.[ku] Two columns of newspaper listed others who also wished to sell property in Boise for the new building. The next year many men of Boise, including Lemp, decided the best spot for the building was the Green Meadow Corral.[kv] They sent the mayor east to lobby for that location.

On 5 December of 1895, John's younger brother Jacob, 45, died of pneumonia.[kw] Death occurred at his home in Boise after only three weeks of illness.[kx] John and Jacob had been in business together in the past. Jacob had been involved with the Stirm brewery in Payette in recent times. Jacob was buried in Pioneer Cemetery in Boise under a simple stone which said "Jacob Lemp 1850-1895."

Two months later, his widow, Mary Stirm Lemp, received a check for $2,000 from the A.O.U.W. local chapter.[ky] A month later a major fire in Payette destroyed the Valley Hotel and an adjacent storage building owned by Jacob's estate.[kz] The building contained 2,000 pounds of grain, two barrels of wine and other insignificant items. There was no insurance.

On December 23, 1895, John's daughter Augusta Julia Margaret (Gussie) married Angus Roderick Grant of Portland, Oregon.[la] The wedding was at the Lemp family residence. Best man was T. P. Kelley of Portland and the Maid of Honor was Ida Lemp. Catholic Bishop A. J. Glorieux performed the ceremony in the presence of a few relatives. The bride wore Duchess satin and carried bride roses. A wedding supper followed and in the morning the couple left for Portland. With the bride's uncle less than three weeks deceased, a large formal wedding was a social impossibility.

An article in the *Idaho Democrat* extolling the qualities of Boise mentioned the exquisite architectural designs of many buildings including the two blocks owned by Lemp.[lb] Mrs. Catherine Lemp was among the many sponsoring the charity ball on New Years Eve.[lc]

John suffered a bout of rheumatism that next month, February of 1896.[ld] My observation is that periods of stress, such as the marriage of a daughter in this case, seemed to always take a physical toll on Lemp and his rheumatism would flare up.

In the district court in February, future U. S. Senator William. E. Borah was made judge pro tem to hear the case of J. S. Bogart vs. John

Lemp's brewery as it was on the fire insurance map of Boise in 1893.

Lemp, and another case involving Bogart.[le] Judge Richards excused himself because he once had an interest in the case. The facts were that Lemp took the land in question in 1864 as a townsite location and paid taxes on it all those years but only got a mayor's deed in 1891. Bogart alleged he had squatted on the land beginning in 1890 but his request for a mayor's deed had been rejected. As in the Lemp-Pence War, the weakness and inconsistency of early land registration rules and procedures had sown the seeds of later disputes.

Lemp was again elected to the board of directors of the Boise Central Railway Company when they met in March of 1896.[lf] That same month Governor William McConnell sent a letter to Captain James M. Wells, Idaho's commissioner at the World's Fair of a few years before, asking him to turn over any money from the fair that he might still have.[lg] Lemp was one of the bondsmen for Wells and he was potentially liable if malfeasance was ever established. As such, Lemp received a copy of the letter from the governor.

On another business front, Lemp was sued that month by J. R. Russell for a Settler's Ditch matter.[lh] Russell contended that he was due $450 for the damages sustained to his farm when the ditch was put through it. The amount had been fixed by arbitration. Lemp, as president, and J.W. Daniels, as secretary of the corporation, gave Mr. Russell a note in December of 1891 for the money, Russell alleged, and now he wanted to collect.

In July of 1896, John paid for his three liquor licenses for the coming quarter.[li] That August the *Statesman* reported that David— not Nathan—Falk was the owner of the General Pettit mine at Atlanta, and had brought down rich specimens of ore from it. Lemp bought mining property from Joseph Pinkham, acting as administrator of the John S. Gray estate, in Custer County.

In August, the political primaries were held. Lemp was one of the "bolting" (according to the *Statesman*'s editor) Republicans.[lj] He was a delegate from East Boise. Shortly after this, another attack of rheumatism confined John to his home.[lk] Perhaps the political disagreement brought him more stress.

In September, there was a robbery at the brewery which created a fairly lengthy court case. One of Lemp's sons said he saw Thomas O'Grady, H. Curtis and a soldier named Grant break into the brewery and they "purloined a number of bottles of hop extract."[ll] O'Grady and Curtis were released on their own recognizance but Grant was held in jail.[lm] Some reports said Grant was in fact not a soldier. Perhaps he did not give the right name when arrested.[ln] The case was heard on the 11th of September and was not concluded the first day.[lo] About a week later Grant was released on his on recognizance and from that time "no trace of him has been found."[lp] Such formal or informal agreements were not uncommon in the West. The county did not want to provide room and board, and the defendant did not want to languish in jail. Such suspects were released on the "get out of town" basis.

Mrs. Lemp donated the use of the Capitol Hotel to the Equal Suffrage Club for its annual ball in October of 1896.[lq] This certainly was one of the few references to indicate her political stances—and her husband's willingness to allow them. The women had a great deal to celebrate at that time because Idaho had become the first Pacific Northwest state to enfranchise women. Historian Carlos Schwantes described the effort as "a quiet inexpensive campaign managed mostly by local women."[lr] The state constitutional amendment was overwhelmingly approved.

This was one of the years the Populist movement in America reached its height. In neighboring Washington, John R. Rogers was elected Populist governor. Only Washington, Kansas and Colorado ever elected Populist Party governors. New political ideas were gaining strength in Idaho as elsewhere at that time. Idaho was the fourth state to allow women the vote.

In December of 1896, there was a suit in the Fourth District court of John Lemp et al vs. Isaac Brockbank et al—application for appointment of a receiver set for hearing 17 December at 11 a.m.[ls] when the listing of all charter members of the New Idaho Mining Exchange was published in February of 1896 Lemp was listed, curiously, as a hotel man.[lt] By the end of the previous year he had added ownership of a dry goods store to his long resume. Lemp took over the clothing store of William B. Connor, his son-in-law, in settlement of a claim he had against him.[lu] This was to cause a great deal of litigation and eventually involve the Idaho State Supreme Court.

Two men entered Lemp's dry goods store late in January of 1896 and tired to steal two suits.^lv Son Albert Lemp grappled with them and a lively struggle ensued. Police Chief Robbins happened to wander by and he placed them under arrest. They refused to give their names.

When Miss Zo Heskett went to work at the Lemp store it was worthy of a mention in the Statesman.^lw Also, when Peter Enebo became a bookkeeper for Lemp it was mentioned.^lx

Lemp's wholesale liquor store got a brief plug in the *Idaho Democrat* in January of 1897. The press said he carried the purest wines and liquors to found in the state and "his home brewed beer is equal to the best."^ly

Lemp was again elected a director at the March 1897 meeting of the Boise Central Railway Company. ^lz Their property was still not occupied by a railroad but the secretary, Charles A. Clark, suggested that they appoint some capable person to see that a railroad into Boise was put there at last. A worthy goal, but one destined for continued frustration and disappointment. It was even not until 1911 that the Oregon Short Line laid double tracks from Nyssa west to Huntington^ma Boise remained off to the side for many decades.

Daughter Ida Lemp went to Portland on a visit in May of 1897.^mb She probably was visiting her sister Gussie, Mrs. Grant. That June, far from his home in Portland, Roderick Grant was on the way to Placerville with J. P. Gately and had gotten as far as Emmett when the king bolt on their buggy broke. Grant, who was driving, was dragged about 30 feet and his hip was dislocated.^mc

The Louisa Lode deed was recorded on 28 May 1897 at the request of Lemp and Falk, as being transferred from the United States to John Lemp, Nathan Falk, Edson Bishop, and Edward Brisbin on 19 September 1892, five years previous.^md This was undoubtably in preparation for the sale that same month to Colonel Coates and Dr. Wood by Messers Lemp, Falk and Patterson.^me Falk and Lemp also recorded the deeds to the Sunrise and the Ohio that same day.^mf

In June, Lemp went to Notus, where he owned land, on

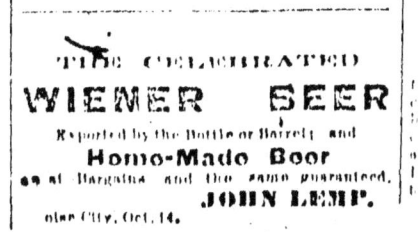

Lemp advertised the Wiener beer of San Francisco that he sold in his saloon.

business.ᵐᵍ During this period most of Lemp's energy seems to have been devoted to his dry goods store which advertised heavily in the *Statesman*.ᵐʰ Son George of Middleton often got back to Boise these months.ᵐⁱ That August, son Albert went fishing on Shafer creek and reported the grouse were plentiful.ᵐʲ

Lemp improved his Main Street property in July by having cement sidewalks placed in front of all of it.ᵐᵏ In a special issue of the *Boise Sentinel* describing Boise businesses, they mentioned Lemp as on the executive committee of the Boise Rapid Transit Company.ᵐˡ

In mid-August of 1897, there was a fire in the Lemp home in Boise.ᵐᵐ It turned out to be only a clogged flu. Firemen quickly fixed the trouble.

In September of 1897, there was an election to select the Queen of Idaho to reign over the state fair.ᵐⁿ Among the vote getters was Ida Lemp, though she did not finish in the top twenty. Father John sold two lots in the Lemp addition to Riley E. Dill that September of 1897, indicating that land investment continued to pay.ᵐᵒ Lemp may have had some cash flow problems that year. He was listed as $2,469.69 delinquent on his property taxes in Boise in September.ᵐᵖ I suspect the financial dealings with the Star mine, mentioned earlier, were taking a toll.

In October of 1897, the pioneers of Idaho paraded in Boise and had their pictures taken. The list of participants included Lemp as an 1863 arrival, as well as his rival brewer John Brodbeck.ᵐᑫ

In December of 1897 Lemp sued J.C. Bane but the case—whatever it was—was dismissed by consent of the counsel.ᵐʳ

RICHARDS, GORDON ET AL VS. JOHN LEMP AND W.B. CONNOR

A law suit of Richards, Gordon et al vs. W. B. Conner and John Lemp which eventually reached the Idaho Supreme Court was first filed in December, 1897.ᵐˢ This all began when those who were owed money by Connor sued. Connor wanted a change of venue, which was denied. The Idaho Supreme Court reversed this.ᵐᵗ Later that month, the case, described as an action for debt, was transferred to Elmore county to be heard by Judge Stockslager.ᵐᵘ Various wholesale houses had liens aggregating $5,000 against Lemp's son-in-law Connor. Lemp held a chattel mortgage under which he took over the stock from Connor and he then refused to pay the old debts since they were not his. In November of 1899, the case was finally heard before Judge Stockslager in fourth district in Mountain Home.[mv] In the questions of fact submitted to the jury, they decided in favor of the plaintiff Gordon et al in each instance. They said there was sufficient stock to pay Lemp his mortgage and the creditors their liens if the problem was handled by liquidating some of the assets.

A year later, in December of 1898 the case was still before Judge Stockslager's court on a rehearing. A motion to strike an answer from the files was overruled and the case was set to be heard further on December 15th.[mw] A week later the case was continued for the term.[mx]

In May of 1899, there was a contempt case against William B. Connor when he refused to give a deposition in the case against him[my] It was dismissed because Connor's failure to appear at the trial would permit judgment to be entered by default.

In April of 1900, Stockslager issued his final decision.[mz] "Judgment to the plaintiff." Goods to be sold off sufficient to pay the $5,000. W. H. Dunton was the referee appointed to collect. If enough money was not raised, a further judgment was to be issued. Lemp and Connor appealed to the State Supreme Court.

The State Supreme Court scheduled the Gordon v. Connor and Lemp case for hearing on 23 May 1901.[na] In the case a "motion was made to supply the record of court below and was taken under advisement by the court."[nb] On 3 June 1901, the Idaho Supreme Court Decision was released.[nc]

Lemp's attorney's were Wyman and Wyman and W.E. Borah, future Senator. A headline in the *Statesman* read: "Lemp Loses Case/ Judgment Entered in the Connor Case Affirmed/Outgrowth of a Failure/ Charges and Denials Resulting from the Agreement Under Which John Lemp Took Possession of the Stock of Goods—What Supreme Court Says." The original complaint alleged that Lemp and his son-in-law Connor entered a secret agreement by which Connor gave Lemp a note and contract for the transfer to Lemp of the stock of merchandise in his dry goods store. Connor then stayed on as the agent in charge of Lemp's store. The note was for $7,740 but Lemp realized $14,000 from sales of the stock. This enabled Connor to effectively stay in business while insolvent. Connor made purchases from the plaintiffs without revealing the existence of the contract and thus kept his stock replenished, stayed in business, and converted $5,000 to his own use. This was done with the knowledge and consent of Mr. Lemp. Justice Sullivan wrote the ten page opinion, Justice Quarles concurred, while Justice Stockslager did not sit because he had originally tried the case.[nd]

The plaintiffs asked the court to adjudge the contract a chattel mortgage, adjudge it void as against the claims of plaintiffs and that they be given prior lien. A general demurrer was interposed and overruled by the lower court. "Thereupon Appellant Lemp answered and put in issue most of the material allegations of the complaint," said the Supreme Court opinion, authored by Justice Sullivan. Lemp's answer averred that the note was for not less than $7,000; he denied that it was secret; admitted that he took possession of about $8,000 worth of goods in good faith in full payment of the indebtedness. The transfer was to satisfy the debt and for no other purpose; purchases made by Connor after 25 March 1896 and alleged to have been taken by Lemp were of a value of $4,500; admitted that the contract was not formally foreclosed and he has not accounted to Connor or the plaintiffs for money derived from the sale of said goods. Lemp denied he made $14,000 on the sales and in fact said it was not over $8,000. The goods were given to Lemp and a bill of sale issued on 18 November 1896 to satisfy the contract of the previous March. The jury in the original case rendered a special verdict which the court adopted, the court made others, and then entered judgment for the plaintiffs. Motion for a new trial was denied and the Supreme Court ruled on the appeal from the denial of that motion. The Supreme Court ruled that the court findings were proper. The instructions given to the jury by the original court, even if they should not have been given, were not reviewable because the jury finding was only advisory. The case was closed.

Other Business

A newspaper article in January of 1898 said Lemp paid $4,600 in state and local taxes.[ne] This compares to J. B. Broadbent, the heaviest tax payer in Boise at the time, whose total was $13,000. Lemp was also on the list of merchants agreeing to close their stores at 6:30 on weekdays from mid-January until March 15.[nf]

Lemp was the mortgagor to the Bunnell-Eno company for $65,000.[ng] It was thought to be the largest mortgage ever filed in Ada County by one man. The *Statesman* said "few men could command so much money on his personal holdings." This was probably needed to finance the canal work he was doing.

That January, "Miss Lemp"—probably Ida—entertained at the Grove Street family home in honor of Miss Pearl McKennon of Portland.[nh] Nearly fifty guests played high five and several prizes were given, including a booby prize, a rabbit's foot, from A. P. Wilson. Miss McKennon enjoyed it so much she extended her visit another week.

C. E. Cole formerly of the Golden Rule Store took a position at Lemp's dry goods store that January.[ni] In March, he fell from a ladder while at work and was severely injured.[nj] In Boise business, Lemp turned over management of his Capitol Hotel to B. F. Locke, formerly of Butte.[nk]

John was one of the charter members of the El Korah temple of the Mystic Shrine when a Boise chapter formed in March of 1898.[nl] This organization is affiliated with the Masons which interestingly by this time had a policy of not admitting those in the liquor business. After the initiation a banquet was held at Lemp's Capitol Hotel for the new members.

Lemp sold 1,000 head of cattle to Thurston Hutchins of Mountain Home area in March of 1898.[nm] Hutchins was reentering the cattle business. When the deal finally closed the number was increased to 1,200 which included three different bands on the range near Middleton.[nn] The price of $30,000 was an average of $25 per head including the calves. Hutchins planned to relocate them to Camas Prairie.

In April of 1898, a packer named Jesus Urquides sent a letter with testimonials to the *Statesman* complaining of the way he had been arrested.[no] Among the 59 signers who said they had known him for 30 years and vouched for his character were Albert and John Lemp.

On May 19, Idaho's Spanish-American War Volunteers left for the Philippines. The Spanish-American war was forty per cent financed by increasing the taxes imposed on beer. [np]

There was a district court case in September of 1898 of State of Idaho vs John Lemp which had been appealed from Police court.[nq] The demurrer was argued and the case taken under advisement. A few days later the trial began but court adjourned for the day before the trial ended.[nr]

Lemp's dry goods store seemed to be doing very well these years. The local newspaper took note when W. E. Tray took a position there.[ns] In November of 1898 A. L. Perry of New York took charge of the clothing department.[nt]

In September of 1898, Lemp was listed as owing $153.84 plus a penalty of $30.76 for a delinquent street sprinkling bill.[nu] In November Lemp was dunned again—$377.89—for the new sewer district.[nv] When the Boise city council set as a board of equalization in late October of 1898 they raised Lemp's assessment on some of his property from $3,000 to $4,000, and his merchandise assessment went from $6,000 to $10,000.[nw] In June of 1899, John again failed to pay all his property taxes and ended up on the delinquent list.[nx] Nearly all his property was listed and the total bill was $1,224.64.

In December of 1898, son George Lemp was thrown from a horse on the ranch at Middleton and seriously hurt.[ny] A day later the newspaper reported no bones were broken but there was a fear of internal injuries.[nz] The next report said he was rapidly improving and was to be brought to Boise.[oa] By mid-January of 1899 he was reported again on the streets "looking thin but natural."[ob]

1899

In 1899 Anna Elizabeth Lemp, John's mother died.[oc] She was about 86 and had been a widow for nearly half a century. After leaving Germany, the last eleven years of her life were lived in Boise with her son John's family and near two of her three daughters.[od] Beside son John, she had daughters Mrs. Elizabeth Jauman, Mrs. Julia Lyerzapf both of Boise, and Mrs. Margaret Bach of St. Louis.[oe] She was found dead in bed and no one had heard anything. "She evidently passed over without a struggle, and fell asleep as gently as a child from sheer old age." She was buried out of John's home.

John had a severe attack of rheumatism when his mother died and it took him two weeks before he was again out on the street.[of] Despite delinquencies on property tax, John's financial rating remained high, for he had signed a bond for $6,000 of the $114,000 posted by new County Treasurer John W. Eagleson in January of 1899.[og] For all his many holdings, Lemp was assessed $1,224.64 in taxes that year.[oh]

Son-in-law E. G. Hurt left his position as manager of Western Union in Boise and took a job as an accountant for the I. X. L. grocery, working for Mr. Spiegel. "He is one of the best accountants in the state, and Mr. Spiegel is to be congratulated on securing so valuable a man," said the *Capital of Boise*.[oi]

During 1899, son George William managed one of his father's farms. Son Albert helped managed the hotel and dry goods store. Edward and Bernard were both in school.[oj] George also filed for title on 320 acres of desert land in March of 1899.[ok]

Mary Medosh filed a civil suit again John Lemp which was heard in Judge Herrick's court in late February of 1899. It was settled "satisfactory to both parties."[ol] This involved waitressing at the Capitol Hotel. The hotel business was not always one of smooth sailing. Lemp brought in waitresses from cities far and wide under contract to work in the hotel dining room.[om] Usually they agreed to stay at least six months and the car fare he had advanced was taken out of their pay during that period. One girl quit before her contract was up but Lemp would not let her have her trunk. She secured it through a replevin suit and then went to Butte. Not long after a Barbara Fritter of Denver sued Lemp for $255.85 for damages under a waitress contract. Justice Herrick heard the case.

On April 29, 1899 the Bunker Hill & Sullivan concentrator at Wardner was dynamited. The Coeur d'Alene mining wars were flaring up again. No part of Idaho would escape the ramifications of this philosophical, economic and criminal conflict.

In July, the *Statesman* reported that Frank Blackinger and Tim Regan intended to sign a five year lease on Lemp's hotel to commence on August first.[on] No one involved would speak to the press. Two days later the deal was confirmed for five years with another five year option.[oo] Extensive changes were planned.

One of Lemp's employees, William Barnes, made the papers in August of 1899 with an ill-advised stunt.[op] While drunk, Barnes went to the Camas Prairie stables on 8th and Grove streets and tried to put a blanket on his horse. He missed his attempt to throw the blanket and fell against the horses hind legs. The steed kicked Barnes who flew against a heavy wagon tongue that cut his scalp and knocked him senseless. Al Lemp was called and he took Barnes to a physician, Dr. Haley, who stitched him and he was all right.

In late spring of 1899, John Lemp came up lame and was on crutches for four months.[oq] The reason was never explained but this sounds like rheumatism again. At the end of his recovery period, Lemp went for an outing at Schafer Creek and came home feeling well enough to walk with only a cane. He planned to visit next one of his cattle ranches with intent to get well enough to drop the cane he was using. In late August he did indeed go to his Snake River ranch for a short stay.[or]

In August of 1899, Lemp bought wholesale and retail liquor licenses from the Boise City Council as usual.[os] He also secured bonds for his saloon on Main Street and wholesale liquor stores with Max Mayfield and Nathan Falk signing as sureties. Lemp's store joined others in Boise to make liberal donations to victims of the great fire in Placerville, Idaho.[ot] The whole center of that Boise Basin village had burned and left many destitute.

In September, a most interesting district court case was listed in the newspaper. John Lemp was suing brother-in-law George W. Kohlepp.[ou] In November, the clerk of the district court published an alias summons for Kohlepp which gave some of the particulars of the action.[ov] Lemp was seeking $1,000 dollars plus six per cent interest per annum from November 12 of 1892, which would have been another $420. Kohlepp had signed a promissory note to Lemp on that date. In January of 1901, the trial was scheduled in civil court in Boise.[ow]

Also that September, Waldo J. Morgan, who worked at Lemp's store returned from a two months trip to the east.[ox] A few weeks later widow Mrs. Emil Lemp and her son John left for her home in Alton, Illinois.[oy] They must have been visiting the Lemp family. John made a brief trip to Weiser to place son Eddie in the Weiser academy for the school term.[oz]

The liquor business had its problems that same March of 1899. John Keane, one of the bartenders at Lemp's saloon on Ninth and Main was arrested for selling liquor to minors.[pa] The jury spent only 15 minutes deciding guilty, and Keane was given the choice of $100 or 50 days in jail. He paid the fine. The complaining witness was Frank Haug Jr. son of the late Idaho City, Idaho, brewer Nicholas "Frank" Haug. The three boys had spent 35 cents on beer—which must have bought a large volume—they drank it in the backroom and got so drunk they could not stand. The boys got arrested for dog stealing that day and the officer then investigated the source of their apparent intoxication.

Boise Mayor Moses Alexander (future first Jewish governor in Idaho and the United States) stated publicly that he would move for revocation of Lemp's liquor license because of this incident.^{pb}

In March of 1899, Lemp was ordered by city authorities to clean out the foul smelling corral near the Lincoln school.^{pc} This was part of the old brewery complex there. The school and the brewery site were to clash for the next decade. John was suffering from ever more frequent and severe bouts of rheumatism by this age. In early May he was reported laid up with the condition.^{pd} In June he was able to be out and about again after an attack.^{pe} This may have been the same attack that lasted over a month.

Perhaps being laid up prevented John from paying his property tax. He was delinquent on lots 1 to 12 of block 72 of Boise and owed $35.37.^{pf} Such a small amount was most likely an oversight.

With the hotel leased out and his health better, John took a three week vacation to his cattle ranch on Shafer Creek.^{pg}

Walter Logus had been a driver for Lemp but then was working as a bartender.^{ph} He apparently robbed Lemp's safe on the night of October 2, 1899. The next morning he was gone and so was over $300. Most of the money belonged to a friend who had deposited it there for safe keeping.^{pi} Logus was finally located at Rawlings, Wyoming well over a year later. At the preliminary hearing held in late December of 1900 he pled innocent. John and his son Albert both testified. Logus was held on $1,000 bail and the trail was to be in February of 1901. That February, Walter Logus, described as a young German, who over a year prior had robbed Lemp's safe, and who had been captured in Wyoming four months before, was sentenced to three years in the penitentiary.^{pj} Lemp had hired Logus as a barkeep but the fellow Deutschlander failed to resist temptation and left town at midnight one night with $200 [not the $300 previously reported]. He then went to Germany to see his aged mother. After a year he returned and went to Wyoming thinking the robbery was all forgotten by that time. Information sent there resulted in his capture and Sheriff Campbell brought him back to Boise. The *Capital* said he "appeared very broken in health."

Just before the winter holiday, *The Weekly Capital* ran a biographical sketch of Lemp as part of a series on the prominent citizens of Boise.[pk] It did not contain much new but served to reiterate the contributions he had made to the city.

In a report on Christmas business in Boise, Manager Morgan of Lemp's dry goods store said it was their best Christmas ever.[pl] Lemp must have been able to afford his taxes that year. A report a week later said the store also had its best whole year ever.[pm]

John and Kate's son George Lemp died on 1 January 1900.[pn] He had been running his father's stock ranch at Middleton and came to Boise for the holidays. He was taken sick with inflammation of the bowels and died suddenly and unexpectedly at his father's home. The funeral was at the family home on Grove Street, and the services were conducted by Rev. C. E. Deuel, Episcopal priest.[po] The Ancient Order of United Workmen conducted their funeral service also.[pp] George was laid to rest in the Masonic cemetery.

A week after the funeral, brother Albert Lemp applied to be the administrator of the estate of George W. J. Lemp.[pq] George had life insurance of $10,000 payable to his estate and also was due $2000 from the A. O. U. W. payable to his mother. His other property of note was 320 acres of desert land. By April, Albert had a notice to creditors published in the *Statesman* which gave such persons ten months to present to him at the Lemp dry goods store the proof of any claim.[pr]

In mid-January of 1900 three hoboes were arrested in Lemp's barn and taken before Judge Koelsch where they pleaded guilty to a minor charge.[ps] "The judge sententiously observed that it was a pity to waste good grub on such worthless characters and they will be given a chance to leave Boise this morning if they will promise never to return."

In February, Lemp's wholesale liquor house was renovated so the Boise Butcher Company could move in.[pt] Liquor was being sold out of Lemp's saloons and Leo Grunbaum's liquor operation was a strong competitor. About this same time Lemp was reported to have turned down an offer of $18,000 for 25 feet of property at the corner of Main and Ninth where "The Market" then stood.[pu] Lemp refused to place a price on the 100 feet he owned there and also refused to lease it for twenty years to a produce firm that wished to erect a brick building at the location.

On another business front, Lemp was sued that month by J.R. Russell for a Settler's Ditch matter.[pv] Russell contended that he was due $450 for the damages sustained to his farm when the ditch was put through it. The amount had been fixed by arbitration. Lemp, as president, and J.W. Daniels, as secretary, gave Mr. Russell a note in December of 1891 for the money, Russell alleged, and now he wanted to collect.

Lemp's canals had some difficulties with the water users in the Spring of 1900.[pw] Lemp had been charging water users $1.50 per acre they owned, but a new law required that the water actually be measured and charged for on a more accurate basis. State Engineer D. W. Ross became the go-between for the settlers with Lemp in regards to their demands for the new system. First Ross met with about forty settlers at the White Cross school house. They came away convinced that proper measurement would be to their benefit. A settlers committee then met with Ross and Mr. Lemp to discuss the matter. The *Statesman* reported that Lemp would put in the main measuring weirs and the settlers would put in the individual weirs.

Under the old system there was no incentive to conserve the water. About 54 inches was being applied to each acre when 30 would have been sufficient. Some places the water went to waste while at the end of the lateral canals there was often an insufficient supply. Only five thousand acres were being irrigated while the canal theoretically carried enough water for 9,000 acres if it was used judiciously. Nearly all the farmers were prepared to increase their acreage if more water was assured.

Under the new system the water would be measured at an inch flowing 24 hours which is very close to an acre foot (an acre covered one foot deep in water). The canal carried 180 acre feet per day and they calculated a loss due to evaporation and seepage of 20 per cent. This left 144 acre-feet per day for irrigation. If the rate charged was 2 cents per unit, the canal owner would reap about $9,000 a season.

Currently Lemp was only taking in $7,500. Using measuring weirs, the farmers would cover the land quickly and then shut the water off without allowing any waste. Another advantage was that use could be planned for more accurately and no one would fail to get what was needed when it was needed.

Lemp published a formal reply to the committee in the *Statesman*.[px] Lemp stated he would charge two cents per inch per 24 hours, as the committee and Mr. Ross had discussed with him. Also he agreed to have "appliances, boxes, weirs and measuring devices" placed in the canal as the state engineer directed.

The whole deal was not quite as smooth as this would seem, for in July the county commissioners had to issue an order to Lemp to place weirs or measuring devices on the three lateral ditches.[py] One lateral was for A. M. Wolfkell and others, one for George Dubois and others, and one for William Lewis and others. The commissioners said if the devices were not installed they would install them at Lemp's expense.

Toward the end of March of 1900, Lemp's long-time bookkeeper at his dry goods store, P. K. Enebo, resigned to take a position with the War Eagle Consolidated Mining Company.[pz] In other business matters, Lemp renewed his two liquor licenses in April of 1900.[qa] In May, the Lemp dry goods store became one of the underwriters for a series of free band concerts put on by the local Columbia Band, directed by Mr. Perkins.[qb]

That summer Albert Wolters, Lemp's old associate in the Hailey area, was running for county commissioner and his technique was to send liquor to various places in hopes of being remunerated with votes.[qc] Wolters sent a keg of beer to the East Fork of Wood River with "that wild Dutchman of Ketchum" Brewery owner Robert Koeninger. Bob sampled the beer and found it good. So he sampled it again and again until it was all gone, and no potential voters could get a drop. A week later Koeninger came to town and told Wolters about the beer. Bob consoled Wolters: "But de peer do ju gude, all the same, Wolters. I vote for you."

In May of 1900, Boise was trying to raise $200,000 in subscriptions for bonds for the Idaho Midland Securities.[qd] There were eventually 676 individuals or corporate entities that subscribed, and the amount was $16,000 more than required. John Lemp personally pledged $5,000. "Mrs. C. Lemp" (nephew Clarence's wife) was also on the list of subscribers. The city had a massive celebration when the goal was met. This railroad proposal would enable the railroad to come to Boise and goods and passengers would no longer have to go to Nampa on the stub to connect to the main line for distant travel. Again this goal was thwarted.

On June 11, 1900 the U. S. Census taker came to Lemp's house. He was listed as 61 years old, 34 years married, and born in Germany. Catherine was 49, mother of 13 with 9 living, and born in Germany. The twins were 25, Albert C. was 23, Edwin H. was 18, Herbert F. 15, Bernard L. 13, Louise B. 11, and nephew George Kohlepp 15 was living with them. This was George Kohlepp's son with second wife Lizzie Garrety. George was also the son of the man Lemp had filed suit against that year.

The New York Canal was completed June 22, 1900, greatly expanding irrigation in the Boise valley. June was also the month that John Brodbeck bought and installed the first ice making equipment in the city.[qe] The warm winter the previous year had made the usual ice harvest insufficient. Many people mistrusted machine-made, "artificial" ice but its time had come.

In July, Lemp had an unwelcome visitor to his ranch.[qf] A porcupine—"porkapine" in western lingo—decided the chicken coop was a cafeteria. An excessive amount of chicken profanity in the house tipped off a couple of men who sought to remove him. The first got "quills enough to keep a pen factory running for a year." The second managed to get the intruder into a meal bag which was hung up for the night on a post of the corral. The beast kept wiggling around and trying to get out and the horses became increasingly curious. "Then one old stagger got very bold and gave the bag a good jolt with his nose. The next instant he was cavorting around the corral sniffing like a man with the grip." The horse had a nose full of quills. The horse kicked at the sky but to no available. Two men who did not know about the location of the porcupine went to see about the enraged horse. One leaned against the porcupine bag and started away from the bag "with the speed of an O.S.L. locomotive, giving up 60-lung power whoops that would have done an Apache credit." One of the ranchmen decided to take the chicken thief to town and put the bag in the back of the wagon. A traveler that hitch hiked a ride sat in the back by the almost forgotten porcupine. He was muttering some thanks when he let out a yell and dived headlong from the wagon to the ditch by the side of the road. The horse took fright at this and ran a quarter of a mile before they could be reigned in. When the ranch man looked back the traveler was looking for a rock to throw at him so he did not see fit to stop his journey to Boise. A friend in Boise got a cage and put the "porkapine" on display. A sign on the cage read: "Porkapine—Captured by Joe Beal on Lemp's ranch. Have a quill. Anyone may have one by sticking his hand in the cage."

Two other men that worked for Lemp had an exciting experience that July of 1900.[qg] They were fording the Boise river with a wagon just south of town when the wagon slipped off the ford and the horses became tangled in the harness. They cut the harness to free the endangered horses. Bill Breen held fast to part of the wagon and was swept downstream a quarter of a mile, nearly drowning.

Among the ranch hands Lemp employed at various times were D. E. Clemmens, and W. E. Fisher. Both went on to sufficient prominence to have biographical sketches published in Hawley's 1920 history of Idaho.[qh] Both men worked as cattle punchers before going on to own their businesses.

In September, General and Mrs. J. L. Weaver announced the engagement of their daughter, Miss Lucille Weaver to Mr. Albert Lemp. [qi] The Lemp family nest was going to lose another child while gaining another set of prominent in-laws.

Fourteen-year-old Bernard Lemp ran into a bunch of bears on Shafer creek late August of 1900.[qj] He shot and killed one weighing 300 pounds and his dog reportedly killed another. He claimed to see no less than twenty of the bruins. That would be an enormous number of bears for an adult to see but about the right number for an excited young teenager to recall.

Long standing rival John Brodbeck sold his brewery to Henry Muntzer of Butte, Montana, for a broadly estimated $30,000 to $50,000.[qk] Expansion was to be the order of the day during the new century for Lemp's local rival. The nature of the competition, however, would not resemble that of the decades past. Muntzer, had just sold his long-time interest in the Butte Brewery.

As a long time friend of Marcus Daly of Montana, Muntzer shared a dislike for William A. Clark, Lemp's old friend. Daly had been feuding with the other "Copper King" of Montana, William A. Clark, for political power in that state for years. Would Muntzer then dislike Lemp due to the association? Lemp's old traveling companion Clark had secured a U. S. Senate seat from Montana through exorbitant bribes to the state legislatures who selected senators before a constitutional amendment brought direct election. The Senate refused to seat him but the state's Lieutenant Governor, acting in the governor's stead appointed Clark to the very same seat vacated when he was refused admittance. Clark secured the Senate seat again, allegedly through bribery again, was admitted this time, and served without distinction from 1901 to 1907.[ql]

The Nineteenth Century closed on John Lemp and his large family and his many friends at the height of their successes. The new century would offer even greater potential for successes and failures.

END NOTES

a   *Idaho Daily Statesman,* 4 January 1890, p. 3, c. 1.
b   *Idaho Daily Statesman,* 15 January 1890, p. 3, c. 2.
c   *Idaho Daily Statesman,* 8 February 1890, p. 3, c. 3.
d   Cochran, *The Pabst Brewing Company: The History of an American Business,* 1948, p. 126-127.
e   *Idaho Daily Statesman,* 22 March 1890, p.p. 3, c. 4.
f   *Idaho Daily Statesman,* 23 March 1890, p. 3, c. 2.
g   *Idaho Daily Statesman,* 25 March 1890, p. 3, c. 2.
h   *Idaho Daily Statesman,* 26 March 1890, p. 3, c. 2.
i   *Idaho Daily Statesman,* 27 March 1890, p. 3, c. 3.
j   *Idaho Daily Statesman,* 3 April 1890, p. 3, c. 3.
k   *Idaho Daily Statesman,* 9 April 1890, p. 3, c.2.
l   *Idaho Daily Statesman,* 12 June 1890, p. 3, c. 2.
m   *Idaho Daily Statesman,* 19 June 1890, p. 3, c. 3.
n   *Idaho Daily Statesman,* 6 August 1890, p. 4, c. 1.
o   Ada County Court Records, Microfilmed Judgment Books, Idaho State Historical Society.
p   *Idaho Daily Statesman,* 7 May 1911, Section II, p. 5, c. 1-5. The old article reprinted in the historical section of the Sunday newspaper was found in the cornerstone of a building and was originally from the *Idaho Democrat.*

q   *Idaho Daily Statesman,* 23 June 1890, p. 3, c. 2. 24 June 1890, p. 3, c. 2.
r   *Idaho Daily Statesman,* 19 June 1890, p. 3, c. 3.
s   *Idaho Daily Statesman,* 10 July 1890, p. 3, c. 2.
t   *Idaho Daily Statesman,* 28 June 1890, p. 3, c. 2.
u   *Idaho Daily Statesman,* 3 May 1890, p. 3, c. 1 & 2. 1 June 1890, p. 2, c. 1.
v   *Idaho Daily Statesman,* 4 July 1890, p. 3, c. 2.
w   Bureau of Land Management, Land Patent Records. Internet. For the Ironclad: Accession Serial # IDIDAA045997, Document # 16510.Description Section 6, 4-N, 20-E and Section 7 4-N, 20-E. For the Concordia: Accession/Serial # IDIDAA 044872, Section 28, Township 2-N, Range 18-E.
x   *Idaho Daily Statesman* 3 August 1890, p. 4, c. 1.
y   *Idaho Daily Statesman,* 14 August 1890, p. 4, c. 1.
z   *Wood River Times,* Hailey, Weekly, 3 September 1890, p. 1, c. 2.
aa *Idaho Daily Statesman,* 17 September 1890, p. 4, c. 1.
ab *Idaho Daily Statesman,* 22 September 1890, p. 4, c. 1.
ac *Idaho Daily Statesman,* 4 October 1890, p. 4, c. 1.
ad *Idaho Daily Statesman,* 7 October 1890, p. 4, c. 1.
ae *Idaho Daily Statesman,* 7 October 1890, p. 4, c. 2.
af *Idaho Daily Statesman* 17 October 1890, p. 4, c. 2.
ag *Idaho World,* Idaho City, 24 October 1890, p. 1, c. 2. *The Elmore Bulletin,* Rocky Bar, 25 October 1890, p. 3, c. 4.
ah *Idaho Daily Statesman,* 19 November 1890, p. 4, c. 1.
ai *Idaho Daily Statesman,* 19 November 1890, p. 2, c. 2.
aj *Idaho Daily Statesman,* 24 November 1890, p. 4, c. 2.
ak *Idaho Daily Statesman,* 22 November 1890, p. 4, c. 1.
al *Idaho Daily Statesman,* 30 December 1890, p. 8, c. 1.
m   *Idaho Daily Statesman,* 13 January, 1891, p. 8, c. 1.
an *The Idaho Democrat (The Weekly Democrat),* Boise, 17 January 1891, p. 4, c. 3 & 4.
ao *The Idaho Democrat,* Boise, 28 February 1891, p. 6, c. 6.
ap *Idaho Daily Statesman,* 5 February 1891, p. 8, c. 2.
aq *Idaho Daily Statesman,* 17 April 1891, p. 8, c.3.
ar *Idaho Daily Statesman,* 30 April 1891, p. 8, c. 2.
as Bureau of Land Management, Land Patent Records. Accession/Serial #IDIDAA 013641, Document 117, Section 34, Township 4-N, Range 2-W.
at *The Idaho Democrat,* Boise, 29 April 1891, p. 3, c. 1.
au *Idaho Daily Statesman,* 17 June 1891, p. 8, c. 1.
av *Idaho Daily Statesman,* 22 June 1891, p. 8, c. 3.
aw *Idaho Daily Statesman,* 28 August 1891, p. 8, c. 3.

ax *Idaho Daily Statesman*, 14 August 1891, p. 8 c. 1. *Idaho World*, Idaho City, 18 August 1891, p. 1, c. 1.
ay *Idaho Falls Times*, 13 August 1891, p. 8, c. 3.
az *Idaho Daily Statesman*, 27 August 1891, p. 8, c. 2.
ba *Idaho Daily Statesman*, 30 June 1891, p. 8, c. 2.
bb *Idaho Daily Statesman*, 1 July 1891, p. 2, c. 1.
bc *Idaho Daily Statesman*, 1 July 1891, p. 8, c. 1.
bd *Idaho Daily Statesman*n, 1 July 1891, p. 2, c. 1.
be *Idaho Daily Statesman*, 2 July 1891, p. 2, c. 2. Judge Milton Kelly had run the Statesman from 1872 to 1889. Despite his temperamental, vindictive and unlikable personality he had never called Lemp any names.
bf *The Daily Evening Citizen*, 8 July 1891, p. 2, c. 1.
bg *The Daily Evening Citizen*, Boise, 7 July 1891, p. 2, c. 1. The only copies extant of this paper are those for the few days before this election.
bh *Idaho Daily Statesman*, 2 July 1891, p. 8, c. 1.
bi *Idaho Daily Statesman*, 2 July 1891, p. 2, c. 1 & 2.
bj *Idaho Daily Statesman*, 3 July 1891, p. 2, c. 1.
bk *Idaho Daily Statesman*, 3 July 1891, p. 8, c. 1.
bl *The Daily Evening Citizen*, 8 July 1891, p. 1, c. 2.
bm *The Daily Evening Citizen*, 10 July 1891, p. 2, c. 1-2.
bn *The Daily Evening Citizen*, 10 July 1891, p. 4, c. 3. 11 July 1891, p. 1, c. 5.
bo *Idaho Daily Statesman*, 14 July 1891, p. 8, c. 1.
bp *Idaho Daily Statesman*, 15 July 1891, p. 2, c. 1.
bq *Idaho Daily Statesman*, 11 July 1891, p. 8, c. 3.
br *Idaho Daily Statesman*, 20 July 1891, p. 2, c. 1.
bs MacGregor, "Founding Community in Boise Idaho, 1882-1910," p. 117. MacGregor, Boise, Idaho, 1882-1910, p. 67-71.
bt *Idaho Daily Statesman*, 2 September 1891, p. 8, c. 1.
bu *Idaho Daily Statesman*, 17 September 1891, p. 8, c. 2.
bv *Idaho World*, Idaho City, 11 September 1891, p. 1, c. 3. Boise County Judicial Records, Judgment Records, Microfilm, Idaho State Historical Society, reel 35.
bw *Idaho Register*, Idaho Falls, 2 October 1891, p. 5, c. 1. *Idaho Daily Statesman*, 30 September 1891, p. 8, c. 1.
bx *Idaho Daily Statesman*, 2 September 1891, p. 8, c. 1. 3 October 1891, p. 4, c. 1.
by *Idaho Daily Statesman*, 5 September 1891, p. 8, c. 2.
bz *Idaho Daily Statesman*, 9 September 1891, p. 2, c. 1.
ca *Idaho Daily Statesman*, 15 September 1891, p. 4, c. 1.
cb *Idaho Daily Statesman*, 17 September 1891, p. 8, c. 2.
cc *Idaho Daily Statesman* 2 October 1891, p. 2, c. 1.
cd *Idaho Daily Statesman* 10 October 1891, p. 2, c. 2.

ce *Idaho Daily Statesman*, 21 October 1891, p. 8, c. 2.
cf *North Idaho Star*, Moscow, 10 October 1891, p. 1, c. 1.
cg *The Elmore Bulletin*, Rocky Bar, 24 October 1891, p. 3, c. 2.
    The Genesee News, 21 October 1891, p. 3, c. 2.
ch *Idaho Daily Statesman*, 21 October 1891, p. 8, c. 2. 30 October 1891, p. 8, c. 2.
ci *Idaho Daily Statesman*, 8 December 1891, p. 8, c. 1.
cj *Idaho Daily Statesman*, 8 December 1891, p. 8, c. 1.
ck *Idaho Daily Statesman*, 24 December 1891, p. 1, c. 1.
cl Maxwell, H. James, and Sullivan, Bob, Jr. *Hometown Beer: A History of Kansas City's Breweries*. Kansas City: Omega Innovative Marketing, 1999, p. 201..
cm *Idaho Daily Statesman*, 8 January 1892, p. 8, c. 2.
cn *Idaho Daily Statesman*, 6 January 1892, p. 8, c. 2.
co *The Elmore Bulletin*, Rocky Bar, 26 March 1892, p. 3, c. 3.
cp Bureau of Land Management, Land Patent Records. Accession/Serial # IDIDAA 030570, Document # 1151. Description was Aliquot NSE Section 35, Township 6-N, Range 2-E and Aliquot SWSE Section 35, Township 6-N, Range 2-E, and Aliquot 2, Section 2, Township 5-N, Range 2-E.
cq *Idaho Daily Statesman*, 5 March 1892, p. 8, c. 1 & 2.
cr *Idaho Daily Statesman*, 18 March 1892, p. 4, c. 3. The newspaper was very late with this report.
cs *Idaho Daily Statesman*, 7 January 1896, p. 3, c. 1.
ct Robbins was the same marshal who's alertness in 1870 saved Lemp property from a fire.
cu *Idaho Daily Statesman*, 10 March 1892, p. 8, c. 1.
cv I*Idaho Daily Statesman*, 19 March 1892, p. 8, c. 1.
cw *Idaho Daily Statesman*, 12 March 1892, p. 4, c. 1.
cx Ada County Court Records, Microfilmed Judgments Books, Idaho State Historical Society.
cy *Idaho Daily Statesman*, 16 March 1892, p. 8, c. 1.
cz *Idaho Daily Statesman*, 25 March 1892, p. 8, c. 1.
da *Evening Capital News*, 5 June 1909, p. 4-5, c. 1-7. This was a history of the water system in Boise.
db *Idaho Daily Statesman*, 6 April 1892, p. 4, c. 2, c. 3.
dc *Idaho Daily Statesman*, 23 March 1892, p. 5, c. 3.
dd *Idaho Daily Statesman*, 27 March 1892, p. 8, c. 2.
de Alturas County Patent Deed Records, Idaho State Historical Society, Blaine County Judicial Records, reel 31, original record on pages 455-457. County realignment creates this seeming discrepancy.
df Alturas County Patent Deed Records, Idaho State Historical Society, Blaine County Judicial Records, reel 31, original record on pages 1-4. They recorded the claim almost one year later on 5 May1883. An added marginal assignment

on this record dated 10 May 1954 was from Kathryn Lemp Langdon to John Lemp. This must have been our grandson, and shows what long time the property remained in the family.

dg *Idaho Tri-Weekly Statesman*, 10 March 1882, p. 3, c. 1. *Ketchum Keystone*, 13 April 1882, p. 1, c. 3.

dh Logan County Deed Records, Volume 13, Idaho State Historical Society, Blaine county Judicial Records, Microfilm reel 10. pages 219-220 in original book. County realignment creates the seeming mislocation of the records.

di Logan County Deed Records, Volume 13, Idaho State Historical Society, Blaine county Judicial Records, Microfilm reel 10. pages 204-206 in original book.

dj *Wood River Times* (Weekly) Hailey, Idaho, 17 December 1884, p. 3, c. 6. 31 December 1884, p. 1, c. 5. Boise City Republican, 20 December 1884, p. 1, c. 1.

dk *Idaho Tri-Weekly Statesman*, 17 March 1885, p. 1, c. 5.

dl *Idaho Daily Statesman*, 16 October 1889, p. 3, c. 1.

dm Blaine County Judicial Records, Idaho State Historical Society, microfilm reel 34, original page 471.

dn *Idaho Daily Statesman*, 1 April 1892, p. 1, c. 6. Wood River Times, 27 April 1892, p. 3, c. 3.

do "Visit the Blaine County Historical Museum," pamphlet, Hailey, Idaho, n.d.

dp *Idaho Register*, Idaho Falls, 8 April 1892, p. 5, c. 3.

dq *The Commonwealth of Idaho*, Boise, 1 April 1892, p. 1, c. 6.

dr *Idaho Daily Statesman*, 18 October 1892, p. 8, c. 2.

ds *Wood River Times*, Hailey, Weekly, 30 November 1892, p. 1, c. 1.

dt *Idaho Daily Statesman*, 26 February 1893, p. 1, c. 5.

du *Wood River Times*, Hailey, 3 May 1893, p. 3, c. 2.

dv *Idaho Daily Statesman*, 22 September 1893, p. 8, c. 1 & 2.

dw *Wood River Times*, Hailey, Daily, 4 October 1893, p. 3, c. 1.

dx *Wood River Times*, 11 October 1893, p. 4, c. 1. *Idaho Daily Statesman*, 7 October 1893, p. 3, c. 1.

dy *Idaho Daily Statesman*, 4 November 1893, p. 8, c. 1.

dz *Wood River Times*, Hailey, Weekly, 18 April 1894, p. 2, c. 3.

ea Blaine County Judicial Records, Idaho State Historical Society, Microfilm reel 30, District Court Records, original page unnumbered. The men were Brockbank, Nichols, Winter?, Rushton, Isaac, Fox, Hardy, Jennings, Morris, and Starrh.

eb Logan County Deeds, Blaine County Judicial Records, Idaho State Historical Society, Microfilm reel 10, double page 248 of original book. Brockbank's partners were A. E. Nichols, Thomas Winter, Edwin Rushton, John R. Isaac, Jesse W. Fox, Jr. Charles W. Hardy, Isaac Jennings, Elias Morris and F. A. Starrh.

ec Logan County Deeds, Blaine County Judicial Records, Idaho State Historical Society, Microfilm reel 10, double page 247 of original book.

ed *Wood River Times*, Hailey, Weekly, 7 October 1896, p. 4, c. 3.

ee *Idaho Daily Statesman*, 15 December 1896, p. 3, c. 2.
ef Alturas County Deeds, Blaine County Judicial Records, Idaho State Historical Society, Microfilm reel 28, double page 28.
eg *Wood River Times*, Hailey, Weekly 4 August 1897, p. 3, c. 1 & 2. 11 August 1897, p. 3, c. 1.
eh *Wood River Times*, Hailey, Weekly, 9 February 1898, p. 3, c. 2.
ei *Idaho Daily Statesman*, 19 August 1897, p. 3, c. 1.
ej *Wood River Times*, Hailey, Weekly, 9 February 1898, p. 3, c. 1.
ek *Wood River Times*, Hailey, Weekly, 25 October 1899, p. 3, c. 2. *Idaho Daily Statesman*, 26 October 1899, p. 6, c.1.
el *Wood River Times*, 1 November 1899, p. 3, c. 1, c. 3.
em *The Weekly Capital*, 4 November 1899, p. 8, c. 1.
en *Wood River Times*, Weekly, Hailey, 4 May 1892, p. 1, c. 1.
eo *Idaho Capital News*, 17 December 1903, p. 4, c. 4.
ep *Idaho Daily Statesman*, 14 December 1903, p. 5, c. 3.
eq *Idaho Daily Statesman*, 15 December 1903, p. 5, c. 5.
er *The Idaho Magazine*, "John Lemp: Foundation Builder of Boise," March, 1904, p. 30. Progressive Men of Southern Idaho, 1904, p. 71.
es *Idaho Capital News*, 4 August 1904, p. 3, c. 6.
et *Evening Capital News*, 6 September 1904, p. 5, c. 5.
eu Blaine County Judicial Records, Idaho State Historical Society, microfilm reel 10, Logan County Deeds, original page 207.
ev Blaine County Judicial Records, Idaho State Historical Society, microfilm reel 30, original page 206.
ew *Evening Capital News*, 9 August 1905, p. 8, c. 3.
ex *Wood River Times*, Hailey, Daily, 7 August 1905, p. 4, c. 1.
ey *Idaho Capital News*, 24 August 1905, p. 10, c. 5. *Evening Capital News*, 17 August 1905, p. 8, c. 4.
ez *Evening Capital News*, 19 September 1905, p. 5, c. 5.
fa *Idaho Daily Statesman*, 7 April 1892, p. 5, c. 1.
fb 1850 to 1951 Marriage Index, CD-ROM.
fc *Idaho Daily Statesman*, 23 April 1892, p. 8, c. 1.
fd *Idaho Daily Statesman*, 23 April 1892, p.8, c. 1.
fe *Idaho Daily Statesman*, 6 May 1892, p. 8, c. 1.
ff *Idaho Daily Statesman*, 17 June 1892, p. 5, c. 1.
fg *The Standard*, Ogden, Utah, 2 June 1892, p. 8, c. 2.
fh *Idaho Daily Statesman*, 13 June 1892, p. 8, c. 1.
fi The Marriage Index: Illinois 1851-1900, Family Tree Maker, CD-ROM # 250 does not list this marriage.
fj *Idaho Daily Statesman*, 31 July 1892, p. 1, c. 1.

fk *Idaho Daily Statesman*, 19 August 1892, p. 5, c. 2. Joseph C. Pence was a lawyer and one of five brothers of an old Dutch family. Joseph Pence later served as mayor of Boise. John Pence lived in Mountain home at the time of this article. See *Evening Capital News*, 27 March 1908, p. 8, c. 6 & 7.

fl *Idaho Daily Statesman*, 22 August 1892, p. 8, c. 1.

fm *Idaho Daily Statesman*, 22 August 1892, p. 8, c. 1.

fn *Idaho Daily Statesman*, 3 September 1892, p. 8, c. 2.

fo *Idaho Daily Statesman*, 5 September 1892, p. 8, c. 2. Lemp went to Sheep Mountain to again look to his mining interests before the trial. He did not seem very worried. *Idaho Daily Statesman*, 19 September 1892, p. 8, c. 1. 20 September 1892, p. 5, c. 2.

fp *Idaho Daily Statesman*, 20 September 1892, p. 8, c. 1.

fq *Idaho Daily Statesman*, 21 September 1892, p. 8, c. 2.

fr *Idaho Daily Statesman*, 22 September 1892, p. 8, c. 2.

fs *Idaho Daily Statesman*, 23 September 1892, p. 8, c. 1.

ft *Idaho Daily Statesman*, 28 September 1892, p. 8, c. 1.

fu *Idaho Daily Statesman*, 17 November 1892, p. 2, c. 1.

fv *Idaho Daily Statesman*, 2 September 1892, p. 5, c. 1.

fw *Idaho Falls Times*, 15 September 1892, p. 8, c. 1. *Idaho Daily Statesman*, 18 September 1892, p. 3, c. 3.

fx *Idaho Daily Statesman*, 4 October 1892, p. 5,c. 1.

fy *Idaho Daily Statesman*, 9 October 1892, p. 8, c. 1 & 2.

fz *Idaho Daily Statesman*, 15 October 1892, p. 1, c. 4.

ga *Idaho Statesman*, 8 January 1973, p. 11, c. 1 – 2.

gb *Idaho Daily Statesman*, 14 October 1892, p. 1, c. 1.

gc MacGregor, Boise, Idaho, 1882-1910, p. 108-9.

gd *Idaho Daily Statesman*, 23 October 1892, p. 1, c. 6.

ge Arthur Hart, "Lemp Helps Boise Grow," Idaho Statesman, 26 July 1993, p. 2D, c. 1-2.

gf Logan County Deeds, Blaine County Judicial Records, Idaho State Historical Society, Microfilm reel 10, item three. page 559 in original book.

gg Ada County Court Records, Microfilmed Judgment Books, Idaho State Historical Society.

gh *Idaho Daily Statesman*, 12 December 1892, p. 1, c. 2. p. 2, c. 5.

gi *Idaho Daily Statesman*, 8 February 1893, p. 8, c. 4.

gj *The Idaho Democrat*, Boise, 18 January 1893, p. 3, c. 2.

gk *Idaho Daily Statesman*, 14 January 1893, p. 8, c. 1.

gl *Idaho Daily Statesman*, 21 January 1893, p. 5, c. 1.

gm *Idaho Daily Statesman*, 4 March 1893, p. 8, c. 4.

gn *Idaho Daily Statesman*, 8 March 1893, p. 5, c. 2.

go *Idaho Daily Statesman*, 8 March 1893, p. 8, c. 1.

gp *Idaho Daily Statesman*, 12 March 1893, p. 8, c. 4.
gq *Idaho Daily Statesman* , 15 March 1893, p. 8, c. 2.
gr *Idaho Daily Statesman*, 18 March 1893, p. 3, all columns.
gs *Idaho Daily Statesman*, 30 March 1893, p. 8, c. 1.
gt Bureau of Land Management. Land Patent Records. Accession/Serial # IDIDAA 044307, Document # 22733. Description was section 23, Township 6-N, Range 16-E, and Section 26, Township 6-N, Range 16-E.
gu Bureau of Land Management. Land Patent Records. Accession/Serial # IDIDAA 044308. Document # 22734. Description was Section 23, Township 6-N, Range 16-E, and Section 26, Township 6-N, Range 16-E.
gv *Idaho Daily Statesman* 19 April 1893, p. 8, c. 1.
gw Bureau of Land Management, Land Patent Records. Accession/Serial # IDIDAA 044309, Document # 22785, description was Section 26, Township 6-N, Range 16-E.
gx *Idaho Daily Statesman*, 24 April 1893, p. 8, c. 1 & 2.
gy *Idaho Daily Statesman*, 25 April 1893, p. 8, c. 4.
gz *Idaho Daily Statesman*, 27 April 1893, p. 5, c. 1.
ha *Idaho Daily Statesman*, 20 May 1893, p. 8, c. 4.
hb *Idaho Daily Statesman*, 26 May 1893, p. 8, c. 1.
hc *Idaho Daily Statesman*, 4 June 1893, p. 1, c. 3.
hd Ogle, *Ambitious Brew*, 2006, p. 125.
he *Idaho Daily Statesman*, 17 June 1893, p. 8, c. 1 & 2.
hf *Idaho Daily Statesman*, 15 July 1893, p. 8, c. 1. 18 July 1893, p. 2 & 3, c. 1 & 2.
hg Bureau of Land Management, Land Patent Records. Accession/Serial # IDIDAA 044889, Document # 23231. Description Section 28, Township 2-N, Range 18-E. This was also under the 1866 mineral patent law.
hh *Wood River Times*, Hailey, Weekly, 9 August 1893, p. 3, c. 1.
hi *Wood River Times*, Hailey, Daily, 16 August 1893, p. 1, c. 6.
hj *Wood River Times*, Hailey, 30 August 1893, p. 1, c. 5.
hk *Idaho Daily Statesman*, 17 August 1893, p. 1, c. 3.
hl *Idaho Daily Statesman*, 26 August 1893, p. 8, c. 2.
hm *Idaho Daily Statesman*, 1 September 1893, p. 8, c. 2.
hn *Idaho Daily Statesman*, 13 September 1893, p. 8, c. 1 & 2.
ho *Idaho Daily Statesman*, 22 September 1893, p. 6, c. 4.
hp *Evening Capital Journal*, Salem, Oregon, 18 September 1893, p. 4, c. 4.
hq *Capital Journal*, Salem, Oregon, 19 September 1893, p. 4, c. 1.
hr *Evening Capital Journal*, Salem, Oregon, Wednesday 20 September 1893, p. 4, c. 1.
hs *Evening Capital Journal*, Salem, Oregon, 25 September 1893, p. 4, c. 1.
ht *Evening Capital Journal*, 26 September 1893, p. 4, c. 2.
hu Internet. salemhistory.org/places/historic-Downtown.

hv The current name is the Semlar building and it is at 315 to 333 State Street in Salem.
hw *Idaho Falls Times*, 5 October 1893, p. 4, c. 1.
hx *Idaho Falls Times*, 2 November 1893, p. 5, c. 2.
hy *Idaho Daily Statesman*, 9 October 1893, p. 8, c. 1.
hz *Idaho Daily Statesman*, 12 October 1893, p. 8, c. 2.
ia *Idaho Daily Statesman*, 13 October 1893, p. 5, c. 5.
ib *Idaho Daily Statesman*, 19 October 1893, p. 8, c. 1. *The Elmore Bulletin*, Mountain Home, 21 October 1893, p. 3, c. 2.
ic *Idaho Daily Statesman*, 20 October 1893, p. 8, c. 1 & 2.
id *Idaho Daily Statesman*, 10 November 1893, p. 3, c. 1.
ie *Idaho Daily Statesman*, 4 November 1893, p. 8, c. 4.
if Ada County Court Records, Microfilmed Judgment Books, Idaho State Historical Society.
ig *Idaho Daily Statesman*, 23 December 1893, p. 3, c. 1.
ih *Idaho Daily Statesman*, 23 February 1894, p. 6, c. 3.
ii *Idaho Daily Statesman*, 4 February 1894, p. 3, c. 1.
ij Correspondence from Karl Lemp, Sr. April 2002.
ik *Idaho Daily Statesman* 14 February 1894, p. 6, c. 1 & 2.
il *Idaho Daily Statesman*, 15 February 1894, p. 6, c. 4.
im *Idaho Daily Statesman*, 23 March 1894, p. 6, c. 1.
in *Idaho Daily Statesman*, 24 March 1894, p. 6, c. 4.
io *Idaho Daily Statesman*, 28 March 1894, p. 4, c. 1.
ip *Idaho Daily Statesman*, 15 March 1894, p. 3, c. 1.
iq *Idaho Daily Statesman*, 31 March 1894, p. 3, c. 1.
ir Ada County court Records, Microfilmed Judgment Books, Idaho State Historical Society.
is *Idaho Daily Statesman*, 30 November 1895, p. 8, c. 4.
it *Idaho Daily Statesman*, 10 December 1895, p. 8, c. 4. *Idaho Reports*. vol. 4, 1894-1896, p. 526. Ruling issued 13 December 1895 in case of Pence v. Lemp.
iu Mrs. Pence died 5 June 1896 at St. Alphonsus hospital after an operation. She was born 21 September 1858, came to Idaho in 1875 and married Pence 22 August 1877 in Owyhee County. She had been an invalid for some time and left four children. *Idaho Daily Statesman* 7 June 1896, p. 4, c. 1.
iv *Idaho Daily Statesman* 12 February 1897, p. 6, c. 2.
iw *Idaho Daily Statesman*, 31 March 1894, p. 5, c. 3-6.
ix *Idaho Daily Statesman*, 22 May 1894, p. 5, c. 4.
iy *Idaho Daily Statesman*, 19 April 1894, p. 6, c. 4.
iz Ada County Court Records, Microfilmed Judgment Books, Idaho State Historical Society.

ja *Idaho Daily Statesman*, 20 April 1894, p. 6, c. 2.
jb *Idaho Daily Statesman*, 27 April 1894, p. 2, c. 3.
jc *Idaho Daily Statesman*, 4 May 1894, p. 3, c. 2.
jd *Idaho Daily Statesman*, 10 May 1894, p. 6, c. 1.
je *Caldwell Tribune*, 19 May 1894, p. 2, c. 2.
jf *Idaho Daily Statesman*, 28 June 1894, p. 3, c. 1.
jg *Idaho Daily Statesman*, 20 July 1894. p. 3, c. 1.
jh *Idaho Daily Statesman*, 22 July 1894, p. 3, c. 2.
ji *Idaho Daily Statesman*, 26 August 1894, p. 3, c. 1.
jj *Idaho Daily Statesman* , 5 September 1894, p. 6, c. 1.
jk *Idaho Daily Statesman*, 20 September 1894, p. 3, c. 1. Custer County Judicial Records, Idaho State Historical Society, Microfilm reel 10 lists the sale of several mining properties from Clark to Benjamin Brown of Houston, Custer County, Idaho.
jl *Idaho Daily Statesman*, 30 September 1894, p. 6, c. 4.
jm *Idaho Daily Statesman*, 11 October 1894, p. 4, c. 3.
jn *Idaho Daily Statesman*n, 29 November 1894, p. 4, c. 3.
jo *Idaho Daily Statesman*, 7 December 1894, p. 3, c. 1.
jp *Idaho Daily Statesman*, 11 December 1894, p. 6, c. 1.
jq *Idaho Daily Statesman*, 23 February 1895, p. 3, c. 3.
jr *Idaho Daily Statesman*, 26 February 1895, p. 11, c. 1-4.
js *Idaho World*, Idaho City, 12 March 1895, p. 1, c. 1. *Idaho Daily Statesman*, 10 March 1895, p. 3, c. 3.
jt Phone interview with Karl H. Lemp, 19 January 2002.
ju *Idaho Daily Statesman*, 12 March 1895, p. 3, c. 2.
jv Correspondence from Karl Lemp, Sr. of St. Louis, April 2002.
jw *Idaho Daily Statesman*, 16 March 1895, p. 6, c. 2.
jx *Idaho Daily Statesman*, 4 June 1895, p. 6, c. 3.
jy *Idaho Daily Statesman*, 5 November 1895, p. 6, c. 4.
jz *Idaho Daily Statesman*, 21 April 1895, p. 3, c. 4.
ka *Idaho Daily Statesman*, 22 April 1895, p. 5, c. 2.
kb *Idaho Daily Statesman*, 27 April 1895, p. 6, c. 2. 30 April 1895, p. 2, c. 3.
kc *Idaho Daily Statesman*, 1 March 1895, p. 6, c. 2.
kd *Idaho Daily Statesman*, 6 March 1895, p. 6, c. 4.
ke *Idaho Daily Statesman*, 28 May 1895, p. 4, c. 3.
kf *Idaho Daily Statesman*, 21 June 1895, p. 6, c. 1.
kg *Idaho Daily Statesman* 27 June 1895, p. 3, c. 2.
kh *Idaho Daily Statesman*, 1 September 1895, p. 2, c. 3.
ki *Idaho Daily Statesman*1 August 1895, p. 5, c. 6.

kj *Idaho Daily Statesman*, 14 September 1895, p. 3, c. 3.
kk *Idaho Daily Statesman*, 16 September 1895, p. 6, c. 4.
kl *Idaho Daily Statesman*, 27 August 1895, p. 6, c. 4.
km His death notice, obituary and funeral report gave the essential details of Jauman's life. *Idaho Daily Statesman*, 8 October 1895, p. 3, c. 3. 9 October 1895, p. 3, c. 3. 10 October 1895, p. 3, c. 3.
kn *Boise City Republican*, 4 April 1885, p. 1, c. 3. Jaumann had been an Ada County Commissioner when it was charged that he accepted pay for his duties there. A case of Rankin V. Jauman was decided on 5 February 1894 (Idaho Reports, February 1894, pp. 53-66) regarding removal from office. A related case of Rankin V. Jauman was decided 7 March 1895 (Idaho Reports March 1895, pp. 395-402) which regarded compensation of county commissioners.
ko Photocopy of the will, Probate Court, Ada county, Idaho.
kp *Idaho Daily Statesman*, 23 March 1897, p. 6, c. 2.
kq *Idaho Daily Statesman*, 5 October 1895, p. 3, c. 2.
kr *Idaho Daily Statesman*, 12 October 1895, p. 6, c. 4.
ks *Idaho Daily Statesman*, 24 October 1895, p. 3, c. 2.
kt *The Idaho Register*, Idaho Falls, 15 November 1895, p. 8, c. 4.
ku *Idaho Daily Statesman*, 10 November 1895, p. 6, c. 4.
kv *Idaho Daily Statesman*, 24 April 1896.
kw *Idaho World*, Idaho City, 10 December 1895, p. 1, c. 3. *Wood River Times*, 11 December 1895, p. 3, c. 1.
kx *Idaho Daily Statesman*, 6 December 1895, p. 6, c. 4.
ky *Idaho Daily Statesman*, 20 February 1896, p. 6, c. 1.
kz *Idaho Daily Statesman*, 29 March 1896, p. 5, c. 2.
la *Idaho Daily Statesman*, 24 December 1895, p. 6, c. 4. 30 December 1895, p. 6, c. 1.
lb *The Idaho Democrat*, Boise, 15 December 1895, p. 3, c. 2.
lc *Idaho Daily Statesman*, 15 December 1895, p. 6, c. 2.
ld *Idaho Daily Statesman*, 19 February 1896, p. 6, c. 4.
le *Idaho Daily Statesman*, 15 February 1896, p. 3, c. 1.
lf *Idaho Daily Statesman*, 4 March 1896, p. 3, c. 4.
lg *Idaho Daily Statesman*, 13 March 1896, p. 4, c. 1.
lh *Idaho Daily Statesman*, 29 March 1893, p. 5, c. 1.
li *Idaho Daily Statesman*, 23 July 1896, p. 4, c. 2.
lj *Idaho Daily Statesman*, 9 August 1896, p. 3, c. 1.
lk *Idaho Daily Statesman*, 20 August 1896, p. 3, c. 2.
ll *Idaho Daily Statesman*, 8 September 1896, p. 6, c. 2.
lm *Idaho Daily Statesman*, 9 September 1896, p. 2, c. 2.
ln *Idaho Daily Statesman*, 10 September 1896, p. 6, c./ 1.

lo *Idaho Daily Statesman*, 12 September 1896, p. 6, c. 1.
lp *Idaho Daily Statesman*, 17 September 1896, p. 6, c. 2.
lq *Idaho Daily Statesman*, 11 October 1896, p. 6, c. 1.
lr Carlos A. Schwantes, *The Pacific Northwest, An interpretative History*. Lincoln: University of Nebraska Press, 1989. p. 134.
ls Wood River Times, 9 December 1896, p. 4, c. 4.
lt *Idaho Daily Statesman*, 23 February 1896, p. 2, c. 1-3.
lu *Idaho Daily Statesman*, 18 November 1896, p. 6, c. 2.
lv *Idaho Daily Statesman*, 29 January 1896, p. 4, c. 3.
lw *Idaho Daily Statesman*, 22 November 1896, p. 6, c. 1.
lx *Idaho Daily Statesman*, 10 July 1897, p. 6, c. 1.
ly *Idaho Democrat*, Boise, 20 January 1897, p. 3, c. 1.
lz *Idaho Daily Statesman*, 16 March 1897, p. 3, c. 2.
ma *Evening Capital News*, 11 May 1911, p. 5, c. 1 & 2.
mb *Idaho Daily Statesman*, 11 May 1897, p. 6, c. 1.
mc *Idaho Daily Statesman*, 26 June 1897, p. 6, c. 1.
md Blaine County Judicial Records, Idaho State Historical Society, Microfilm reel 31, original page 618-621.
me *Idaho Daily Statesman*, 27 May 1897, p. 6, c. 1 & 2.
mf Blaine County Judicial Records, Idaho State Historical Society, Microfilm reel 31, original pages 622-625, and 626-629. The Sunrise was owned by Lemp, Falk, W. H. Savidge and B. B. Eldred and had been first claimed on 19 September 1892. The same men owned the Ohio which had originally been claimed the same day.
mg *Idaho Daily Statesman* 8 June 1897, p. 6, c. 1.
mh *Idaho Daily Statesman*, 20 March 1897, p. 30, c. 2 & 3. This is just an example of the many ads.
mi *Idaho Daily Statesman* 13 April 1897, p. 6, c. 1.
mj *Idaho Daily Statesman*, 13 August 1897, p. 6, c. 2.
mk *Idaho Daily Statesman*, 14 July 1897, p. 6, c. 2.
ml *Boise Sentinel*, 10 June 1897, p. 17, c. 3.
mm *Idaho Daily Statesman*, 15 August 1897, p. 6, c. 1.
mn *Idaho Daily Statesman*, 26 September 1897, p. 3, c. 1.
mo *Idaho Daily Statesman*, 12 September 1897, p. 6, c. 3.
mp *Idaho Daily Statesman*, 16 September 1897, p. 4, c. 4.
mq *Idaho Daily Statesman*, 17 October 1897, p. 2, c. 1 & 2.
mr *Idaho Daily Statesman*, 11 December 1897, p. 4, c. 1.
ms *Idaho Daily Statesman*, 21 December 1897, p. 5, . 3.
mt *Idaho Daily Statesman*, 21 December 1897, p. 5, c. 3.
mu *Idaho Daily Statesman*, 25 January 1898, p. 6, c. 1.

mv *The Weekly Capital*, Boise, 4 November 1899, p. 2, c. 3.
mw *The Elmore Bulletin*, Mountain Home, 15 December 1898, p. 3, c. 3.
mx *The Elmore Bulletin*, Mountain Home, 22 December 1898, p. 3, c. 5.
my *The Teton Peak*, Saint Anthony, Idaho, 13 May 1899, p. 2, c. 1.
mz *The Capital*, 28 April 1900, p. 3, c. 1.
na *The Evening Capital News*, 14 May 1901, p. 6, c. 2.
nb *The Evening Capital News*, 13 May 1901, p. 4, c. 2.
nc *Idaho Reports*, vol. 7, 1900-1901, pp. 677-686.
nd *Idaho Reports*, vol. 7, 1900-1901, pp. 677-686.
ne *Idaho Daily Statesman*, 4 January 1898, p. 6, c. 3.
nf *Idaho Daily Statesman*, 8 January 1898, p. 6, c. 2.
ng Idaho Daily Statesman, 23 January 1898, p. 5, c. 2.
nh *Idaho Daily Press*, 23 January 1898, p. 5, c. 2.
ni *Idaho Daily Statesman*, 16 December 1898, p. 6, c. 1 & 2.
nj *Idaho Daily Statesman*, 8 March 1898, p. 6, c. 2.
nk *Idaho Daily Statesman*, 24 February 1898, p. 6, c. 1.
nl *Idaho Daily Statesman*, 24 March 1898, p. 6, c. 1.
nm *The Elmore Bulletin*, Mountain Home, 30 March 1898, p. 3, c. 1.
nn *Elmore Bulletin*, Mountain Home, 6 April 1898, p. 3, c. 3.
no *Idaho Daily Statesman*, 24 April 1898, p. 6, c. 1.
np Mittelman, Amy. "The Politics of Alcohol Production: The Liquor Industry and the Federal Government, 1862-1900." Dissertation, Columbia University, 1986, p. 184.
nq *Idaho Daily Statesman*, 16 September 1898, p. 4, c. 1.
nr *Idaho Daily Statesman*, 20 September 1898, p. 4, c. 1.
ns *Idaho Daily Statesman*, 17 September 1898, p. 8, c. 1.
nt *Idaho Daily Statesman*, 10 November 1898, p. 6, c. 1.
nu *Idaho Daily Statesman*, 27 September 1898, p. 5, c. 3.
nv *Idaho Daily Statesman*, 8 November 1898, p. 4, c. 2-3.
nw *Idaho Daily Statesman* , 29 October 1898, p. 4, c. 3-6.
nx *Idaho Daily Statesman*, 20 June 1899, p. 2, c. 4.
ny *Idaho Daily Statesman*, 17 December 1898, p. 4, c. 2.
nz *Idaho Daily Statesman*, 18 December 1898, p. 4, c. 2.
oa *Idaho Daily Statesman*, 21 December 1898, p. 4, c. 2.
ob *Daily Capital News*, 14 January 1899, p. 4, c. 1.
oc *Daily Capital*, 19 January 1899, p. 4, c. 1.
od Hawley, *History of Idaho*, vol. 2, p. 18.
oe *The Capital News*, 26 January 1899, p. 8, c. 1.
of *Daily Capital*, 24 January 1899, p. 4, c. 2.

og *Idaho Daily Statesman*, 10 January 1899, p. 6, c. 1.
oh *Idaho Daily Statesman*, 20 January 1899, p. 2, c. 4.
oi *The Capital*, 20 February 1899, p. 1, c. 3.
oj *An Illustrated History of the State of Idaho*, 1899, p. 499.
ok *Idaho Daily Statesman*, 10 March 1899, p. 5, c. 2. 11 March 1899, p. 4, c. 2.
ol *The Capital*, 27 February 1899, p. 4, c. 2.
om *Idaho Daily Statesman*, 16 March 1899, p. 4, c. 2.
on *Idaho Daily Statesman*, 23 July 1899, p. 6, c. 2.
oo *Idaho Daily Statesman*, 25 July 1899, p. 4, c. 3.
op *Idaho Daily Statesman*, 1 August 1899, p. 6, c. 2.
oq *Idaho Daily Statesman*, 9 August 1899, p. 4, c. 2.
or *Idaho Daily Statesman*, 27 August 1899, p. 5, c. 2.
os *Idaho Daily Statesman*, 14 August 1899, p. 5, c. 3-4.
ot *Idaho Daily Statesman*, 19 August 1899, p. 3, c. 1-3.
ou *Idaho Daily Statesman*, 6 September 1899, p. 5, c. 1.
ov *Idaho Daily Statesman*, 19 November 1899, p. 8, c. 3.
ow *Idaho Daily Statesman*, 26 January 1901, p. 3, c. 3.
ox *Idaho Daily Statesman*, 12 September 1899, p. 4, c. 1.
oy *Idaho Daily Statesman*, 4 October 1899, p. 4, c. 1.
oz *Idaho Daily Statesman*, 5 October 1899, p. 4, c. 2.
pa *Idaho Daily Statesman*, 11 March 1899, p. 5, c. 2.
pb *Idaho Daily Statesman*, 26 March 1899, p. 4, c. 1.
pc *Idaho Daily Statesman*, 16 March 1899, p. 6, c. 1.
pd *Idaho Daily Statesman*, 13 May 1899, p. 5, c. 2. 21 May 1899, p. 4, c. 4. 28 May 1899, p. 4, c. 2.
pe *The Weekly Capital*, 10 June 1899, p. 7, c. 1. Idaho Daily Statesman, 7 June 1899, p. 4, c. 1.
pf *Idaho Daily Statesman*, 23 May 1899, p. 2, c. 3.
pg *Idaho Daily Statesman*, 30 July 1899, p. 8, c. 1.
ph *Idaho Daily Statesman*, 29 December 1900, p. 4, c. 3.
pi *The Teton Peak*, Saint Anthony, Idaho, 14 October 1899, p. 2, c. 1.
pj *The Capital*, 9 February 1901, p. 8, c. 3. 8 December 1900, p. 3, c. 2. At first the amount was reported as $300.
pk *The Weekly Capital*, 23 December 1899, p. 14, c. 4.
pl *Idaho Daily Statesman*, 24 December 1899, p. 12, c. 1.
pm *Idaho Daily Statesman*, 1 January 1900, p. 2, c. 1.
pn *Idaho Daily Statesman*, 2 January 1900, p. 6, c. 2.
po *Idaho Daily Statesman*, 3 January 1900, p. 6, c. 2.

pp *The Weekly Capital*, 6 January 1900, p.4, c. 4. Idaho Daily Statesman, 4 January 1900, p. 6, c. 2.
pq *Idaho Daily Statesman*n, 9 January 1900, p. 4, c. 4.
pr *Idaho Daily Statesman*, 12 April 1900, p. 5, c. 4.
ps *Idaho Daily Statesman*, 19 January 1900, p. 4, c. 4.
pt *Idaho Daily Statesman*, 3 February 1900, p. 4, c. 1.
pu *Idaho Daily Statesman*, 24 February 1900, p. 6, c. 2.
pv *Idaho Daily Statesman*, 29 March 1900, p. 5, c. 1.
pw *Idaho Daily Statesman*, 21 March 1900, p. 6, c. 1.
px *Idaho Daily Statesman*, 22 March 1900, p. 4, c. 3.
py *Idaho Daily Statesman*, 20 July 1900, p. 4, c. 3.
pz *Idaho Daily Statesman*, 29 March 1900, p. 6, c. 1.
qa *Idaho Daily Statesman*, 4 April 1900, p. 6, c. 1.
qb *Idaho Daily Statesman*, 12 May 1900, p. 4, c. 1.
qc *Wood River Times*, Weekly, Hailey, 14 November 1900, p. 4, c. 2.
qd *Idaho Daily Statesman*, 27 May 1900, p. 3, c. 1. 31 May 1900, p. 3, c. 1-3.
qe *Idaho Daily Statesman*, 30 June 1900, p. 6, c. 1.
qf *Idaho Daily Statesman*, 12 July 1900, p. 4, c. 2-3.
qg *Idaho Daily Statesman*, 13 July 1900, p. 3, c. 2.
qh Hawley, *History of Idaho, The Gem of the Mountains*, vol. 3, p. 622, p. ?
qi *Idaho Daily Statesman*, 16 September 1900, p. 7, c. 3.
qj *The Teton Peak*, Saint Anthony, Idaho, 6 September 1900, p. 2, c. 1.
qk *Idaho Daily Statesman*, 23 December 1900, p. 4, c. 1.
ql George Everett, *Champagne in a Tin Cup: Uptown Butte and the Stories Behind the Facades*. p. 25.

Part III

1901 to 1912

ON 3 JANUARY 1901, Albert C. Lemp, son of John and Catherine, took Lucile Weaver, daughter of General and Mrs. J. L. Weaver, as his bride.[a] The ceremony was at the bride's Boise home and only twenty-seven immediate family members were present. The Episcopal Priest, C. E. Deuel, officiated. There was a luncheon after the ceremony and the bride and groom then left to their new apartment. The Lemp nest was inexorably emptying as the new century arrived.

Five days later, on January 8 of 1901, John Lemp filed a land patent on 73.541 acres in Custer County, Idaho, under the authority of the Mineral Patent-Lode Act of 1866.[b] His interest in investing in mines was not flagging as he entered the middle of his seventh decade.

On the 25th, John was coming home and about to enter his house when he slipped on the ice on the porch and broke a small bone just above his ankle.[c] The press described John as over 60 and weighing over 200 pounds, yet the injury was not terribly serious. "It would seem quite serious but the doctors in attendance think he can get out on crutches in about two week's time."[d] A couple of days later the word was that he was doing nicely and would be able to sit up about the house in a few days.[e] This was fortunate since his daughter Ida was being married the next day.

On 29 January 1901, Ida Catherine Lemp married Edward H. Kessberger of Springfield, Illinois. Reverend Deuel, rector of the Episcopal church, again—as he had with Albert four weeks before—performed the ceremony which was held at the Lemp residence at high noon.[f] Kessberger was described as an enterprising businessman of Springfield, Illinois. The bride wore a "beautiful white dress of Cross-grain silk, cut en train and trimmed with white chiffon and rare laces. The family veil was worn and the bride carried in her hand a beautiful bouquet of white carnations and a real lace handkerchief, the present of her sister, Mrs. E. G. Hurt. Brother Edward Lemp was groom's man and Miss Louise Lemp acted as maid. The happy couple took the train for Springfield and their new residence the next morning." Two marriages in one month was quite a way to start a new century.

John Lemp's new brewing rival in Boise was Alsace-born Henry Muntzer, principal owner of the Idaho Brewing Company. He came from Butte where he had owned The Butte Brewing Company, and planned to continue living in Montana. Lemp never developed any obvious business or personal connections with Muntzer as he had with his predecessor, John Brodbeck. Muntzer's manager was Rupert Maxgut, also from Butte but he had worked at the rival Centennial Brewery.

Lemp renewed his county liquor license bond at about this time.[g] In February, Mr. and Mrs. A. Roderick Grant returned to Boise from a two month trip to the East.[h] They reported that they had visited all the principle points of interest and had a most enjoyable time.[i] This was Grant's first trip east in ten years and his wife's—the former Miss Lemp—first trip ever across the Rockies. She had apparently missed her sister's wedding.

Work on a new headgate for the Lemp Canal was progressing in late February of 1901.[j] A report the next month gave the detail that the whole canal had been enlarged from a capacity of 7,000 inches to 10,000. This was needed because more acres were constantly being put under cultivation.[k] In July, the Lemp Canal at Boise, ten miles long with seventy-five miles of laterals, was sold for $100,000.[l] The canal took water from the Boise River just below the railway bridges and irrigated the area around White Cross. President B. F. Olden of the Bank of Commerce was reported to be the representative of the buyers.[m] The next day the *Statesman* corrected its original report that eastern parties were buying it, and said the sale was to a local, newly formed corporation.[n]

John Lemp • The Beer Baron of Boise 199

Many who were originally involved with the canal had lost heart and were discouraged by the difficulties of construction. Lemp had never faltered though it cost him a fortune. There had been difficulties with slides, breaks, and quicksand, but when completed, it had been a great

Ida Catherine Lemp
Photo, Idaho State Historical Society

boon to the area.º One source said the canal "is understood to have crippled [Lemp]."ᵖ The actual transfer of the canal was in October.ᑫ The officers of the new company were B. F. Olden, president; C. E. Brainard, vice president; H. N. Elkington; manager; and Charles Fifer. The board included these men plus General George M. Parsons. They planned to increase the 12,000 acres it watered by adding over

Typical newspaper ad for Lemp's Dry Goods store. Idaho Statesman.

60 miles of new laterals, and to change the terminus, which was near Nampa. Lemp was paid $100,000 in bonds of the canal company and they took out an option on his 1800 acres of land in the area.[r] The company was actively recruiting in the East for more farmers to come settle the new area which their expansion of the canal would make tillable for the first time.

A biographical sketch of Lemp from 1902 praised his canal work and said it "now waters hundreds of producing acres and enables many people to have pretty incomes returning homes that otherwise must have plodded along surrounded by sand and sage brush."[s] On Smith Prairie in the northwest part of adjacent Canyon County the old BVTRR (Boise Valley Traction) station adopted the name "Lemp Town."[t] The area lived by irrigation and it was honoring the supporter of that irrigation. The original Post Office was established in 1869 as Lower Boise but later discontinued. The Post Office, with Lemp's name, lasted from 1901 to 1904. This was near to the town later called "Notus."

W. E. Pierce and Company, "The old reliable Real Estate Dealers," were advertising lots in the Lemp Addition for "a home, or a safe and profitable investment."[u] By late March, Lemp was out on the street with the aid of crutches.[v] In April of 1901, while the canal business was progressing, John and Catherine Lemp continued to sell lots in their addition which then cost about $150 each.[w] Lemp, as many others, renewed his county liquor license for a whole year at this time. Nathan Falk and Max Mayfield were his sureties on both licenses, while son Albert Lemp joined with Leo Grunbaum to guarantee the bond of O. B. Truesdale for his saloon.[x]

THE LEMP DRY GOODS STORE

The Lemp dry goods store featured orchestra music on Saturday, April the 6th, to help sell their "Matchless Spring Merchandise."[y] In May, 1901, *The Evening Capital News* ran a contest to see which self-supporting lady of Boise would get the most votes for a free trip to the Pan-American Exposition in Buffalo, New York.[z] Mae Oliver, an employee at the Lemps Dry Goods Store was in fourth place throughout much of the contest. She finally finished third with 9,388 votes behind Mabel O'Connor and winner Emily L. Driscoll.[aa]

Another Lemp employee, Ed Weiser, took his family to Schafer Creek for a summer outing and to hopeful kill a cougar reported in the vicinity.[ab] The store had attractive display ads in *The Evening Capital News* during the Fall clothing season.[ac] The largest shipment of children's ready to wear dresses, from 50 cents to $7.50, as well as jackets in all colors, sizes, and prices, were offered.

In March, 1902, Lemp's Dry Goods Store donated $25 to the fund for a road to the latest and greatest mineral discovery in Idaho, Thunder Mountain.[ad] Lemp's store advertised blankets from $1 to $9, twenty-five cent socks, $2 quilts and 50 cent underwear in April of 1902.[ae] The store offered a $15 suit of clothes as one of the prizes in a bicycle race that June.[af] Bicycle races were the rage at that time. Lemp's Dry Goods Store was shown in a special photo section on the delights of Boise in *The Evening Capital News* in August of 1902.[ag] In September, W. B. Connor returned from his buying trip to the east. He had been making purchases for the Lemp store.[ah] He said the trip was pleasant but he was kept busy, and the many novelties turned out in the East assured there would be many more choices for his consumers in the months ahead. Clerk Olga Bengston left her employment at Lemp's Dry Goods store to return to her home in Minnesota.[ai] In 1904 son-in-law William Connor, who was still working for Lemp, again returned from his annual purchasing trip to the East—New York in particular.[aj]

The Lemp Dry Goods Store, "one of the most enterprising stores [in Boise]," came up with the idea of providing free lunch to its customers between 1 and 2 p.m. "The luncheon proved to be a success in every way from the number of people who called during the hour and the shoppers took advantage of it as in this way they could do what shopping they wished during the hourly sales the store had on, and not have to leave the store during the noon hour for their luncheon."[ak]

As plans for the Fourth of July developed in 1905, Lemp's dry goods store pledged to put a float in the parade.[al] Meanwhile, W.B. Connor left for New York one more time to make more fall purchases for the Lemp dry goods store.[am] The store also received interior improvements to make it lighter and more attractive.[an] More storage space was allowed to meet the increased demand, the management claimed.

Another big contest in *The Evening Capital News* encouraged votes for young women and the winner was to get a free piano.[ao] Miss Alice Russell who worked at Lemp's Dry Goods Store received a lot of votes but was between 5th and 10th place most of the time.

Lew W. Ensign, one of the most prominent men of Meadows in Washington County, was visiting Boise in October, 1907 when he went into Lemp's Drygoods store to buy a hat.[ap] Soon a detective grabbed him for passing a counterfeit bill.

Newspaper ad for Lemp's Dry Goods store. *Idaho Statesman.*

He was taken to the police station and made to furnish a $10 bond before being released. When he went to lunch later he learned it was all a practical joke—a payback for the joke he pulled on Harry Shellworth when that Boiseian had visited Ensign's hometown the summer before. On that occasion Ensign made up a yarn that Shellworth shot at a chicken and killed a pig. Shellworth had suffered greatly from that story for a year but had now gained revenge.

When Wilfred Gardiner who had worked in the clothing department of the Wheeler-Motter Store left to go to the dress goods department of Lemp's Dry Goods Store it was worthy of mention in the press.[aq] A report on Boise business conditions in November of 1907, gave information from an unnamed source that the Lemp Dry Goods Store was doing just as well as it had ever been and expected good sales to continue.[ar] A recession was causing many to question how well America's businesses were doing at that time.

A piece that was a cross between an advertisement and a news report appeared in *The Evening Capital News* on April 4, 1908 under the headline "Police Called Out to Stop Mule Show."[as] Lemp's clothing store conducted a "Dynamic sale" in which they cut prices in two and even threw away merchandise from the roof of the store to the crowd of several thousand onlookers "who furnished amusement to all by their wild scramble for the articles." P. A. Pyles, special sale agent of Baltimore had the idea for the sale. When "Mary and Ezra" drove the store's prize mule, hitched to a barrel, up and down the street the police ordered them to go to a back street so as not to disrupt traffic. "The sale was one of the most successful conducted in Boise and decidedly one of the most novel."

Newspaper advertisements throughout April, 1908 extolled the continuance of the Lemp's Dynamic Sale.[at] Crowds, they claimed, were immense. In May, they offered a prize of $25 to the largest load of women brought to town. J. H. Peters brought 40 to 50 on one hayrack which had a sign on the side: "Lemp's or Bust."[au]

The window at Lemp's store displayed some handsome pheasant cocks and the afternoon newspaper took the occasion to remind people that they were not native and had only been loose in America about twenty years.[av] The first had been released in Oregon and afforded five years of protection during which they had multiplied rapidly. The ones in Lemp's window were from the Steven's ranch on the Boise bench where large number were being prepared to be released into the wilds of Idaho.

The dry goods store was soon advertising their greatest sale in history.[aw] The trophies to be awarded to the winners of the second annual tournament of the Idaho State Sportsman's association were put on display in the window in May.[ax] Then a shock came. Lemp's dry goods store ran large newspaper ads in May and June, 1908, that they were going to quit business, and everything was being sold at a great discount.[ay] There were a number of clothing stores in Boise including the long established Falk store and the Cohen & McDevitt store. Profits must have declined.

By July, the Lemp store was selling shoes for 98 cents and continuing to liquidate the store.[az] Miss Alice Russell left the employ of the store and went back home to New Ulm, Minnesota.[ba] At some point that Fall the door was shut for good.

Lemp's real estate was involved with another contribution to new technology in Boise about this time. The store room of his defunct dry goods store was remodeled into the Dreamland Moving Picture Company which would feature "high class moving picture show [s]."[bb]

About the end of that December a new shoe store run by William G. Schmelzel and Mr. Ray took over part of the building.[bc]

BACK TO 1901

The new company headed by Henry Muntzer began massive remodeling on Brodbeck's old brewery all during January, February and beyond in 1901. There was a new bottling works, new refrigeration equipment, and a new smoke stack. The era of fewer, larger breweries was noticeably beginning in Idaho. The Lemp brewery inadvertently received some bad publicity in late May when 24 Salvation Army members decided to march through "the alley", the quasi-legal prostitution area in Boise, to protest that institution.[bd] They marched from their barracks to the rear of Lemp's brewery and conducted their devotional exercises there. Eventually they addressed a crowd of 300. The police chief believed they had gone too far and were guilty of blocking a thoroughfare.

Meanwhile, Albert Lemp and his recent bride moved into the house owned by Mr. H. Neiberding.[be] The city council of Boise took action to establish a sewer system in the north section of town. The rapid settlement of people in the Lemp, Bannock, McCarty, Arnold, Bryon, Locust Grove, Hyde Park and Resseguie additions made this a necessity.[bf]

In mid-April, John was recovered enough from his broken ankle to visit several of his businesses with the aid of crutches.[bg] It had taken considerably longer than two weeks. The Rocky Mountain Bell Telephone company published a list of their subscribers in late April of 1901.[bh] This was like a small phone book on one page of the newspaper. Phones were far from ubiquitous at that time. John Lemp's residence was 62-N, Lemp Dry Goods Store was 112-N, The Capitol Hotel (operated by Frank Blackinger) was 132.

The Rocky Mountain Bell Company had been organized out of Ogden, Utah in 1883, and reached Boise in 1891. At that time it had extra stations at Silver City and Idaho City and long distance calls went through the company's first Idaho site at Hailey.[bi] A single operator was sufficient in the early days.

The Capital Evening News polled prominent men on the issue of municipal ownership of the water system in Boise in April, 1901.[bj]

The old system could be purchased, or a new one built, either option would involve a $120,000 bond issue. Albert Lemp was one of those consulted. Al replied : "No, to all four of the questions. Taxes are too high now."

Lemp's son-in-law A. Roderick Grant, "well known traveling man of Portland," was at the Capitol Hotel in early May and reported that business in the northwest was "never in a more flourishing condition than now."[bk]

Louise Lemp and Bernard Lemp enjoyed a day with many other children celebrating the 12th birthday of Alice Springer at Green Meadow ranch in May of 1901.[bl] Bernard's future wife, Leona Tucker, was returning home to Placerville after a visit to Garden Valley at this time.[bm] In late May, John was healed and navigating well enough to visit Meridian and look after affairs on his ranch there.[bn] Lemp's old friend Senator William A. Clark of Montana married off his son William Jr. to Miss Mabel Foster that month.[bo] The Senator gave them a magnificent home on Fifth Avenue in New York and a million dollars for a wedding gift. This didn't break the Senator, for the next month he bought the *Salt Lake Herald* for $60,000.[bp]

In June, the Boise City Council passed an ordinance to build a six foot cement sidewalk in several areas of Boise and to dun the property owners for the cost.[bq] Herr Lemp was accessed $138.99 for one piece of property, $236.98 for another, and $111.11 for frontage on blocks 34, 72 and 73 that he owned.[br] Apparently Lemp was not too badly crippled financially for he was listed as the second highest taxpayer in Ada county in August of 1901 with $185,436 in assessed property.[bs] As nearly always, improvements in the city of Boise cost John Lemp more than anyone else.

The next month, Lemp sold the west half of lot 10, block 3, to Fong Suey for $3,800.[bt] Fong Suey was an American-born citizen and was acting on behalf of the Chinese Masonic tong.[bu] They planned to build a three story building with retail space on street level, sleeping rooms on the second floor, and a lodge hall and temple on the third. The project was assisted by a $13,000 loan from a local banker.

In July of 1901, an International Mining Congress was held in Boise and a special issue of the *Evening Capital News* described the mining and business conditions in all of Idaho.[bv] In their description of the

Artesian Hot and Cold Water Company, John Lemp was listed as one of the original and current directors. The company had a history of good management and large dividends.

That same month, Julius Grunbaum, brother of liquor dealer Leo, visited Chicago and scouted out the available types and makes of that new invention, the automobile.[bw] O. B. Truesdale had decided to purchase one and be the first to bring a horseless carriage to the streets of Boise. Before long John Lemp would follow the trend and have one also.

That August, Harry McDonald, a 37 year old Californian in the employ of Lemp, died. He had been ill about a month and the diagnosis was muscular rheumatism.[bx] A large number of Boiseans, including Mrs. John Lemp and party, spent August at Payette Lakes.[by] This area near McCall has been a recreation site ever since. After two weeks, Mrs. Lemp and family, and sister-in-law Mrs. Jaumann returned to Boise. "Ed and Bernard Lemp acted as scouts and conducted the party home overland."[bz]

Lemp's son-in-law, W. B. Connor, was selected for the trial jury pool for the upcoming September session.[ca] Other son-in-law A. Roderick Grant was visiting Boise representing the Blumauer-Frank Company of Portland.[cb]

Mrs. Lemp and daughter Louise went to Portland and Salem for a visit in the Fall of 1901. In Portland, they visited daughter and sister, Mrs. Grant, and in Salem they saw Mrs. Lemp's sister, Mrs. Adolph and her daughter.[cc] Mrs. Lemp's niece, Miss Adolph, came back to Boise for a visit with her aunt when the group returned in November.[cd]

In September of 1901, the Boise Rapid Transit Company directors met and announced that earnings had doubled and ridership was up due to the new 20 minute service and the increased population and business level in Boise.[ce] Lemp was on their board of directors and a member of the executive committee.

There was a move at this time to annex the housing addition built by former brewery owner John Krall to the city limits of Boise.[cf] Albert Lemp and his wife signed the petition to the Boise City Council asking for a special election on the issue.

John Lemp sold 50 feet of property on the corner of Ninth and Main to the Western Surety and Trust Company late in that month of September, 1901.^{cg} The *Evening Capital News* ran a headline that said "The Big Lemp Deal a Certainty," and gloated about how they had scooped the *Statesman* on this news.^{ch} This was the 50 by 122 foot lot then occupied by "The Market," and for which Lemp was paid $30,000.^{ci} The purchasing company in this case was a Boise and Chicago financial institution.^{cj} Mr. Day and Mr. Everett, Chicago members of the company, had been in Boise working on the deal for some time. They planned to build a six story steel business building on the newly acquired land. John agreed to put up a structure that was an exact duplicate of this new building on adjoining lots that he still owned. It was to be the largest and best business structure between Salt Lake and Portland. A few weeks later Lemp's intentions were reconfirmed in the newspaper and the report said the building would cost him $100,000.^{ck} In late October, the sale was reported in escrow and a Chicago architect was preparing a sketch.^{cl} As Winter reached the mid-point, the next February, the *Statesman* again confirmed that Lemp would erect a 5-story building and the two together would have 100 feet of frontage.^{cm}

The Odd Fellows held their state-wide yearly convention in Boise in October of 1901, among the many festivities was honoring and having a photo taken for the newspaper of the seven men who had been in continuous service in the lodge for 25 years.^{cn} The picture showed H. Sellers, Nathan Falk, D. F. Baker, John Atkinson, R. E. Emerson, J. H. Van Pelt, and, in the rear center of the photo, John Lemp.

John Lemp and Nathan Falk signed a power of attorney dated 22 October 1901 for Lyttleton Price of Blaine County, where most of their mining interests were, to represent them in the purchase and patent of government mineral lands.^{co} The W. E. Pierce real estate company continued to advertise choice lots in the Lemp Addition for only $150 with easy terms.^{cp}

In late October, the Boise City Council held a special session to consider building a new flume for carrying the waters from Hull's gulch in the north part of the city, to the Perrault ditch.^{cq} The current flume of 1950 feet was built of one inch planks and was not sufficient to handle heavy run off. They considered building a new flume or condemning a new right of way along the mountain side on the property of John Lemp. Boise city filed suit in December of 1901 against John

Lemp and three others to condemn a right-of-way through their property to put in a waste ditch from Hull's gulch.[cr] In Caldwell, Lemp sued A.B. Anderson, as administrator of the estate of John Nelson, for a foreclosure.[cs] Anderson entered a default.

John Ruckdaschel, long time Lemp employee, died of dropsy in Mid-November of 1901. He was remembered as a German immigrant, former navy and later infantry man, a member of the Ancient Order of United Workman—who conducted the funeral—and a father of six.

Son-in-law and former business partner W. B. Connor managed to get himself arrested by the sheriff of Boise County in December of 1901.[ct] In September, he had gone through the Basin area soliciting and taking order for clothing on behalf Wanamaker & Brown, Philadelphia clothiers.[cu] Since he still worked for his father-in-law, most likely the clothing was to be sold via Lemp's store. He had no peddler's license and when told of this shortcoming allegedly said he would get one. He did not get one but then said he would if he were allowed to leave Boise County. He returned to Boise city (Ada County) but still did not get a license. A warrant was issued for his arrest and Sheriff Mills went down the mountain to serve it. Conner was arrested but he was immediately released on his own recognizance and a writ of habeus corpus was filed on his behalf. Judge Stewart denied the writ and and remanded Connor to the custody of Sheriff J. Mills.[cv] The case centered on the right of the legislature to pass a tax on peddlers. This turned out to be a minor event.

John and son Albert both signed a published petition opposing the newly passed Boise ordinance against laundries and wash houses in town. [cw]

1902

Lemp donated $500 to the fund for the purchase of a fair grounds and the building of a permanent structure for the state fair.[cx]

GIBBARD VS. LEMP

William H. Gibbard sued Lemp in the district Court that January of 1902.[cy] Gibbard had been superintendent of the Lemp Canal and was due, he alleged, $714.56 in back pay for 1 January to 1 November of 1901, and $200 for 20 tons of hay he furnished to Lemp. At the initial court session the demurrer was withdrawn and Lemp was given a few days to answer.[cz] H.S. Worthman represented Gibbard.[da] The case drug on through legal delays but was finally before the Idaho Supreme Court in December of 1905.[db] H. S. Worthman and S. Tipton represented Gibbard, while Morrison and Pence were the attorneys of record for Lemp. Yes, this was J. C. Pence of the Lemp-Pence War. John Lemp seemed incapable of holding a grudge. In early February, Gibbard, "superintendent of the Settlers Canal Company," hurriedly returned to Ripon, Wisconsin, after receiving a telegram informing him of the death of his father.[dc] This may have postponed the court date. In early May, the execution in the case of W. H. Gibbard vs. Lemp was reported stayed until May 20th.[dd] It was actually rescheduled in District Court for the 18th of May 1905.[de] Judge Smith denied the motion for judgment against the surety (John Lemp) on the appeal bond.[df] Attorney S. L. Tipton argued the appeal of John Lemp.[dg] Lemp claimed he gave Gibbard $298.02 worth of clothing, dry goods, wines, liquors and cigars, paid him cash of $168.55 and delivered him $168.57 worth of water for irrigation. The referee, Frank Wyman, had come up with the judgment amount. Gibbard had appealed but it was dismissed because it had not been filed or served in the required time. S. L. Tipton and Harry S. Worthman appeared for Gibbard, and Morrison and Pence represented Lemp. The court took the matter under advisement.

Coincidentally, the grading outfit of Wilkerson and Thompson was in Boise to begin expanding the Settlers Canal. The newspaper report mentioned that the canal was formerly known as the Lemp Canal.[dh] Lemp was also granted $7.10 for a tax rebate by Ada County in early February.[di]

The Germans of Boise—in fact, all the Teutons of Idaho—were invited to a social on the 11th of February in 1902 at the G.A.R. hall.[dj] The committee organizing this was John Lemp; former brewery owner John Brodbeck; Lemp brother-in-law, Charles Leyerzaph; General John Greene; brewery manager, Rupert Maxgut; former Moscow and Spokane brewer, Louis Koehler; John Nagel; M. Klinge; Ben Kurs; and August J. Moritz. The Gambrinus (brewers) brotherhood was well represented. They sent out a call for all Germans of Boise to join them at the Grand Army of the Republic hall for a social.[dk] Dancing

and speechmaking in the German language were the order of the day.
[dl] Refreshments were served at intervals throughout the evening. John Lemp made a short address in which he spoke of the pleasure it gave him to see the German citizens all gathered together after so many years, and he hoped it would be the first of many gastherings to be held in the future. Rupert Maxgut, Idaho Brewery manager, then spoke, followed by a humerous recitation by Mrs. Heuschel and C. E. Kaufer.

Son-in-law Roderick Grant of Portland was in Boise again during March.[dm]

John Lemp had a direct involvement in the first production of sugar beets in the Boise Valley when he sold 60 acres in section 25, 11 miles east of Boise to Jacob Burblock, formerly of Nebraska.[dn] The beet processing factory was to provide the seed, and twenty to twenty-five tons of beets per acre were the expected yield. If the project proved successful more German families from Nebraska would come to farm the same crop.

L. L. Lemp (Albert's wife Lucille) was one of nine who filed on a placer location near the Charcoal Gulch and Boise River confluence in early April of 1902.[do] Her parents, the Weavers, were also owners. It seems unlikely that she was personally prospecting. In December of 1903, a placer claim was filed on 160 acres for each individual located in township 5, range 3 east. The mining areas were the Grey Wolf, White Swan, Lucille, Mallard Duck, Butter Ball, Coyote, Gray Swan, Red Fox and Porcupine claims, and Lucile Lemp was again one of the owners of this collective enterprise.[dp]

On 9 April 1902, Albert Carl Lemp and his wife had a new daughter, and John and Catherine a new granddaughter: Katherine Ida Lemp was born.[dq] Adjutant General Weaver was now a proud grandfather too.

Also in April of 1902, the Sons of Hermann, a branch of the German American Alliance, was organized in Boise with 54 charter members. "Officers elected included C. Kauffen, C. Hummel, John Salfer, W. E. Steineck, Henry Konrad, Charles Koehler, and Drs. Blitz and Boeck."[dr] Lemp was pleased.

That same month, the Ada County Commissioners approved Lemp's bonds for his two saloon licenses.[ds] Lemp also filed a suit that month for $203 in the justice court of T. M. Herrick against Frances and John Keegan to recover a long standing board bill.[dt] An alias summons was published which explained that the debt was incurred between 1 January 1897 and 1 May 1898 in Boise, and Lemp was charging them seven percent interest.[du]

Mrs. E. H. Kessberger and her brother-in-law A. W. Kessberger came to Boise from Illinois to visit her parents, the Lemps.[dv] The visitors probably also wanted to see her new niece, the infant daughter of Mr. and Mrs. Albert Lemp. Albert returned from a two-week trip to the St. Louis area about this time, having sold six carloads of horses for the southern market.[dw] He said market conditions were satisfactory and he disposed of the shipment at good prices.

On May 28 at 8:00 p.m., Lemp's niece, Jennie Leyerzaph married Martin Kline at the home of the bride in Boise.[dx] Catholic Bishop Glorieux performed the ceremony. The bride wore a white silk mull gown and carried bride's roses. Miss Annie Leyerzaph, sister of the bride, was the maid of honor. Mr. Hurt was best man. The house was decorated in white calla lilies, carnations and roses.

A break in the Phylls Canal near Caldwell in May of 1902 created a real hardship for the settlers who had been counting on the water.[dy] Mr. Charles Fifer, manager of the "Lemp Canal," and Mr. R. E. Green, manager of the Ridenbaugh, each allowed about 2,000 inches of water from their canals to run in free to help the situation. They even had to dig a small stretch to allow the connection. They were warmly thanked. Of course, Mr. Lemp was no longer the owner of the canal which still was popularly known by his name.

A month later, the Boise City Irrigation Canal and Land Company (Ridenbaugh Canal Company) sued the Settlers Ditch Company, the Bank of Commerce, John Lemp and B. F. Olden.[dz] The complainants said they had built ditches to catch waste water and return it to the main canals. The respondents, it was alleged, had taken possession of some of these ditches. They sought a perpetual injunction. Lemp was probably involved because he held the paper on the canal and had not yet been paid in full.

In early June, another listing of the donations to the Thunder Mountain road fund was published with John Lemp one of the $200 donors.[ea] John suffered a badly fractured left arm in mid-June as the result of a runaway in which he nearly lost his life.[eb] John, with son Edward, was on Shafer Creek on business driving between Emmett and Boise when they left George Cartwright's place early in the morning with two horses and a top buggy. They were twenty-two miles from Boise, almost at the top of the steepest mountain road in the country, known, ironically, as Lemp's hill, when their team was frightened by a pack train of burros. The horses became unmanageable, so Edward jumped down and seized them by their heads. He seemed to be quieting them when they suddenly whirled around and headed down the grade at breakneck speed. Edward had the lines in his hands and was dragged some distance before he became entangled in the underbrush and had to let go. John sat helpless in the buggy, clinging to the seat and expecting imminent death, as the horses plunged down the slope.

At the very bottom of the ravine the wheels struck a large rock and the buggy was capsized, throwing John into the air. Edward made his way down to the spot of the wreck to find his father unconscious. John had fallen among thick briar bushes which cushioned his landing and saved his life. Another buggy was rounded up to bring John back to Boise and he arrived about 3:00 p.m. Dr. Springer found many bruises, cuts and a left arm broken badly just above the elbow. Springer put the severely swollen arm in a temporary cast to wait until the swelling subsided. Lemp was resting after this ordeal but his rheumatism began to bother him. The break was probably caused by his arm being twisted in the ribs of the buggy as he was hurled into the air. The plan was to take him to St. Alphonsus hospital to examine the arm with the new medical invention, an x-ray machine. Overall, it was quite an ordeal for a 64 year old man.

A few days later, the evening newspaper reported that Lemp spent a most restless night but was somewhat improved.[ec] Mayor Moses Alexander paid his respects to John Lemp at a special meeting of the city council.[ed] Mr. Lemp, through his attorneys, asked for a rebate on the $57.68 he was charged in penalties for failure to pay the special assessment in sewer district No. 3. John Haynes and county attorney Frawley appeared at the meeting in Lemp's behalf.

That July, John installed a set of luxurious transom lights in his main street store to allow light into the back of the room.[ee] These were Luxifer prism transoms which were designed to light up the whole room.[ef] Maybe this made John seem wealthier, for when the county board of equalization met that August, his lots 11 and 12 of block 10 were raised in value from $20,625 to $30,625.[eg]

A biographical sketch of Lemp published in the *Evening Capital News* summer supplement told Lemp's life story with some new details, and gave a snapshot study of the brewery at that time.[ch] They said it turned out several thousand barrels per year of pure malt and hops beer with no adulterants. Worries about pure food and drugs had captured the public imagination at this time. Lemp employed 210 men per year but the article did not break down the number for each of his businesses. Lemp continued to daily attend to his business affairs with son Albert being his chief of staff.

Lemp's house was shown in the *Statesman* that July and the article emphasized the majestic maple tree that they said he had planted in 1868.[ei] It was symmetrical, 80 feet high and branched into four limbs at eight feet above the ground. The *Evening Capital News* had a similar photo in late August.[ej]

Mrs. Albert Lemp and daughter, Miss Ida Katherine Lemp, were among the guests at a lawn party in honor of the birthday of Miss Mary Kenneth Ross in late August of 1902.[ek] The little child was being introduced to the Boise social scene.

In September, John Lemp was healed enough to be back visiting Hailey for a few days.[el] When he returned to Boise he entered his horses in the Ada County Fair. John won a first for the best three year old and up Clydesdale stallion; a first for the best three year old Purcheron stallion; first for a three year old mare with foal; first for a one-year old filley; second for best foal of 1902; second for best stallion of any age; first for best stallion with those of his gait over seven years old; first for best pair of matched draft horses; first and second for best 1902 filly or entire; first for best filly or entire, one year old.[em] Quite a show of excellence for one entrant.

Lemp sold five lots in his addition to C.P. Rader for $1,000 that month also.[en] The government tax on beer was lowered to $1 per barrel from the Spanish-American War increase to $2.

At the Boise Rapid Transit Company's stockholder meeting that September of 1902 Lemp was again elected to the executive committee.[eo] The company vowed to secure new power and make other new improvements.

At the Republican primaries in September of 1902 there was a major factional schism between the Borah ticket that favored the future Senator and the Anti-Borah ticket that obviously did not.[ep] Albert Lemp was nominated as a delegate to the party convention from precinct two. He finally received 146 votes on the Borah ticket and 36 on the Anti-Borah ticket to assure his selection.[eq] Borah won overwhelmingly and earned the support of the entire Republican Party in his bid to be United States Senator. He needed to be elected by the state legislature, not the voters.

The next month, daughter Ida won second place at the Canyon County fair for her dairy cheese.[er] A Lemp, with no other name listed, also won second for patchwork quilt, and crazy bedspread.[es]

W. B. Conner, no longer in legal trouble in Boise Basin, left for Chicago to visit with friends in late November.[et]

Lemp sold some Custer County mining property to John P. Gray near the end of December.

1903

In January of 1903, John made a brief business trip to Caldwell to welcome the new year.[eu] A. R. Grant (listed now as a resident of Walla Walla, not Portland), son-in-law, left for home at that time after a long visit with John.[ev] John and many others paid their $500 for their county liquor licenses at the April second meeting of the county commissioners.[ew]

At Lemp's ranch in Crane gulch there was a fatal shooting in early April of 1903.[ex] W. A. Graham, who was employed by his father J. M. Graham to cut cottonwood on the Lemp ranch, came into Boise with the message that Charley Hygh had shot and killed Lee "Jim" Singh. Singh was a cook at the ranch.[ey] A deputy went to the ranch and brought Hygh to the jail, and Singh to Glover's undertaking parlor. Hygh, who was described as a weak-minded old man, told his version of the events. He and Singh had disagreed about who should use a certain cooking basin and the "Chinaman" got so quarrelsome Hygh ordered him off the ranch. A few minutes later Sing appeared in Hygh's bedroom with an ax. Hygh picked up a Winchester rifle intending, he said, to hit Jim with it. Unbeknownst to him it was cocked and loaded and went off accidentally with an immediate fatal effect.

Both Grahams testified at the coroner's inquest that Hygh told Singh to drop the ax which he did. The shot was fired immediately after that. W.A. Graham said he saw Hygh work a cartridge into the chamber and afterwards point the gun directly at Singh and fire. Graham Sr. said Sing was an inoffensive old Chinaman and did not provoke the assault. Hygh was a partial invalid who was easily provoked to uncontrollable anger. Singh had been in America for forty-one of his sixty-three years and had worked for John Lemp doing odd jobs the last ten years. Charley Hygh was sixty-five and had been a freighter for twenty-eight years. He was employed cutting wood at the ranch. The coroner's jury ruled that Hygh shot and killed Sing but they did not add any reference to criminal intent. In March of 1903, Judge Herrick bound over Charles Hygh to answer a charge of murder.[ez] Hygh was described as a paralytic and mentally deficient.

Lemp's horse ranch at Middleton was in the news in early April of 1903.[fa] His famous stallions, "Douglas," and "Dewey," were brought to Middleton by ranch foreman Robert F. Long. Long then took "King's Pride" and "Nancy Brown" to Boise to be kept there. John and his son Edward Lemp paid the ranch a visit about this time. Hundreds of Boise residents mourned when Lemp's faithful old work horse "Old Capitol" had to be put down due to age and infirmity.[fb] He was "about the first horse bred and raised in Idaho," as the *Statesman* remembered him. He was about 35 years old and had hauled every brick used to build the Capitol hotel in Boise. All the hands at the Middleton ranch had looked after him but when he began to fail and suffer they drew lots to see who would end his misery. Foreman Robert Long with one blow euthanized "the pride of John Lemp, and of late the reminder of his early struggles." "Surely, if there is any beautiful, green pastuerage in the equine world beyond, 'Old Capitol' is welcome and entitled to admittance."

The city of Boise decided to asphalt the streets of the original townsite late in May of 1903 and published a list of all the many property owners. Each owner also had listed the assessment they owed for the street work adjacent to their lots. Lemp owned nine separate parcels with a total of $3,909.10 assessed.[fc]

In July of 1903, Lemp traveled to Idaho City to conduct some business before the probate judge in connection with the estate of

Constantine Wirtz.[fd] He stayed two days. Lemp and Nathan Falk were joint patentees on 20.661 acres of mineral land, named "Washington" in Blaine County on July 1, 1903.[fe] They were not destined to be jointly involved in this for long. Lemp's long time co-owner of mining property in Hailey, Nathan Falk, became ill from a bowel obstruction while in Hailey that July and eventually died.[ff]

In August, Albert Lemp's wife and daughter enjoyed an outing at the seashore—exactly where was not mentioned in the newspaper.[fg] The Oregon coast was a typical spot for Idaho people to vacation. An indication of the wide spread nature of Lemp's holdings was that the Board of Equalization of Elmore County raised his property tax holdings from 300 head of cattle to 400, and also added on twenty saddle horses to be taxed.[fh]

In the Mountain Home area, George Graham who was tending Lemp's cattle, met with an accident because he did not keep his feet in the stirrups while riding a mule.[fi] The local press there advised him to keep his feet in the stirrups and do a little string pulling even if it didn't look quite so well to spectators. Also they said "beware of the mule; don't let his innocent looks deceive you."

THE SLOW, PAINFUL, UNLAMENTED DEATH OF THE LEMP BREWERY

An indication of how Lemp's brewery was viewed by 1901 was given by the evening newspaper when it said the new billboard erected near it was "a welcome innovation to the scenery of that neighborhood."[fj] Apparently they thought the brewery an eye sore.

The Lemp brewery received a short mention in the newspaper in August of 1903 when the roof of a shed on the grounds at 312 West Main caught fire about one in the morning, presumably due to a careless pedestrian.[fk] A few buckets of water extinguished the problem. This may have been the beginning of the end of the existence of that symbol of Boise's early days.

The Brewery made news again in November of 1903 in a way that surely John Lemp would have wished to avoid.[fl] The school board made a request to the Boise city council that Lemp's brewery be declared a nuisance because it was adjacent to Lincoln school. A health committee was formed of Councilman Gumbert, Barber and liquor dealer Grunbaum, to study the situation and make a recommendation. The majority report from Grunbaum and Gumbert said: "we do not consider said Lemp property a nuisance or in any way objectionable to the school, and that we do not approve that the same should be condemned or any action taken in this matter other than to notify Mr. John Lemp that these premises will have to be kept in perfect sanitary condition in the future and all garbage and refuse will have to be removed promptly."

Barber's minority report recommended that the main brick building be left standing but that "the surrounding shacks and piles of rubbish should be condemned as a nuisance and ordered removed." He went on to say that the general appearance of the city as well as the health and morals of the children were at stake. He called the brewery buildings "filthy, unsightly, unsanitary and a disgrace to the city."

John Lemp was present and made an "impassioned speech" defending his brewery buildings. Lemp pointed out that he had been there forty-one years and the school board should have kept away if they did not favor the location for a school. He protested that Barber had attacked his brewing business itself, and while he was at it, citizen Lemp criticized the macadamizing of Main Street. John suggested the tax payers take care of that with 6 % bonds paid over ten years instead of levying against the property owners who had already paid enough for street improvements.

Barber said he had no intention of attacking Mr. Lemp's business. The whole board then stated their positions on the matter. Liquor dealer Grunbaum favored keeping the premises in good repair. Dressler wanted to do as the school board asked and condemn the site. Grunbaum moved to table the minority report. The no votes were Barber, Dressler, Logan and Roberts. The yes votes were from Grunbaum, Gumbert, Smith, Sloan, and the deciding vote was that of acting Mayor Good. The majority report was then adopted by the same vote except Barber voted for it, noting that in terms of the sanitary conditions he would accept half a loaf instead of none. The brewery was saved! Temporarily.

In August 1904, Mr. and Mrs. Lemp mortgaged a number of lots in the old section of Boise, the Capitol Hotel building and the Lemp brewery to John B. Broadbent to secure a loan of $70,000.[fm] John soon asked the city council for permission to rebuild one of his buildings at the brewery complex and the matter was referred to the fire and water committee.[fn]

The city council had not finished considering the Lemp brewery.[fo] The vote of the previous year postponed, rather than settled, the issues. Councilman Dressler moved the appointment of a committee to investigate conditions there. He said the conditions there might not be detrimental to the health of the Lincoln school pupils but it was surely detrimental to their morals. He knew of events there that were a disgrace. He asked not to be on the committee himself since he feared his prior knowledge would prejudice his judgment. His motion was unanimously adopted and Mayor Hawley appointed a committee of Latham and Roberts, with Dressler as the head, despite his wish to be excused.

Lemp's brewery saloon was back in the news in late October of 1905.[fp] Police magistrate Locke issued an arrest warrant for the manager of the brewery on the charge of selling liquor without a license. A complaint was filed alleging that the place was open in violation of the Sunday and midnight closing act. According to the report at this time, the brewery had never taken out a license for the sale of intoxicating liquors not withstanding the law that said all dealers whether retail or wholesale had to have such a license. The decision was that the closing law applied only to those places selling by right of a city license. Therefore the charge was amended to include failure to secure a license. When officers went on Sunday to serve the warrant, the brewery was closed up tight and fast and they had to wait to serve it. The case was not going to be swept under any rug. The powers that be in Boise seemed to no longer hold Lemp in the reverence they once did. Perhaps the liquor business in general was no longer held in high esteem.

About this time, Judge Smith upheld the validity of the Boise Sunday closing ordinance.[fq] That avenue of defense was closed. A week later the matter of the closing law and the burned building were both back in the news. As the *Statesman* said "John Lemp had the unique distinction yesterday of appearing twice the same day in police court to answer for his alleged misdeeds."[fr] The first case involved the selling of beer on Sunday at his brewery on Fourth and Main. He was convicted of this and Judge Locke fined him $50 and costs. Notice of appeal was given at once.

The brewery continued to limp along during the next two years but there was no desire to upgrade the brewery. On the 1907 fire insurance map, the brewery was described as "old and dilapidated."[fs] Across the street was the Ridenbaugh's Lumber Yard.

A headline in the *Evening Capital News* on 8 August 1907 said "Old Lemp Brewery is to be Replaced by Elegant Dwelling: Herbert Lemp will Have Old Building Torn Down and Modern Residence Will be Built—Work to Begin this Fall."[ft] Herbert, identified as the manager of the Lemp Drygoods Store, agreed a short time ago to close down the Lemp brewery and rent his saloon to Boise's Idaho Brewing Company. As soon as the farm hands were done harvesting crops, he would put them to work tearing down the old buildings and getting the ground in shape for new buildings. The article mentioned the dilapidated condition of the brewery, the ongoing problem with the adjacent school, and the relief the neighbors would feel to know this news. The razing of the building did not take place as predicted.

According to the *American Brewers Review*, John Lemp's brewery in Boise closed 1 December 1907.[fu] It had been effectively closed for some time. Lemp's empire had long before outgrown the seed from which it sprung. The actual closing was little noted in Boise. It deserved a headline, and maybe a parade: "Boise's beer baron no longer brews beer!!"

The Boise school board was becoming increasingly concerned about the condition of the old Lemp brewery site adjacent to Lincoln School.[fv] They passed a detailed resolution and sent it on the city council for action. "To the common council of Boise City: Your memorialists, the board of trustees of the independent school district of Boise City, respectfully represent that the south half of the east half of the north half of block 34 of the original townsite of Boise City, being the property of Mr. John Lemp, is in a most unsanitary condition and is a continuous menace to the health of the pupils attending the Lincoln school situated on the northwest quarter of said block, and that by reason of the unsanitary condition of the premises mentioned, many cases of diphtheria have developed among the pupils attending said school, thereby necessitating the closing of said school for fumigation and for such periods as were required under the rules of the board of health, in order to avoid a general contagion or epidemic among the pupils of said school: that the closing of said school results in a direct financial loss to the district of at least forty dollars ($40) per day, and considerable expense has also been incurred by the district by reason of the unsanitary conditions of said premises in fumigating and disinfecting the Lincoln school, and we have been required by the board of health to destroy books and other property in some of the rooms of said building, at considerable financial loss to the district, all of which is directly the result of the unclean and unsanitary condition of the premises mentioned. Wherefore, we respectfully urge your honorable body to take such action, and without delay, as may be necessary to place the said premises in a clean and sanitary condition." Obviously, a great number of Boise folks would not miss the old brewery if it were to suddenly combust. But blaming diphtheria on a building seems a scientific stretch.

An omen of the future occurred in February when the Lemp brewery was found ablaze at 1 O'clock in the morning.[fw] Presumably the fire started in a pile of old rags lying on the west side of the building. A couple of young men walking by saw the blaze, sounded the alarm, and the firemen of Chemical Company No. 1 extinguished it before it made significant headway.

On 7 August, the old, unused Lemp Brewery finally did burn.[fx] The oldest part of the building, dating back 45 years to 1864, burned to the ground. Officer Bostwick noticed the fire a few minutes before 3 o'clock in the morning and gave the alarm.[fy] Hundreds of people gathered to watch the spectacular blaze. The fire department arrived quickly but found the sheds and storage building completely in flames. They had no chance to save anything on the Main Street side. They directed their efforts to saving the granary and the stables which they succeeded in doing. The big brick ice house shielded the Lincoln school which was adjacent. The horses in the corral were let loose. A shed at the nearby Ridenbaugh's lumber yard caught fire but the flames were quickly extinguished. "The prevailing opinion was to the effect that the old buildings were an eye sore to the community and there was little regret that they were destroyed."[fz]

Later, fire chief Fulton said the pressure gauge on the fire engine

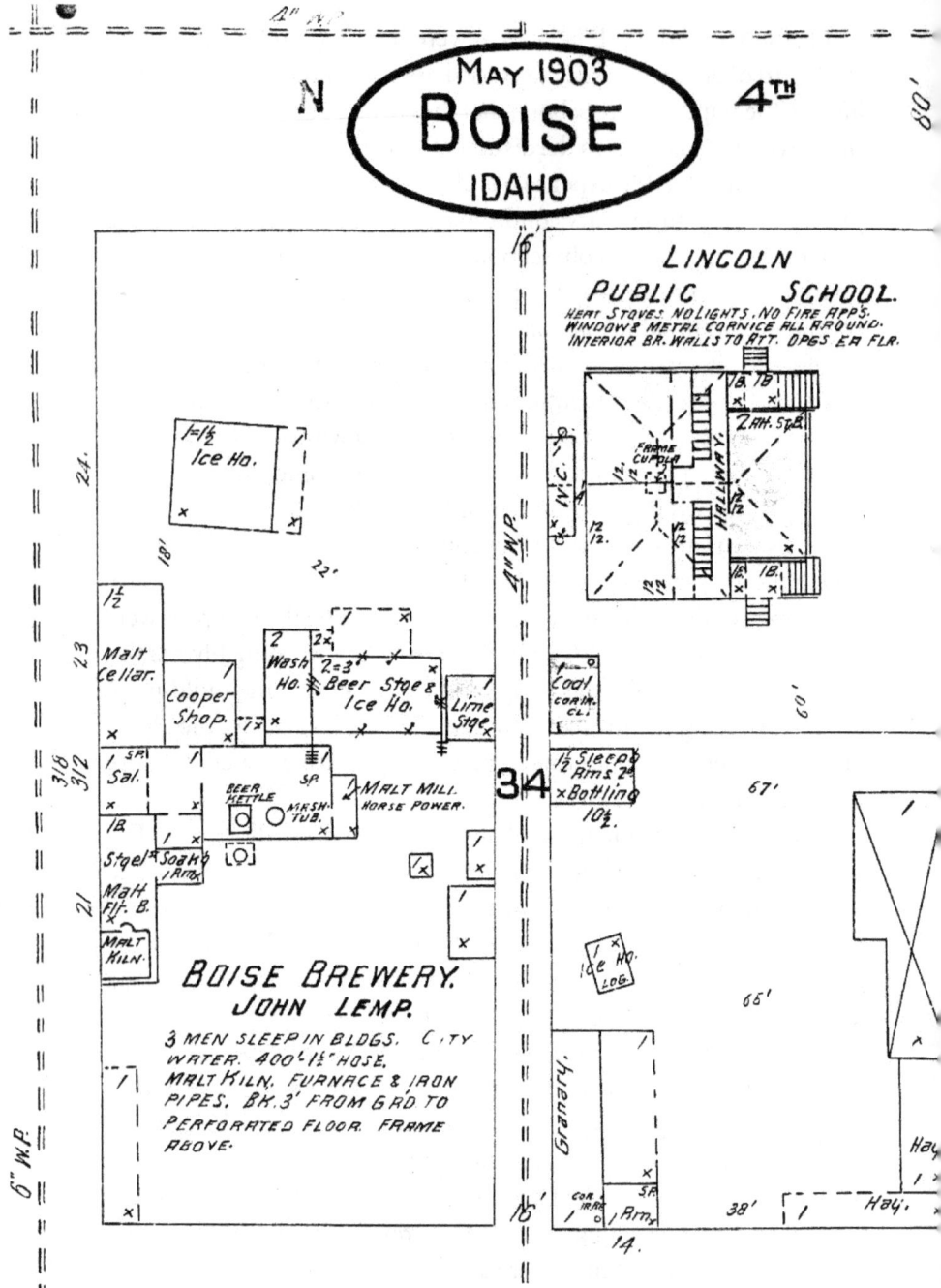

The Lemp brewery as it appeared on the fire insurance map of 1903. The proximity of the Lincoln School became a serious problem.

ran from 85 to 90 pounds for three hours.[ga] It would not have been possible to keep such a flow if many small hydrants around the city had been watering lawns. He wanted all property owners to turn off irrigation during fires. However, if all fires occurred at such an early hour there would be no problem.

The next day the *Statesman* offered a more detailed, historically-based, photo-illustrated account of the fire and the brewery.[gb] The fire punctuated and completed the passing of one of the oldest landmarks in the city. The brewery had been built in 1864, and, according to their questionable recollection, it was the first brewery in the city. Other breweries were absorbed by Lemp's establishment, and, for years, it was the only brewery, they said erroneously, in the southern part of Idaho. The *Statesman* was exercising inventive counter-factual myth-making. Since the brewery had been shut down, adjacent property owners asked Lemp to raze it, but he had refused. He seemed to have a sentimental attraction to this symbol of his early years in Boise. Lemp said his loss was $2,500 which was not covered by insurance. The contents of the brick building were entirely destroyed but first they gave the firemen a hard battle. Lemp had definitely lost a link with his early days in town, and Boise had lost a link with its early days. The Boise Beer Baron who had not brewed for nearly two years, no longer had a brewery! The main focus of John Lemp's life was over.

The fire at the Lemp brewery became the arguing point for fire chief Fulton to request better equipment and more hose for his department.[gc] He said they could not possibly have saved the buildings, but, had they been of slower burning materials, just double the present amount of hose would have been needed to save them. He warned that "If any of the large business blocks or hotels catch fire, we haven't half enough hoses at present to do as effective work as I know my men are capable of if they are properly equipped."[gd]

After the fire at the brewery several valuable brass fixtures were taken to John Lemp's home and locked in his barn to protect them.[ge] A young man—apparently a professional criminal—Joseph Bethal got in through a window and was about to abscond with them when Herbert caught him in the act. He was soon before Judge W. C. Dunbar.

On the last day of September, 1910, over a year after the fire, the City council of Boise again instructed the city health officer, building inspector, and fire chief to inspect the old Lemp brewery with a view to bringing about the removal of the building.[gf] Most of the buildings had been quickly removed by Mr. Lemp and the council noted this when they visited the site.[gg] Boise was in the midst of a drive to create "Boise the Beautiful." This was a sort of urban renewal as frontier buildings were replaced by modern structures, many of which in deed beautified the city for the next century.[gh]

Fire chief Harry W. Fulton, building inspector Thomas Weston, and city health officer M.S. Parker submitted a report to the city council in October 1910 regarding Lemp's property.[gi] "To the honorable mayor and common council: We, the undersigned, requested by your honorable body to inspect and report, from a fire and sanitary standpoint, upon the remaining buildings of the Lemp brewery plant on the block situated between Idaho and Main streets and Third and Fourth streets, beg leave to say that we carefully examined the structures in question and are fully convinced that all of the frame and the small brick buildings are both a fire and a health menace to the city, particularly to the Lincoln public school, which is in proximity to them, and we recommend that they be razed and removed. We further recommend the removal of the gable ends and the contents of the brick malthouse of cold storage buildings (sic), also the frame outside portion of the same.

We respectfully ask that you make an investigation of the matter at your earliest convenience."

The Boise city council inspected the burned out ruin of the Lemp Brewery in October of 1910 as part of a health and safety inspection of several sites.[gj] They concluded the site must be cleaned up and undestroyed portions locked up. The crumbling walls and unsightly holes must be eradicated at once. Nothing seemed to be happening and in early December John Lemp was summoned into court and fined $15.[gk] "This is the first time I was ever fined in my life, declared Mr. Lemp as he slowly counted out $15 in currency and silver and handed it to City Health Officer Parker." Lemp then asked Parker sarcastically "there can't be very much money in the city treasury can there?" Parker said he did not have access to the exchequer. According to the *Evening News* Lemp was angry and chagrined. He told the court that his troubles began when the Lincoln School was built. "If it had not been for that school building, it would not have burned down." "It don't make much difference what the nature of the business was, it did a great deal for the growth of Boise and was one of its biggest concerns." "I told Mr. Stewart who was a school director when the site for the building was selected that it was no place for a public school and do good could come from placing it there. After the business burned down they have been after me about the property and its one trouble after another ever since."

A year later, health officer Parker, City detective Roeder and a janitor from the school all testified to the city council that the stench from the filthy corrals filled the school when the wind was right. Witnesses for Mr. Lemp said he tried to fill in holes with cinders and such things but the premises had not really been improved in the last twelve months.

At the Boise City Council meeting on Halloween that month in 1911 they again tried to take action—"about the fifty seventh attempt"—to get the old Lemp barns and brewery torn down.[gl] The buildings between Idaho and Main streets and Third and Fourth streets were declared nuisances and the building inspector was told to serve the necessary notices and if they were not torn down within a week to raze them himself. Another Lemp property, an old tower at the rear of the Capitol Hotel, was also condemned and ordered torn down.

The council's discussion started with a report from building inspector Cody on the condition of the old tower which he said had settled so much it was thirty inches out of plumb, was still in use, and was a menace to the safety of every person who passed by. This led them to again discuss the brewery. It seems that near the end of John Lemp's life, his brewery, despite having burned and not been in operation for several years, was reclaiming the important position it held in the early days. During the middle decades of Lemp's time in Boise the brewery never seemed that important. It was always there but a minor player in the drama of his life. The brewery and the brewer had aged together and become decrepit, yet were still dependent on each other.

True to form, the Lemps did not take these orders from the City Council at face value. Herbert, on behalf of his father, said he would raze the leaning tower but would go to court to avoid pulling down the other buildings at this time.^gm "In the near future we intend to clean up that block on which the stable and burned ice house stand, but it is impossible to do it at this time, and if the city attempts to pull down those buildings I will ask the courts for an injunction."

"Next spring it may be possible for us to remove that stable, but just at this time of the year we must have it for our teams and for storing hay. In case conditions are right we intend to do considerable building next spring, and in that event we would use the bricks in the old ice house. Tearing that down and stacking the bricks up at this time would mean that they would have to be handled at least twice, and that would be a big expense. I admit that the building looks none too well, but it is neither a fire trap nor a health menace. Everything inflammable about it has already been burned, and as the walls are three feet thick I do not believe there is much danger of their falling in." "It may be that the council can force this issue but I will take the matter into the courts and see before I will comply with this order. The council is right about the old tower back of the Capitol Hotel building. I intend to have it torn down as soon as possible." Building

Old Lemp Brewery which was destroyed by fire early yesterday morning and which was one of the landmarks of the city.

The newspaper photo that was published after the fire.

inspector Cody had served notice about the tower, Herbert said, and it would probably be torn down within the next few days.

The next day another chapter in the story unfolded.[gn] At the city council meeting Building Inspector Cody reported that he had talked the matter over with Herbert Lemp. Lemp steadfastly refused to tear down the barn but said he might be willing to tear down the old ice house and brewery buildings on the block. Cody was to have further discussions with Lemp on the issue.

Eventually the brewery site was cleared and then occupied by the First Ward of the LDS Church. Later, the building was made the Club for Women.[go] Then a property of St. Luke's Hospital, and still later an office building. In late 1937, workmen building a Latter Day Saints chapel dug into an old empty cellar which the press identified, incongruously, as a wine cellar from a former brewery.[gp] It was empty, save cobwebs and a musty smell.

1903

In October of 1903, Mrs. Lucille Lemp, Albert's wife, was taken suddenly ill with what was described as a "nervous attack" at the home of her parents at 712 Franklin street.[gq] Family problems were becoming public knowledge, and were destined to increase.

A local Nampa man named George Duffey forged John Lemp's name to a check for $65.[gr] He found himself arrested and lodged in the county jail at Caldwell.

John entered many of his draft horses in the competition at the Idaho State Fair in the fall of 1903.[gs] The *Statesman* described them as a credit to the county and they "repaid him by winning quite a number of prizes." Lemp did almost as well as he had at the Ada County fair. He took first place for his Clydesdale stallion, three years old and up.[gt] He was second in the category of three-year-old English Shire stallion. He was second for his three year old Purcheron stallion. His two year-old Purcheron mares with foals at foot won both first and second. For two-year old mare he took first. His one year-old filly entry won both first and second. For foal of 1903, Lemp won both first and second. In the Championship category Lemp won second for his stallion of any age. He also took second for matched pair of draft horses.

In November, Boise was again levying a special assessment on property owners along a portion of Main street to pay for macadamizing, curbing, and surface drainage.[gu] Lemp owned nine parcels in that area with a total tax owed of $1, 665.66.

1904

The Boise Rapid Transit Company was sold to investors from the east—a Mr. I. W. Anderson, in particular, from Philadelphia—in January of 1904.[gv] This involved buying the outstanding stock. Lemp had been a stockholder and director of the company for years. Anderson came to Boise to close the deal and said the only way to make the company profitable was to improve service.[gw]

In Ohio, the state Grand Master of the Odd Fellows, Charles C. Pavey, gave all saloon men an ultimatum.[gx] Change your occupation or be expelled. The anti-liquor movement had not reached Idaho yet but was an omen of the future. John Lemp was steadfastly committed to his lodge and his profession.

In the Boise society pages, Mr. Lemp, was at a card party with many other young people of Boise. At another party there was a Mr. "C." Lemp. These references were to John's nephew Clarence Lemp.[gy]

When H. Smith Woolley was appointed Idaho state assayer by President Theodore Roosevelt some Idaho people were not pleased. As one of his defenders said, the opponents brought up "old, almost forgotten and long discredited yarns about an unsuccessful business enterprise of Mr. Woolley's, John Lemp's revenue stamps, and a money order romance with the postmaster of Lewiston."[gz] This certainly implies that someone in the past raised some issue about Lemp's brewers tax stamps. The exact nature of the problem was vague.

L. N. B. Carpenter, the ranchman on one of Lemp's spreads was a visitor to Boise in February of 1904 and was mentioned in the press.[ha]

In 1904, the *Idaho Magazine* carried a portrait article on Lemp subtitled "Foundation Builder of Boise."[hb] At that time a portion of his original brewery still stood as a landmark of the state capital. Lemp owned 5,000 acres and was considered a founder of the Settlers, Middleton, Central Park and Sebree canals. He had pushed lateral canals to within one and one-half miles of Nampa and three and one-half miles of Caldwell. He still owned the Star mines and was hoping to produce Galena ore there. The magazine said he still had a keen mind and was ready to "take occasion by the beard" as when he was in his prime.

The Boise street improvement question was not resolved. Lemp was among the many property owners hit with a special tax so that Boise could afford to pave and improve Main street. He was assessed $17.44 for 33 feet, 8 inches of lot 4, Block 3, and $3.62 for 7 feet of lot 5, block 3.[hc] This issue had been going on for some months.

In St. Louis, Beer Baron William J. Lemp ended his life with a gunshot wound on 13 February 1904. William had lost his son Frederick in December of 1901, and then his best friend, Frederick Pabst, Milwaukee brewer, died on 1 January 1904. He was despondent over these events. William J. Lemp, Jr. then took over the reigns of the giant Missouri brewery. This was important enough national news to get a column in a Boise newspaper and other Idaho papers, and must have impacted John's thinking.[hd]

John's future brother-in-law Albert Wolters sold two lots in Hailey in February of 1904 to Frank H. Parson for $800.[he] In early May, he sold a half interest in another lot to the Friedman Company for $250.[hf] He was seemingly liquidating an ever increasing number of his assets.

In March, Albert Lemp returned to Boise after an eight week pleasure and business trip through the eastern and southern states.[hg] He had been to St. Louis, New Orleans, Philadelphia and other cities. [hh] There was no mention of his wife being with him. This was another vague hint of trouble in that household. Less than two months later, Albert was off on the afternoon train to St. Louis to be present when the World's Fair opened on April 30.[hi] He knew people in the city and was able to get good accommodations for himself and other Idahoans. His aunt, Mrs. Frederich Bach, lived there, as well as the Lemp brewing family, his distant relatives.

The lots in Lemp addition were advertised by "the old reliable real estate dealers" W. E. Pierce & Co. for $175 with easy terms.[hj] That same month the Settler's Canal farmers were organizing an irrigation district under the new law. Its former name of Lemp Canal was mentioned so everyone would know which canal was being discussed.[hk] Lemp's Niece Anna Leyerzaph, clerk in the state auditor's office, was reported ill at home in April.[hl]

In late May, Lemp's old buddy Senator W. A. Clark of Montana married Miss Anna L. La Chappelle of Butte, Montana, at Marseilles, France. Along with the marriage announcement, which was not made until June, came the announcement that they were the parents of a two year-old daughter.[hm]

Mrs. John Lemp and daughter Louise left on June 7 for a trip to St. Louis to the Fair and to Springfield, Illinois to see her daughter, Mrs. Kessberger.[hn] They expected to be away all summer. Mrs. Lemp seemed to be taking ever more trips without John. Was he too infirmed to go, or too busy, or was their marital closeness breaking down?

Daughter Ada's husband, E. G. Hurt, described as the agent for Mrs. Adams, lessee of the Old Ironside mine in the Black Warrior district, opened an office in the First National Bank building.[ho] George Wyman, formerly superintendent of the Checkmate mine in the Pearl district, was made superintendent of the Ironside. A ten stamp mill was to be started up within a week.

A news item from Blue Valley, Idaho, said that Miss Neal from Boise was visiting the Lemp ranch for a few days.[hp]

In late June, the trouble between Lucille and Albert Lemp reached a climax. She sued for divorce in District Court; three witnesses were heard in court on the 28th of June.[hq] Albert did not deny her accusations and Judge T. M. Herrick gave Lucille custody of their child Kathryn.[hr]

Son Herbert Lemp joined three other local men and headed to the Fair in St. Louis in late June.[hs] Albert returned to Boise in early July after two months spent mostly at the fair.[ht] Its not certain if they were ever there simultaneously.

On June 29 1904, a large gathering of Idaho pioneers went to the Overland Hotel for one last visit.[hu] Many had been there in September of 1864 when it was first dedicated. Now, after forty years of service to the city, it was to be replaced with a new seven-story up-to-date version. Among the throng enjoying the nostalgia was John Lemp, pioneer of 1863.

Also in late June, a protest was sent to the Boise city council about the macadam paving of Main Street which Lemp had disagreed with when he addressed the council the previous November.[hv] They believed the work was not being done according to the specifications that had been prescribed. Among the twenty-two land owners who signed was John Lemp.

On 7 July 1904, daughter Ida Catherine Lemp Kessberger died. She was only 29. By shear chance, Mrs. John Lemp had been at her daughter's side in Springfield, Illinois, at the time of death. The Statesman predicted correctly that her body would be shipped to Boise for internment.[hw] Cause of death was given as blood poisoning induced by quinsy (an antiquated term for tonsillitis). The body was escorted home by her mother Mrs. John Lemp, Ida's brother Herbert, who had been at St. Louis, as well as sister Louise Lemp, and Mr. Edward H. Kessberger, her husband.[hx] John and another of her brothers met the group in Nampa. The funeral was held at the family residence on Grove Street, and burial was in the Masonic cemetery. The home was overflowing with those who came to pay last respects. The service was conducted by the Christian Science church. The evening newspaper said she was a member of the Episcopal church.[hy] She was buried beside her three brothers and one sister that had preceded her in death. There were four Lemp sons and four Lemp daughters remaining. All the members of the family were able to be in Boise for the service.[hz] Sister Mrs. Grant of Walla Walla had to return home quickly after the funeral because of the illness of her husband.[ia] A few days later the *Statesman* carried a nice article remembering that she and her sister Ada Lemp Hurt were the first twins born in Boise.[ib] Mr. Kessberger returned to Illinois on July 26.[ic]

Niece Anna Leyerzaph returned to Boise about this time. She had been to the fair in St. Louis and also went to New York City to see her parents off on their voyage to Germany.[id]

The Anti-Saloon League held a meeting in Boise this July to try to organize a local chapter.[ie] They blamed poor attendance on the many other meetings that night. The national organization demonstrated a bulldog attitude which was determined to push total abstinence through legal edict until it became the law of the nation.

In August 1904, Mr. and Mrs. Lemp mortgaged a number of lots in the old section of Boise, the Capitol Hotel building and the Lemp brewery to John B. Broadbent to secure a loan of $70,000.[if] Their mortgage was alternately reported to be for $80,000. Broadbent was at this time the wealthiest land owner in Boise. Just why Lemp needed so much cash is unclear.

The R. G. Dun Idaho business list for 1904 (p. 4) had John Lemp as a brewery owner in Boise, and the the Lemp Dry Goods Co. (not inc.) as another business. The Elmore County Equalization Board also raised his assessment in Mountain Home from 350 head of cattle valued at $2,625 to 650 head valued at $4,875.[ig]

The women of the Columbia Club of Boise held a meeting to expound on the national irrigation act. Mr. Pinchot, chief of the forestry bureau, spoke and mentioned a silver maple tree he had seen in Boise which was the most beautiful tree he had ever seen. It was on the lawn of John Lemp's Grove Street home.[ih]

Late in August, a colorful character usually known as "Hogan, the stiff"—although he preferred the name Jimmy—was found guilt of vagrancy for the umpteenth time.[ii] He had kept his word about staying out of Boise until his previous sentence was up but then he returned to exercise his inordinate appetite for liquor. The judge fulfilled Hogan's wishes and sentenced him to work on one of Lemp's ranches and fixed the sentence so Hogan could return to town to see the fair in the fall. In late November, Hogan was back in court and sentenced to 90 days in jail.[ij] Justice Johnson suspended the sentence if he again stayed on Lemp's ranch. Hogan was allowed to come to town for Christmas and New Years.

Lemp's late mining partner Nathan Falk's cemetery monument—the most expensive ever brought to the Boise area—was unloaded by the White Line Transfer Company.[ik] It was a mammoth three piece column of granite that required three train cars to transport. The base weighed 62,000 pounds, the second section 42,000 and the top section 30,000. It was put on Falk's grave in the Masonic cemetery.

In 1904, Lemp was one of only five surviving members of the original Turnverein society. That year the organization was given a veritable new life through John's efforts and new members were enrolling.[il] All over the United States German-America or Deutschtum, a cultural not a physical entity, was rallying for a decade of growth and energy before The Great War in Europe caused its final brutal demise.

In Mid-September, Mr. and Mrs. William Lemp of New York, John's nephew and wife, came to visit John and Catherine.[im] The only other Lemp brother found to date who could have been William's father, was Johann. William was connected with the North German Lloyd Steamship Company. John's sister, Mrs. William Jaumann, went to St. Louis for a trip of two or three months in late September.[in] No doubt the world's fair attracted her and she could stay with her sister's family.

ABC Bohemian (American Brewing Company of St. Louis) beer was now being heavily advertised in Boise.[io] Charles L. McKinnell was the wholesaler of this additional rival to the local brewers.

The State meeting of the Odd Fellows was held in Boise that autumn. At the keynote address John Lemp was honored for being the first Grand Treasurer of the lodge in Idaho.[ip]

The City of Boise wished to pave the alleys in some sections of the city with brick and held a meeting for property owners to voice their concerns. A special assessment was to be used to pay for the improvement. John Lemp was listed as owning four pieces of the property involved and was to be taxed $1,257.71.[iq]

As a further city improvement, a very large sewer improvement district was contemplated. All the property was listed with its legal description and ownership which took up several pages and several issues of the Evening Capital News.[ir] John Lemp was listed more than anyone, with the possible exception of John Broadbent. Lemp had 53 pieces of property listed, according to my count, with a total proposed cost to him exceeding $9,168.53. When Boise improved itself, a large share of the bill always went to John Lemp.

John Lemp again made a very fine showing at the Idaho State Fair in October of 1904.[is] He won a first place for a three year-old Clydesdale stallion, fifth for a three year-old Purcheron stallion, first for a one year-old Purcheron stallion, second and third for two year-old Purcheron mares, first for a one year-old Purcheron filly, second in the any age draft horse stallion, second in any age draft horse mare, third in matched pair of draft horses second and third for two year-old general purpose fillies, and first for one year-old general purpose filly. Apparently Lemp beer was delivered by powerful horses that would make anyone proud.

The Pioneer Association displayed an old Bird's Eye View map of Boise in October of 1904. The *Statesman* commented that among the houses shown around the border of the map was the Lemp house, still standing.[it]

With all his family having seen the world's fair, John decided it was his turn. In late October, he went with Colonel M. W. Woods to the city where his relatives owned the giant Lemp Brewery.[iu] Lemp's St. Louis trip went poorly.[iv] He had an attack of rheumatism and was badly crippled for a while. He ended up in a St. Louis hospital. For a while he was in bad enough shape that his relatives were uneasy as to the outcome, but than he rallied.[iw]

At the Boise city council meeting plumbing inspector Conklin reported on buildings that had their downspouts still connected with the city sewers contrary to compliance with city orders. John Lemp had several buildings on the list that still needed to disconnect downspouts.[ix] On the list of Ada county property tax payers in November of 1904 was John Lemp at $8,289.28, the third highest total.[iy] In Boise, the great growth in the number of new homes in the city during 1904 was celebrated.[iz] In particular, citizens praised the growth in the Lemp addition and the Locust Grove area where there were forty new houses, costing an aggregate $45,450.

1905

The inaugural ball in Boise to honor the newly elected state officials was held at the Natorium on January third 1905. One member of the committee, in charge of the floor, was Herbert Lemp.[ja] His political career was continuing.

The Boise City Railway & Terminal Company filed suites against Mr. and Mrs. John Lemp, Mr. and Mrs. Joseph Perrault and John Gray, et al to condemn property for right of way purposes.[jb] The first week of January of 1905 three appraisers, John McMillan, A. J. Glorieux and Harry M. Hughes, were appointed by the court to serve in all these cases. At the end of January of 1905 the Lemps sold a 100 foot strip of land across several lots to the company for $1,250.[jc] The suit of Boise Railway & Terminal company vs. John Lemp on the 31st of January was dismissed on motion of the plaintiff at plantiff's cost.[jd] This may have settled the situation.

Albert's ex-wife Lucille married Nate E. Gardner in Columbus, Nebraska in late January.[je] They planned to live in Gregory, South Dakota.

In March, Lemp made a much bigger real estate deal. He sold his property on the northeast corner of Main and Ninth, commonly known as the Plouhead market to the Idaho Trust and Savings company for $36,000.[jf] There was a front of zero feet on Main but 122 feet on Ninth. This made a price of $735 per front foot. The new owners were to put up a brick building for an office and a clothing store and said it would be "an ornament to the city." The deed listed the property as lot 12 in block 10 of Boise City.[jg] The warranty deed was recorded 29 March with no mortgage attached to anyone.[jh]

John Morris filed suit in Judge Stewart's District Court at the end of January 1905 against John Lemp for $2,594.50 for services rendered.[ji] Late in February, Lemp's legal team argued his demurrer but were overruled.[jj] Lemp was given permission to file a motion to require the plaintiff to separate his causes of action which would cover in better form the same idea as in the demurrer. The case was scheduled for the second of March at 2:00 p.m. But this would not be the end.[jk] The case was destined to drag on. In May, it was again on the court calendar as "demurrer to amend complaint; Davidson & Stoutemyer and Morrison & Pence, attorneys."[jl] Within days, leave was granted to amend the complaint.[jm] The Morris vs. Lemp case was set for trial in mid-May, 1905, but was postponed again.[jn] Lemp barely got home from Hailey in August 1905, before John Morris' old suit for debt came up again in the District Court.[jo] The Morris v. Lemp lawsuit finally was given its day in court.[jp] It was scheduled for September 6; then Morris was allowed to amend the complaint. The case was reset to be heard on October 5 at 10:00 a.m.[jq] The Jury returned a verdict for the plaintiff of $1,031.49.[jr] Costs of $73 were also added on and the plaintiff had execution against the property of Mr. Lemp.[js] An appended note in the court records states that on 3 May 1906 the lien against Lemp's property was waived. The case was appealed to the state Supreme Court which finally ruled on one February of 1907.[jt] The original decision of Judge Frank J. Smith of the District Court for Ada County was modified. Originally Morris sued Lemp to collect a balance on an account he believed he was entitled to. The original judge granted extended time for Lemp to file for a new trial which the court found was proper despite law which said no one could extend the time. However, at the original trial the court-appointed referee did not list every credit Lemp believed he was entitled to and he wished to prove his additional claims. Lemp was not allowed to do so. The Supreme Court ruled this an error. They remanded the case back to the lower court and said the judgment should be modified by deducting the credits the defendant (Lemp) offered to prove or allowing a new trial at which he could present these.

In late February, John was reported taking message baths at Mrs. Robbins for his rheumatism and feeling as good as new.[ju] He planned to walk downtown for the first time in several days.

Theodore Roosevelt was inaugurated President of the United States in March of 1905. Idaho sent many people to the far off national capital to witness the inauguration. General George H. Roberts went to represent Governor Gooding. A platoon of high school cadets went to march in the parade. The high school delegation had a good place in the line of march and when they passed the reviewing stand the President, noticing the Idaho banner, cheered and exclaimed "Good for Idaho. Think how far those boys have come."[jv] These boys of the Gem state, Morris of Lewiston, John Glantzman of Idaho Falls, John M. Gooding, the governor's son from Shoshone, Herbert Dunton and Bernard Lemp of Boise, "acquitted themselves with credit during their stay."[jw]

John Lemp sued S. E. Sparber and the case was placed on the calendar but then dismissed.[jx] The cause of action was not given.

Herbert Lemp was elected to the board of directors of the Boise Baseball Association (a.k.a. Boise Athletic Association) along with Frank H. Plaisted, James R. Lusk, John W. Cage, and Albert B. Kohny.[jy] The following day they met again to select company officers. They were capitalized at $25,000 and filed their incorporation papers with the Idaho Secretary of State.

In Payette, in April, the horse team pulling a wagon load of hay driven by George Wilson ran away.[jz] Both Wilson and his passenger, Clarence Lemp, the son of John's late brother Jacob, were thrown out. Clarence was bruised on the head.

Albert Wolters bought a 1/3 interest in the Fairplay mining claim in Blaine County for $1 that April from George Chillingsworth.[ka] In August, Wolters bought another 1/3 interest from Arthur Smith, also for one dollar.[kb]

John, as many others, paid $1,000 for his yearly county liquor license dating from 1 April 1905.[kc] His sureties were L. H. Cox and W. E. Pierce. The ever increasing cost of a license was a deliberate attempt to increase county revenue and to decrease the number of liquor retailers.

In early May, Boise opened its new Carnegie library building with great ceremony. A formal reception, followed by a ball, was held with a full string orchestra to provide dance music for two and a half hours. Herbert Lemp was a floor manager for the ball.[kd] There were appropriate speeches and ceremonies that evening as well as the next day at the formal dedication. Among the nineteen dignitaries on the stage who gave these dedication speeches was John Lemp.[ke]

A great effort to raise sugar beets for the Sugar City factory to process was in full blast. A sugar beet planting of five thousand acres were needed to make the project practical and give the factory owners enough confidence to order the new machinery for the new brick and stone factory. John Lemp symbolically led the way for other land owners by contracting to grow 100 acres of beets.[kf] There were hopes

A group portrait of Boise Pioneers. Lemp is the back, middle individual labeled with a numeral two. 1. Mr. Sellers 2. Lemp. 3. R. E. Emerson 4. Mr. Van Pelt 5. Nathan Falk 6. Mr. Davies 7. John Atkinson. Photo, Idaho State Historical Society

to build a similar sugar factory in Boise Valley or perhaps at Meridian.

By early 1907, there were 21,000 acres of Idaho land in sugar beets, and four factories to make sugar. Sugar City turned out 850 sacks a day, or 23,000,000 pounds per season; Idaho Falls make 20,000,000 pounds, Nampa 10,000,000 pounds, and Blackfoot 11,000,000 pounds.[kg] Lemp had helped to start a major industry.

John's brother-in-law Charles Leyerzaph sold a city lot to Mrs. Jennie Klinge, his daughter, for love and affection, and another to his unmarried daughter Anna Leyerzaph, also for love and affection.[kh]

The Boise Chamber of Commerce had a plan to advertise their area at the Lewis and Clark Exposition in Seattle. Lemp donated $10 per month to the total of $300 per month they needed to meet their goals.[ki]

John Lemp, and the rival Idaho Brewing Company, each gave $5.00 to the Memorial Day exercises which was a very large event in Boise that year.[kj]

One of the persistent mysteries of the frontier remains how did huge pieces of machinery get into remote areas where backpackers a century later find the trail narrow and difficult. Part of the answer is that sometimes they didn't get there. For instance, a 14,000 pound (7 ton) boiler promised to the Placerville dredge was en route to that Boise Basin town on two wagons and was laboriously pulled up the Shafer Creek hill one day in June of 1905.[kk] This is near one of the Lemp ranches. Like Sisyphus of classical myth, at the top the load came loose and rolled to the bottom again, smashing the wagons to kindling wood. No one was hurt.

Herbert Lemp was one of the directors of the baseball team which was to play on the July 4th holiday.[kl] Herb was also one of the men in charge of the horseback feature in the parade.[km]

On July third, the fire department came on the run to Lemp's house. Luckily, it only turned out to be a back draught from the chimney that filled the basement with smoke.[kn] No damage was done.

After the Fourth of July, Boise liquor dealers complained that the retail establishments all were closed on that day in compliance with the law, but that the Larson wholesale establishment sold over 1,000 bottles of beer and a great deal of whiskey flasks.[ko] This, they viewed as discrimination.

John Lemp • The Beer Baron of Boise 239

The Boise City Council made their first meeting after the holiday one to remember. The Evening Capital News said they "opened in a humdrum, listless sort of way," but then "came a solar plexus blow, as a Republican member made a proposal, 'for the political fakirs who shout about reform every two years.'"[kp] The proposal was to close saloons on Sunday and after Midnight everyday. The council would not even allow their legal counsel to study the measure first, they passed ordinance #623 with only Smith voting against. Then came a proposal to raise the business tax on saloons from $50 per quarter to $150 per quarter. The council had already passed new salaries for themselves and needed the money to be able to pay them. This was approved too. Lemp's saloons had been struck two mighty blows with no warning and no chance to protest or resist.

In early August, a petition was presented to the city council signed by dozens of the business and professional men of the city asking that the ordinance be repealed. W. B. Connor of Lemp Dry Goods store was one of the signers.[kq]

Lemp was one of the investors mentioned in a new electric railroad company which was capitalized at $5,000,000.[kr] The plans were to run lines in several directions to small cities in the Boise area. Lemp next extended the lease on his Capitol Hotel to Mr. Regan and Mr. Blackinger for another year.[ks] Senator William Clark of Montana, Lemp's old traveling companion, made the newspapers when he had an abscess removed from his mastoid bone involving chiseling away two inches of bone.[kt]

Boise suffered a large fire in August of 1905.[ku] The fire began for an unknown reason in the second-floor "resort" in the Whitechapel district known as the "Red Light" at 716 Main Street about 9:00 a.m. On the ground floor was a saloon called the Anheuser Busch. The flames spread quickly and the "inmates" had to be taken out by a ladder. One woman was overcome by fear and smoke and had to be carried down the ladder. The women lost everything they owned. Five streams of water soon had the flames under control but the weight of the water did as much damage as the fire. The floor gave way and the furniture crashed through the door into the Anheuser Busch saloon. The adjacent building at 714 Main was owned by John Lemp and it was badly damaged by both fire and water. It was occupied by the Palace restaurant below with rooms above. The restaurant personnel quickly carried their furniture into the street. Lemp carried $2,000 insurance with W. E. Pierce & Co. The building with address number 712, also owned by Lemp, received slight damage from water, but was fully covered by insurance, according to the *Capitol News*, while the *Statesman* said the loss was $3,000, fully covered by insurance.

The buildings were among the oldest in the business district. Lemp's was about twenty years old, which demonstrates the youth of the frontier city of Boise. The fire fighters were hampered by the many backdoors that had afforded undetected entrance to the premises but also created drafts for the flames on this occasion. Total losses for the fire were about $16,000.

Louise Lemp was listed among the visitors in Portland in late August for the Lewis and Clark fair and also to visit her sister.[kv] Louise was often listed with those attending society dances.[kw] Son Herbert went hunting with Ben Pettingill in the hills around Boise in early September.[kx] Right after that he was visiting in Portland.[ky]

With no warning to friends or acquaintances, Mrs. Elise Jaumann, John Lemp's widowed sister, married Albert Wolters. Mayor Pinney solemnized the marriage at her home at 7:00 the same evening they secured their marriage license. Wolters was described as a former county commissioner of Blaine County.[kz] She had been a widow nearly ten years.

Son Herbert was visiting the great exposition in Portland, and reported when he returned to Boise he had enjoyed a delightful time.[la] In September of 1905 the rival Idaho Brewing and Malting Company tore down the old wooden bottling house and put up a 50x70 three-story building, with a Eclipse bottle soaking wheel, a Tornelius bottle washer, and up-to-date pasteurizing equipment. All these would have a capacity of 40 barrels per day, and cost $10,000. The old rivalry with Lemp matching improvement against improvement was over.

Lemp did not respond.

In late October, John was still listed as the third biggest property tax payer in Ada County right behind John Broadbent, and the railroad. He paid $7,438.27.[lb] Lemp also owned land in a township called Victory.[lc] He was in that neighborhood having a large section of sagebrush cleared for spring planting at this time.[ld]

In early September, John Broadbent began to tear down his building which had been fire damaged that summer in the notorious Red Light conflagration, and the *Evening Capital News* said that Lemp would have to tear down his adjoining building to keep it from falling.[le] Not necessarily. While work went on during

September, Lemp developed an idea.[lf] He presented a petition to the Boise city council in October to be able to roof his building that had burned in the bawdy house fire the previous August.[lg] The Council had refused requests to repair the buildings, condemned them and ordered them torn down. The owners, including Lemp, began razing them. When the top floor had been removed the work on Lemp's building stopped. It was then that he requested that he be allowed to roof it and leave it standing as a one story structure. The Council unanimously refused to change their former decision and ordered the building completely torn down.

John Lemp sold twenty acres to J. W. McLean, vice president and general manager of the new brick plant.[lh] McLean also bought 16 adjoining acres from Mrs. Blair. Access to the railroad was an important consideration in selecting the location.

The other case was about his failure to comply the order of the city council to tear down his building at 714 Main. Lemp was charged with maintaining a nuisance. Both Lemp's building and the adjacent building belonging to J. B. Broadbent had been taken down to one level but the city Council would not approve building permits. Lemp signified his intention to comply and therefore asked for the case against him to be dismissed. Judge Locke agreed but kept the case on the docket for another week in case Lemp had a change of mind. This matter, as seemingly with all Lemp court cases, was not over until it was over.

On November 13 of 1905, a patent was issued on 320 acres of land in Canyon county under the 1877 Desert Land Act to the heirs of George W. J. Lemp.[li]

In Mid-November, at a city Council meeting, councilman Mr. Koelsch asked who gave John Lemp permission to make improvements on his Main Street building.[lj] He said the place was dangerous because a new cellar was being dug and poles were being used to keep the walls from caving in during construction. The city attorney explained that the ordinances were defective and failed to make it necessary to get permission from the city to make brick and stone improvements on brick and stone buildings in the fire limits. Councilman Kahn thought the ordinances ought to be amended. Councilman Annett agree with Koelsch that the Lemp building was in bad shape. Councilman Clinton moved that the building committee inspect the building and if it was found unsafe, to notify the builders to quit work immediately, pending action by the Council. It was so ordered. Lemp seemed to take this all in stride.

Miss Lemp was in the society section for helping Mrs. W. T. Booth serve luncheon at her elegant card party.[lk] This gives an idea of how the Lemp daughters passed the time.

The Gibbard problem had not caused Lemp to disavow the canal business. In December of 1905, the Lemp Co-Operative Lateral Co. Ltd. filed articles with the Secretary of State as a new corporation.[ll] Capital stock was $17,400, of which $15,200 had been subscribed by the incorporators, namely W. S. Kingsbury, J. L. Hanna, H. W. Sutton and B. F. Halford, all of Caldwell, and John Lemp of Boise. The expressed purpose of the company was to build a ditch from the dam in Marquam slough, running 8,000 feet, and such other ditches as the stockholders may decide.

As 1905 drew rapidly to a close, Lemp sold 13 acres just north of the Locust Grove addition to John D. Daly for $8,000.00.[lm] Daly intended to plat the land for city lots.

On December 31, former Governor Frank Steunenberg was assassinated at his Caldwell, Idaho home. The foul and murderous deed was in retribution for his heavy-handed dealing with the miners' strike in the Coeur d'Alenes while in office. The deed had vast implications for Idaho and American history in general, and was a major topic of conversation in Idaho for years to come. Lemp had been at the State Constitutional Convention in 1889 with Steunenberg. The assassin, usually known by his alias Harry Orchard, was turned in by Lizzie Vorberg, daughter of Hailey, Idaho brewer Herman Vorberg.

THE LEMP TRIANGLE

As Boise grew and wished to acquire more modern amenities, the push for public parks developed. This led to a complex land ownership question.[ln] The "Lemp Triangle" on West Fort street had for many years had no legal owner. The city then acquired title through a federal patent which was mislaid before it could be filed. After several years a duplicate was obtained and filed. Meanwhile John Lemp had occupied the land and at the present time had it rented out as a Chinese vegetable garden. City Attorney Kahn was researching to see if the title was clear, and a park could be put there, or if Lemp had a legitimate claim. At the 21 December City Council meeting, Kahn said the the triangle belonged to the city of Boise in his opinion, but Lemp was likely to deed it to the city for park purposes, so he would not go into the legal history of the matter.[lo] It was not that cut-and-dried.

At the City Council meeting in March 1906, a report was made by Chairman Davis of the fire and water committee about the Lemp Triangle land. Lemp's lawyer said he claimed the land and would resist any attempt by the city to take possession.[lp] Davis said the land in question had been definitely located and consisted of an acre and three quarters in the heart of the Lemp triangle. They wanted to erect a fire station there and hoped to resolve this as soon as possible. The city attorney hoped to exchange the land in the middle for a similar sized plot on the edge. Negotiations had taken place but were not yet concluded. The council planned to meet again when it was time to make a final decision.

Two weeks later, the matter resurfaced and ownership was not as clear as it had first seemed. In fact, City Attorney Kahn held that the land belonged to Lemp who had claimed it fully fifteen years.[lq] Under the law the mayor should have advertised the fact when he received the government patent, then allowed squatters to apply for a mayor's deed, and then sold unclaimed lands at auction. As is so often the case, government bodies proved incapable of obeying their own rules. Lemp would have been entitled to a title under this law. Therefore all the city ever held was an estate in trust, and not in fee simple. The report was placed on file and Chairman Davis was instructed to advertise for bids to build new fire stations at Hay Market and at Resseguie street near Tenth.

In December, the Boise City Council took up the question of the rightful ownership of a "block of land outside the city limits," the Lemp Triangle.[lr] Lemp had occupied the land for years and the city attorney reported that the city had no claim whatsoever to it. The mayor had merely been the trustee when the land was patented from the United States government.

The February, 25 city council meeting was devoted to hearing objections to giving John Lemp a deed to the disputed land at Thirteenth and Resseguie streets.[ls] No less than five attorneys were at the meeting. J. C. Pence, the old combatant in the Lemp-Pence War, was the only one opposed to the issuance of a deed. He had a written formal statement of his objections. The first was that the Interior Department, years before, had said Lemp was not entitled to a deed; second, Lemp could not acquire title since it was owned by the city and not subject to taxes; and thirdly, Lemp was not an occupant of the land and thus not eligible under the townsite acts of Congress. After all had spoken their piece, John Lemp was given a deed by Mayor John Haines to the "Lemp Triangle," about 1.13 acres or one-eighth of the tract enclosed at the corner.[lt] The *Statesman* editorialized that this was a "grave mistake" and plead to the city fathers to "save the Triangle," but to no avail. Many thought the land perfect for a park but it became the site of Boise's first junior high school. In June of 1908, one disgruntled "Taxpayer" believed Boise could easily acquire the Lemp Triangle or similar small plot for a city park and a large expenditure was unneeded.[lu]

Lemp was improved enough from his illness to be out and about and appeared before the city council to request that he be given until July to plat the Lemp triangle.[lv] The council granted the request.

In August 1909, Lemp announced he would remove the portions of fencing at points where the projected streets in the recently platted tracts in the Lemp triangle would cross the land.[lw] Former city engineer Tolman would survey the land and set stakes at the points where the fence was to be taken down. Cooperation was the theme of the day.

Boise City Councilman E. H. McAuley had a strong desire to make Boise live up to its reputation as "The City Beautiful" and was looking at the Lemp triangle and another piece of land as possible parks sites. [lx] "I am convinced that Boise should be provided with a park system

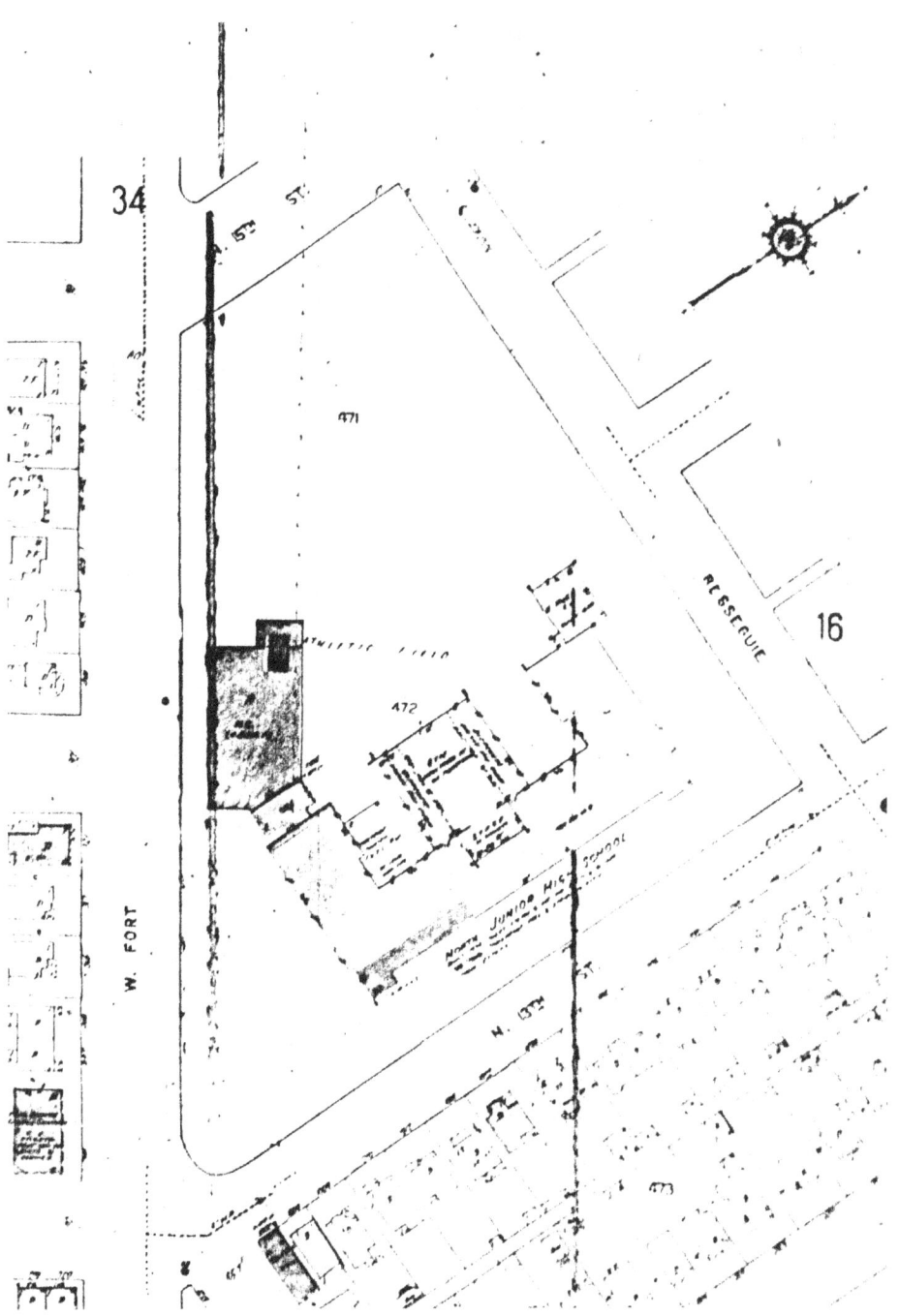

Section of fire insurance map showing the Lemp Triangle.

like other cities of the northwest," he explained to the press. He had his eye on he Lemp triangle. Lemp's land, which was available for about $40,000, was over ten acres and much less expensive than the other tract under consideration. Lemp's triangle was reached by two street car lines and was in easy walking distance of the heart of the city. McAuley was sure the citizens would vote for the bonds since the value of the park would far out weigh the expense. McAuley described his vision of the future park: "The Lemp tract for instance could be made into a very beautiful park at comparatively small expense and it is large enough to at least make a good beginning in this direction. Walks could be laid out, trees planted, fountains constructed and tennis courts and croquet grounds laid out that would furnish amusement for many. Later on concerts might be arranged with the excellent band and orchestra that Boise now boasts, and in time the place would surely become one of the chief attractions of the city—a place to which visitors might be taken and where they would certainly receive a pleasing impression of the city."

New mayor Pence pointed out that the city was in excellent financial shape.[ly] McAuley believed that Lemp's 10.6 acres was the best tract he had examined.

In October, the city council again considered the park question under the urging of Councilman McAuley.[lz] He wanted the city to purchase either Lemp's land for $40,000 or the land of Mr. McCarty for $80,000. Lemp had been offered $50,000 by a Boise real estate firm but he rejected the offer to see what the city fathers would decide.

In early March, Boise received news about the proposed $125,000 bond issue they would vote on later in the month.[ma] $40,000 of the amount was for the purchase of the Lemp Triangle. It was measured at 6.36 acres according to the plat in the city engineer's office. The city had an option from Lemp on the land which expired on the fifth of February, but Lemp agreed to extend it three months until May 5th.

In August of 1910, there was a weed fire on the Lemp triangle.[mb] It originated from an unknown cause on the Thirteenth street side of the plot. Fire Chief H.W. Fulton called the land the "worst fire menace in Boise." He regretted he was not authorized to take some men out and burn all the weed covered lots. That summer of 1910 the greatest fire in Idaho history destroyed many square miles of the pine forests in the panhandle of the state. Wildfire was certainly more strongly on the minds of civic leaders that year than most.

In January 1911, the new owners of the Lemp Triangle submitted their plat to the city council for approval.^{mc} The mid-week meeting lacked a quorum but a couple of days late the matter was handled.^{md} They planned to install sewers, curbs and sidewalks. The council did not inspect the area but made arrangements for collecting the special improvement taxes on the addition.^{me}

By early February, Van Valkenburg and Harris were advertising lots in the Lemp Triangle Addition and claimed twenty-one had been sold the previous week.^{mf} Their advertisements touted the lots as "beautiful, close in, convenient, sure to save street car fare, available on easy terms, and no shacks would be allowed."^{mg} In April, the realtors said they had sold two more lots last week and expected to close more deals shortly.^{mh}

In May, W. S. Clarke and A.C. Worthington, who were among the first purchasers in the Lemp Triangle, had completed a five room bungalow there.^{mi} They were contemplating building three or four more such homes on their tract. Each was expected to cost $2,000. Advertisements for the house lots in the triangle were placed by Van Valkenburg and Harris, the exclusive agents.^{mj} The City council selected lot 1, block 1 of the Lemp Triangle addition for a new fire station in late June of 1911.^{mk}

In July, John sold a lot in the Lemp Triangle to A. C. Worthington for $1400.^{ml} Over a year later the Boise city council was still discussing the possibility of a bond issue to allow purchase of the triangle (or what was still unsold of it) and the creation of a park there.^{mm} The old issue would not die.

1906

The Boise City Council learned that Lemp's building at 823 Main lacked fire escapes and they notified him to comply with city ordinances.^{mn} Meanwhile Lemp's old friend Montana Senator Clark, principal owner of the Sunset group in northern Idaho's Silver Valley, sought capital for that area from Butte, Montana mining men.^{mo}

The Pabst Brewing Company of Milwaukee lost the annex and shed at their warehouse by the tracks in Boise to a fire in January.^{mp} Mr.

A. Bundy just missed losing the $2,000 worth of beer he had stored there. The point here is that many eastern brewers were shipping vast amounts of beer into Boise and competition was fierce.

Julia Lemp, widow of brewer William Lemp, Sr. died in St. Louis in March of 1906. She was the richest woman in St. Louis at the time of her death. The extended Lemp family was dealt another blow.

John Lemp secured his quarterly liquor license for 621 Main, the Brewery Saloon, in March of 1906.[mq]

In February, the notices for the assessments against each piece of city property for the new sewer system in Boise was published in the newspaper several times.[mr] John Lemp was listed with 140 pieces of property. Some of these were jointly held with individuals who were mortgaged, but still it was an impressive list which covered nearly three columns of the newspaper.

Among the many saloon licenses issued in Boise in March was John Lemp's for the "Old Hickory" saloon. Also, the city claimed one and three-quarters acres in the middle of the Lemp triangular tract on Thirteenth street.[ms]

In April of 1906, John Lemp joined the citizens of Boise in raising money for relief of the San Francisco earthquake victims.[mt] Lemp pledged $100 to aid a city he had visited in the past. San Francisco had 24 breweries, 20 of which were damaged in the quake. Six came down but 18, including that of John Wieland, who had retailed through John Lemp's saloons, continued on.

On 9 May 1906, Herbert Frederick Lemp married Marguerite Ann Nolan, and Bernard Louis Lemp married Leona Caroline Tucker. There was no double wedding. Herbert's wedding was held in Hancock, Michigan near Marguerite's childhood home. She had been born in Roscommon, Michigan in 1882, and graduated from Michigan State College at Lansing at age 20 before coming to Idaho in 1902.[mu] Bernard's wedding was in Idaho.

Marguerite taught in Weiser, Idaho, for two years from 1902 until 1904 when she began teaching in Boise.[mv] While a teacher at Boise High School, Miss Nolan was credited with beginning the domestic science courses, which included cooking and sewing.[mw] The fall 1970 issue of *Idaho Yesterdays*, the state histrical society journal, had two pages of photos of her and her children.

Mr. and Mrs. Herbert Lemp returned from their wedding trip and were staying with his parents until June 1st when they were to take the home of Mr. and Mrs. Haines for the summer while the Haines family went East.[mx] Herb barely got back before he was back shooting with the Boise Gun Club at its regular shoots.[my] He also had to take a brief business trip to La Grande, Oregon before the end of May.[mz]

In June, the issue of selling liquor to minors made a small splash in Boise. Charles Phelps, bartender at Lemp's Brewery saloon, was charged with asking no questions when a youth that looked only 17 or so asked for a drink.[na] He pleaded not guilty but was convicted and fined $20, which he paid.[nb] The messenger services of the city were warned that boys could no longer be sent to saloons to pickup beer.[nc] It was a tradition all over America for office workers to chip in a few coins in the late afternoon and send a messenger boy to the saloon for a growler of beer.

When the National Irrigation Congress prepared to meet in Boise,

Louise Lemp is the girl in the middle left with her index finger touching her temple. The group were in a play. Photo, Idaho State Historical Society.

citizens pledged nearly $5,000 for the entertainment of the delegates. John Lemp pledged $100.nd

The City of Boise planned to pave a number of streets and property owners were invited to a meeting with the mayor to discuss the proposal and the assessments needed. Lemp owned four pieces of property listed and would owe well over $1,000 if approved.[ne]

Lemp accused Len Hart of stealing his horse back on June 25, almost two months before.[nf] Justice of the Peace Savidge dismissed the complaint on the motion of the prosecuting attorney. The evidence was insufficient for a conviction.[ng]

In August of 1906, incorporation papers were filed for the Boulder Consolidated Mining Company, Limited. John Lemp was the vice president.[nh] Son Herbert was elected a Republican delegate to the county convention from the fourth precinct of Boise.[ni]

Most of Lemp's business in the late summer and fall of 1906 involved selling more housing lots. Mrs. A. Roderick Grant of Portland came to visit and her brothers Herbert and Edward went to Nampa to meet her at the train.[nj] Another report from Nampa said A. F. (sic) Lemp and Ed Lemp were among those registered at the Dewey Hotel.

In the Fall of 1906, Louise Lemp was a student at the overcrowded Boise High School.[nk] John meanwhile had J. E. Tourtellotte, the noted architect, preparing plans for two connected buildings and basements on Main Street between Seventh and Eighth.[nl] It was to be a brick store building with stone trim and two business sites on the ground floor. There would be apartments or a hotel on the second and third floors. It was to be on the present location of the Pioneer Saloon and the vacant lot adjacent.[nm]

Despite a quiet spell in the Boise real estate market, John, via the W. E. Pierce Co., continued to sell housing lots.[nn] That very week John was reported confined to his bed with another attack of rheumatism.[no] He was improving but still in bed two weeks later.[np]

In late November, one of John's employees, William Stone, was found dead in the Wood River barn on Main Street.[nq] Stone asked to sleep at the barn about 1:30 A.M. and to be called at 5:00 A.M. When George Hilt, the night man, tried to wake him at 5:00 he was dead. Stone, 54, was born at Rock Island, Illinois, and had been a blacksmith in Boise for 20 years. A short time before, he had cared for Lemp's horses and of late had worked some in the Mint Saloon. Coroner Schreibe took charge of the remains and no inquest was planned.[nr] His death was attributed to heavy drinking.

John Lemp was "reported very ill at his home in this city" in early December.[ns] He had no activities mentioned in the local newspapers for some time. The city council renewed liquor licenses for many dealers, including John Lemp. Before 1906 came to an end, local butcher Harry Graham was accused by John Lemp of stealing a fat cow.[nt] The cow was found in Graham's killing pen, and County Attorney Charles Koelsch appeared for the prosecution in Judge Savidge's court. J. E. Schooler represented the defendant. The outcome was not reported.

1907

In early January of 1907, Chairman W. E. Pierce of the finance committee of the entertainment committee of the Commercial Club was busy soliciting money to entertain members of the legislature.[nu] Among the 87 enlightened citizens of Boise who contributed a total of $6,750 was John Lemp who subscribed $100. Lemp was able to afford his largess; he had just sold two lots.[nv]

On 19 February 1907, Herbert Frederick and Marguerite Ann Lemp celebrated the birth of nine-pound son "John."[nw] The senior John Lemp had a new grandson and second namesake. This young man would have an important role to play decades in the future when World War II came. Herbert pursued his political ambitions and was a delegate to the local Republican caucus that March.[nx]

Lemp held the liquor license for the Alcove Bar in Boise in 1907.[ny] He renewed at the $500 rate on 31 March, just before the price rose to $750 on April first.[nz]

In early April, The Settlers Irrigation District sued Settlers Canal Co. Ltd., the Bank of Commerce, the Idaho Trust & Savings Bank, Ltd., John Lemp, Dave McMullen and the County of Ada, Idaho for foreclosure of mortgage.[oa] Three days were granted for the defendants to file an amended answer. On 16 April the complaint was dismissed and the plaintiff ordered to pay costs.[ob] However, the case was not final yet.

On the 18th, an appeal of the case of the Settler's Irrigation District vs. the Settlers' Canal Company, limited, John Lemp, Dave McMullen and the County of Ada, was filed with the clerk of the supreme court. The appeal was taken from he third judicial district by the plaintiff against whom a demurrer on the part of the defendants was sustained by Judge Woods.[oc] In September of 1907, a "friendly " suit was filed with Idaho Trust & Savings Bank and John Lemp vs. Settlers' Canal Co. et al. for foreclosure of mortgage.[od] A related action was The Settlers Irrigation District vs. The Settlers Canal Company Limited, and John Lemp. This was to determine if actions were properly taken in the issuance of $120,000 in bonds by the corporation.[oe] The next March, the Idaho State Supreme Court handed down their opinion which confirmed the validity of a proposal by the Canal Company to issue $120,000 worth of bonds.[of] In June of 1908 the Idaho State Supreme Court dismissed a suit of the Settlers' Irrigation district vs. Settlers' Canal Company at cost of plaintiff and appellant.[og]

Lemp was the victim of the theft of two kegs of beer from his brewery in April of 1907.[oh] James Mullin and Pat Breen were arrested by City Detective Dowd and being unable to furnish $500 ($50 according to the *Evening Capital News*) each bail, were taken to jail. They broke a window at the brewery, entered the cellar on Main between Third and Fourth, and purloined the kegs which they shared with several friends. The brewery manager and city detective Dowd found the kegs at Breen's home. When found, one of the kegs marked "John Lemp" was empty and one was still on tap. Attorney's Edwards and Miller appeared for the defendants while County Attorney Koelsch prosecuted the case.[oi] After a hearing in Justice Dunbar's court, Breen was bound over on a charge of receiving stolen property, and Mullin was charged with burglary.

The big news of nation-wide importance in Boise in 1907 was the trial of Big Bill Haywood and other mining union officials for complicity in the assassination of former Governor Steunnenberg. Herbert Lemp was on the second open panel of prospective jurors but was excused because his father John was sick and he had to run the family businesses for him.[oj]

John Broadbent, who was possibly the richest man in Boise at this point, purchased the property on Main Street between Sixth and Seventh where John Lemp operated his saloon.[ok]

When Herbert was not running the business, he was often shooting at the gun club. At one competition he won the Con W. Hesse medal for highest average with 92%, at another he finished 7th breaking 110 out of 135 shots.[ol] In team shooting, his group was third on the second occasion. At the state-wide "Idaho State Sportsmen's Association Tournament" shooting competition in May of 1907 Herbert finished 7th one day, and was elected state treasurer of the organization.[om] He shot at 425 birds and broke 269.[on]

The mayor of Boise called a meeting of former mayors and prominent citizens to discuss the advisability of selling the municipal building and erecting a much larger one in its place.[oo] John Lemp spoke, and was one of four that did not favor erecting a new building while the present one was not paid for. Generally, those that attended favored a combined city and county building.

J. L. Waggoner of the Settlers' Irrigation District in Ada County published a Delinquent Assessment sale list in May of 1907. On the 30th of June the properties were to be sold. On the list was John Lemp—Northwest quarter, section 35, township 4, 560 acres. $61.85.[op] One of the few court decisions of this era that did not restrict alcohol further was rendered in May of 1907.[oq] The Idaho State Supreme Court ruled unconstitutional the liquor law of 1903 which prohibited the sale of alcohol near public works, grading camps of canals and kindred enterprises. Their reasoning was that the title of the act was too restrictive to cover the provisions of the act.

This same month the Boise City council decided to set up a paving district to pave nearly four miles of downtown Boise.[or] There was a special tax assessment to pay for this. Large property owners such as John Lemp would be hard hit once again.

In July, Mrs. Lemp and daughter Louise went to the cooler climes of Portland for a visit.[os] In August, word reached Boise of the death of Mrs. George Kohlepp, sister-in-law of the Lemps, in Seattle of cancer.[ot] She and her husband had left Boise nine years before, according to the report, but she was an old-timer, having come here with her parents, Mr. and Mrs. Edwin Crouch in 1860. This was George's third wife. A few days later there was a report that Henry Kohlepp and wife of Middleton paid a call on the Lemp's.[ou] I suspect this meeting related to the grieving process in the Kohlepp family. Before long Henry moved to Boise and was deemed a visitor when he went back to Middleton on business in September.[ov]

In a legal notice of land to be sold for taxes, penalties and costs assessed in 1906 by the Settlers Irrigation District of Ada County were several parcels owned by John Lemp for which he was $62.10 in arrears.[ow]

On August 7, the first through car traveled from Boise to Caldwell on the new Boise & Interurban train.[ox] About 30 city, county and state officials, businessmen and reporters—including John Lemp – – made the initial run. The 28 1/2 miles run was made in less than two hours, counting stops at the barn and substations. Their first stop was at Soldiers Home where the company had built a small depot. Next, they stopped to inspect the steel bridge being built over the Farmer's Union Canal. The company's barn at the 4 1/2 miles mark was reached next. It was large enough to hold 12 of the company's cars. Then it was on to Eagle and Middleton. The 550 foot steel bridge across the Boise river near Caldwell was the great surprise of the trip. On the return the train reached speeds of 50 miles per hour. All the guest passengers were delighted with the trip.

A short time later, speaking of the positive effect of the Boise-Interurban railroad, The Boise Citizen noted that since its inception John Lemp's ranch at Middleton had increased in value from $5 per acre to $100.[oy] The increased value resulting from improved transportation. A 20 fold increase seems extreme, but the trains' usefulness was indisputable. A Caldwell forwarding company, for instance, was able to send a reaper to the Lemp ranch with noteworthy ease.[oz]

At a regular city council meeting, the Fathers of Boise accepted the report of their street and alley committee which rejected the request of John Lemp and M. A. Wilcox for rebates on the street sprinkling fees they had paid.[pa]

In late August of 1907, Lemp leased the Boston Grill to Otto Klein for $150 per month until April of 1913.[pb] Klein also leased the Capitol hotel from the Idaho Brewing Company at the same time for $500 per month.

Ed Lemp was mentioned as a visitor to Star in early September of 1907.[pc] About this time, the man in charge of the Lemp vineyard three miles west of Boise came upon two women filling their pails with the luscious fruit. He did not actually see them for they saw him first and scrammed minus their hats and the half-filled buckets.[pd] Lemp had published warnings about hunting not being allowed on his Middleton ranch or his Island ranch.[pe] Lemp advertised once again that there was no hunting allowed on his Middleton or Island ranches.[pf]

Perhaps not quite coincidentally, Judge Bryan in Caldwell rendered a decision that the new state liquor law allowing county commissioners to refuse to grant liquor licenses was constitutional.[pg] Eventually the state Supreme Court concurred.

Otto Scholtz, employed on the Lemp ranch "down the valley" was arrested after making a disturbance on the interurban car at State and Tenth Streets. He had five pint bottles of whiskey on him at the time. His case was rapidly disposed of in Municipal court the next morning.[ph]

Christmas of 1907 at the Lemp home was not noted in any public mention but it was the first John had known for 43 years without being in the brewing business, and, tragically, it was to be the last he and Catherine would have together.

THE DEATH OF CATHERINE LEMP

Without public warning, on Tuesday, 7 January 1908 at 7:00 in the evening, Catherine Lemp, "aged pioneer," died at 57. [pi] She had been ill for a year but only severely for a week. John had been confined to his bed for several weeks—"since December 21"—at the time and was not there at the final moment. Seven of her eight living children, all except Augusta, who lived in Portland, were there at the end. The end was calm and peaceful. Catherine was described as a "woman of most beautiful character, kindly, generous, ever thoughtful and considerate of the comfort and happiness of others;" and "a woman of sterling worth having a beautiful character making her a devoted mother, and a loyal friend always ready to administer to the needs of others." Her husband and eight children survived her.

She was buried from her home on Fifth and Grove streets at 10 O'clock on Friday.[pj] Friends could view her remains until 10 o'clock the morning of the funeral. The casket was closed then, never to reopen. She was interned in the Masonic portion of Pioneer Cemetery beside her late children. Pall bearers were all old friends and pioneers of Boise: R. C. Adelman, Charles Himrod, Judge J. H. Richards, Joseph Pinkham, C. Tatro, Tim Regan, John Maloney, and John Haines.[pk] The Hailey newspaper described Catherine as the wife of the wealthy Boise brewer and sister of George Kohlepp who had started the first brewery in Hailey.[pl] Augusta Lemp Grant arrived in Boise from Portland in time for her mother's funeral.[pm] The loss John must have felt with the death of his wife of forty-three years, the mother of his thirteen children, can only be imagined.

Catherine's will, dated 22 December 1896, was entered into probate on 31 January and probated at 10 o'clock on February 3.[pn] Mrs. Lemp was half owner of all the Lemp property which was conservatively estimated at $1,000,000. Her will had been written by Judge George H. Stewart. She left everything to her husband and he was also named executor to serve without bond. The Lemps had decided not to give an inheritance to the children while either one of them survived.

The daily concerns of life continued through John's grief. Lemp was the third highest—behind John Broadbent and The Oregon Shortline railway—property tax payer in Ada County in 1908 with a total due of $8,047.79.[po] He had held this third place position for several years at this point. In 1908, Tourtellotte and Hummel designed a brick store building for Lemp at 823 1/2 Main.[pp] This architecture firm was very productive during this decade.

In January 1908, Mayor John Haines addressed the Ladies of the Columbian Club about the need for parks in Boise which was a current topic because two months before the city had accepted park land from Tom Davis.[pq] This was to be Julia Davis Park and an integral part of Boise for the next century.

The Odd Fellows were eighty-nine years old in America and celebrating their 40th year of the Ada Lodge in March.[pr] Lemp's lodge was building a new $75,000 hall in Boise.

The Capital State Bank of Boise was forced to close but by March of 1908 was seeking agreement of the depositors for a plan to continue business. An informal poll of businessmen found most favored this. Among the opinions expressed was one from "Mr. Lemp" [Bernard, I believe] who said "there is no question in my mind that the reopening of the bank would be a good thing..."[ps]

On 13 April 1908, the "stork visited the home of Mr. and Mrs. Herbert Lemp."[pt] The family added their first daughter and second, and last, child, Mary Catherine. Obviously the middle name was for Herbert's recently deceased mother.

In April of 1908, a group of Montana mine owners purchased a northern Idaho smelter. Among the men in this group was Senator W. A. Clarke, described as the world's largest individual mine operator.[pu] This was the man who traveled the Oregon trail with John Lemp nearly half a century before.[pv]

As the Odd Fellows of Boise prepared to celebrate the 89th anniversary of the founding of the lodge in America, they recalled how in 1881 they had moved the lodge into the Lemp Hall while they purchased lots to build their own building.[pw]

B. F. Neal wrote a multi-column letter to the *Capital News* in May offering his thoughtful ideas about the location of parks in Boise.[px] He favored buying a portion of the Lemp tract even though the initial price was higher. It would be a good investment.

In late June, the Bank of Idaho filed for incorporation after the stockholders put up $100,000 to begin business. The 17 owners listed included John Lemp.[py] Soon the officers were named and the commercial nature of the bank was described for the public.[pz] Advertisements showed an outline map for the state of Idaho and at the bottom a list of prominent stockholders, including John Lemp.[qa]

Four Boise men, James Latimer, William Sullivan, Bert Haug and Bert Harris went to the Lemp ranch twenty-two miles below the city to hunt frogs and managed to capture a hundred of them.[qb] This was a large number for the area.

Louise Lemp rode in an automobile with her friends Ethel and Avice Sheridan and Hazel Grigsby in the 4th of July parade in 1908.[qc] Things had changed from the days of the old liberty car floats. Many people of Boise had probably seen only a handful of Tin Lizzies by this time. That same month son Herbert was nominated as a delegate to the Republican convention from precinct four of Boise.[qd] He was actually elected a couple of weeks later.[qe]

In July of 1908, the Imperial Potentate of the Mystic Shrine, the national headman, decreed that all Shrine banquets should be "dry."[qf] As a long time member, Lemp must have been struck by this change in policy and how it reflected on him and the profession he had chosen.

W. C. Tatro, Lemp's Oregon trail companion of 1863, suffered a fatal stroke of apoplexy while working as a night watchman at the statehouse.[qg] He had been in the mercantile business in Rocky Bar and started the stage line there from 1870 to 1882. Next he had been marshal in Hailey for eight years. He had worked at the state house for four years, and left a wife, two daughters, and his son W. C. Tatro, Jr. of Everett, Washington.

J. E. Tourtellotte & Co., architects, began preparing plans for a two story brick building to be erected on Main between Seventh and Eighth streets for John Lemp.[qh] It was to have a 21 foot front, extend 122 feet, to be two stories and to be made of brick and cut stone. The ground floor was to be a store room and the second story to be divided into eight rooms. The estimated cost was $10,000. Within a month the architects let the contract to W. M. Clifton for $5,800 with Lemp furnishing the brick.[qi] When the *Evening Capital News* listed the great new buildings of 1908 in Boise in their welcome the new year edition, Lemp's building, costing about $7,000, was on the list.[qj]

In early October of 1908, the *Statesman* printed the Boise business census of 1868—forty years before—which included five breweries, two distilleries, and twenty saloons for 365 voters in the whole of Ada county.[qk] The newspaper went on to contrast that with the present list which included twenty saloons, one brewery and no distilleries for a vastly increased population. They believed the question "Is the city growing better?" was thus easily answered. Clearly breweries, such as Lemps, had lost the attraction they held in the early days. Rather than their presence being a sign of growth, stability and business, their absence was a sign of improved morals.

A small ad in the *Evening Capital News* in October of 1908 informed the public that Faust's art store had moved to Main street in Lemp's building opposite the Mode.[ql]

A giant charity drive in Boise featured "Tag Day" with a charity ball to follow in a few days to raise money for the homeless children of Idaho.[qm] Among the initial contributions was $25 from John Lemp, $50 from the retail liquor Dealers Association and $50 from the Idaho State Brewers Association. At that point the total received was only $320, so these were sizable amounts.

W. A. Goulder, the newspaper reporter emeritus of Idaho wrote a brief biographical sketch of John Lemp for the pioneer section of the Sunday *Statesman* in November of 1908.[qn] The article was headlined "How a Penniless German Boy Made It Go in the Early Days of Idaho." Goulder mostly relied on his memory as a source and a few of his details were weak or erroneous, but the tone and direction of the piece were admirable. He knew and admired John Lemp and he had sincere emotions to convey. There was also a photo of Lemp as a young man. Goulder said Lemp was born in Germany near Butzbach at a date Goulder could not remember. Lemp came penniless but strong willed and determined to make a home. Gould said Lemp followed the business of a brewer from age fourteen (sic) and "I am sure Mr. Lemp has no cause to regret his choice of an occupation for there are few lines of business that have helped more materially in building up cities and in giving employment to multitudes of men." "Being a strict and uncompromising prohibitionist myself I seldom drink beer, unless the weather is extremely cold and then my natural preference drives me irresistible to Tom and Jerry. But I can very distinctly remember having tasted some of 'Lemp's Best' which I pronounced it very good but Mr. Lemp's industry and enterprise were far from being confined to the manufacture of that delicious beverage which 'jeers but does not ingogsify.' The impress of his indefatigable industry and far seeing business sagacity in many other branches of enterprise are seen here in Boise and in many sections of Ada county. In 1866 Mr. Lemp was married to Miss Katherine Kohlepp, a native of Prussia, whose mother and other relatives resided here for many years. The worthy couple were the parents of eight children, four boys and four girls." "During his short sojourn of 43 years in Boise Mr. Lemp has filled several posts of honor and responsibility the duties of which were always met and fulfilled by him with both credit to himself and to the best interests of the people. He was for several years president of the First National bank of Idaho, whose affairs he managed to the entire satisfaction of all parties concerned or in any way interested. He has been one of Boise's best mayors and at a time when the struggling young city needed just the help which he was fitted and always able to give. For several years past Mr. Lemp has been grievously afflicted with rheumatism which besides the suffering which it has brought to him, has for much of the time kept him in his home, so that his host of friends have seen and felt but little of his welcome and genial presence. All this with other afflictions and sorrows, he has borne with the bravery and fortitude that has always marked and dignified his life and that fits so gracefully and grandly into his declining years of a true and genuine Idaho pioneer. Very truly, W. A. Goulder." Goulder's memory earned some pluses and some minus marks. Goulder had been saved by Lemp when he was being carried away by a flood years before, and they had known each other for decades.

In November of 1908, Lemp again advertised against hunting on his property.[qo]

When the old Central school building in Boise burned in 1908 it was remembered in the press of Boise. They mentioned that Lemp was one of the school board members when the building was erected in 1881.[qp] He had been functioning as a school for the Deaf, Dumb, and Blind in its recent years.

Also in November, long-time rival and shirt-tail relative, John Brodbeck, caught a severe cold which developed into bronchial trouble, then pneumonia, and he died at the home of his daughter Mrs. T. P. Woodcock.[qq] Brodbeck was arguably the second or third most significant brewer in early Idaho history. The Boise brewing fraternity lost a patriarch. The Lemp and Brodbeck plots in Pioneer cemetery are very close together and their homes in Boise were very near each other.

LEMP PARK

Lemp began to advertise 85 tracts of land from 8 1/2 to 17 acres each carved from his holdings in the Boise Valley.[qr] The allotment system of the Carey Act (desert land act) was to be used to determine who got the land. The Boise and Interurban electric railroad went through the area and access was quick and easy to Boise, Caldwell or Nampa, proclaimed the full page ad. Later in the month, a follow up ad in the shape of a letter said inquiries from all the surrounding states and all over Idaho had been pouring in.[qs] A full page ad the next January said the date of February 17 had been selected for the allotment.[qt] Only those who had deposited part of the first payment by then would be eligible. Each tract in "Lemp Park" was $1,290 regardless of size or location.[qu] A February 6th ad the next year reminded everyone that the time for the allotment was approaching, on the 13th the ad said "the last call," and on the 15th it said "Fair Warning."[qv] Quite a few hopefuls were reported in Caldwell on the 17th of February 1909 for the drawing, and a lucky Caldwell man secured the first chance to select one of the lots for himself.[qw]

Three months later, Lemp was still advertising ten-acre irrigated garden and orchard tracts at Middleton in what was being called Lemp Park.[qx] For a small down payment and easy monthly payments one could have immediate possession. The area was a one hour ride from Boise, three miles from Star, and on the Boise & Interurban Electric Railway. The Colonists Trustee Company Lts. on the ground floor at 107 North Tenth St. was the agent. Lemp's farm of 1200 acres was the largest in the area and the railroad went through for nearly a mile.[qy] Great development for that section was predicted.

1908

After the November, 1908 state elections, the Local Option issue was on the minds of many. "The big Republican majority in the upcoming legislature undeniably worries the heads of the Brewers' cabinet," according to the *Statesman*.[qz] Hopes for a change in the law were unlikely and saloons all over the state were worried. As a life-long Republican, Lemp found himself allied with a group opposed to his own interests.

1909

The Bank of Idaho advertised the value of depositing one's salary and then writing checks to cover obligations.[ra] In January of 1909, this was not yet a widely established concept. Many people used cashier's checks. The bank bragged about its $100,000 in capital and listed its officers and stockholders. Third on that list was John Lemp. He was still involved in the bank and his name was still a symbol of stability.

The St. Louis branch of the Lemp family endured a very public messy divorce case which ended on 18 February 1909. Lillian was granted a divorce from her multimillionaire husband William, Jr. but given only $6,000 per year in alimony.[rb] She appealed, and in 1913 the Missouri State Supreme Court granted her $100,000 per year.

In late March, John Lemp returned to Boise from Hot Lake, Oregon where he had spent some time for his health—most certainly treating his rheumatism.[rc] Son Herbert and daughter Louise accompanied him. The 65,000 square foot main brick building was completed at the lake, halfway between La Grande and Union, in 1908. At its height it was a sanitarium, spa, and teaching hospital using the lake water which bubbles out at 208 degrees. Many famous Americans, including the the Mayo brothers of the famed medical clinic visited.[rd]

John still held a retail liquor license. In April 1909, he put up bond with W. F. Pierce and L. H. Cox as sureties for one year's license.[re]

A Lemp employee died late in April and his story was published in the *Statesman*.[rf] Harry Curtis was working on the Lemp hog farm on the south side of the river when he was taken violently ill one day. His brother William got him into the tent they shared with Mr. Briggs. Harry died there and the newspaper mentioned that the trio were victims of the morphine habit. Supposedly the drug had weakened Harry's system enough that he could not resist an illness. He was the son of the late Judge Curtis who at one time had been the secretary of the Idaho Territory, acting governor and a leading attorney. Drugs were a societal problem then as ever since.

In May, the Columbian Club of Boise picked Bishop Funsten and C. C. Anderson as members of the advisory committee to replace John Lemp and the late Alfred Eoff.[rg] The Club had just paid off the lot it bought at the corner of Franklin and Ninth and was basking in the glow of success at the time.

June 1, 1909 was a banner day for the Northwest. In Seattle, on the University of Washington campus, the Alaska-Yukon-Pacific Exposition opened when President Taft, 3,000 miles away in Washington, D.C., moved an Alaskan gold nugget attached to a telegraph key to complete a circuit and send a telegraphic impulse across the continent to officially open the fair. June first was also the day that Mayor J. T. Pence issued an order outlawing the sale of liquor in the Boise Red Light district.[rh] This did not affect Lemp's businesses but it was symbolic of the ever tightening squeeze being put on the beverage alcohol business.

In June, the *Evening Capital News* published a long history of the water system in Boise.[ri] They spoke of the fine quality of the water in the system and mentioned the first stock holders—including John Lemp—of the Artesian Hot and Cold Water Company that formed in March of 1891.

In July of 1909, the number of saloons in Boise dropped from 29 to 27.[rj] One of the two closing was the Old Hickory run by John Lemp, who failed to apply for renewal of its liquor license. The excessive cost of liquor licenses was an effective way to diminish the number of saloons.

Boise, and all of Ada county, was facing an election on the local option issue in September of 1909. Lemp still owned liquor licenses and had a concern in the outcome. Headed by attorney Gustave Kroeger, the Wets made one of their most effective campaigns ever in Idaho and carried the day by 840 votes.[rk]

That Fall, Bernard Lemp charged Fred Harris with stealing a load of grain from the Lemp stable on Main Street between Third and Fourth streets.[rl] Harris pled guilty and Judge Dunbar sentenced him to three months in the county jail. Meanwhile Miss Louise Lemp was assisting Mrs. Purcell at her bridge party.[rm] Social life and business life always coincided.

A small court case in Boise attracted considerable attention because the mayor represented one side and the city attorney the other. The plaintiffs were the socially prominent Mr. and Mrs. Herbert Lemp.[rn] Mrs. Lemp received a set of black lynx furs for Christmas but when she went to put them away in May discovered two moth millers on them and feared their might be hidden eggs from them. Mrs. A. A. Austin ran a fur store and she said she could bake the furs to kill any eggs. Mrs. Lemp took the furs in on the 28th of May and was to pick them up on June 2nd. On the second Mrs. Austin called to say that the furs had been ready the day before and she had laid them on some other furs near the cash register. When she went to look for them later they had disappeared. Mrs. Lemp claimed she paid $75, the wholesale price, but they were worth $150. Mrs. Austin offered to pay $100 but Mrs. Lemp ask her to order a new set from the Anderson-Bloomquist company. Mrs. Austin did this but when they arrived they were priced at $240. She then consulted an attorney who said she was not liable for the theft if she had not been negligent. The case took all day with many witnesses. The jury finally awarded $70 to the plaintiff.

Lemp's building at 714 Main had a new tenant in November of 1909: a billiard parlor.ʳᵒ E. M. Rogers gave up his post as district manager of the Boise branch of the Bell Telephone company to open this new business. He had worked his way up in the phone company from the very bottom, but now wanted to open a first rate recreational resort and be his own boss.

1910

Brother-in-law George Kohlepp, recently made a widower, returned to the Boise area after being a saloonist in Spokane and commenced a court action against John Lemp to quiet title to a piece of property.ʳᵖ The property was about forty acres described as the south half of the northeast quarter of the southeast quarter of section 19, and lot 9 of section 30, all township 3 north, range 3 east. The newspaper article mentioned Kohlepp's late sister, Mrs. Lemp. George and John were no longer the close friends they had been in the early years when they were both involved in horse racing.

In January of 1910, the Statesman lauded Lemp's impending construction that would make Boise more metropolitan than ever before.ʳᑫ Lemp was having plans drawn for a nine-story building on the southeast corner of Ninth and Main. In early March, Lemp said that though he had not even selected an architect yet, he would spend not less than $150,000.ʳʳ Unnamed individuals who heard him speak of his proposal believed it would be six to nine stories, and modern in every way. The fire fighting capacity of the city at that time was inadequate to fight a fire on a building so tall, and also the city ordinances prohibited a structure over six stories. Supposedly a local restaurateur already had designs on the ground floor. The *Statesman* commented how many times in the past conservative businessmen thought Lemp was exceeding the needs of the city but each time his vision had proved prophetic and profitable. This was the essence of Lemp's business success: going beyond the immediate situation and looking to the future. The *Evening Capital News* asked Herbert Lemp what his father's plans were, said they were not ready to announce anything.ʳˢ In February, they added the Lemp building to the list that they believed assured the capital city of the busiest building season ever.ʳᵗ

Also in March, Lemp was issued a building permit for a two-story brick on Main between Seventh and Eight next to the existing Lemp building.[ru] It was to be 18 X 122, to be used as a lodging house, and to cost $20,000. Soon the tenants in Lemp's building at Ninth and Main had been told to vacate by the first of June when materials for the new building would be on the ground.[rv] The *Evening Capital News* in mid-May proclaimed that the Lemp building might go to ten stories and be part of a "skyscraper row" in Boise.[rw] By mid-August, the project had been postponed until at least the following year due to a tight money market.[rx]

Meanwhile "Miss Lemp" was busy with such things as the "Young Girls Sewing Club" which not only sewed but gave dinners to honor members.[ry]

On 6 April 1910, Bernard Louis and Leona Caroline Lemp became parents of their first child, Bernard Louis, Jr.[rz] Mrs. Grant, Bernard's sister Augusta, had returned to Portland about the 28th of March, just before the birth.[sa] She had been visiting her father and sisters in Boise.

Little Catherine Lemp danced "The Irish Washerwoman" at the recital of Breach's Dancing Academy.[sb] Meanwhile, Mrs. Herbert Lemp was co-hostess with Mrs. J. H. Haines at a card party for a very large number of women.[sc] She passed much of her time in social activity. The next month, Herbert accompanied Mrs. Lemp and his son as far as Salt Lake on their trip back to Chicago and Michigan where she was to visit her relatives.[sd] By early June she was back in Boise.[se]

The 1910 Census listed the various Lemp families in Boise. John had sons Albert and Edward and daughter Louise listed at his address. Albert's daughter Catherine was not living with her father. Harold and Clarence Lemp, sons of the late Jacob Lemp were in Twin Falls with their mother and step-father William Breckon.

In late June, "Miss Lemp" (Louise) was chairman of a dance held in the pavilion at Pierce park to raise money for the children's ward at St. Luke's hospital. Some danced, some watched, and some went boating on the lake.[sf]

On June 27, John Lemp and Catherine Lemp *each* filed a land patent on Boise county acreage, according to Bureau of Land Management Records. John's was 166.7 acres and Catherine's was 173.62 acres.

These were cash entry sales.^{sg} It may be that Catherine had initiated the purchase before her death and her estate was finishing the purchase, or the estate was filing in her name.

In August, John announced the engagement of his daughter Louise to Marshall C. Simonson who worked in the city clerk's office.[sh] Louise Lemp and Marshall Simonson obtained their marriage license early in October.[si]

In late August, Louisa Lemp went to Portland to visit her sister, Mrs. Grant.[sj] Little Miss Katherine Lemp, Albert's daughter, visited her mother in Nebraska and returned to Boise as school began in September.[sk]

Boise pioneer James A. Pinney gave a large dinner in his apartment at the Pinney theater on the occasion of his 75th birthday.[sl] He invited many other Idaho pioneers and complied some information to share about each. Among his guests, Pinney listed John Lemp, 72, as a native of Germany who came to Idaho in 1859 via an ox team. The date should have been 1863.

One of Lemp's buildings, at 714 Main street, which had recently been a billiard hall, caught fire from a cigar stump one morning but suffered little damage. The pool hall had moved up the street and some of the building was used for storage by the Dan Brown Liquor Wholesale Company.[sm]

On 5 October 1910, Louise Bernice Lemp married Marshall C. Simonson. The round of parties for the bride took two weeks so every possible hostess from the Boise social set had the chance to hold a society event. The Misses Sheridan began on Monday, more than a week before the wedding, with a small party. Then came Miss Booth and Mrs. Ormund Booth's event was held. Miss Hazel Cohen gave a dinner on a Thursday. Mrs. Ferguson and Mrs. Mendenhall did likewise. Mrs. Charles Shriver, Mrs. Julius Myers, and Mrs. Eugene Hale gave a bridge party just before the wedding. Miss Hazel Grigsby continued the round on the next Tuesday. The Grigsby party featured heart shaped cards and candlesticks intertwined with nasturtiums. Louisa's sister-in-law, Mrs. Herbert Lemp, also gave a party with a sit down supper. A luncheon was given by Miss Helen Furnell, one of the maids of honor.[sn]

The Society section of the *Daily Statesman* predicted the wedding would attract "a large number of the younger set."[so] The wedding was performed by Dan Smith at John Lemp's home in the drawing room.[sp] The Statesman gave the event itself a large report and told every detail. The furniture was removed except for the grand piano. Between the two front windows a canopy of clematis with a cluster of electric lights hidden in the foliage sheltered the bridal party. The only other decoration in the room was a huge brass bowl of yellow chrysanthemums on the piano. In the dining room was a large cut glass bowl filled with white carnations and lighted with pink shaded candles. The table holding the wedding cake was ornamented with a bowl of pink roses, with the same flowers banking the buffet. The archway between the drawing room and the dining room had a grill of Virginia creeper.

The wedding march was played by Mrs. Gamble and Miss Morehouse. The huge wedding party than began to appear. First six friends of the bride came in—Misses Avis and Ethel Sheridan, Lennie Korts, Marguerite Helfrich, Hazel Cohen, and Audrey Lowe—and they formed a ribbon isle through which passed the honored maid, Hazel Grigsby, followed by two maids of honor, Helen Pursell and Hazel Booth. Then came the flower girl, Katherine Lemp, Herbert's daughter, niece of the bride, with a basket of pink and white sweet peas. The bride came down the stairway unattended and met her "aged father" at the bottom. John Lemp escorted his daughter to the alter where she met the bridegroom and the best man, Jack Adelman.

The bride wore cream Empire satin made in a simple but beautiful style. The frock itself was perfectly plain with a long court train. "Over it was a slip of embroidered tulle which formed a decollette corsage with shoulder sleeve caps and fell in straight panels, both back and front to within a few inches of the hem of the skirt, the ends being edged with deep silk fringe. A high necked guimpe, hand embroidered, with a flow of pearls at the top of the collar was worn with the gown. The veil was the same one worn by her older sister, Mrs. O'Connor, 21 years ago, and covered the entire gown." It was arranged in a cap-like fashion on the coiffure, ornamented with a circlet of pearls. The bride carried a shower bouquet of bride roses.

The honored maid wore white crepe with a border of pink roses over pink messaline. Miss Pursell wore white chiffon over pink and Miss

Booth white marquisette over pink. All carried pink roses. The frocks of the ribbon bearers blended in soft pastel shades, Miss Helfrich wearing white over yellow, Miss Ethel Sheridan pink crepe, Miss Avis Sheridan yellow crepe, Miss Cohen pale green messaline, Miss Lowe yellow chiffon and Miss Khortz white lace. Mrs. Roderick Grant, of Portland, sister of the bride, wore a handsome gown of rose colored Ninon, trimmed with cut jet; Mrs. O'Connor, another sister, wore pale grey chiffon cloth over gray messaline.

Miss Avis Sheridan caught the bride's bouquet and cut the ring as well. Mr. and Mrs. Simonson planned to make their home with the bride's father, John Lemp. This was what a fashionable 1910 wedding in Boise, Idaho was like. Also, the situation reveals that John Lemp needed family around to care for him at this stage of his life.

The bride's sister Mrs. Grant immediately returned to Portland after the wedding and the visit with her father.[sq] Life for John Lemp returned to normal.

Marshall C. Simonson was born in Marion County, Illinois on 17 October 1882, the son of John M. and Bessie Johnston Simonson.[sr] His father died in 1908 in that county. Marshall was educated at Salem, Illinois and then attended Washington University in St. Louis and learned to be a civil engineer. He came to Boise in 1903 and worked as an engineer. From 1908 to 1912 he held the office of deputy city clerk of Boise. After that he went on to work for his firm of Atkinson and Simonson which represented building material manufacturers.

1911

On New Year's, a large dance was held in the Rose Room of the Owyhee Hotel.[ss] Mr. and Mrs. Herbert Lemp attended. A few days later the inaugural ball for Governor Hawley was held, and Herbert Lemp was a member of the floor committee that night.[st]

Early that January of 1911, Herbert was elected second vice president and executive committee member for the Idaho State Life Insurance company.[su] Herbert seemed to be pursuing numerous business situations simultaneously as his father always had done.

Boise was continuing to modernize in the second decade of the century. A petition to install cluster street lights was submitted to the city council with the signatures of some of the heaviest property owners—"some of whom were never before known to have fallen in line for any special improvement of any description."[sv] John Lemp was among the 195 signers.

On the Polk City Directory of 1911 for Boise and Ada County, John was listed as a capitalist whose office was at 208 Overland Building, Bell Telephone 68, Independent Telephone 386. His home was still 507 Grove with Bell number 62-L and Independent number 686-M.[sw] Albert and Edward were listed as livestock men, working out of the Grove Street home. Herbert lived at 108 S. Fifth. Bernard was listed as a bookkeeper who lived at 1711 W. Franklin.

Boise appeared to have a murder mystery on its hand for a brief time in March of 1911 when workmen digging a basement beneath the Broadbent building, occupied by Leo Seller, came across a number of bones.[sx] They found what appeared to be a child's skull, as well as a foot, arm bones, shoulder blade and teeth of an adult. Some recalled the story of a man who was found forty years before with his skull crushed in the saloon that once occupied the spot. John Lemp had owned the saloon back then, and when told of the find scoffed at any hint of a crime in connection with the bones. He said that boys used to dig up bones from the Indian cemetery behind the fort and scare people by reconstructing skeletons. Since these parts didn't match one individual they were probably thrown into some dump and gradually buried. A physician said the skull was from some animal, but the other bones were human. A dentist said the molars were also human. Apparently no one there knew enough to determine gender, ethnicity, or age of the bones. This whole incident reveals the casual attitude of the majority society toward the human remains of Native Americans.

John's old friend former Senator William A. Clark made the news when his wife underwent an operation for appendicitis.[sy]

In April, 3,000 head of John Lemp's cattle were driven through Boise en route from Winter quarters at Parma and Middleton to their Summer range on Smith's Prairie.[sz] Herbert and his wife returned to Boise after a trip to Salt Lake City.[ta] There was always something going on to remind the folk of Boise of Lemp's wealth and influence.

Mrs. A. Wolters returned from an extended eastern trip that June on which she had taken her grandnephew, Herbert's son, John Lemp, Jr., four and a half years old.[tb]

There was a small blaze near the roof in the old building John Lemp owned at the corner of Ninth and Main that July.[tc] The Exchange Bar occupied the site and the fire was quickly extinguished with a garden hose.

Mr. and Mrs. Herbert Lemp went on a camping and fishing trip with Mr. and Mrs. W. F. Bee.[td] They went initially by auto, switching to pack horses for the last leg, and enjoyed a two weeks stay at Trinity lakes.

Albert Lemp carelessly left his team unhitched on the street one day and paid a $5 fee in court the next morning.[te] He commended the officer who cited him, was glad to pay his fine, and believed the ordinance should be enforced.

In August, the Ada County Board of Equalization ruled on several assessments on Lemp property.[tf] Lots 9-10 of block 9 of the Boise original townsite went from $45,000 to $35,000; lots 3-4 and 10 W 1/2 11 and 5 of block 24, Boise original townsite, from $3,000 to $2,000; and lots 1-6, block 128 of Boise original townsite from $11,250 to $10,250.

An interesting story came out of rural Boise in August of 1911. Its only direct connection to John Lemp is that it took place in Lemp Gulch but it explains the conditions in rural Idaho in 1911.[tg] Rancher W. M. Butterbaugh had been missing chickens for some days but could not tell what kind of an animal had been doing the mischief. Sport, his medium-sized coach dog, figured it out. One morning Butterbaugh heard Sport take off after something and he got up as soon as he could and followed the trail up the gulch. When he overtook his dog he found him lying nearly dead on the ground, and beside him, thoroughly dead, was a six-foot bobcat. The poor dog was mauled and ripped from end to end with some scratches going to the bone, but he had won the day. The fight, Butterbaugh suspected, must have lasted fifteen minutes. Surprisingly, he succeeded in nursing the dog back to health.

For the Labor Day contests of 1911, the *Statesman* joked that John Lemp was rumored to be "riding the 'joy wheel' at the White City recently," and they surmised he was training for the fat man's race.[th] Of course, John's days as an athlete were over.

Herbert's family moved to 1801 Resseguie Street about the end of

August.^ti Mrs. Lemp returned to Boise from a trip to her old home in Michigan a week later.^tj

In October, United States President William Howard Taft came to Boise on an official visit. The town spared no effort to make this a big day. A parade included all the national level politicians from Idaho on down to local leaders. Car # 17 was Herbert Lemp's and included passengers J. M. Roberts, Stephen Utter, H. Ellsworth, Mrs. Maud L. Cleary, Miss Ivy M. Wilson.^tk Herbert's political climb was becoming increasingly obvious. The report on the parade in the *Statesman* had a photo of father John Lemp in an automobile in the parade. They said he rode "for once without using the familiar Phaeton."^tl A Phaeton at that point in history was an open, four-wheeled carriage. According to the *Evening Capital News* in the second division of the parade was a contingent of eighteen of Boise's pioneer firefighters in the uniforms of the old days.^tm Those in the contingent included Messrs. Lemp and Lyerzapf. This must have been John. Perhaps he rode after marching part of the way. John was not listed with the pioneers of the early 1860s that were honored at the parade.

The *Evening Capital News* published a large "Progress" issue in mid-October and described many businesses and prominent individuals of southern Idaho.^tn The only listing of John Lemp was as an officer in the Pacific National Bank of Boise.

Polo

Herbert's real interest at this time was not old buildings but polo. Polo, "the popular field game of the east," had been introduced to Boise in September of 1909 by the cavalry at Fort Boise.^to The cavalry team was first going to play the town team-Lemp's team at the barracks one weekend in early November.^tp Herbert Lemp was captain of the town team which also featured teammates Waterbury, Falk and Ostner.

On November 19th, the Cavalry team and the town team continued their series of matches.^tq The town team won and "one of the factors that contributed much toward the Boise victory was the work of Herbert Lemp and his horses." "Lemp's mounts easily outdistanced anything else on the field. His horsemanship was almost desperate, and his spectacular rushes carried the ball many yards toward the army goal during the course of the game." There was some dispute about the army's one goal as Lemp had just been unseated. Since there was no perceived danger to man or horse, play went on and the goal counted. Later, during the fifth period, Lemp broke loose with a fast horse and drove the ball from one end of the field to the other. Later, an off side play by Lemp and Falk netted another goal. Falk made a nearly impossible shot to Lemp, who then carried it down the field.

For the second game in the series of matches Herbert Lemp was again riding in the number two position for the town team.[tr] Reserved seats were sold this time to defer some of the expenses. The army won this one 4 to 1 1/2 setting up the final match for the championship of Idaho's capital city.[ts] They sold tickets for this match and intended the proceeds to go to charity.[tt]

Captain C. O. Thomas, Jr. of the U. S. Army selected an All-Northwest, all-star polo team for the *Statesman* before this last game could be played.[tu] He selected one cavalry man, two men from Portland, and Herbert Lemp in the number three position. Lemp was selected for his "ability as a horseman, his perfectly reined horse, his powerful right hand drive, and his good eye for hitting to place."

In the last game of the season the Boise team again beat the cavalry.[tv] Lemp scored the first goal in the first few minutes. He scored again in the third period. At that end of that period he took the ball from the cavalry and rushed it to the other end of the field to disrupt their desperate effort to score. In the fourth period Lemp scored again. Lemp committed a foul near the end which cost his team a half a point but as time ran out he scored yet another goal to give his team victory. Polo season for 1911 was over.

With the arrival of Spring in 1912, came the new polo season. Two teams, the Yellows and the Reds, were organized to put on the first competition at the field by the barracks in a series of preseason matches.[tw] Herbert Lemp was the captain of the Yellows. A week later the first clash between the Boise men and the men of the fort was held.[tx] In late March, the soldiers won a match despite Herbert's goal shot.[ty] In April, the *Statesman* published a big cartoon under the caption "Boise is Just Crazy for Polo."[tz]

Also in June, two of the polo team, Charles T. Barringer and Ed Ostner, were injured severely enough to need hospitalization.[ua] Ostner was struck in the forehead by a mallet; Barringer collided with a member of the Army team. Herbert Lemp was playing at the time of their injuries.

1911

In the Society section of the *Statesman* on 12 November was a photo of Mrs. Herbert Lemp and "her two charming children."[ub] There was an article on the same page about a bridge luncheon at the Owyhee Hotel where the guests included Mrs. Herbert Lemp.

On the second Sunday in December, the *Statesman* carried an historical article listing and showing a portrait of every mayor ever elected in Boise.[uc] John Lemp, the fifth mayor, serving from 1874 to 1876, was among them.

Later that month, daughter Julia, Mrs. A. R. Grant of Portland, came home to Boise to visit her father.[ud]

Harry Steiner, an employee of John Lemp at the Arc Light Saloon, had to testify in a murder case in Boise.[ue] Steiner had seen the victim holding his abdomen and the knife which had stabbed him. S. J. Clark was the accused. Despite all the years, the violence associated with the saloon kept reappearing, and Lemp could not completely disassociate himself from that old stigma associated with the liquor traffic.

1912

In the early months of 1912, Boise was embroiled in a feud over the form of its city government. A list of those actively supporting the current charter for Boise city government included Herbert Lemp of John Lemp & Co., and John Lemp, capitalist.[uf] The *Statesman* said Frank Martin, who supported the Black Law (proposed new law), would just as soon these political opponents left town.

While her husband was riding up and down a field hitting a ball, Mrs. Herbert Lemp was passing time holding bridge teas to entertain the society ladies of Boise.[ug] She also attended those held by others.[uh]

In May of 1912, Lemp's Extra Pale Beer was advertised in the Boise *Statesman*.[ui] No, John Lemp's burned down brewery was not making a comeback; this was the Lemp brewery of St. Louis, Missouri, forerunner to Falstaff, and a large national shipper of beer at that early date whose sales territory had then reached Idaho's capital. There was no brand conflict or name confusion in Boise by this time. One

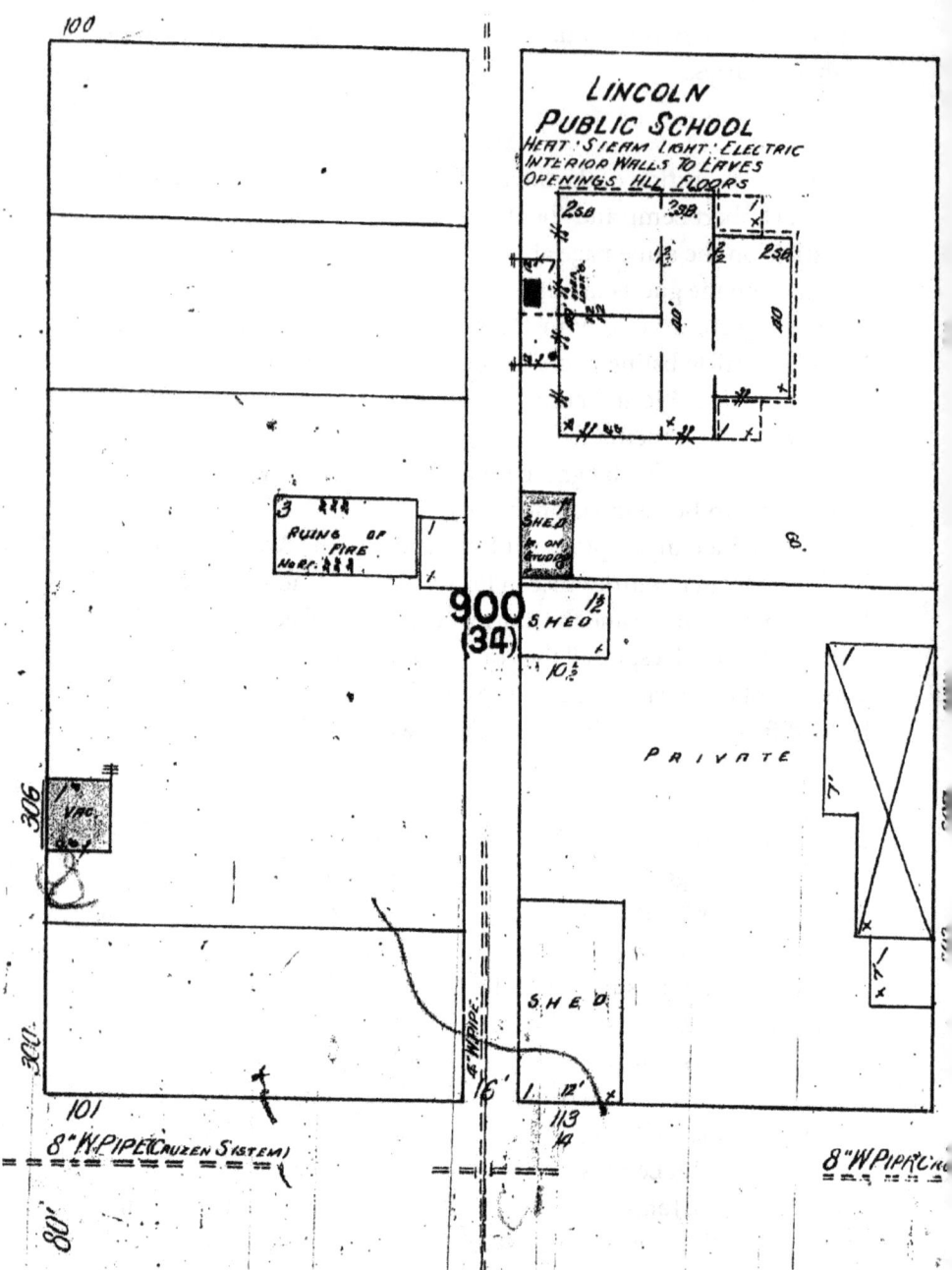

The site where the Lemp brewery had previously stood. The area was almost clear of buildings. 1913 Fire insurance map.

can only speculate about what John Lemp felt when he first saw an advertisement in Boise for the beer brewed by his St. Louis cousins.

Ada county in which Boise city is located had a local option election on 19 June of 1912.[uj] There were 6,288 votes against local option and 4,477 for it, making an official wet majority of 1,811. Lemp's saloons would be allowed to continue in business.

About this same time the Republicans were making preliminary nominations for all state offices.[uk] Many candidates were proposed for each office prior to making final selections. Lyon Cobb nominated Herbert Lemp for representative. Little came of this directly, but Herbert was clearly accepting the political legacy of his father.

THE DEATH OF JOHN LEMP

Without any warning about life threatening illness in the local media, the citizens of Boise met with sad news when on 18 July 1912, John Lemp died at age 74.[ul] The *Statesman* said that while it was known he was seriously ill "his rugged constitution was depended upon to stave off death and his passing will come as a shock to the many friends in the city and state." The first report of his death mentioned that he belonged to an old family of the Fatherland. He left three sons and three daughters. His children were listed as "John Emil who died in 1895, George William also dead, Elizabeth, wife of W. B. Connor, Augusta, wife of Roderick Grant, Ida and Ada, Twins; William who died in 1881; Albert, Herbert, Bernard and Marie, the latter dying in 1896."

John was remembered as a member of the Masons, Odd Fellows, Knights Templar, and the Ancient Order of United Workmen.

The portrait article in the *Statesman* the next day emphasized Lemp's fortune, many positions of responsibility and large family.[um] The funeral was delayed until Mrs. Roderick (Augusta Julia Margaret Lemp) Grant of Walla Walla (they had moved from Portland temporarily), the only Lemp child not in Boise, could arrive. Episcopal Bishop Funsten was to officiate at the Lemp home and the Masons would officiate at the grave.

The *Statesman* said Lemp was not a politician in any sense of the word but served as a council man for a time. Twenty years on the Council would have been more accurate. He had been at the state's constitutional convention. He was a great reader of history and specialized in knowing dates in Idaho's past. He was the oldest pioneer living continuously in Idaho at the time of his death.[un] His many buildings and companies were noted, such as the Lemp Block, the Shainwald Block, the Capitol Hotel, and the ranch land in Ada and Canyon Counties. They said at least twenty pioneers had been buried at his expense.

His first home was the present home of Mrs. Peter Sonna. His current Grove Street home, which he owned after that, was now forty-five years old and had the most perfect trees in the valley. His estate was estimated at $1,000,000. Mrs. Lemp had died four and a half years previously. Five of his thirteen children were already deceased. There were four grandchildren; a daughter by Albert, a son by John Emil and a son and a daughter of Herbert. The *Evening Capital News* mentioned his sisters, Mrs. A. Wolters and Mrs. Charles Leyerzapf of Boise, and Mrs. Fred Bach of St. Louis.[uo]

Many pioneers visited the Lemp home before the funeral to tell the children of the many good deeds their father had done, most of which the children were unaware. He had lent a helping hand to those who were down and had provided for old men who were no longer able to work and had no means with which to live.[up] It was characteristic that Lemp never told his own children of these deeds. He cared not for publicity about his philanthropy.

William Stoehr, manager of the Idaho Brewing and Malting Company and president of the Turn Verein, put a notice in the newspaper for all members to meet at the hall so they could attend the funeral of their brother as a group.[uq] Likewise, Frank G. House, Worshipful Master of the Masons, released a similar notice to his members.[ur]

The Boise City Council passed a resolution on July 20 to honor John Lemp.[us] They mentioned he was a former mayor and a council member for many years and he gave "this city and the state of Idaho proof of his great ability and frugality in her early territorial days: that he endured the hardships of pioneer life with zeal, fidelity and loyalty befitting the manhood of the early pioneer; that he left enduring land marks of his ability and industry upon the hearts of our people..." They went on to say "we loved his genial, yet rugged nature, and his many companionable qualities and we do not see anyone who can quite fill his place."

At the funeral, Bishop Funsten read the Episcopal service; the Episcopal quartet sang several hymns.[ut] The honorary pallbearers—all Odd Fellows—were Richard Adelmann, Amos G. Thompson, Robert Mobley, Robert Aikman, William McGuffin, Oric Cole and Charles Chinn. The

Lemp Lane sign keeps his legacy in mind where his namesake town once thrived. Photo by the author.

active pallbearers were from the Shriners: Charles Himrod, Frank Coffin, Alvin Regan, Frank Parsons, George Fletcher, Jerre Robinson, Theodore Daniel, and Sigmund Falk. Large floral arrangements were from the Shriners, Idaho Commandery Knights Templar, Boise Lodge No. 2, A. F. & A. M. (Free and Accepted Masons); Boise Lodge No. 3, R. A. M. (Royal Arch Masons), Canton Columbia and Encampment; Ivanhoe lodge, K of P; F.O.E. lodge and the Boise Turnverein. John Lemp was laid to rest beside his wife and other family members in the Pioneer Cemetery. The Beer Baron of Boise would brew no more.

The entire text of Lemp's will appeared in both Boise Newspapers immediately.[uu] Sons Herbert and Bernard got equal shares of all cattle, horses and other livestock. The remainder was divided among all the living children—Herbert, Bernard, Elizabeth Connor, Ada Hurt, Edward, Louise Simonson, Augusta Grant,—and grandson, John F. Lemp, son of deceased son Emil Lemp, in equal one-ninth portions. Herbert was the executor, having been in charge of his father's affairs for some time. Bernard was the alternate executor if needed. The will contained the usual provisions to meet expenses and pay debts. Real estate could be held for up to five years before dividing if necessary for an advantageous selling price.

The *Statesman* commented on the goodly sum the state of Idaho would gain from the taxes on the Lemp estate.[uv] They believed the estate would eventually be worth $1,500,000 and the tax $40,000. The rate was 1 per cent up to a $25,000 inheritance, then 1 1/2 per cent from $25.000 to $50,000, then 2 per cent up to $100,000, 2 1/2 per cent from $100,000 to $500,000, and 3 per cent for amounts over $500,000. Adult heirs could exempt $4,000 and minors could exempt $10,000. No interest was charged on the tax if paid in a year and a discount of 5 per cent was given if paid within six months.

The newspaper notice was dated 20 July when the court set the date for proving the will and issuing letters of testamentary to Herbert.[uw] There was no contest when the will was admitted to probate on August 3. Judge Dunbar appointed W. E. Pierce, Leo J. Falk and E. W. "Walter" Yeomans as appraisers in Ada County.[ux] Leo had been the treasurer of the Falk Mercantile Company for some time.

Herbert put the customary and required notice in the newspaper for those with claims to come forward.[uy] Herbert had many complicated decisions to make, and years to wait before the whole estate was settled as we will see in his section of the chapter on the "Legacy of John Lemp." In mid-September the appraisers report was published. John Lemp had $144,994.86 in personal property; $445,721.40 real estate in Ada County; totaling $600,716.26.[uz] He owned an additional $89,978.22 in Canyon County, mostly in ranches; in Blaine County $660 in personal property; in Boise County $2,026.40.

The Lemp family plot in Pioneer Cemetery, Boise, Idaho. Photo by the author.

In *Roughing It,* Mark Twain opined that "the cheapest and easiest way to become an influential man and be looked up to by the community at large, was to stand behind a bar, wear a cluster diamond pin, and sell whiskey . . . I am not sure but that the saloon keeper held a shade higher rank than any other member of society. His opinion had weight. It was his privilege to say how elections should run. No great movement could succeed without the countenance and direction of the saloon keeper." Adding brewer to his early title of saloon keeper certainly set Lemp off on a course to prosperity and influence. He never looked back.

The mortal John Lemp was gone but his businesses, property, and eight of his children continued his legacy. He had built a massive foundation for his descendants to continue to build upon. Their stories are the next chapter, The Legacy of John Lemp.

In the words of Herbert Pocket a character in Charles Dickens' *Great Expectations,* "I don't know why it should be such a crack thing to be a brewer; but it is indisputable that while you can not possibly be genteel and bake, you can be genteel as never was and brew. You see it every day." Boise's beer baron, John Lemp, was genteel as never was—you saw it everyday.

Auf Wiedersehn, Herr Lemp!

END NOTES

a *The Capital,* 5 January 1901, p. 1, c. 3. *Idaho Daily Statesman,* 5 January 1901, p. 6, c. 2-3.

b Bureau of Land Management, Land Patent Records. Accession/Serial # IDIDAA 043895. Document # 33354. The geographic name was Blue, and the description was Sections 5, 8, 9 of Township 14-N, Range 12-E.

c *The Capital,* 2 February 1901, p. 7, c. 3. *Idaho Daily Statesman,* 27 January 1901, p. 8, c. 2.

d *Daily Capital,* 26 January 1901, p. 4, c. 1.

e *The Capital,* 28 January 1901, p. 4, c. 1.

f *Idaho Daily Statesman,* 31 January 1901, p. 8, c. 2. *Daily Capital,* 30 January 1901, p. 4, c. 2.

g *Idaho Daily Statesman,* 31 January 1901, p. 8, c. 1.

h *The Capital,* 4 February 1908, p. 8, c. 1.

i *Evening Capital News,* 5 February 1901, p. 4, c. 1.

j *Idaho Daily Statesman,* 23 February 1901, p. 3, c. 4.

k   *Idaho Daily Statesman*, 11 March 1901, p. 6, c. 1. *Elmore Bulletin*, Mountain Home, 21 March 1901, p. 1, c. 7.

l   *Idaho Falls Times*, 1 August 1901, p. 4, c. 1 *Elmore Bulletin*, Mountain Home, 1 August 1901, p. 1, c. 1.

m   *Idaho Daily Statesman*, 19 July 1901, p. 5, c. 2-3.

n   *Idaho Daily Statesman*, 20 July 1901, p. 8, c. 1.

o   Hawley, *History of Idaho*, 1920, vol. II, p. 23

p   Flenner, *Syringa Blossoms*, 1912, p. 169.

q   *Idaho Capital News*, 3 October 1901, p. 5, c. 6.

r   *Idaho Daily Statesman*, 1 October 1901, p. 6, c. 2-3. *Elmore Bulletin*, Mountain Home, 10 October 1901, p. 1, c. 1. *Evening Capital News*, 1 October 1901, p. 1, c. 7

s   *The Evening Capital News: Mid-Summer Supplement*, 30 August 1902, p. 11, c. 4-5.

t   Boone, *Idaho Place Names, A Geographical Dictionary*, p. 222. The location was 2150'. T4N R2W, section 3.

u   *The Evening Capital News*, 27 March 1901, p. 1, c. 6 & 7.

v   *Idaho Daily Statesman*, 28 March 1901, p. 6, c. 2.

w   *Idaho Daily Statesman*, 13 April 1901, p. 6, c. 1. See the appendix for the individual sale data.

x   *Idaho Daily Statesman*, 22 April 1901, p. 4, c. 3.

y   *Evening Capital News*, 5 April 1901, p. 6, c. 3-5.

z   *The Evening Capital News*, 27 May 1901, p. 6, c. 1.

aa *The Evening Capital News*, 1 August 1901, p. 1, c. 3-5. A photo of the top three contestants was printed.

ab *Evening Capital News*, 16 August 1901, p. 6, c. 1.

ac *Evening Capital News*, 4 October 1901, p. 6, c. 5-7.

ad *Evening Capital News*, 20 march 1902, p. 1, c. 7.

ae *Idaho Daily Statesman*, 14 April 1902, p. 8, c. 4 & 5.

af *Idaho Daily Statesman*, 18 June 1902, p. 5, c. 1.

ag *The Evening Capital News*, 30 August 1902, p. 5.

ah *Idaho Daily Statesman*, 8 September 1903, p. 5, c. 6.

ai *Evening Capital News*, 30 April 1904, p. 5, c. 1.

aj *Idaho Daily Statesman*, 7 September 1904, p. 5, c. 4. *Evening Capital News*, 6 September 1904, p. 5, c. 3.

ak *Evening Capital News*, 27 May 1905, p. 5, c. 6.

al *Idaho Daily Statesman*, 29 June 1905, p. 5, c. 3.

am *Idaho Daily Statesman*, 17 August 1905, p. 5, c. 2.

an *Evening Capital News*, 12 January 1907, p. 5, c. 3.

ao *Evening Capital News*, 14 September 1907, p. 2, c. 5.

John Lemp • The Beer Baron of Boise   281

ap *Evening Capital News*, 25 October 1907, p. 10, c. 1 & 2.
aq *Evening Capital News*, 25 November 1907, p. 5, c. 4.
ar *Evening Capital News*, 28 November 1907, p. 5, c. 1-4.
as *Evening Capital News*, 4 April 1908, p. 2, c. 4.
at *Evening Capital News*, 21 April 1908, p.12, c. 1-7.
au *Evening Capital News*, 11 May 1905, p. 2, c. 3.
av *Evening Capital News*, 15 April 1908, p. 5, c. 2-3.
aw *Evening Capital News*, 15 April 1908, p. 10, c. 1-7.
ax *Idaho Daily Statesman*, 6 May 1908, p. 5, c. 5.
ay *Evening Capital News*, 13 May 1908, p. 5, c. 5-7, *Idaho Daily Statesman*, 6 June 1908, p. 3, c. 1-7.
az *Evening Capital News*, 18 July 1908, p. 8, c. 4-7.
ba *Evening Capital News*, 11 July 1908, p. 7, c. 3.
bb *Evening Capital News*, 15 October 1908, p. 5, c. 3.
bc *Evening Capital News*, 29 December 1908, p. 8, c. 2.
bd *Evening Capital News*, 31 May 1901, p. 1, c. 6.
be *The Evening Capital News*, 6 April 1901, p. 3, c. 3 & 4.
bf *The Evening Capital News*, 17 April 1901, p. 6, c. 4.
bg *The Evening Capital News*, 19 April 1901, p. 6, c. 1.
bh *The Evening Capital News*, 30 April 1901, p. 3, c. 1-4.
bi *Evening Capital News*, 23 July 1911, p. 2, c. 5.
bj *The Evening Capital News,* 26 April 1901, p. 1, c. 3-5.
bk *The Evening Capital News*, 7 May 1901, p. 6, c. 1.
bl *The Evening Capital News*, 18 May 1901, p. 3, c. 2.
bm *The Evening Capital News*, 11 May 1901, p. 2, c. 3.
bn *The Evening Capital News*, 24 May 1901, p. 5, c. 3.
bo *The Evening Capital News*, 11 June 1901, p. 3, c. 2-4.
bp *The Evening Capital News*, 4 July 1901, p. 2, c. 3.
bq *The Evening Capital News*, 17 June 1901, p. 1, c. 5-6.
br *Idaho Daily Statesman*, 20 June 1901, p. 6, c. 2
bs *Idaho Capital News*, 15 August 1901, p. 5, c. 5-6. *Idaho Daily Statesman*, 10 August 1901, p. 5, c. 1 – 2.
bt *The Evening Capital News*, 16 July 1901, p. 3, c. 4.
bu Hart, *Chinatown, Boise, Idaho, 1870-1970*, p. 101.
bv *The Evening Capital News*, Special Issue, 23 July 1901, p. 8, c. 3
bw *The Evening Capital News,* 23 July 1901, p. 8, c. 1.
bx *Idaho Capital News*, 8 August 1901, p. 2, c. 3.
by *Evening Capital News*, 9 August 1901, p. 1, c. 2.
bz *Evening Capital News*, 15 August 1901, p. 6, c. 1.

ca *Evening Capital News*, 28 August 1901, p. 6, c. 4.
cb *Evening Capital News*, 31 August 1901, p. 6, c. 2.
cc *Idaho Daily Statesman*, 25 September 1901, p. 5, c. 3. *Evening Capital News*, 25 September 1901, p. 6, c. 1.
cd *Idaho Daily Statesman*, 15 November 1901, p. 5, c. 4.
ce *Idaho Daily Statesman*, 11 September, 1901, p. 6, c. 4.
cf *Idaho Daily Statesman*, 22 September 1901, p. 7, c. 1.
cg *Idaho Daily Statesman*, 28 September 1901, p. 6, c. 4.
ch *Evening Capital News*, 25 September 1901, p. 6, c. 2.
ci *Idaho Daily Statesman*, 1 October 1901, p. 5, c. 3. *Evening Capital News*, 30 September 1901, p. 1, c. 2.
cj *Idaho Daily Statesman*, 25 September 1901, p. 6, c. 1.
ck *Idaho Daily Statesman*, 13 October 1901, p. 9, c. 2.
cl *Evening Capital News*, 25 October 1901, p. 1, c. 3-5.
cm *Idaho Daily Statesman*, 26 February 1902, p. 6, c. 2.
cn *Evening Capital News*, 14 October 1901, p. 4, c. 2-4.
co Blaine County Judicial Records, Idaho State Historical Society, microfilm reel 34.
cp *Evening Capital News*, 4 November 1901, p. 1, c. 6 & 7.
cq *Evening Capital News*, 29 October 1901, p. 5, c. 2.
cr *Idaho Daily Statesman*, 4 December 1901, p. 5, c. 3.
cs *Idaho Daily Statesman*, 7 December 1901, p. 2, c. 4.
ct *Idaho Daily Statesman*, 23 December 1901, p. 5, c. 2.
cu *Evening Capital News*, 21 December 1901, p. 8, c. 3.
cv *Idaho Daily Statesman*, 24 December 1901, p. 8, c. 1. *Idaho Capital News*, 26 December 1901, p. 6, c. 2.
cw *Idaho Daily Statesman*, 11 December 1901, p. 6, c. 3.
cx *Idaho Daily Statesman*, 17 January 1902, p. 8, c. 1.
cy *Idaho Daily Statesman*, 16 January 1902, p. 5, c. 4.
cz *Idaho Daily Statesman*, 30 January 1902, p. 6, c. 2.
da *Idaho Daily Statesman*, 25 January 1902, p. 6, c. 1.
db *Evening Capital News*, 21 January 1905, p. 1, c. 1.
dc *Evening Capital News*, 2 February 1905, p. 5, c. 3.
dd *Evening Capital News*, 5 May 1905, p. 5, c. 1 & 3.
de *Idaho Capital News*, 18 May 1905, p. 7, c. 1. *Idaho Daily Statesman*, 16 May 1905, p. 4, c. 3.
df *Idaho Daily Statesman*, 2 December 1905, p. 3, c. 3.
dg *Evening Capital News*, 1 December 1905, p. 8, c. 4.
dh *Evening Capital News*, 23 January 1902, p. 9, c. 3.
di *Idaho Daily Statesman*, 3 February 1902, p. 2, c. 5.

dj *Evening Capital News*, 10 February 1902, p. 6, c. 1.
dk *Idaho Daily Statesman*, 10 February 1902, p. 5, c. 4. *Evening Capital News*, 10 February 1902, p. 6, c. 1.
dl *Idaho Daily Statesman*, 12 February 1902, p. 5, c. 2.
dm *Evening Capital News*, 21 March 1902, p. 2, c. 3.
dn *Evening Capital News*, 28 March 1902, p. 3, c. 1.
do *Idaho Daily Statesman*, 3 April 1902, p. 5, c. 3.
dp *Idaho Daily Statesman*, 15 December 1903, p. 6, c. 2.
dq *Idaho Daily Statesman*, 11 April 1902, p. 5, c. 2.
dr MacGregor, *Boise, Idaho, 1882-1910*, p. 37.
ds *Idaho Daily Statesman*, 17 April 1902, p. 6, c. 3.
dt *Idaho Daily Statesman*, 26 April 1902, p. 6, c. 2.
du *Idaho Daily Statesman*, 9 May 1902, p. 6, c. 4.
dv *Idaho Daily Statesman*, 6 May 1902, p. 6, c. 4.
dw *Evening Capital News*, 10 May 1902, p. 8, c. 2.
dx *Evening Capital News*, 31 May 1902, p. 8, c. 2. Jennie's mother was John Lemp's sister.
dy *The Capital News*, 29 May 1902, p. 7, c. 7. *Evening Capital News*, 27 May 1902, p. 5, c. 4.
dz *Idaho Daily Statesman*, 19 June 1902, p. 6, c. 3.
ea *Idaho Daily Statesman*, 8 June 1902, p. 5, c. 1.
eb *Idaho Daily Statesman*, 14 June 1902, p. 5, c. 3. *Evening Capital News*, 13 June 1902, p. 1, c. 5.
ec *Evening Capital News* 16 June 1902, p. 5, c. 2.
ed *Evening Capital News*, 19 June 1902, p. 8, c. 4.
ee *Idaho Capital News*, 10 July 1902, p. 2, c. 3.
ef *Idaho Daily Statesman*, 8 July 1902, p. 6, c. 2.
eg *Idaho Capital News*, 7 August 1902, p. 7, c. 2.
eh *The Evening Capital News*, Summer supplement, 30 August 1902, p. 11, c. 4-5.
ei *Idaho Daily Statesman*, 20 July 1902, p. 9, c. 2-3.
ej *Evening Capital News*, 30 August 1902, p. 7, c. 1.
ek *Idaho Daily Statesman*, 31 August 1902, p. 7, c. 1.
el *Wood River Times*, Hailey, Idaho, 2 September 1902, p. 4, c. 1.
em *Idaho Capital News*, 23 October 1902, p. 1, c. 5 & 6.
en *Idaho Daily Statesman*, 3 August 1902, p. 8, c. 1.Mr. and Mrs. Albert Wolters sold a town lot
in Hailey for $300 that same month. See Blaine County Judicial Records, Idaho State Historical Society, microfilm reel 10, Logan county Deeds, item three, original page 374.
eo *Idaho Daily Statesman*, 10 September 1902, p. 6, c. 1.

ep *Idaho Daily Statesman*, 13 September 1902, p. 6, c. 1.
eq *Idaho Daily Statesman*, 14 September 1902, p. 5, c. 1-3.
er *Idaho Daily Statesman*, 12 October 1902, p. 12, c. 1.
es *Idaho Daily Statesman*, 15 October 1902, p. 3, c. 3.
et *Idaho Daily Statesman*, 29 November 1902, p. 3, c. 2.
eu *Idaho Daily Statesman*, 5 January 1903, p. 2, c. 2.
ev *Idaho Daily Statesman*, 11 January 1903, p. 7, c. 4.
ew *Idaho Daily Statesman*, 3 April 1903, p. 6, c. 4.
ex *Idaho Capital News,* 4 April 1903, p. 7, c. 2. The whole story from the coroner's inquest is from this article.
ey *Idaho Daily Statesman*, 14 March 1903, p. 5, c. 3.
ez *Idaho Daily Statesman*, 19 March 1903, p. 5, c. 3.
fa *Idaho Capital News*, 4 April 1903, p. 7, c. 2.
fb *Idaho Daily Statesman*, 18 April 1903, p. 3, c. 4-5. MacGregor, *Boise, Idaho, 1882-1910*, p.60.
fc *Idaho Daily Statesman*, 25 May 1903, p. 2, c. 4 & 5. The lots were 1. E. 33 feet 8 inches of lot 4, block 3. 2. W. 7 feet of lot 5, block 3. 3. lot 11, block 10. 4. lot 12, block 10. 5. lot 7, block 9. 6. E. half lot 8, block 9. 7. lot 9, block 9. 8. lot 10, block 9. 9. W. half lot 11, block 9.
fd *Idaho Capital News*, 23 July 1903, p. 5, c. 3.
fe Bureau of Land Management, Land Patent Records, on line. Accession/Serial # IDIDAA 045195. Document # 36810. The location was Section 33, Township 3-N, Range 17-E.
ff *Idaho Daily Statesman*, 22 July 1903, p. 5, c. 3.
fg *Idaho Daily Statesman*, 23 August 1903, p. 7, c. 2.
fh *Elmore Bulletin*, Mountain Home, 13 August 1903, p. 4, c. 5.
fi *Elmore Bulletin*, Mountain Home, 17 September 1903, p. 1, c. 4.
fj *Evening Capital News*, 20 August 1901, p. 6, c. 1.
fk *Idaho Daily Statesman*, 22 August 1903, p. 5, c. 4.
fl *Idaho Daily Statesman*, 20 November 1903, p. 5, c. 1-2. This long article provides all the information on this city council matter.fm*Idaho Daily Statesman*, 10 July 1904, p. 7, c. 4.
fn *Idaho Daily Statesman*, 2 September 1904, p. 5, c. 3.
fo *Idaho Daily Statesman*, 27 November 1904, p. 6, c. 3.
fp *Idaho Daily Statesman*, 23 October 1905, p. 3, c. 2.
fq *Idaho Daily Statesman*, 27 October 1905, p. 3, c. 1.
fr *Idaho Daily Statesman* 31 October 1905, p. 3, c. 3.
fs *Chapter Three Background Report. East End Neighborhood Policy Guide.* (Boise) Internet site. p. 6.
ft *Evening Capital News*, 8 August 1907, p. 5, c. 1 & 2.
fu *American Brewers Review*, 1907, p. 600

fv *Idaho Daily Statesman*, January 1908, p. 2, c. 1.
fw *Idaho Daily Statesman*, 21 February 1909, p. 2, c. 2.
fx *Western Brewer*, 34:9 , September 1909, p. 472. They called the brewery a state landmark.
fy *Idaho Daily Statesman*, 7 August, 1909, p. 2, c. 2.
fz *Idaho Daily Statesman*, 7 August, 1909, p. 2, c. 2.
ga *Idaho Daily Statesman*, 9 August 1909, p. 8, c. 2.
gb *Idaho Daily Statesman*, 8 August 1909, p. 4, c. 3-5.
gc *Idaho Daily Statesman*, 9 August 1909, p. 8, c. 2.
gd *Idaho Daily Statesman*, 9 August 1909, p. 8, c. 2.
ge *Evening Capital News*, 13 September 1910, p. 8, c. 4.
gf *Evening Capital News*, 1 October 1910, p. 12, c. 4. 5 October 1910, p. 5, c. 3.
gg *Evening Capital News*, 5 October 1910, p. 3, c. 1
gh MacGregor, *Boise, Idaho, 1882-1910*, p. 219.
gi *Idaho Daily Statesman*, 5 October 1910, p. 3, c. 6.
gj *Idaho Daily Statesman*, 6 October 1910, p. 6, c. 3.
gk *Evening Capital News*, 2 December 1910, p. 7, c. 3.
gl *Idaho Daily Statesman*, 1 November 1911, p. 3, c. 1. *Evening Capital News*, 1 November 1911, p. 7, c. 4.
gm *Idaho Daily Statesman*, 3 November 1911, p. 5, c. 3.
gn *Idaho Daily Statesman*, 4 November 1911, p. 3, c. 4.
go *Chapter Three, East End Neighborhood Policy Guide*, (Boise) Internet site, p. 7.
gp *Post Register*, Idaho Falls, 3 December 1937, p. 6, c. 6.
gq *Idaho Daily Statesman*, 7 October 1903, p. 5, c. 4.
gr *Idaho Capital News* (weekly) 8 October 1903, p. 3, c. 3.
gs *Idaho Daily Statesman*, 17 October 1903, p. 6, c. 4.
gt *Capital News*, 22 October 1903, p. 6, c. 5.
gu *Idaho Daily Statesman*, 9 November 1903, p. 2, c. 2-3. Lemp's land was: 1. Lot 4, block 22. 2. Lot 5, block 22. 3. Lot 6 block 22. 4. lot 1, block 34. 5. Lot 2, block 34. 6. Lot 3, block 34. 7. Lot 4, block 34. 8. Lot 5, block 34. 9. Lot 6 Block 34.
gv *Idaho Daily Statesman*, 23 January 1904, p. 5, c. 2.
gw *Evening Capital News*, 30 January 1904, p. 5, c. 1-2.
gx *Evening Capital News*, 9 January 1904, p. 1, c. 6.
gy *Evening Capital News*, 16 January 1904, p. 7, c. 1. p. 7, c. 2.
gz *Evening Capital News*, 30 January 1904, p. 4, c. 1-2.
ha *Idaho Daily Statesman*, 26 February 1904, p. 5, c. 4.
hb *The Idaho Magazine*, "John Lemp: Foundation Builder of Boise," March, 1904, p. 30. *Progressive Men of Southern Idaho*, 1904, p. 71.
hc *Idaho Daily Statesman*, 11 February 1904, p. 2, c. 4-7.

hd *Evening Capital News*, 13 February 1904, p. 5, c. 3. *Idanha Chieftain*, Soda Springs, 11 February 1904, 6, c. 3.

he Blaine County Judicial Records, Idaho State Historical Society, microfilm reel 10, Logan County Deeds, item three, original page 560.

hf Blaine County Judicial Records, Idaho State Historical Society, microfilm reel 10, Logan County Deeds, item three, original page 586.

hg *Idaho Daily Statesman*, 2 March 1904, p. 5, c. 2.

hh *Evening Capital News*, 1 March 1904, p. 4, c. 3.

hi *Idaho Daily Statesman*, 26 April 1904, p. 5, c. 4. *Evening Capital News*, 26 April 1904, p. 8, c. 2.

hj *Evening Capital News*, 3 May 1904, p. 3, c. 4.

hk *Evening Capital News*, 21 March 1904, p. 1, c. 3-4.

hl *Evening Capital News*, 21 April 1904, p. , c. 6.

hm *Evening Capital News*, 12 July 1904, p. 5, c. 3.

hn *Evening Capital News*, 8 June 1904, p. 5, c. 2.

ho *Evening Capital News*, 22 June 1904, p. 5, c. 2.

hp *Evening Capital News*, 25 June 1904, p. 6, c. 3.

hq Ada County Court Records, Microfilmed Judgment Books, Idaho State Historical Society.

hr *Idaho Daily Statesman*, 29 June 1904, p. 5, c. 4. *Evening Capital News*, 28 June 1904, p. 1, c. 7. The child's name was spelled differently in various sources. I believe this one is the correct one.

hs *Idaho Daily Statesman*, 30 June 1904, p. 5, c. 4.

ht *Idaho Daily Statesman*, 6 July 1904, p. 5, c. 4.

hu *Idaho Daily Statesman*, 30 June 1904, p. 3, c. 1-2.

hv *Idaho Daily Statesman*, 1 July 1904, p. 3, c. 3-4. The petition was dated 20 June 1904.

hw *Idaho Daily Statesman*, 8 July 1904, p. 5, c. 4.

hx *Idaho Daily Statesman*, 13 July 1904, p. 5, c. 3-4.

hy *Evening Capital News*, 12 July 1904, p. 5, c. 3.

hz *Evening Capital News*, 12 July 1904, p. 5, c. 3.

ia *Idaho Daily Statesman*, 17 July 1904, p. 9, c. 1.

ib *Idaho Daily Statesman*, 15 July 1904, p. 3, c. 3.

ic *Idaho Daily Statesman*, 27 July 1904, p. 5, c. 2. The Grants may have been living there briefly but were in Portland both before and after this period.

id *Evening Capital News*, 11 July 1904, p. 5, c. 2.

ie *Evening Capital News*, 12 July 1904, p. 1, c. 7.

if *Idaho Daily Statesman*, 10 July 1904, p. 7, c. 4.

ig *Elmore Bulletin*, Mountain Home, 4 August 1904, p. 4, c. 1.

ih *Evening Capital News*, 9 August 1904, p. 3, c. 1.

John Lemp • The Beer Baron of Boise   287

ii *Idaho Daily Statesman* 31 August 1904, p. 6, c. 4.
ij *Evening Capital News*, 1 December 1904, p. 5. c. 1.
ik *Evening Capital News*, 31 August 1904, p. 8, c. 3.
il *Progressive Men of Southern Idaho*, 1904, p. 71.
im *Idaho Daily Statesman*, 22 September 1904, p. 5, c. 2.
in *Idaho Daily Statesman*, 28 September 1904, p. 5, c. 2.
io *Evening Capital News*, 23 September 1904, p. 6, c. 4-5.
ip *Evening Capital News*, 18 October 1904, p. 2, c. 2.
q   *Evening Capital News*, 10 October 1904, p. 6, c. 3-5.
ir *Evening Capital News*, 7 November 1904, p. 9-12, c. 1-7.
is *Idaho Capital News*, 27 October 1904, p. 3, c. 2. *Idaho Daily Statesman*, 22 October 1904, p. 7, c. 3-4. *Evening Capital News*, 22 October 1904, p. 4, c. 3-4.
it *Idaho Daily Statesman*, 20 October 1904, p. 5, c. 3-4 This is extant a century later.
iu *Idaho Daily Statesman*, 26 October 1904, p. 5, c. 4.
iv *Idaho Daily Statesman*, 3 December 1904, p. 5, c. 2.
iw *Evening Capital News*, 3 December 1904, p. 5, c. 3.
ix *Evening Capital News*, 31 October 1904, p. 2, c. 1-2.
iy *Evening Capital News*, ? November 1904, p. 2, c. 1.
iz *Evening Capital News*, 14 December 1904, p. 6, c. 1-2.
ja *Idaho Daily Statesman*, 25 December 1904, p. 3, c. 3.
jb *Idaho Daily Statesman*, 5 January 1905, p. 5, c. 4.
jc *Idaho Daily Statesman*, 31 January 1905, p. 6, c. 5.
jd *Evening Capital News*, 1 February 1905, p. 5, c. 3.
je *Idaho Daily Statesman*, 25 January 1905, p. 5, c. 1.
jf *Idaho Capital News*, 16 March 1905, p. 12, c. 3.
jg *Idaho Capital News*, 30 March 1905, p. 4, c. 6.
jh *Idaho Daily Statesman*, 30 March 1905, p. 5, c. 2. *Evening Capital News*, 29 March 1905, p. 8, c. 4.
ji *Idaho Daily Statesman*, 1 February 1905, p. 5, c. 3.
jj *Idaho Daily Statesman*, 28 February 1905, p. 6, c. 3. *Evening Capital News*, 27 February 1905, p. 5, c. 4.
jk *Evening Capital News*, 1 March 1905, p. 5, c. 1.
jl *Idaho Daily Statesman*, 1 May 1905, p. 3, c. 2.
jm *Idaho Daily Statesman*, 3 May 1905, p. 6, c. 1.
jn *Idaho Daily Statesman*, 19 May 1905, p. 8, c. 1.
jo *The Idaho Capital News*, 7 September 1905, p. 2, c. 3.
jp *Evening Capital News*, 5 September 1905, p. 5, c. 3. 16 September 1905, p. 5, c. 1. Scheduling was an on-going, ever-changing process.
jq *Idaho Capital News*, 21 September 1905, p. 3, c. 5.

jr *Idaho Daily Statesman*, 6 September 1905, p. 5, c. 2. 8 September 1905, p. 8, c. 3 17 September 1905, p. 4, c. 1. 7 October 1905, p. 7, c. 4.

js Ada County Court Records, Microfilmed Judgment Books, Idaho State Historical Society.

jt The Case of Morris vs. Lemp, 13 Idaho, Feb. 1907, pp. 116-122 was afterward used as a precedent in case involving the granting of new trials. *Idaho Daily Statesman*, 3 February 1907, p. 3, c. 5.

ju *Evening Capital News*, 27 February 1905, p. 5, c. 3.

jv *The Teton Peak-Chronicle*, St. Anthony, Idaho, 16 March 1905, p. 1, c. 3.

jw *Evening Capital News*, 22 February 1905, p. 8, c. 3.

jx *Idaho Daily Statesman*, 16 March 1905, p. 3, c. 3.

jy *Evening Capital News*, 6 April 1905, p. 4, c. 5. 7 April 1905, p. 8, c. 1.

jz *Idaho Capital News*, 20 April 1905, p. 7, c. 1.

ka Blaine County Judicial Records, Idaho State Historical Society, microfilm reel 30, item three, original page 283.

kb Blaine County Judicial Records, Idaho State Historical Society, microfilm reel 30, original page 269.

kc *Idaho Daily Statesman*, 17 April 1905, p. 6, c. 5.

kd *Evening Capital News*, 1 May 1905, p. 5, c. 3.

ke *Idaho Daily Statesman*, 4 May 1905, p. 5, c. 1. *Evening Capital News*, 3 May 1905, p. 8, c. 4.

kf *Evening Capital News*, 4 May 105, p. 5, c. 1.

kg *The Genesee News*, 15 February 1907, p. 1, c. 1-2.

kh *Evening Capital News*, 3 May 1905, p. 8, c. 4.

ki *Idaho Daily Statesman*, 24 May 1905, p. 3, c. 2. *Evening Capital News*, 26 May 1905, p. 9, c. 1.

kj *Evening Capital News*, 3 June 1905, p. 4, c. 2.

kk *Evening Capital News*, 23 June 1905, p. 6, c. 3.

kl *Idaho Daily Statesman*, 2 July 1905, p. 7, c. 1.

km *Idaho Daily Statesman*, 3 July 1905, p. 5, c. 1.

kn *Idaho Daily Statesman*, 4 July 1905, p. 2, c. 2.

ko *Idaho Daily Statesman*, 10 July 1905, p. 3, c. 4.

kp *Evening Capital News*, 7 July 1905, p. 8, c.1-4.

kq *Evening Capital News*, 3 August 1905, p. 5, c. 1-3.

kr *Idaho Daily Statesman*, 12 July 1905, p. 5, c. 1-2.

ks *Idaho Daily Statesman*, 3 August 1905, p. 5, c. 5.

kt *Evening Capital News*, 9 August 1905, p. 5, c. 5-6.

ku *Idaho Capital News*, 24 August 1905, p. 6, c. 1. *Idaho Daily Statesman*, 21 August 1905, p. 3, c. 5.

kv *Idaho Daily Statesman*, 27 August 1905, p. 6, c. 2. *Evening Capital News*, 21 August 1905, p. 5, c. 2.

John Lemp • The Beer Baron of Boise 289

kw *Evening Capital News*, 26 August 1905, p. 6, c. 1-2.
kx *Idaho Daily Statesman*, 3 September 1905, p. 5, c. 3.
ky *Idaho Daily Statesman*, 17 September 1905, p. 3, c. 3.
kz *Evening Capital News*, 1 September 1905, p. 4, c. 4.
la *Evening Capital News*, 25 September 1905, p. 1, c. 4.
lb *Idaho Capital News*, 26 October 1905, p. 10, c. 6. *Evening Capital News*, 21 October 1905, p. 1, c. 7.
lc *Idaho Capital News*, 2 November 1905, p. 6, c. 5.
ld *Evening Capital News*, 26 October 1905, p. 2, c. 1.
le *Evening Capital News*, 12 September 1905, p. 5, c. 4.
lf *Evening Capital News,* 25 September 1905, p. 5, c. 4.
lg *Idaho Daily Statesman*, 20 October 1905, p. 5, c. 1-2.
lh *Evening Capital News*, 22 September 1905, p. 1, c. 5.
li Bureau of Land Management, Land Patent Records. Accession/Serial # IDIDAA 013705. Document 468. Description was Aliquot Parts E, Section 31, Township 4-N, Range 2-W.
lj *Idaho Daily Statesman*, 17 November 1905, p. 5, c. 1-2.
lk *Evening Capital News*, 9 December 1905, p. 6, c. 4.
ll *Idaho Daily Statesman*, 7 December 1905, p. 8, c. 1.
lm *Idaho Daily Statesman*, 30 December 1905, p. 2, c. 4.
ln *Idaho Daily Statesman*, 20 December 1905, p. 12, c. 3-4.
lo *Evening Capital News*, 22 December 1905, p. 2, c. 1-3.
lp *Idaho Daily Statesman*, 23 March 1906, p. 3, c. 2.
lq *Idaho Daily Statesman*, 6 April 1906, p. 3, c. 2.
lr *Idaho Daily Statesman*, 28 December 1906, p. 5, c. 3.
ls *Evening Capital News*, 26 February 1908, p. 6, c. 1 & 2.
lt J. M. Neil, "The Impossible Dream," *Idaho Yesterdays*, vol. 42, no. 4, Winter, 1999, p. 14.
lu *The Boise Citizen,* 26 June 1908, p. 1, c. 1-2.
lv *Idaho Daily Statesman*, 15 May 1909, p. 5, c. 2.
lw *Idaho Daily Statesman*, 22 August 1909, p. 5, c. 2.
lx *Idaho Daily Statesman*, 24 September 1909, p. 3, c. 2. *Evening Capital News*, 23 August 1909, p. 10, c. 1-2. 23 September 1909, p. 1 & 2, c. 6 & 7.
ly *Evening Capital News*, 25 September 1909, 25 September 1909, p. 3, c. 4-5.
lz *Evening Capital News*, 25 October 1909, p. 2, c. 3-4.
ma *Idaho Daily Statesman*, 9 March 1910, p. 5, c. 1.
mb *Idaho Daily Statesman*, 4 August 1910, p. 3, c. 2.
mc *Idaho Daily Statesman*, 27 January 1911, p. 3, c. 5.
md *Evening Capital News* 25 January 1911, p. 8, c. 2.
me *Idaho Daily Statesman*, 31 January 1911, p. 10, c. 3.

mf *Evening Capital News*, 5 February 1911, p. 8, c. 1-4.
mg *Evening Capital News*, 24 February 1911, p. 8, c. 6 & 7.
mh *Evening Capital News*, 2 April 1911, p.8, c. 4.
mi *Idaho Daily Statesman*, 8 May 1911, p. 8, c. 3.
mj *Idaho Daily Statesman*, 14 May 1911, p. 12, c. 4.
mk *Evening Capital News*, 28 June 1911, p. 2, c. 2.
ml *Idaho Daily Statesman*, 30 July 1911, p. 13, c. 2.
mm *Idaho Daily Statesman*, 7 September 1912, p. 10, c. 3 & 4.
mn *Evening Capital News*, 2 February 1906, p. 3, c. 1-2.
mo *Evening Capital News*, 7 February 1906, p. 6, c. 1-2.
mp *Idaho Daily Statesman*, 30 January 1906, p. 5, c. 6.
mq *Idaho Daily Statesman*, 23 March 1906, p. 3, c. 3.
mr *Evening Capital News*, 21 February 1906, p. 9, c. 1-3.
ms *Evening Capital News*, 23 March 1906, p. 8, c. 2 & 3.
mt *Idaho Daily Statesman,* 20 April 1906, p. 3, c. 2-3.
mu *Idaho Sunday Statesman*, 9 July 1967, p. 2-D, c. 5.
mv "Those Were the Days, Growing Up in Style," *Idaho Yesterdays*, Fall, 1970, p.28-29.
mw "History of the Boise School District. *Independent School District of Boise City.* Internet site. www.sd0.1.k12.id.us/administration/dist1st.html.
mx *Evening Capital News*, 26 May 1906, p. 7, c. 3.
my *Evening Capital News*, 21 May 1906, p. 6, c. 2. 28 May 1906, p. 3, c. 4. 31 May 1906, p. 2, c. 2.
mz *Evening Capital News*, 30 May 1906, p. [5, c. 5.]
na *Idaho Daily Statesman*, 15 June 1906, p. 5, c. 2.
nb *Idaho Daily Statesman*, 17 June 1906, p. 5, c. 2.
nc *Idaho Daily Statesman*, 17 June 1906, p. 4, c. 2.
nd *Idaho Daily Statesman*, 30 June 1906, p. 5, c. 1.
ne *Evening Capital News*, 4 July 1906, p. 4, c. 5-7. The list was published numerous days.
nf *Idaho Daily Statesman*, 11 August 1906, p. 5, c. 4.
This poorly written account seemed to imply that Lemp was the one accused.
ng *Evening Capital News*, 11 August 1906, p. 5, c. 2-3.
nh *Wood River Times*, Hailey, Daily, 7 August 1906, p. 4, c. 3.
ni *Idaho Daily Statesman*, 25 September 1906, p. 2, c. 1.
nj *Evening Capital News*, 12 September 1906, p. 5, c. 4, p. 8, c. 4.
nk *Idaho Daily Statesman*, 24 September 1906, p. 4, c. 2.
nl   *Idaho Daily Statesman*, 21 October 1906, p. 12, c. 2.
nm *Evening Capital News*, 27 October 1906, p. 8, c. 6-7.

nn *Idaho Daily Statesman*, 11 November 1906, p. 8, c. 3.
no *Idaho Daily Statesman*, 14 November 1906, p. 3, c. 3.
np *Idaho Daily Statesman*, 15 November 1906, p. 3, c. 1, 23 November 1906, p. 3, c. 4.
nq *Idaho Daily Statesman*, 28 November 1906, p. 8, c. 2.
nr *Evening Capital News*, 26 November 1906, p. 3, c. 4.
s   *Evening Capital News*, 5 December 1906, p. 3, c. 5.
nt *Idaho Daily Statesman*, 30 December 1906, p. 3, c. 3.
nu *Idaho Daily Statesman*, 8 January 1907, p. 8, c. 3.
nv *Idaho Daily Statesman*, 8 January 1907, p. 8, c. 3.
nw *Idaho Daily Statesman*, 20 February 1907, p. 3, c. 4.
nx *Idaho Daily Statesman*, 10 March 1907, p. 4, c. 1.
ny *Idaho Register*, Idaho Falls, 22 March 1907, p. 2, c. 6.
nz *Idaho Daily Statesman*, 20 March 1907, p. 5, c. 3.
oa *Idaho Daily Statesman*, 2 April 1907, p. 5, c. 2.
b   Ada County Court Records, Microfilmed Judgment Books, Idaho State Historical Society.
oc *Evening Capital News*, 18 May 1907, p. 12, c. 4.
od *Idaho Daily Statesman*, 7 September 1907, p. 5, c. 1.
oe Ada County Court Records, Microfilmed Judgment Books, Idaho State Historical Society.
of *Idaho Daily Statesman*, 14 March 1908, p. 3, c. 4.
og *Idaho Daily Statesman* 19 June 1908, p. 6, c. 4.
oh *Idaho Daily Statesman*, 24 April 1907, p. 5, c. 2. p. 8, c. 2. One article spells one culprits name Brean and the other spells it Breen, the other gentleman is alternately Mullin and Mullen.
i   *Evening Capital News*, 23 April 1907, p. 8, c. 3.
oj *Idaho Daily Statesman*, 24 May 1907, p. 2, c. 1. 25 May 1907, p. 9, c. 1.
ok *Idaho Daily Statesman*, 26 May 1907, p. 14, c. 1.
ol *Idaho Daily Statesman*, 31 May 1907, p. 3, c. 4. *Evening Capital News*, 6 May 1907, p. 8, c. 4.
om *Evening Capital News*, 10 May 1907, p. 2, c. 4.
on *Evening Capital News*, 11 May 1907, p. 2, c. 3.
oo *Evening Capital News*, 17 May 1907, p. 10, c. 1.
op *Evening Capital News*, 23 May 1907, p. 6, c. 3.
oq *Evening Capital News*, 22 May 1907, p. 8, c. 4.
or *Evening Capital News*, 15 June 1907, p. 3, c. 4-5.
os *Idaho Daily Statesman*, 23 July 1907, p. 5, c. 2.
ot *Idaho Daily Statesman*, 2 August 1907, p. 6, c. 4.
ou *Idaho Daily Statesman*, 17 August 1907, p. 6, c. 4.

ov Evening Capital News, 14 September 1907, p. 12, c. 2.
ow Evening Capital News, 7 august 1907, p. 8, c. 5.
ox Evening Capital News, 7 August 1907, p. 5, c. 5 &6.
oy The Boise Citizen, 9 August 1907, p. 3, c. 1-3.
oz Evening Capital News, 21 August 1907, p. 2, c. 3.
pa Evening Capital News, 17 August 1907, p. 2, c. 5.
pb Idaho Daily Statesman, 31 August 1907, p. 6, c. 1.
pc Evening Capital News, 12 September 1907, p. 3, c. 3.
pd Idaho Daily Statesman, 18 September 1907, p. 5, c. 2.
pe Idaho Daily Statesman, 14 September 1907, p. 2, c. 1.
pf Evening Capital News, 24 October 1907, p. 3, c. 4.
pg Evening Capital News, 3 December 1907, p. 1 & 2, C. 3, 4, 5.
ph Idaho Daily Statesman, 7 December 1907, p. 5, c. 4-5.
pi Idaho Daily Statesman, 8 January 1908, p. 5, c. 3. Evening Capital News, 8 January 1908, p. 1, c. 4.
pj Evening Capital News, 9 January 1908, p. 5, c. 1.
pk Idaho Daily Statesman, 9 January 1908, p. 5, c. 2. 10 January 1908, p. 3, c. 4. 11 January 1908, p. 5, c. 1.
pl Wood River Times, 9 January 1908, p. 4, c. 2.
pm Idaho Daily Statesman, 9 January 1908, p. 3, c. 2.
pn Idaho Daily Statesman, 23 January 1908,p. 3, c. 3. Photocopy of the will. Probate court, Ada county, Idaho. Evening Capital News, 23 January 1908, p. 5, c. 3.
po Idaho Daily Statesman, 11 January 1908, p. 3, c. 1 & 2.
pp Wright and Reitzes, Tourtellotte & Hummel, p. 91.
pq J. M. Neil, 1890-1917 Boise Gets Julia Davis Park," Idaho Yesterdays, Vol. 46, No. 1, Winter 2005, p. 45.
pr Evening Capital News 20 March 1908, p. 10, c. 1-4.
ps Evening Capital News, 2 April 1908, p. 2, c. 7.
pt Evening Capital News, 13 April 1908, p. 6, c. 5.
pu Idaho Daily Statesman, 18 April 1908, p. 1, c. 2.
pv The W. A. Clark mansion was a museum and bed and breakfast in Butte, Montana in the Twenty First Century.
pw Evening Capital News, 27 April 1908, p. 5, c. 1.
px Evening Capital News, 19 May 1908, p. 2, c. 1-4.
py Evening Capital News, 24 June 1908, p. 1, c. 1-2.
pz Evening Capital News, 25 June 1908, p. 5, c. 3.
qa Evening Capital News, 4 September 1908, p. 2, c. 5.
qb Evening Capital News, 29 June 1908, p. 5, c. 1.
qc Idaho Daily Statesman, 4 July 1908, p. 4, c. 4.

qd *Idaho Daily Statesman*, 18 July 1908, p. 2, c. 1.
qe *Idaho Daily Statesman* 21 July 1908, 21 July 1908, p. 5, c. 1 & 2.
qf *Idaho Daily Statesman*, 19 July 1908, p. 2, c. 4 & 5.
qg *Evening Capital News*, 18 August 1908, p. 1, c. 5.
qh *Idaho Daily Statesman*, 15 September 1908, p. 5, c. 3. *Evening Capital News*, 14 September 1908, p. 8, c. 3.
qi *Idaho Daily Statesman*, 30 October 1908, p. 3, c. 3.
qj *Evening Capital News*, 1 January 1909, p. 3, c. 1.
qk *Idaho Daily Statesman*, 4 October 1908, Section II, p. 6, c. 2-4. Forty Years Ago column.
ql *Evening Capital News*, 5 October 1908, p. 2, c. 5.
qm *Evening Capital News*, 2 November 1908, p. 1-2.
qn *Idaho Daily Statesman*, 15 November 1908,p. 5, c. 3 & 4. W. A. Goulder, "How a Penniless German Boy Made It Go in the Early Days of Idaho."
qo *Idaho Daily Statesman*, 1 November 1908, p. 6, c. 3.
qp *Idaho Daily Statesman*, 4 December 1908, p. 7, c. 3*Evening Capital News*, 4 December 1908, p. 1, c. 3-4.
qq *Idaho Daily Statesman*, 25 November 1908, p. 2, c. 4. 26 November 1908, p.5, c. 5. 27 November 1908, p. 5, c. 2.
qr *Evening Capital News*, 21 November 1908, p. 8, c. 1-7.
qs *Evening Capital News*, 28 November 1908, p. 12, c. 1-7.
qt *Evening Capital News*, 16 January 1909, p. 12, c. 1-7.
qu *Evening Capital News*, 23 January 1909, p. 12, c. 1-7. 26 January 1909, p. 10, c. 6 & 7.
qv *Evening Capital News*, 6 February 1909, p. 8, c. 1-7. 13 February 1909, p. 8, c. 3-7. 15 February 1909, p. 8, c. 1-3.
qw *Evening Capital News*, 18 February 1909, p. 6, c. 3.
qx *Idaho Daily Statesman*, 9 May 1909, p. 6, c. 1 & 2.
qy *Idaho Daily Statesman*, 22 November 1908, Section II, p. 6, c. 2. A full page ad was on p. 4.
qz *Idaho Daily Statesman*, Section II, 22 November 1908, p. 3, c. 1 & 2.
ra *Idaho Daily Statesman* 12 January 1909, p. 2, c. 3.
rb A detailed account of the divorce trail appeared in the *Evening Capital News*, 8 February 1909, p. 8, c. 3. See also *Evening Capital News*, 18 February 1909, p. 1, c. 3.
rc *Idaho Daily Statesman*, 28 March 1909, p. 5, c. 4. *Evening Capital News*, 27 March 1909, p. 2, c. 4.
rd *Lewiston Tribune*, 18 March 2007, p. 1D and 6D.
re *Idaho Daily Statesman*, 23 April 1909, p. 12, c. 7.
rf *Idaho Daily Statesman*, 30 April 1909, p. 4, c. 3.
rg *Idaho Daily Statesman*, 2 May 1909, p. 5, c. 1.

rh *Evening Capital News*, 1 June 1909, p. 2, c. 1-2.
ri *Evening Capital News*, 5 June 1909, p. 4-5, c. 1-7.
rj *Idaho Daily Statesman*, 2 July 1909, p. 2, c. 4.
rk *Evening Capital News*, 8 September 1909, p. 1, c. 5. The Wets were organized for several months before the election. See *Evening Capital News*, 30 July 1909, p. 3, c. 4.
rl *Idaho Daily Statesman*, 2 October 1909, p. 4, c. 3.
rm *Evening Capital News*, 25 September 1909, p. 3, c. 1.
rn *Idaho Daily Statesman*, 5 November 1909, p. 7, c. 2.
ro *Idaho Daily Statesman*, 11 November 1909, p. 8, c. 2.
rp *Evening Capital News*, 24 January 1910, p. 2, c. 2.
rq *Idaho Daily Statesman*, 30 January 1910, p. 4, c. 1.
rr *Idaho Daily Statesman*, 5 March 1910, p. 6, c. 1.
rs *Evening Capital News*, 29 January 1910, p. 6, c. 1-2.
rt *Evening Capital News*, 12 February 1910, p. 8, c. 1-2.
ru *Idaho Daily Statesman*, 23 March 1910, p. 6, c. 2.
rv *Evening Capital News*, 2 April 1910, p. 2, c. 2.
rw *Evening Capital News*, 14 May 1910, p. 5, c. 3 & 4.
rx *Evening Capital News*, 13 August 1910, p. 5, c. 3-4.
ry *Evening Capital News*, 12 February 1910, p. 10, c. 1.
rz *Evening Capital News*, 8 April 1910, p. 2, c. 2.
sa *Idaho Daily Statesman*, 29 March 1910, p. 3, c. 2.
sb *Evening Capital News*, 29 March 1910, p. 2, c. 1.
sc *Idaho Daily Statesman*, 24 April 1910, Section II, p. 8, c. 2.
sd *Idaho Daily Statesman*, 12 May 1910, p. 5, c. 1.
se *Idaho Daily Statesman*, 5 June 1910, p. 2, c. 3.
sf *Idaho Daily Statesman*, 29 June 1910, p. 5, c. 3.
sg Bureau of Land Management, Land Patent Records, John's was Accession/Serial # 141545. BLM Serial # IDB 0007444. Document 07444. Description was Aliquot Parts, SNE, Section 2, Township 5-N, Range 2-E, and Aliquot SESE Section 35, Township 6-N, Range 2-E, and Aliquot 1, Section 2, Township 5-N, Range 2-E. Catherine's was Aliquot SNW Section 1, Township 5-N, Range 2-E. And Aliquot 3, Section 1, Township 5-N, Range 2-E. And Aliquot Parts 4, Section 1, Township 5-N, Range 2-E.
sh *Evening Capital News*, 13 August 1910, p. 12, c. 1.
si *Evening Capital News*, 6 October 1910, p. 2, c. 3.
sj *Idaho Daily Statesman*, 24 August 1910. p. 4, c. 5.
sk *Idaho Daily Statesman*, 2 September 1910, p. 5, c. 2.
sl *Idaho Daily Statesman*, 2 October 1910, p. 6, c. 1-3. *Evening Capital News*, 1 October 1910, p. 4, c. 1 & 2.

John Lemp • The Beer Baron of Boise   295

sm *Evening Capital News*, 6 October 1910, p. 2, c. 3.
sn *Idaho Daily Statesman*, 25 September 1910, Section II, p. 8, c. 1 & 2. *Evening Capital News*, 24 September 1910, p. 4, c. 1 & 2. 1 October 1910, p. 4, c. 1 & 2.
so *Idaho Daily Statesman*, 2 October 1910, Section II, p. 5, c. 1 & 2.
sp *Idaho Daily Statesman*, 9 October 1910, Section II, p. 1, c. 1-3. The following quotes about the wedding are all from this newspaper article.
sq *Idaho Daily Statesman*, 9 October 1910, p. 5, c. 4.
sr French, *History of Idaho*, vol. II, p. 598.
ss *Idaho Daily Statesman*, 1 January 1911, p. 5, c. 1.
st *Idaho Daily Statesman*, 6 January 1911, p. 3, c. 1-3.
su *Idaho Daily Statesman*, 14 January 1911, p. 3, c. 5.
sv *Idaho Daily Statesman*, 11 February 1911, p. 3, c. 1.
sw R. L. Polk & Co.'s *Boise City and Ada County Directory, 1911*, Vol. VII.
sx *Idaho Daily Statesman*, 19 February 1911, p. 10, c. 3-4.
sy *Evening Capital News*, 20 February 1911, p. 1, c. 7.
sz *Idaho Daily Statesman*, 3 April 1911, p. 3, c. 4.
ta *Evening Capital News*, 7 April 1911, p. 2, c. 4.
tb *Idaho Daily Statesman*, 23 June 1911, p. 2, c. 2. The lad was listed as John Jr. which is not technically correct.
tc *Evening Capital News*, 5 July 1911, p. 8, c. 3.
td *Idaho Daily Statesman*, 13 August 1911, p. 2, c. 2.
te *Evening Capital News*, 15 August 1911, p. 2, c. 3.
tf *Idaho Daily Statesman*, 29 August 1911, p. 9, c. 2-7.
tg *Idaho Daily Statesman*, 29 August 1911, p. 7, c. 4.
th *Idaho Daily Statesman*, 3 September 1911, p. 6, c. 1.
ti *Evening Capital News*, 3 September 1911, p. 2, c. 3.
tj *Evening Capital News*, 7 September 1911, p. 3, c. 3.
tk *Idaho Daily Statesman*, 6 October 1911, p. 3, c. 5.
tl *Idaho Daily Statesman*, 13 October 1911, p. 3, c. 1-6.
tm *Evening Capital News*, 12 October 1911, p. 1, c. 1, and p. 2, c. 5-7.
tn *Evening Capital News*, [14] October 1911, p. 10, c. 2-3.
to *Evening Capital News*, 20 September 1909, p. 3, c. 2.
tp *Idaho Daily Statesman*, 3 November 1911, p. 10, c. 5.
tq *Idaho Daily Statesman*, 20 November 1911, p. 3, c. 1-2.
tr *Idaho Daily Statesman*, 25 November 1911, p. 8, c. 3.
ts *Idaho Daily Statesman*, 27 November 1911, p. 5, c. 3.
tt *Idaho Daily Statesman*, 3 December 1911, p. 11, c. 1.
tu *Idaho Daily Statesman*, 10 December 1911, p. 8, c. 1-4.
tv *Idaho Daily Statesman*, 11 December 1911, p. 5, c. 1-2.

tw *Idaho Daily Statesman*, 24 March 1912, p. 8, c. 3 – 4.
tx *Idaho Daily Statesman*, 31 March 1912, p. 7, c. 4-5.
ty *Idaho Daily Statesman*, 1 April 1912, p. 4, c. 5.
tz *Idaho Daily Statesman*, 14 April 1912, p. 9, c. 2-5.
ua *The Evening Capital News*, 10 June 1912, p. 1, c. 5.
ub *Idaho Daily Statesman*, 12 November 1911, . 4, c. 2-4.
uc *Idaho Daily Statesman*, 10 December 1911, Section II, p. 1, c. 1-7. From 1867 to 1911 the list included Prickett, Hart, Himrod, Twitchell, Lemp, Logan, Himrod, Jacobs, Bilderback, Pinney, Hasbrouck, Huston, Pefley, Pinney, Sonna, Pierce, Alexander, Richards, Alexander, Hawley, Pinney, Haines, Pence, and Fritchman.
ud *Idaho Daily Statesman*, 15 December 1911, p. 4, c. 4.
ue *Idaho Daily Statesman*, 16 December 1911, p. 10, c. 1-2.
uf *Idaho Daily Statesman*, 11 February 1912, p. 11, c. 1-3.
ug *Idaho Daily Statesman*, 31 March 1912, p. 4, c. 1.
uh *Idaho Daily Statesman*, 14 April 1912, p. 5, c. 2.
ui *Idaho Daily Statesman*, 11 May 1912, p. 7, c. 4.
uj *Idaho Daily Statesman*, 20 June 1912, p. 5, c. 3-4. 1 July 1912, p. 3, c. 2.
uk *Idaho Daily Statesman*, 1 July 1912, p. 4, c. 2. *The Evening Capital News*, 30 June 1912, p. 16, c. 1-3.
ul *Idaho Daily Statesman*, 18 July 1912, p. 2, c. 3. *Idaho Death Index, 1911-51*, certificate number 002592.
um *Idaho Daily Statesman*, 19 July 1912, p. 3, c. 3-5. *Idaho Weekly Statesman*, 22 July 1912, p. 2, c. 2.
un C.W. Moore also lived in Boise from 1863 to 1916.
uo *Evening Capital News*, Boise, 18 July 1912, p. 7, c. 1.
up Hawley, *History of Idaho*, vol. 2, p. 18.
uq *Idaho Daily Statesman*, 20 July 1912, p. 10, c. 2.
ur *Idaho Daily Statesman*, 20 July 1912, p. 10, c. 3.
us *Evening Capital News*, 21 July 1912, p. 8, c. 3.
ut *Idaho Daily Statesman*, 21 July 1912, p. 11, c. 1.
uu *Sunday Capital News*, 21 July 1912, p. 11, c. 3 & 4. *Idaho Daily Statesman*, 22 July 1912, p. 3, c. 1 & 2. See the appendix for the complete text of the will.
uv *Idaho Daily Statesman*, 22 July 1912, p. 3, c. 3. *Idaho Weekly Statesman*, 22 July 1912, p. 7, c. 3.
uw *Idaho Daily Statesman*, 22 July 1912, p. 13, c. 7.
ux *Idaho Daily Statesman*, 4 August 1912, p. 16, c. 2.
uy *Idaho Daily Statesman*, 8 August 1912, p. 8, c. 3.
uz *Evening Capital News*, 13 September 1912, p. 2, c. 3.

The Legacy of John Lemp

"I'M NOT PREJUDICED AGAINST THEM MIND YE. They made good beer an' good citizens and mod-rate policemen, an' they are fond of their families an' cheese. But wanst German, always Dutch. Ye cudden't make Americans iv them if ye called them all Perkins an' brought them up in Worcester."[a] Mr. Dooley, the fictional Irish bartender-philosopher who bespoke the satirical philosophy of his creator, Chicago humorist Finley Peter Dunne, in the newspapers of the early Twentieth Century, offered this ethnically biased summation of German American character. John Lemp made good beer, a first rate citizen, featured cheese with the free lunches at his saloon, and he was extraordinarily fond of his family. He left a tradition for them, and they carried on his legacy. John Lemp disproved part of Dunne's theory, however. John Lemp died a complete American.

John Lemp's Place Among Idaho's Brewers

My study of Idaho's other brewers has generated a great deal of data about their lives, backgrounds and activities. How does Lemp stand in relation to the group which he leads? I have data on about 150 Idaho brewers to compare. For very few, if any, of these individuals do I know as many aspects of their lives as with Lemp, but much is known. About three-fourths of Idaho brewers were of German descent, some with only one Germanic parent. Lemp is certainly in with the majority on this account.

Lemp Street remains a part of Boise.

Less than three per cent of Idaho's brewers were formally trained in brewing academies, and Lemp, like the majority, learned from experience. Lemp was a business clerk and then a miner before brewing. Idaho's brewers followed many prior professions and there is little to indicate that any one of these was a gateway to brewing. More saloonists were involved with brewing than any other profession, but was it a case of saloonists learning to brew, or brewers learning to retail their product? Retailing liquor requires no understanding of organic chemistry as brewing does. Nine other brewers were involved with fire departments, as was Lemp.

Many Idaho brewers—23 on my list—were, like Lemp, involved with mining. I find no direct correlation in the businesses. Mining required capital and brewers had capital, and probably they got to know many full-time miners or prospectors in their saloons. Opportunities for formal investment or just the "grubstacking" of a customer thus occurred and occasionally paid huge dividends. Successful investments in mining necessarily became public due to deeds and contracts being recorded, but investment in other things remained unrecorded. Also, Idaho virtually worshipped mineral wealth as somehow superior to any other basis for becoming rich.

Many Idaho brewers had relatives who were also in brewing. Lemp's extended family is the prime example of this. His brother Jacob brewed; his brothers-in-law George Kohlepp, and Samuel Adolph brewed. William Stirm, Jacob's brother-in-law brewed. John Lemp's sons worked in his brewery. Many Lemp employees went on to start their own brewing businesses. No other brewer in the state, with the possible exception of John Brodbeck, had so many familial tentacles reaching out to the brew kettles of others. With his thirteen children, twelve of whom survived infancy, Lemp also led the drive to reproduce. Christian Weisgerber of Lewiston, who was married twice, holds second place with eight offspring that survived infancy.

Only three brewers beside Lemp were Knights Templar; nine other brewers were Odd Fellows; eighteen other brewers were Masons; Lemp was one of three Shriners; the Ancient Order of United Workmen claimed two brewers beside Lemp.

Lemp was christened a Lutheran, buried an Episcopalian, and his children were married into various denominations. Only five other Idaho brewers were found to be various kinds of Protestants. There were six Catholic brewers in Idaho, five Jews, and four Later Day Saints. All the many others were unknown, undeclared or uninterested.

Lemp was one of eighteen Republican brewers. Likewise, there were eighteen Democratic brewers. When Lemp briefly joined the fusion party he was one of five who ever belonged to any "Third" party. Many brewers were active in local Politics. Lemp was one of five brewers to serve on a school board. Lemp was one of six to serve on a city council, and one of nine to be a city mayor.

Lemp endured many injuries but the only chronic medical condition noted with Lemp was rheumatism. Six other brewers were afflicted with the same condition. Informally, that is without medical confirmation, the problem is often ascribed to doing heavy labor in the cold of the brewery ice house. If this is not a cause, it may certainly be an irritant to the condition. Though I have no exact comparative figures, Lemp was apparently in many more civil and criminal court cases, whether as plaintiff, defendant, witness, or juror than any other brewer of early Idaho and possibly more than any other man of his time and place.

When the World War I draft came, all men born between 1872 and 1900 were required to register. John's sons Albert Carl Lemp, born 7 February 1877 of Boise, Bernard Louis Lemp, 8 November

Letterhead of the St. Louis Lemp Brewing Company.

Six descendants of John Lemp, all named John Lemp. Left to right, back row: John Lemp, Jr., Col. John Lemp, John Frederick Lemp, Sr., John Frederick Lemp, Jr. Front row: John Lemp, John Louis Lemp. 5 July 1969, Laurel Glen, Jack Mountain, near Greenstone, PA. Photo from Karl Lemp.

1886 of Boise, Herbert Frederick Lemp, 24 June 1884, of Boise and nephew Clarence J. Lemp, 27 July 1897, of Twin Falls all registered.[b] Millions of Americans of German descent, like the Lemps, signed up to face the possibility of a return to Europe to wage war on their own extended families.

As with the Biblical Father Abraham, John Lemp was what anthropologists term an apical ancestor; the progenitor from whom a whole genetic line traces its roots. This was true because he was the first of his immediate family to come to a new country on a new continent, because John's own father died so young that many of his children never really knew him, and because John sired so many children to carry forth his family line and legacy.

EDWARD H. LEMP

On 6 September 1912, at 5 o'clock in the morning, about six weeks after his father's death, Edward Henry Lemp, died.[c] He was at the family home at 507 Grove Street, and the cause was ascribed to complication of diseases from which he had been suffering for about two years. He was thirty years old and single. The funeral was held at the home at 4:30 on Saturday the 7th. Episcopal Bishop Funsten was in charge according to the *Statesman* and Reverend D. H. Jones of Christ Church according to the *Evening Capital News*. There were many floral tributes. The Elks Lodge officiated at the grave. Burial was at the Elks Rest in Morris Hill Cemetery, not at the Pioneer Cemetery where most family members were interred.[d]

Edward's will, dated 23 July 1912, two weeks before his death, left half of his property to brother Herbert and half to brother Bernard. Herbert was named executor with Bernard the alternate. It was filed for probate on 10 September 1912.

AUGUSTA JULIA MARGARET LEMP GRANT

In May of 1926, John Lemp's daughter Mrs. Augusta Grant of Portland died.[e] Boise remembered that she was the daughter of John and Kate, that she was born in Boise, and she had been in Portland about 15 years. She had three brothers (Herbert, Bernard and Albert) and three sisters (Mrs. W. B. Connor, Mrs. E. G. Hurt, and Mrs. Marshall Simmons) surviving. The Boise members of the family drove to Portland for the funeral.

Augusta's will was dated 21 December 1912 and was probated in Ada County as well as in Multnomah County, Oregon.[f] Some of her assets must have still been in the John Lemp estate. She left everything to her husband and named him executor. The will was first admitted to probate on 15 November 1926.

HERBERT FREDERICK LEMP

Herbert Frederick Lemp was executor for his father's estate which was no small task. When he took on that job Herbert was already active in the management and ownership of many companies in Boise.[g] The mantle of alpha male in the Lemp extended family fell to him. Herbert's office manager for the estate, until at least 1920, was Watt Piercy, a man with stenographic and legal training.[h] He was a Hoosier who had worked for mining companies in Idaho before working for the Lemp estate.

Herbert clashed with Arthur Hodges, the Mayor of Boise, almost immediately over ownership of the Lemp Triangle land in Boise, and the case ended in the Idaho State Supreme Court after Mayor Hodges appealed. The case involved several points: Henry E. Prickett, as Mayor of Boise filed a plat of Boise City in the office of the Ada County Recorder on 23 November 1867, he filed the plat with the United State Interior Department on 13 January 1868, and the Interior Department issued a patent to the Mayor on 2 May 1870. The problem was that the Interior Department's patent covered 442 acres while the original plat was for 410 acres, and thus 32 acres were not platted.

HERBERT F. LEMP,

Executor Estate of John Lemp (deceased), Falk Building, Boise, Idaho.

Director, Boise Traction Co.

Director, Boise Stone Co.

Director, Pacific National Bank.

Director, Idaho State Life Insurance Co.

President, Idaho Provision & Packing Co.

Director, Guarantee Guardian & Casualty Co., Salt Lake.

Born: Boise, Idaho, June 24, 1884; son of John and Catherine (Kohlhepp) Lemp.

Educated: Boise Public Schools; Boise Business College.

During vacation as a boy of 15 took an executive part in the management of his father's diversified business interests, 1899-1902; executor of his father's estate since, 1912, and feeding 3,000 head of beef cattle.

Member of the famous Boise Polo Club that went to California for the P. P. I. E., the International Polo Meet, winning the Sacramento Handicap event, and in no game did they have to use handicap.

Married Marguerite N. Nolan, Hancock, Mich., May 9, 1906; has one son and one daughter.

Clubs: Rotary; Commercial; Elks; Country.

Societies: A. F. & A. M.; B. P. O. E.

Recreations: Fishing; hunting; polo.

Republican.

Christian Scientist.

Residence: 105 E. Idaho Street, Boise, Idaho.

Undated resume for Herbert F. Lemp. Idaho State Historical Society

The Mayor James A. Pinney, on 5 June 1891, for $1, gave John Lemp a deed to 4.55 acres which were within the 32 non-platted acres. In 1910 John Lemp platted the land and placed it upon the market. Hodges who was Mayor of Boise in 1912 discovered these facts in September of 1912 about two months after the death of John Lemp. If this was not complicated enough there was a second cause of action. When Walter E. Pierce was Mayor of Boise on 25 June 1897 he made application for more townsite lands which were patented to him by the government on 23 May 1898. These 1.13 acres were deeded to John Lemp by then Mayor John M. Haines on 26 February 1908 for $5. In 1910 John Lemp platted this land and placed it upon the market. The majority sided with Mayor Hodges and the opinion was written by Judge C.J. Ailshie. They ruled that a rehearing of the case could be made. Justice J. Stewart dissented. He cited the long time period in which Lemp held the land without anyone else claiming a right to it. If there was deception it should have been discovered long before. Also the "mayor" under the Boise form of government was in name only and should not have been allowed to initiate such an action. In July of 1915, the Lemp claim to the "Lemp Triangle" was upheld over the city claim by Judge Bryan of the Seventh District.[i]

Herbert's undated resume at the State Historical Society listed his primary job as executor of his father's estate.[j] He was feeding 3,000 head of cattle. He was also a director of the Boise Traction Co., Boise Stone Co., Pacific National Bank, Idaho State Life insurance Co., Guarantee Guardian & Casualty Co. of Salt Lake, and president of the Idaho Provision and Packing Co. He was in the Rotary, Elks, Commercial Club and Country Club. Fishing, hunting and polo were his chief sports.

In 1914, Herbert won a default judgment against the Western Bottling and Packing Company for $2,425.55 plus costs and attorney fees.[k]

The noted local architecture firm of Tourtellotte and Hummel did various remodeling projects on Lemp estate holdings on Main Street in Boise during 1916, 1918, and 1919, as well as the Lemp store building at 112 S. 9th in 1927.[l]

Here is a quick scan of Herbert's life after his father's death. Polo became in fact more of a passion than a pastime for him. Herbert F.

Lemp returned to Boise in April of 1915 elated over the success of his Boise polo team in contests in California. They returned with their most coveted award, earned under Lemp's leadership, the Sacramento Cup.ᵐ

In the 1915 Boise City Directory, Herbert was listed as executor of the Lemp estate, and also as half of the livestock firm of H. F. Lemp and F. J. Pinkham. His office was at 37 Falk Building, telephone 685. His residence was 701 North 17th, telephone 2188. In November of 1916, the Lemp estate sold $97,000 worth of cattle to Portland buyers.ᵒ Four hundred eighty head were shipped from Nampa in the first lot and a similar number sent out a week later. This was an enormous dollar amount at that time in history. On the last day of November Herbert purchased the nine year-old home of Mrs. Georgia Pierce at First and Idaho streets for $12,000. It occupied 70 feet of ground and was "modern in every respect."ᵖ At this time Herbert had business advertisements in the Statesman for five-year farm loans available at his office at 37 Falk Building, in Boise.ᑫ

On November 9 of 1917 a patent was filed on 160 acres of Boise County land by Albert C. Lemp, Herbert F. Lemp, and John F. Lemp (Herbert's son) under the cash entry law of 1820.ʳ Lemp tradition of land ownership continued.

In James H. Hawley's 1920 multi-volume history of Idaho a biographical sketch of Herbert points out that he was born and educated in Boise and expressed an interest in ranching and livestock raising. ˢ At that time he was a director of the Pacific National Bank of Boise, the Idaho Life Insurance Company, and the Boise Stone Company. His company, the Idaho Packing and Provision Company, and as general manager of the H. F. Lemp Livestock Company, had as many as 6,000 "feeders" in his yards in a single season. Much of the development of the livestock industry in Idaho and adjacent states was attributed to Herbert's influence.

In December of 1920, Herbert was named the Republican County chairman for Ada County, District 2 of Idaho.ᵗ He had the same political affiliation as his father had. That same month Herbert presented a petition to the Boise city council, signed by nineteen businessmen, opposing any move from horse-drawn street equipment to motorized.ᵘ

Herbert continued with the Boise polo team in the years to come. The original members, Lemp, Harry Falk, Ed Ostner, and Charles Barringer, —"Four Horsemen"—played together from 1910 to 1927.[v] When Herbert was elected mayor of the Capital in 1927, he called Beverly Hills Mayor, famous movie star and social critic, Will Rogers to arrange a tournament in Boise. The competition with Rogers' team was canceled after Herbert was injured. A newspaper article in 2001 gave a history of the team based on the clippings, trophies and photos collected by John Barringer, son of Charles, the original member of the team. The cavalry had brought the sport to Boise in 1909 and the town team began the next year. The team lasted until 1954 when Peter Hirschburg and Charles Barringer were the only members of the original—or almost original—team left.

Herbert, chairman of the Ada County Commissioners, had to be absent while at the funeral of his sister Augusta Grant in May of 1926.[w] The Boise polo team was getting ready to play the team from Fort D. A. Russell that had won the nickname of the "Yellow Typhoon." His team eagerly awaited Herbert's return.

In early May of 1927 Herbert Lemp resigned his position as Ada County Commissioner.[x] He had been elected Mayor of Boise. He soon named most of his appointments and was ready to take the oath of office. The same issue of the *Capital News* had a photo of Lemp in the sports section showing him and Ed Ostner at a polo scrimmage under the caption, "Lemp About to Swat the Pill." The polo schedule for the next two months was published there also. The *Capital News* had a third article and second photo of Lemp in the same issue when they discussed "Newly Elected Mayor and Council of Boise City," and "Boise Starts Its New Fiscal Year Under Complete Change in System of City Government."[y] The old Black Law clothed all five commissioners with equal authority and nothing was ever accomplished. Some members of the old council claimed the new election was illegal but the Idaho State Supreme Court in a unanimous decision upheld the validity of the proceedings. Lemp, with no city level experience, defeated incumbent Ern G. Eagleson by a "tremendous majority."

Herb Lemp seemed to be stepping into the starting blocks for a long successful political career. His karma was elsewhere. On Sunday the first of May the polo team which had played together for so many

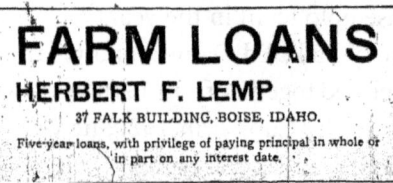

Newspaper Ad for the loans Lemp offered.

seasons held a practice at the Boise barracks.[z] The "Regulars" faced "Harry Falk's "Pirates." During the fourth chukker Lemp and "Lucky Johnson" who usually played on the Green cavalry team were riding the ball toward the goal. Lemp's horse "Craven" stumbled, or tripped and fell, and Lemp was thrown on his head. Despite his heavy helmet he was carried from the field with blood flowing from his right ear. Teammates called an ambulance and together with Dr. Magruder he went to St. Luke's hospital.

He was conscious and resting and friends believed his helmet had prevented serious injury. He was even expected at the inauguration the next day. The first morning in the hospital he greeted his attendants with a cheerful "good morning" and said he felt "just fine." The four new city councilmen took their oath in unison, appointed Clarence T. Ward as the new city attorney, and sought to send him to Lemp's bedside to administer Lemp's mayoral oath to him. The out-going mayor raised an objection that there was no formal appointment of the attorney by the new mayor. The council decided to wait until it heard from Lemp. At 5:15 p.m. Mrs. Angela Hopper, city clerk, journeyed to Lemp's bedside and, with the attending physician and Mrs. Lemp as the only witnesses, administered the oath of office.

At a special meeting of the out-going council on Monday morning they passed the following resolution framed by Councilman Edward Smith: "Resolved, that it is with unfeigned regret that this council has learned of the unfortunate accident sustained by our newly-elected mayor and fellow citizen, Herbert F. Lemp, on the eve of his inauguration to the honors and office to which he was elected. Herb is equally as dear to his friends—the retiring council—as those of the new council, and all citizens who admire good class sportsmanship and gentlemanly qualities; therefore this council in regular session assembled desire to extend to the mayor-elect and his family, our sincere wishes for his early and complete recovery, together with the enjoyment of a successful reign as mayor of Boise city."[aa]

The news from the hospital on Tuesday was that Lemp was resting well and showing every sign of early recovery. The Doctor, William F. Smith, decided not to X-ray his head since what he needed most was rest and quiet. The physician told the *Capital News* that he therefore could not say for certain if a fracture of the skull was present.[ab] The family said he was much improved, resting comfortably and sleeping naturally. "Mr. Lemp himself, said members of his family, had expressed a wish that his friends and the public generally be assured that there was no cause for alarm in his condition."[ac]

Herbert Lemp on his favorite polo pony, Scrambled Eggs, on the steps of the Idaho State Capitol building.

The morning of Wednesday the fourth of May the *Statesman* announced that Lemp had been taken home form the hospital, and no physician was now attending him.[ad] The family wanted him to receive family care in familiar surroundings and he was happy to be home at 105 East Idaho street. Dr. Smith was more cautious. He said the mayor was "little changed" and "was not making rapid progress." By that afternoon when the *Capital News* was issued, little had changed.[ae] Bernard Lemp said his brother's condition seemed about the same but he had not spoken with him since he was brought home.

Will Rogers, of Hollywood, issued this note of concern which was published in Boise on Thursday morning the 5th of May.[af] "Just heard the sad news of the accident to Herb Lemp and I know that I join with everybody in that country in their good wishes for his recovery. I had only met him and was with him one day, but that's all you needed with him to find out what he was. I feel like I had a life-long friend that was ill. Good luck to everybody there and save that man. We can't afford to lose any like him." They had previously met when they competed against each other in polo.

Thursday morning more details of the situation began to emerge. What was not explained seemed to supplement what was said. The "Lemp residence" denied he had failed to show improvement and said he was "resting peacefully and holding his own."[ag] Relatives, however, reported that when they saw him for brief periods, he was asleep. Since he left the hospital J. H. Richardson, Christian Science practitioner, had been put in charge of the case. He reported, "I was with Mr. Lemp practically all the afternoon Wednesday and I found him resting quietly and breathing easily. He seemed to be quiet restful, and I consider that he is improving." He added that Lemp was not conscious all of the time.

By Thursday evening's newspaper Mrs. Lemp said her husband "shows slight improvement and is resting comfortably. He has a good clear color and we are sure that he is improving."[ah] The *Capital News* reporter commented on the fragrance from the many flowers sent to the house in tribute to his popularity.

Within hours the battle between religion and science turned again. The immediate family began to worry, and about 9:30 that evening Lemp was returned to St. Luke's where Dr. James L. Stewart, assisted by Dr. L. R. Quilliam of the United States Veteran's Hospital and Dr. Calvin Cowles, performed an operation on Lemp's skull.[ai] A basal skull fracture was at last diagnosed. The de-compression operation removed a portion of bone from the fractured area and revealed a moderate sized blood clot. After the operation the surgeon reported Lemp's breathing seemed better and his pulse good but it was too early to make predictions. "His splendid vitality is in his favor."

In city business, Walter F. Hansen, president of the council, was acting mayor in Lemp's absence. He was reluctant to do much under the circumstances and left old department heads temporarily in their positions.

By the time the Friday afternoon newspapers hit the stand, Herbert Frederick Lemp was dead.[aj] He had seemed to rally after the surgery but slipped into a coma and died at 7 o'clock Friday morning, the 6th of May. The first Boise Mayor to die in office had barely served. On the front page of the *Capital News* were photos of Lemp on his polo mount "Scrambled Eggs," and a regular portrait shot.

Lemp's biographical sketch in the *Statesman* mentioned his parents, his attending Hoffman's Business College in Boise, and his entering business with his father.[ak] All the events and diversions in Boise were canceled or postponed. Herbert's sister Louise Simonson of Alhambra, California was unable to attend the funeral. His daughter Catherine was at the University of Washington and was heading to Boise. Herbert was a member of the Boise lodge No. 2 of the A. F. & A. M. (Masons), the Elks, the Scottish Rite Masons, Rotary, board of directors of the First Church of Christ, Scientist, Boise Chamber of Commerce, Ada County Grange, Volunteer Fireman, past president of the Sons of Idaho, Country Club, during World War I had been a member of the United States Food Commission. "It was perhaps as president of the Boise welfare board, representing the county commissioners, that Mr. Lemp found work, nearest his heart in the civic world. Stories of distress received his first consideration and at such times other business being put aside."

The city council issued this statement "To the People of Boise:

'The death of Mayor Herbert F. Lemp, so unexpected, is a public catastrophe which the members of your city council feel most keenly. It comes to those of us who were but recently elected to the council, as a genuine shock, almost unbelievable, it is so sudden. There has been taken from the people of Boise by Divine Will the man whom they so graciously elected by an unprecedented vote to be their chief executive, their mayor, their official head of civic government, their leader.

'Coming at a time in the inauguration of a new city administration and of a new era for Boise, the calling of Mayor Lemp, virtually leaves your council, for the time being, passing through a period of necessary reorganization and reconstruction.

'Words at this time fail to express our deep sorrow over the death of our beloved and honored mayor. He was a man among men. Able, genial, energetic, always a friend ready to champion a righteous cause, Mayor Lemp won and held the highest respect of us all. Few men had more admirers or friends held more closely than Mr. Lemp. We feel his administration as mayor, had he been permitted to live, would have ranked as one of, if not the best, in the history of this city.

'His death is a distinct loss to Boise, to the people of Boise and to this council, collectively and individually. We will all miss him more than we can say.

'To those near and dear to him we take this opportunity to express our deep sorrow in this their hour of bereavement and to officially extend to them the good offices of the city of Boise of which their husband, father, and son was the official head."[al]

The Ada county commissioners passed this resolution.

"Whereas this board has heard with profound regret of the death this morning of Herbert F. Lemp, who was a member of this board for a period of over four years, and up to April 30 last, at which time he resigned to become mayor of Boise city. During the years . . . faithful served this board as its chairman.

'Our feeling of regret at his death in the prime of his splendid manhood is entirely beyond our powers of expression. We feel that it is a privilege indeed to have had the close acquaintance and association with him that we have so long enjoyed, and that his passing is a grievous loss, not only to his friends, but to the community at large.

'During the time of our association with him, we have found him loyal, conscientious and ever faithful to his trust. He worked with characteristic energy, on any problem presented to him, be it great or small, and strove always for its fair and just disposition, regardless or consequences or criticism.

'Therefore, Be it Resolved, that as a token of our respect and esteem for our late member, Herbert F. Lemp, this board do now recess till 10 o'clock a,m,, May 9, 1927, and be it

'Further Resolved that this resolution be spread upon the minutes of this board and that a copy hereof be sent to the bereaved family of the deceased."

Idaho Governor H. C. Baldridge issued the following statement:

"So unexpected and such a shock is the death of Mayor Herbert Lemp, it is difficult to realize he is gone from our midst, or to collect one's thoughts so soon after his passing to give adequate expression to the tribute his life well deserves.

'The citizens of Boise fully realize their loss. This morning the city is bowed in grief and his name is on every lip. A native son of Boise, amiable and kindly in disposition, interested in charitable, civic and social affairs, he has year by year added numbers to the list of admirers, until all who knew him well were happy to claim him as a friend. Not only the city of Boise losses its young and well-loved mayor, but the state of Idaho as a whole shall miss him.

'In his passing a personal friend has gone, which I regret very keenly. A man among men, the type of man the city of Boise and the state can ill afford to lose. We can but accept this bereavement in the plan of an All-wise Providence and in resignation to Divine Will."

There were briefer statements from at least six other civic leaders. Herb's father was mentioned, and his surviving two brothers and three sisters were listed. Herb had been active in organizing the Sons of Idaho in 1925 and had served as its first president. He was largely responsible for Idaho buying a tract of land at Grimes pass and erecting

Newspaper mentions of Herbert's accident.

a monument for the man who discovered gold in Boise basin. The responsibility for administration of his father's estate had been his chief activity. In particularly, he managed the business buildings in the 800 block of Main street. The Lemp Triangle had been sold to the Boise Independent School District just one year before. That long standing problem had at last been solved.

Lemp's first political experience was on the staff of Governor Haines but finally he was induced to run for county commissioner.

Some of the great outpouring of support for Lemp came from the pride Boise felt over his polo success. Boise had been a national polo center for fifteen years, Army officers at the barracks in 1911 coached Lemp and others to greatness. Lemp also raised and trained famous polo ponies. He sold "Big Jim" to one of the noted Waterbury brothers and the pony took part in many matches in the East and in England. "Scrambled Eggs" was a veteran of many tournaments and was voted the best polo horse in the section.

On the 7th the funeral plans were published.[am] He was to be buried from the family home at 105 East Idaho Street at 3:00 P.M. on Sunday. Will Rogers asked Boise friends to send flowers on his behalf and he wired: "I know what this must mean to that town, If I were in the West anywhere, I would come over by plane. Sympathy to the family, town, county and state."

Eleven Chinese business people of Boise sent flowers and condolence on traditional red paper.

The active pallbearers were 20 year-old John Lemp, the mayor's son, John Heinen, Ed Ostner, Andrew Little, Laurel Elam and Steen Fletcher.[an] Honorary pallbearers were J. H. Richards, Tom McMillan, F. F. Johnson, Lester W. Ellis, J. P. Congdon and R. D. Leonardson. The service was Christian Science, presided over by Arthur C. Williams. A largest throng to ever attend a funeral in Boise filled the area. Ten car loads of flowers preceded the cortege.[ao] "Scrambled Eggs" with Herb's boots and stirrups hanging from wreaths of carnations, and "Midget" another of his polo ponies followed the hearse. He was buried in the Elks portion of Morris Hill Cemetery.

Politicians after the funeral advertised that voting for the bonds for a new Ada County Court House would be a tribute to Herb Lemp. Supporters proposed a memorial tablet be put in the new building.

The voters rejected the bond issue.

A few days later a poem, "We Mourn for Mayor Lemp" by Alzena Grossman was published in the *Capital News*.[ap] The same issue contained some of the tributes that continued to pour into the newspaper.

Herbert's will, dated 2 October 1912, was entered into probate 25 May 1927.[aq] Herbert left half of community property to his wife and 1/4 to each child. His separate property, inherited from his father was divided 1/3 to each, of his three survivors.

On the official list of Boise City Mayors. Herbert F. Lemp was listed as elected 1927 and died 1927.[ar] His father is listed as mayor from 1875 to 1876. As late as 1954, the Sons and Daughter of Idaho Pioneers remembered Herbert Lemp as their first president.[as]

DAUGHTER-IN-LAW MARGUERITE ANN NOLAN (MRS. HERBERT) LEMP

Mrs. Herbert Lemp lived until 1967, forty years after the loss of her husband. Marguerite Ann Nolan Lemp died 8 July 1967 at a Boise nursing home.[at] She was remembered for starting the home economics class in Boise under the auspices of the Columbian Club. She was survived by her son and daughter, a sister Mary Ellen Nolan of Hollywood, California, three grandchildren and four great grandchildren.

GRANDDAUGHTER MARY CATHERINE LEMP
(DAUGHTER OF HERBERT FREDERICK LEMP)

Mary Lemp died on Monday August 4, 1969 in a Boise hospital.[au] She graduated from Boise High School in 1925, attended Princespia Junior College in St. Louis and then graduated from the University of Washington in 1930. She taught in Idaho and Montana for 15 years. The She was a business secretary for the Mine Workers of America in Washington, D.C. Returning to Boise she was a secretary for the American Federation of Labor from 1956 to 1958. She was also a secretary for the Lemp Development Company. Her grandfather and father were mentioned in her obituary. She was a member of the First Church of Religious Science and was survived by her brother, Col. John Lemp of Washington, D.C.

John Frederick Lemp (Son of Emil)

This John Lemp descendant and namesake was a chemist on the Manhattan Project of World War II which produced the first atomic bomb.[av] His son, John Frederick Lemp, Jr. born in 1928, was listed in many biographical dictionaries of science.

Louise Bernice Lemp Simonson

On 6 October 1912, less than three months after the death of his grandfather, Marshall Lemp Simonson was born to Louise Bernice Lemp Simonson and husband. In 1928 she lived in San Gabriel, California. Louise died 3 November 1966 at Seal Beach, California. Marshall died on 16 June 1988 in Los Angeles.

Martha Elizabeth Lemp Conner

John Lemp's son-in-law William Brower Conner had a biographical sketch published in 1920.[aw] He was born and educated in Berks County, Pennsylvania, and at the age of twenty went west to Chicago where he worked for Marshall Field & Company for seven years. He then moved to Boise. After the court troubles involving his father-in-law that have been covered, he started "The Toggery," a clothing store. By 1920 he and Martha Elizabeth had a 400 acre ranch nine miles west of Boise which had 200 acres planted in wheat. They were also raising alfalfa and hogs and doing very well.

John Lemp's daughter Martha Elizabeth died in Boise at age 58 on Sunday 23 September 1928.[ax] She had been ill for 10 or 11 months. She had no children but her husband, brothers Albert and Bernard, and sisters Mrs. Edwin G. Hurt of Boise and Mrs. Louise Simonson of San Gabriel, California, survived her. Her father, John Lemp was mentioned and her brother, Herbert who had died a year before was also mentioned. The funeral was at the family home at 205 State Street, on Tuesday 25 September. Reverend Walter Ashton officiated. She was Episcopal and was buried at Pioneer Cemetery.[ay]

Her will, dated 2 December 1920 was entered for probate on 7 November 1928.[az] She left everything to her "dear husband William B. Conner" and named him executor.

ALBERT C. LEMP

In 1915, Albert was listed as still a resident of the 507 Grove Street Lemp home.[ba] On the 1930 U. S. Census Albert was living in Payette, Idaho with his wife Lillian. Albert died at age 60 on 28 March 1937. [bb] He died at the Lynn Dobson ranch near Horseshoe Bend, Idaho, where he had been living for about six months. He was remembered as a son of John and Kate Lemp and a brother of former Mayor Herbert Lemp. He had attended Boise public schools and a military academy in St. Louis. He had been in business with his father and later was in the ranching business. His daughter Kathryn (Katherine?) was living in Shanghai, China. Funeral arrangements awaited the return of brother Bernard who was in Portland on business.

His ex-wife, Lucille L. Weaver Lemp, was not mentioned. There was a marriage license listed for Albert and Ethel Velma States in 1907. Either this is an error, or they got the license and then gave in to second thoughts. She married Earl Glenn in Weiser in late June of 1907.[bc]

BERNARD LOUIS LEMP

Bernard was the second youngest of the Thirteen Lemp children, and was educated in Boise where he made a study of bookkeeeping.[bd] Bernard married Leona Tucker and they had four children, Bernard Louis, Jr. born in 1910, George Tucker Lemp, born in 1915, and twins, Leona Marie and Edna who were born on 20 March 1920. In the 1915 Boise Directory,

Bernard was listed as a livestock man who lived at 1103 North 11th Street and had an office in the Falk building at number 37 where his brother Herbert conducted business.[be] In 1915 Bernard sued the Idaho Farms Company before Judge Davis in the District Court over the right to the waters of Dry Creek which both parties claimed.[bf]

In 1920 Bernard had large interests in farming and ranching in Ada and Canyon Counties and running cattle on forest reserve lands. He raised many thousands of head annually for the Omaha and Kansas City Markets.

In 1932, Mrs. Lemp suffered a ruptured appendix and under went surgery.[bg] Peritonitis set in and she was operated on again. A call went out for volunteers to give her a blood transfusion but of the thirty that showed up not one had the "proper blood count," and the Doctors gave up. This was before blood transfusions had become routine. Her son Bernard Jr. returned home from Moscow and the University of Idaho. She developed influenza and the Boise society matron died in the hospital.[bh] She was a native of Placerville in Boise Basin and an active member of St. Michael's Episcopal Church. She was survived by her husband and four children, two brothers Edward and William Tucker, and a sister, Mrs. T. N. Shackleford.

The funeral was at St. Michael's Cathedral with the Very Reverend Frank Rhea officiating.[bi] Several groups and individuals sang. The pall bearers were Byron E. Hyatt, John McDevitt, Harry Bigham, A. A. Walker, James Fennell and Henry Ashcroft.

Bernard was an Elk, a member of the Boise Country Club, the Boise Commercial Club and was a member of the Episcopal Church.

Leona Marie Lemp

John's granddaughter and Bernard's daughter, Leona Marie Lemp, died in Arco, Idaho in 1976 of natural causes.[bj] Brothers Bernard and George were her only survivors. She had lived in Darlington since 1964 and had worked in several Boise grocery stores in her earlier years.

Ada Anna Lemp Hurt

Ada Lemp married Edwin Garland Hurt on 11 October 1896, her 21st birthday.

Edwin had a biographical sketch published in 1920.[bk] He was born in Barry, Pike County, Illinois, 12 June 1866 and came to Boise while an employee of the Oregon Short Line Railroad. Soon he was a manager for the Western Union Telegraph Company. He then invested in ranching and changed professions. He owned a retail store in Caldwell for years and later was manager of the Capitol Hotel block in the John Lemp estate.

Hurt killed himself in 1928.[bl] Despondent over financial troubles, the prominent Idaho "pioneer" opened a gas jet in his upstairs bathroom at 1805 Harrison boulevard. Ada Hurt found him crumpled on the floor with a loaded revolver on a nearby chair. She called Dr. S. W. Forney but Hurt had been dead for two hours when the doctor arrived. His lengthy note, addressed to "Darling," in part it said: " .

Edna and Marie Lemp, daughters of Bernard and Leona Tucker Lemp. They were born 20 March 1920.

. you would understand the circumstances. It may seem strange to end it all this way. But I have lost my health and my strength, our money, our credit and nearly all our friends." . . . "Please have my body cremated as soon as possible and without any services whatsoever. Ed. The bank turned me down."

Hurt's will, signed 7 May 1920 made wife Ada the executrix and her brother Bernard Lemp was named as the alternate.[bm] His body was taken to the Summers and Krebs chapel. A short service was held and the body was taken to Portland for cremation.[bn] The will was entered into probate on the 26th of March 1928.

COLONEL JOHN LEMP

Herbert's son, John Lemp, graduated from Princeton with a B.S. degree in 1930. He was commissioned a second lieutenant in the U. S. Army that year.

"Fortune Favors the Brave," and "Morning Report" are chronological histories of the 644th Tank Destroyer Battalion on Internet sites. Their story begins on 2 July 1941 when 69th Field Artillery Brigade,

44th Infantry Divison was reformed into the 44th Anti-Tank Battalion (Provisional) under the command of Lt. Colonel John Lemp. They trained near Fredericksburg, Virginia first, then in the Carolinas. In December they were redesignated the 644th Tank Destroyer Battalion. Soon they were in Camp Claiborne, Louisiana. In February they went by rail to Fort Lewis, Washington. The highlight of July 1942 was the presentation of the National colors to the Battalion by its Battalion Commander, Lt. Colonel John Lemp, and Reviewing Officer at retreat formation on July 16, 1942.[bo] In August of 1942 Lt. Colonel John Lemp was relieved of command of this battalion and ordered to duty with the Tank Destroyer Command, Camp Hood, Texas. Lemp relinquished command on August 19 and Major Ephraim F. Graham replaced him.[bp] The unit went on to train more in Texas and eventually performed excellently in Germany and France.

After the War, Colonel John Lemp was awarded the Bronze Star for bravery.[bq] In a photo story in the Boise newspaper: [Photo caption] "Col. John Lemp, above, field artillery officer of Boise, who is now a member of the ground plans and training section, Army ground force headquarters, Washington, is shown here as he receives the bronze star medal for heroism against the enemy on Saipan in June 1944. Pinning the medal on him is Maj. Gen. James G. Christiansen, Army ground forces chief of staff. Col. Lemp recently promoted from lieutenant colonel, is the son of Mrs. Herbert Lemp, language teacher in the Boise school system. A graduate of Princeton University, he was executive secretary to the state commissioner of charitable institutions in New Jersey at the outbreak of hostilities. His wife and two sons residing in Trenton, N. J. The colonel was reared here, however, and he is one of the pioneer families of Boise. His father, the late Herbert Lemp, was killed in a polo accident in 1927, shortly after being elected mayor of the city. Col. Lemp is in the plans and training section, AGF.

With representatives from nearly all of the AGF headquarters staff sections present, the medal was awarded for meritorious service in connection with military operations against the enemy at Saipan, Marianas island, during the period of June 17-24, 1944.

Grave marker for Mary Catherine Lemp

As War department observer attached to an infantry division, Col. Lemp "was of invaluable assistance to the commanding general and assistant chief of staff, G-3, during the early phases of the operation," states the citation.

"He gave unstintingly of his time and energy, and without regard to personal safety, voluntarily put himself in positions of danger in order to report accurate front-line observations to the commanding general" concludes the citation.

"Attending the ceremony in addition to Gen. Christiansen, were Maj. Gen. Frederick A. Blesse, chief of ground medical section; Brig. Gen. Robert W. Crichlow, ground requirements section; Brig. Gen. Loyal M. Haynes, assistant chief of staff, ground G-4; Brig. Gen. Bethel W. Simpson, chief of ground ordinance' Brig Gen. R. O. Starr, ground anti-aircraft liaison officer; Col. Leo G. Clarke, ground G-1 section; Col. Syril E. Faine, ground G-3 section; Col. William L. Mitchell, deputy chief of staff; Col. Paul K. Porch, ground G-3 section; Col. Gordon B. Rogers, ground G-2 section; and Lt. Col. Donald G. McLennan, secretary, general staff."

Grandson of John Lemp, son of Herbert Frederick Lemp, namesake of Idaho's Beer King, John Lemp, noted World War II military officer, died in Washington, D.C. in October of 1974.[br] He donated a major collection of family photos to the Idaho Historical Society. Many of those are in this book.

LEMP BREWERY OF ST. LOUIS

In 1922, the Lemp family of St. Louis decided to get out of the brewing business. They sold their giant brewery complex to the International Shoe Company. When the shoe company folded, the brewery sat idle for many years. After 2000 a group hoped to remodel the building. One part was to be devoted to a brewing museum allied with the Brewery Collectibles Club of America. If this ever comes about, it will be a perfect tribute to all the Lemp brewers of American history.

END NOTES

a   O'Connor, *The German-Americans*, pp. 275-276.
b   World War I Draft Registrations, Internet, RootsWeb.Com.
c   *Idaho Daily Statesman*, 7 September 1912, p. 4, c. 7. *Evening Capital News*. 6 September 1912, p. 2 c. 2. 8 September 1912, p. 2, c. 4.
d   The *Statesman* said he was buried in the Masonic cemetery.
e   *Evening Capital News*, 10 May 1926, p. 7, c. 7. 11 May 1926, p. 3, c. 5. *Idaho Statesman*, 11 May 1926, p. 3, c. 1.
f   Photocopy. Probate Court, Ada county, Idaho
g   Hiram T. French, History of Idaho, 1914, "Herbert Frederick Lemp," p. 597. See also the Idaho State Historical Society Manuscript file 178.
h   Hawley, History of Idaho, the Gem of the Mountains, 1920, vol. 3, pp. 560-561.
i   Soda Springs Sun, Soda Springs, Idaho, 22 July 1915, p. 5, c. 3.
j   Idaho State Historical Society, Manuscript File 178.
k   Ada County Judicial Records, Idaho State Historical Society, Microfilm reel 34, Book K, original page 382.
l   Wright and Reitzes, *Tourtellotte & Hummel*, p. 95.
m   *The Idaho Review*, Boise, 16 April 1915, p. 7, c. 2.
n   Boise City and Ada County Directory, Volume X, 1915, R. L. Polk & Co.,
o   *Soda Springs Chieftain*, Soda Springs, Idaho, 30 November 1916, p. 3, c. 3.
p   *Idaho Daily Statesman*, 3 December 1916, p. 5, c. 3.
q   *Idaho Daily Statesman*, 27 November 1916, p. 6, c. 3-4.
r   Bureau of Land Management, Land Patent Records. Accession/Serial # 607048. BLM Serial # IDB 0017687. Description was Aliquot Parts WSW Section 1, Township 5-N, Range 2-E. Aliquot Parts SESW Section 1, 5-N, 2-E, and Aliquot Parts NWSE, Section 1, Township 5-N, Range 2-E.
s   James H. Hawley, *History of Idaho, The Gem of the Mountains*, vol. 2, p. 9.
t   *Soda Springs Chieftain*, 30 December 1920, p. 4, c. 2.
u   *Idaho Daily Statesman*, 29 December 1920, p. 3, c. 3.
v   Mike Butts, *Idaho Daily Statesman*, "Boise's Polo Club," Internet site. November 2001.
w   *Evening Capital News*, 11 May 1926, p. 3, c. 4.
x   *Evening Capital News*, 1 May 1927, p. 12, c. 2.
y   *Boise Capital News*, Anniversary Edition, 1 May 1927, p. 7, c. 2-3.
z   *Boise Capital News*, 2 May 1927, p. 1, c. 7. Idaho Daily Statesman, 2 May 1927, p. 1, c. 7 & 8.
aa *Boise Capital News*, 2 May 1927, p. 10, c. 3. Idaho Daily Statesman, 3 May 1927, p. 2, c. 2.
ab *Boise Capital News*, 3 May 1927, p. 1, c. 4.
ac *Idaho Daily Statesman*, p. 1, c. 8.
ad *Idaho Daily Statesman*, 4 May 1926, p. 1, c. 5.

ae *Boise Capital News*, 4 May 1927, p. 1, c. 4.
af *Idaho Daily Statesman*, 5 May 1927, p. 1, c. 5.
ag *Idaho Daily Statesman*, 5 May 1927, p. 1, c. 5.
ah *Boise Capital News*, 5 May 1927, p. 1, c. 8.
ai *Idaho Daily Statesman*, 6 May 1927, p. 1, c. 8, etc.
aj *Boise Capital News*, 6 May 1927, p. 1 & 2, Columns 2-8.
ak *Idaho Daily Statesman*, 7 May 1927, p. 1, c. 2.
al *Boise Capital News*, 6 May 1927, p. 1, c. 6, p. 3, c. 5.
am *Boise Capital News*, 7 May 1927, p. 1, c. 2.
an *Idaho Daily Statesman*, 8 May 1927, p. 1, c. 6.
ao *Boise Capital News*, 9 May 1927, p. 1, c. 2.
ap *Boise Capital News*, 11 May 1927, p. 4, c. 6.
aq Photocopy of the Will, Probate Court, Ada County, Idaho.
ar "Boise City Mayors." Internet site. www.ci.Boise.id.us/city-clerk/records-%mayors.shtml.
as *Idaho Evening Statesman*, 14 December 1954, p. 8, c. 1 & 2.
at *Idaho Sunday Statesman*, 9 July 1967, p. 2-D, c. 5.
au *Idaho Statesman*, 8 August 1969, p. 2-D, c. 6.
av Phone interview with Karl H. Lemp, January 2002.
aw James H. Hawley, *History of Idaho, The Gem of the Mountains*, vol. 2, p. 957.
ax *Idaho Statesman*, 24 September 1928, p. 2, c. 3. *Boise Capital News*, 24 September 1928, p. 3, c. 5.
ay *Idaho Statesman*, 25 September 1928, p. 4, c. 6.
az Photocopy of the will, Probate Court, Ada county, Idaho.
ba *Boise City and Ada County Directory*, Volume X, 1915, R. L. Polk & Co.
bb *Idaho Statesman*, 30 March 1937, p. 1, c. 5.
bc *Weiser Signal*, 1 July 1926, p. 1, c. 3.
bd James H. Hawley, *History of Idaho, The Gem of the Mountains*, vol. 2, p. 844.
be *Boise City and Ada County Directory*, Volume X, 1915, R. L. Polk & Co.
bf *Idaho Daily Statesman*, 15 April 1915, p. 9, c. 2.
bg *Idaho Daily Statesman*, 2 March 1932, p. 8, c. 3 & 4.
bh *Idaho Daily Statesman*, 2 March 1932, p. 8, c. 3 & 4.
bi *Idaho Daily Statesman*, 5 March 1932, p. 2, c. 3.
bj *Idaho Statesman*, 28 March 1976, p. 3D, c. 4.
bk James H. Hawley, *History of Idaho, The Gem of the Mountains*, vol. 2, p. 857,
bl *Idaho Daily Statesman*, 1 March 1928, p. 1, c. 7. *Boise Capital News*, 1 March 1928, p. 1, c. 2.
bm Photocopy of the will from the Probate Court, Ada county, Idaho.
bn *Idaho Daily Statesman*, 2 March 1928, p. 5, c. 3.

bo Morning Report: Chronological History of the 644th Tank Destroyer Battalion for the Calendar Year 1942. Declassified per executive order 12356, Section 3.3, NND735017. Internet site.www.644tf.com/morning.htm. page 5 of document. Fortune Favors the Brave, internet site. http://www.644td.com/fortunbe.htm.

bp Morning Report: Chronological History of the 644th Tank Destroyer Battalion for the Calendar Year 1942. Declassified per executive order 12356, Section 3.3, NND735017. Internet site.www.644tf.com/morning.htm. page 6 of document.

bq Article from Scrap book of Lemp family. No provenance. Boise, Idaho, Friday, after June of 1944.

br *Social Security Death Index.*

Appendices
Appendix I
John Lemp's Will

Know all men that I, John Lemp of Boise City in the state of Idaho, being of sound and disposing mind and memory and not acting under duress, menace, fraud or any undue influence of any person whomsoever, do make, publish and declare this my last will and testament, in manner and form following to wit:

First—I give and bequeath unto my sons, Herbert and Bernard Lemp, share and share alike, all my horses, cattle and other livestock.

Second—It is my will and I do order, that all my just debts and funeral expenses and expenses of my last sickness be duly paid as soon as conveniently can be done after my decease.

Third—I give, bequeath and devise all the rest, residue and remainder of my estate, or whatsoever kind or nature, and wherever situated, to my children and grandchildren hereinafter named, each receiving one-ninth thereof, and subject to the conditions named in this will, to wit:

To my daughter, Elizabeth Connor, one-ninth.
To my daughter, Ada Hurt, one-ninth.
To my son Edward Lemp, one-ninth.
To my son Herbert Lemp, one-ninth.
To my son Bernard Lemp, one-ninth.

To my daughter Louise Simonson, one-ninth.
To my daughter Augusta Grant, one-ninth.
To my grandson, John F. Lemp, of Alton, Ill., one-ninth.
To my son, Albert Lemp, one-ninth.

Fourth—Said John F. Lemp is the son of my deceased son, Emil Lemp, and I direct that my executor shall hold and retain in trust the interest of said John F. Lemp until he shall have reached 21 years of age, paying the income from said interest to his lawful guardian until said time, said income being payable annually on the first day of January of each and every year.

Fifth—I direct that my just debts, funeral expenses, expenses of my last sickness and the expenses of thee administration of my estate shall be paid out of the proceeds of my personal property, as soon as the same can be conveniently be disposed of after my decease, save and except such personal property as I give and bequeath to my sons Herbert Lemp and Bernard Lemp; provided, however, that in the event the proceeds of the sale of said personal property shall not be sufficient thereof, I direct that sufficient of my real estate be sold to satisfy the same, such real estate so sold to be selected by and at the discretion of my executor, hereinafter named.

Sixth—I direct that all my real estate of whatsoever kind or nature and wherever situated, save and except such as may be selected and sold to pay my debts, as herein provided for, shall be held in trust by my executor for a period not exceeding five (5) years from the date of my death, with power, and in his discretion to sell the same at any time prior thereto, if in his judgment the same may be deemed expedient and for the best interest of my estate, and I do hereby authorize and empower my executor to sell and convey, for such prices as he may deem proper, all or any part of my lands and tenements aforesaid, in order to carry out the purposes of this will.

Seventh—In the event my executor in his discretion, shall decide to hold in trust and intact my real estate, or any portion thereof, for said term of five years or by a shorter time, as in his judgment may seem wise, and not sell and dispose of the same, he shall, during said time, annually on the first day of January, each and every year pay to the beneficiaries his or her net income thereof, after deducting the necessary expenses of administration, taxes, making improvements and other expenses which in the discretion of my executor are necessary and advisable.

Eighth—I authorize and empower my executor, hereinafter named, to sell and dispose of all or any of the real estate of which I shall die seized or possessed, subject to the terms and conditions of the will, at public or private sale and without an order of court, at such times and on such terms and conditions as he shall deem meet or proper, and to execute, acknowledge and deliver all proper writings, deeds of conveyance and transfers therefor (sic).

Ninth—My son, Herbert Lemp, having had especial charge of the management and conduct of my business and reposing special confidence in him, I do hereby nominate, constitute and appoint him, my said son, Herbert Lemp, to be executor of this my last will and testament, and I direct that he be not required to give bonds, either as executor or as trustee.

Tenth—In the event of the death, refusal or inability to act of my said son Herbert Lemp, as executor and trustee as aforesaid, I hereby nominate and appoint, as his successor and in his place ad stead, my son Bernard Lemp, giving him the same power and authority in such an event as I hereby repose in my son Herbert Lemp.

Eleventh—I hereby revoke all former or other wills and testamentary dispositions by me made at any time heretofore made.

Twelfth—Should any of the beneficiaries under this my will, object to the probate thereof or in any wise, directly or indirectly, contest or aid in the contesting of the same or any of the provisions thereof, or the distribution of my estate thereunder, then, in that event, I annul any bequest made herein to such beneficiary, and it is my will that such beneficiary shall be absolutely barred and cut off from any share in my estate.

In witness whereof, I have there unto set my hand, this 30th day of December in the year of our Lord one thousand nine hundred and eleven.

John Lemp

The will was filed for probate 3 August 1912.[1]

Appendix II

LEMP'S POSITIONS OF TRUST

A. Lemps Service as a Business Trustee, Director, or Officer, Etc.

1870 Administrator of estate of William Kohlepp, father-in-law
1870 Trustee of corporation for telegraph line to Boise, etc.
1876 Director of First National Bank, Boise
1877 Trustee First National Bank
1877 Trustee of the Idaho Agricultural Park Association.
1878 Trustee First National Bank
1880 St. Michael's School trustee
1881 Investor in fruit drying company
1879 Vice-President First National Bank
1882 Executor of estate of Andrew Coyle
1882 President of First National Bank
1884 Incorporator of the Idaho, Utah and Oregon Railway Co. Inc.
1886 Director Boise Light Company
1890 Director of First National Bank
1890 Treasurer and member of directors of the Boise Central Railway Company
1891 Re-elected Trustee of Boise Rapid Transit Company
1891 Original stockholder in new corporation to promote mining in Idaho
1892 Director of newly formed Artesian Hot and Cold Water Company of Boise
1892 Re-elected board member of the Boise Rapid Transit Company
1893 Re-elected to board of directors of the Boise Central Railway Company.
1893 Executive committee of the Boise Rapid Transit Company.
1894 Re-elected director of the Artesian Hot and Cold Water company.
1894 Director Boise Rapid Transit company.
1895 Re-elected Boise Central Railway Co. director.
1895 Elected director and executive committee member of the Rapid Transit Company.
1896 Director of Boise Central Railway Co.
1897 Director of Boise Central Railway Company.
1897 Executive committee of the Boise Rapid Transit Company.
1900 Lemp pledges $5,000 for the Idaho Midland Securities to bring a railroad branch to Boise from Nampa.
1901 Director and executive committee member of the Boise Rapid Transit Company.
1902 Executive committee of the Boise Rapid Transit Company. (Company sold in December of 1903)

1905 Lemp invests in new electric railroad company.
1905 Lemp co-operative Lateral Company incorporates.
1906 Lemp vice-president of the newly incorporated Boulder Consolidated Mining Company.
1908 Listed as stockholder in new Bank of Idaho.
1909 Listed as third largest stockholder in the Bank of Idaho.

B. Public Committees

1871 Committee to select 4th of July speaker for Boise
1872 Committee to organize 4th of July celebration, Boise
1874 4th of July Superintendent of Grounds
1876 4th of July Committee on fireworks, and committee on music
1877 December. On the committee to get a military road from Fort Boise to Fort Lapwai.
1878 4th of July Committee
1878 Member of Homeguards during Bannock War
1879 Committee for a new school in Boise
1879 July 4th, Stands Committee
1879 October, Judge at Horse Races
1880 Committee to set up a horse racing program
1881 Idaho Agricultural Park Association
1884 Committee to solicit funds for a wagon road to Atlanta, Idaho
1886 4th of July celebration committee
1887 Committee to organize a celebration over the new school
1889 Committee to dedicate Boise's new opera house
1889 Committee to organize July 4th celebration
1891 Committee to complain to the Union Pacific about insufficient number of trains on the new schedule

C. Political Delegate and Committee Member

1872 Republican County Convention delegate
1876 Republican Convention Ada County
1878 Republican Central Committee Secretary
1880 Republican Territorial Convention
1884 Republican Convention Delegate
1886 Republican Territorial convention
1888 Republican Central Committee
1888 Republican convention
1890 Republican club lists Lemp more than anyone as a possible nominee

1890 Republican committee to consider permanent organization and order of business
1890 Lemp loses Republican nomination for state treasurer to Frank Coffin
1891 Lemp get most votes from Republican caucus for city council nomination
1891 Lemp is nominated for city council by the Fusion Party
1892 Attended Ada County Republican Convention
1895 Many Lemp family members attend ball to honor state legislature.
1895 Elected delegate to the local Republican convention.

D. Jury Duty

1870, November, Grand Jury
1873, November, Territorial Grand Jury
1878, March, U.S. Grand Jury
1879, April, Grand Jury
1880, January, Territorial Grand Jury
1887, April, in District Court Jury pool
1893, March, Third District Court Grand Jury
1894, March, Grand Juror

E. Court Cases of Any Type

The People vs. John Lemp, February 1873, Idaho Supreme court denies Lemp's appeal and confirms the decision of the Boise justice court. Found in the Minutes of the Idaho State Supreme Court, pp. 45-46.
Lemp vs. J. B. Oldham, et all. Mortgage foreclosed. 15 November 1877.
Lemp sued Peter Olson of Weiser, July 1880.
Lemp sued Frances Beck, won $45.12, 1880.
Lemp sued E. Moudy, November 1882. Ad Co. Court Records, Judgment Book, roll 31.
United States vs. John Lemp, May 1884. Lemp acquitted.
Lemp sued Fred Schaffer, et al. October 1884
Lemp vs. Joel Jones over horses ownership, 1885 (Supreme Court March 1886)
John Lemp vs. Arabella C. Maxon, Executrix and Sole Devisee off the last will of Hamilton J. G. Maxon and Arabella Maxon. April 1887. Ada County Court Records, Judgment Book, roll 31.
Lemp sued Idaho Gold and Silver Mining Company limited, District court, March 1889. Ada County Court Records, Judgment Book, roll 31.
John Lemp vs. William F. Blair, September 1889. Ada County Court Records, Judgment Books, roll 31.

John Lemp against Henry Riggs, Foreclosure, March 1890, Ada County Court Records, Judgment Books, roll 31.

Lemp sued the Idaho gold and Silver Mines Limited, September 1891. He wins.

John Lemp vs. The Settlers Ditch Company. December 1891. Ada County Court Records, Judgment Books, Roll 31.

John Lemp vs. Settlers Ditch Company, a Corporation, December 1891, Ada County Court Records, Judgment Books, roll 31.

John Lemp vs. W. B. Biggerstaff. March 1892. Ada County Court Records, Judgment Books, roll 31.

Lemp arrested on complaint of Joseph Pence charging "procuring and inciting another to use force and violence in entering upon and detaining the possessions of another." Lemp acquitted. August 1892.

John Lemp vs. Albert Fritsch. November 1892. Ada County Court Records, Judgment Books, roll 31.

1893, March. J. R. Russell sues Lemp for Settler's Ditch damage to his farm.

1893, October, as trustee of Odd Fellows Home in Idaho Falls, Lemp was unable to get there to defend a lawsuit filed against the home by Charles Carson & Co.

John Lemp vs. James H. Butler. December 1893. Ada County Court Records, Judgment Books, roll 31.

Joseph C. Pence vs. John Lemp. March, 1894. Pence sues Lemp for damages from the destruction of his house. Ada County Court Records, Judgment Books, roll 31.

R. L. Sabin vs. John Lemp. March 1894. Ada County Court Records, Judgment Books, roll 31.

1894, November, James Collins charged with stealing 25 of Lemp's hogs.

1895, November, State Supreme Court dismisses the Pence suit.

1896, February, J. S. Bogart sues John Lemp over ownership of a site in Boise.

1896, October, Lemp and David Falk sue to foreclose mortgage on the Star group of mines

1896, September, trial of soldier Grant for stealing Lemp beer.

1896, December, John Lemp vs Isaac Brockbank in 4th District Court

1897, December, Lemp sued J. C. Bane. Case was dismissed.

1897, December, Richards, Gordon et al vs. W. B. Connor and John Lemp

1899, Nov. case heard in 4th District, in Mt. home) (Judge Stockslager issues opinion in April 1900. June 1902 State Supreme Court rules against Lemp.

1898, September, State of Idaho vs. John Lemp, in district court on appeal.

1899, March. Barbara Fritter sued Lemp for damages under contract.

1899, September. John Lemp sued George W. Kohlepp for $1,000 plus interest. January 1901 trial was scheduled in civil court in Boise.

1899, March, John Keane, Lemp bartender, charges with selling to minors.

1900, December Lemp testified again his bartender Walter Logus for theft.

1902, January. William H. Gibbard sued Lemp for back wages in District court. December 1905 State Supreme Court rules.

1902, April. Lemp sued Frances and John Keegan to recover old bill for $203.

1902, June. Boise Irrigation and Canal and Land company sued Settlers Ditch, Bank of Commerce, John Lemp and B. F. Olden.

1904, June. Lucile L. Lemp vs. Albert C. Lemp. Ada County Court Records. Judgment Books, roll 32.

1905, January. John Morris vs. John Lemp. Case heard October 1905. John Morris sued John Lemp for services rendered. Ada County Court Records, Judgment Books, roll 32. (Feb. 1907 State supreme court rules.)

1905, March. Lemp sues S. E. Sparber, cases dismissed.

1905, October. Lemp in police court on two separate charges. Selling beer on Sunday at the brewery. Other about failure to tear down building at 714 Main Street.

1905, October. Gibbard's suit against Lemp reaches State Supreme Court.

1906, August. Len Hart accused Lemp of Stealing a horse on June 25.

1906, June, Lemp's bartender Charles Phelps convicted of selling beer to a minor.

1906, December Lemp accuses butcher Harry Graham of stealing a fat cow.

The Settlers Irrigation District vs. Settlers Canal Company, Ltd. a Corporation; the Bank of Com-merce, a corporation; the Idaho Trust & Savings Bank. Ltd. a corporation; John Lemp, Dave McMullen, and the County of Ada in the State of Idaho. 1907, April, Idaho Trust & Savings Bank and John Lemp sued Settlers Canal Company. (Suit refiled in September) Ada County Court Records, Judgment Books, roll 32.

The Settlers Irrigation District vs. The Settlers Canal Company Limited, and John Lemp. (after October of 1907) Ada County Court Records, Judgment Books, roll 32.

F. Lodge Offices and Activities

1868 Odd Fellows Annual Ball Committee
1870 Odd Fellows Treasurer
1871 President of the Boise Turn Verein
1873, Committee on reception for the ball, Ada County Jockey Club
1876 Original one of nine members of Odd Fellows Encampment No. 1.
1877 "C. P." in Odd Fellows
1877 "Second W" of Odd Fellows
1877 September, 10th Annual Idaho Masonic Convention
1878 Elected "S" in Masonic Lodge
1879 Odd Fellows Treasurer
1882 Treasurer of Odd Fellows
1883 Trustee of the Ancient Order of United Workmen

1883 Treasurer of Odd Fellows
1884 Treasurer of Odd Fellows
1885 Committee of Masons to pick up a member's body at the train station
1885 State Odd Fellows convention
1886 Odd Fellows State convention, re-elected state treasurer
1887 Odd Fellows State convention, re-elected treasurer
1888 Odd Fellows convention
1889 Odd Fellows yearly convention
1890 October, Odd Fellows Grand Ball
1890 October, Odd Fellows Grand Treasurer
1891 October, Odd Fellows Convention in Moscow
1891 Odd Fellows Grand Treasurer
1892 July, attended laying of the corner stone at Odd Fellows home in Idaho Falls
1892 October, Odd Fellows Grand Lodge and Grand encampment. Reelected treasurer by acclamation
1892 Germania Singing Society member
1893 President of the Turn Verein.
1893 Grand Treasurer of the grand lodge of the Odd Fellows.
1893 Trustee of the Odd Fellows Home in Idaho Falls.
1894 Attended Knights Templar grand ceremonies and banquet.
1898 Initial member of the El Korah temple of the Mystic Shrine.
1904 One of five surviving original Turnverein members.
1908-1909 Advisory Committee of the Columbia Club.

G. Political Offices

1874 Nominated for Boise City council by Tax Payer's Party
1875 Mayor of Boise, Idaho by 80 to 60 vote
1876 Defeated for Ada County Treasurer
1878 Elected Boise City Council as Republican
1881 Elected Boise City Council
1883 Elected Boise City Council
1887 Boise City Council and substitute chair
1888 Re-elected to the school board
1889 Nominated for city council by the Republicans
1889 State Constitutional convention
1891 Elected to City Council with most votes, was on Fusion ticket
1893 Treasurer of newly formed State Bimetallic League
1894 Lemp's school board term ended.

H. Community Involvement

1876 February, Treasurer Boise Fire Company
1877 Treasurer Boise Fire Commissioners
1880 August, member Boise Fire Company
1889 April, member of Boise Engine Company no. 1
1891 subscribed $1,000 to fund to bring Mr. McIntyre's woolen mill to Boise
1891 Subscribed $500 for fund to advertise Boise
1895 Attended February meeting of the Historical Society of Idaho Pioneers, first meeting since 1887.
1902, June, Lemp donated $200 to the Thunder Mountain road fund.
1902, June, Lemp clothing stores offered $15 suit as a prize in a bicycle race.
1906, April, Lemp donated $100 for San Francisco earthquake victims.
1906, June. Lemp donated $100 to entertain guests of the National Irrigation Congress in Boise.

I. Charity Work and Donations

1870 Subscription Drive for German Widows and Orphans, Chair of Committee
1871 Helped raise money for victims of the Chicago fire
1877 Donated to fund for public square and statue of Washington in Boise
1890 Donated for stricken settlers on Camas Prairie
1895 Mrs. Lemp helped sponsors New Year's Eve charity ball

J. Religious Affiliations of Lemp Family Members

John Lemp, as a youth, confirmed Lutheran, at time of death (1912) Episcopal funeral

Wife, Catherine, funeral (1908), no religion mentioned

Son, William Adam, at time of death (1881) no religion mentioned in newspapers

Daughter, Martha Elizabeth Lemp Connor, Married Episcopal (1889), at time of death (1928), Episcopal

Son John Emil, at time of death (1895) Episcopal

Daughter, Ada Anna, married by Methodist minister (1895)

Daughter Augusta Julia Margaret, married (1895) performed by Bishop A. J. Glorieux, Roman Catholic

Daughter Marie Anna, funeral (1896) no religion mentioned

Mother, Anna Elizabeth Lemp, funeral (1898), no religion mentioned

Son, George, funeral (1900), reverend Duel, Episcopal

Son, Albert C. married (1901) Episcopal

Daughter, Ida Catherine, married (1901) Episcopal

Daughter, Ida Catherine Lemp Kessburger, funeral (1904) Christian Science.

Evening Capital News said she was a member of the Episcopal Church.
Son, Herbert, married (1906) no religion mentioned
Son Bernard, married 1906, no religion mentioned
Son Edward Henry, funeral (1912) One newspaper credited Bishop Funsten, Episcopal, other said D. H. Jones, Christ Church.
Daughter, Augusta Julia Margaret Lemp Grant, at time of funeral (1926) no religion mentioned Son, Herbert Lemp, at death (1927), First Church of Christ, Scientist
Daughter, Martha Elizabeth Lemp Conner, at Funeral (1928) Episcopal
Daughter-in-law, Marguerite Nolan Lemp, at time of death (1967) no religion mentioned
Granddaughter through Herbert, Mary Catherine Lemp, at time of death (1969), First Church of Religious Science, (funeral conducted by First Presbyterian Church)
Note: Idaho was about 25% Roman Catholic in 1910; 45% Mormon; 10% Methodist and no other denomination had over 5%. See Carlos Schwantes, *The Pacific Northwest*, 1989, p. 129.

K. Mines and Mining Claims Owned by Lemp

1. Star Mine, Hailey. Star Gulch, Hailey 1885. (later called the Vanderbilt).
2. Shaw's Mountain, north of Boise. March 1892 files claim.
3. Grand Prize, bought 1/3 interest for $1,000. April 1886.
4. Crown Point, 1/3 interest, April 1886.
5. Elmira, Banner, Idaho 1886.
6. Sheep Mountain, 1892, near Ketchum.
7. Graham Mine, attachment against in 1889
8. Iron Clad, July 1890. Filed on by John Lemp and Nathan Falk. 18.1 acres.
9. Concordia, July 1890. Filed on by John Lemp and Nathan Falk. 20.661 Acres.
10. Alta-Johnson
11. Lemp and Nathan Falk took possession of the Hancock Lode which was not recorded until 17 March of 1892.[2] A marginal addendum in the deed book shows Kathryn Lemp Langdon to John Lemp on 28 September 1953.
12. Louisa, March 1893, Blaine Co., Idaho.
13. Lemp and Edson Bishop, Edward Brisbin and Nathan Falk filed on 13.361 acres Warms Springs District. Sold to Coats and Wood by Lemp, Falk & Patterson in 1897.
14. Sunrise, March, 1893, Blaine Co., Idaho, Filed by John Lemp, Eldred, Savidge, and Nathan Falk. 15.588 Acres. Appears to be beside the Louisa.
15. Centre, July 1893, Blaine Co., Idaho. Filed on by John Lemp and Nathan Falk. 15.9 Acres.
16. Ohio, 1893, John Lemp, Eldred Savidge and Nathan Falk file. 20.07 acres in Blaine County, Idaho.

17. "Washington", July 1903, Blaine Co, Lemp and Nathan Falk.
18. January 8, 1901, John Lemp filed a land patent on 73.541 acres in Custer County, Idaho, under the authority of the Mineral Patent-Lode Act of 1866.[3]
19. August, 1906, incorporation papers were filed for the Boulder Consolidated Mining Company, Limited. John Lemp was the vice president.[4]

L. Other Brewers Who Were Affiliated with John Lemp

George Kohlepp. Brother-in-law; later owned brewery in Hailey.

Jacob Lemp. Brother; worked at Lemp's South Mountain brewery. Later involved with brewery in Payette.

Charles Sonnleitner, brewer in Hailey, was foreman of the Star mine owned by Lemp in 1893 and again in 1905.

Philip Paul, Atlanta Brewer, moved to Boise to drive a team for Lemp. Died at that job in 1885.

Herman Hildebrandt in 1878 had worked for John Lemp in Boise and was noted for escaping injury when a new beer cellar caved in on him and John Mops. He ran the Leadville Brewery in Hailey in 1881.

Topp Consorting, Boise brewery worker, worked for Lemp.

Joe Miller, former Lemp employee, reported building a brewery at Payette in December 1886.

John Rost brewed for Lemp for many years then bought the Haug brewery in Idaho City from Nichlaus Haug's widow.

M. John Lemp's Minor Real Estate Transactions

(List is not comprehensive.)

April of 1898 lots 8, 9,10 of Block 10 of Lemp's addition from John Lemp and wife to Katherine Heer for $650.[5]

November, 1899. John sold lots 7 and 12 in block 72 of the original Boise Townsite to John W. Cage and Ed Strauss for $4,200.[6]

April 1901, John and Catherine sold two lots in the Lemp addition to Minnie Drake for $300.[7]

September 1901, John and Catherine sold two pieces of property: one, lot 8 of block 4, to Pard M. Bowman for $225; and the other, lot 2 in block 72, to C.C. Anderson for $1,000.[8]

December 1901, John and Catherine sold a piece of property in the Lemp Addition, south of Resseguie Street and east of Harrison Boulevard, to May Ninemire for $400.[9]

January 1902, John Lemp and wife sold several pieces of property; one for $1,600, and for another $3,450.[10]

January of 1902. Alger W. Woods paid $1600 for 1/16 of a section, and C.W. McClurg paid $2,450 for a larger farm site.[11] Carrie F. Bisby paid $1,600 for a

1/16 of a section of Lemp land.[12] R. W. Chilson bought two lots for $550 on Thirteenth Street in the Lemp addition.[13]

June, 1902, Lemp sold lots 5 and 6 of block 72 in the original townsite of Boise to Perry L. Randall for $2,750.[14] He also sold 1/8 of a section of land to James Prow for $3,200.[15] This was 80 acres located two and a half miles north of Meridian, and the sale was made through the agency of Good and Roberts.[16] Mr. Prow, who was from Car Linda, Iowa, intended to move on to the property.

August, 1902. Lemp sold two more lots in his addition to Frank M. Avery for $550.[17]

September 1902, John and Catherine sold lot 7, block 4 of the Lemp addition to Pard M.Bowen for $350.[18]

March 1903, Lemp and wife sold another piece of property in the Lemp addition to William E. McFarland.[19]

August, 1903, John and Catherine sold two lots in their addition to Mr. and Mrs. Charles May for $350, and two lots to Jane E. Wylie for $500.[20]

March, 1904, Lemp sold two lots to Martin R. Fuller for $500, and in mid-June of 1904, Lemp sold 23 lots in his addition to 9 individuals for a total of $4,925.[21]

June, 1904, John and wife sold a city lot in Lemp Addition to Ida M. St. John for $200.[22]

July 1904, Lemp closed a transaction for two lots with C.B. Starling for $350.[23]

September 1904, Lemp sold two lots in his addition to Mrs. Rebecca Hubbard for $350 and 6 lots to E. C. Cook for $1050.[24]

September and October, 1904, Lemp sold two lots to Albert E. Small for $475, two lots to Fred W. Witham for $400, one lot to Ida M. St. John for $300, and three lots to Guy E. Mathews for $700.[25]

In November, 1904, Lemp sold two lots in his addition to William C. Dunbar for $425;[26] three lots went to Menzo E. Johnston and wife for $700.[27]

January, 1905, Lemp sold two lots to James H. Watson for $350,[28] two lots to Gardner G. Adams and Millard H. Adams for $475.[29] The buyers of this particular sale lots was alternately listed as Mr. and Mrs. Millard H. Adams.[30] The same month, the Lemps sold six lots to J. F. Miller for $1,325, and two lots to Maud J. Bassett for $400.[31]

March, 1905, John Lemp sold two lots in his addition for $450 and two more later in the month.[32] He closed the month by selling two more lots to a Grace M. Joy for $500.[33]

April, 1905, W. E. Pierce bought two for $325, E. G. Jeffries, Jr. bought three for $775, H.C. Miller bought two for $700, Lizzie Millerke bought one for $175, and Felix M. Ferrell purchased two lots for $350.[34]

May, 1905, Lemp sold two lots in his addition, to Harry C. Shellworth, for $500.[35]

June, 1905, Frank M. Avery bought two-and-a-half lots in Lemp Addition for $550.[36]

July, 1905, Lemp sold two lots to Robert L. Creek for $400.[37]

August 1905, Mr. and Mrs. Lemp sold two lots in Lemp's addition to Eliza J. Longmaid for $500.[38]

September, 1905, Lemp sold two lots to Leander Mason for $450 in mid-September, and then two to A. Q. Ariz for $700.[39]

October, 1905, Robert O. Bragg bought two lots for $700, Mr. Oakes bought one, and Mr. Looney got one for $350.[40]

December, 1905, Lemp and wife sold a lot and a portion of a second lot in their housing addition to Ernest Varold for $400.[41]

January, 1906, Lemp sold city subdivision lots: two went to Mary E. Graves (Gravestock?) for $500; two to Robert Dewey Jefferson for $450; and two to Bertha C. Moore for $350, and two to Ona Burke for $350, and two to Phoebe Cleworth for $350.[42]

March, 1906, Lemp sold a lot and a part of another lot in the Lemp addition to W. H. Leonard for $800; in April, Lemp sold two lots to Charles E. Marion for $800.[43]

May, 1906, Mildred M. Selby bought two lots for $400.[44]

August, 1906, Lemp sold two lots to Frank C. Smith for $450; two to Harvey Hile for $450; two to Diedrich Dorsten for $525; two to M. L. Phelps for $1100; one to Hardi L. Allen for $200, and to Margaret Kinney, two for $500.[45]

October, 1906, John, via the W. E. Pierce Co., sold lots 14 and 15 in Lemp's addition to E. L. Wendle for $550.[46]

November, 1906, Lemp sold 2 lots to Otto F. Peterson for $1.[47]

November 1906, Lemp sold two lots in his addition to Lillian A. Walker for $400.[48]

January, 1907, Lemp sold lots 14 and 15 of block 13 in Lemp's addition to Ernest L. Wendle for $550.[49]

February, 1907, Lemp sold two lots in his subdivision to E. N. Parish for $700.[50] Lemp later that month issued a warranty deed to Arthur E. Cunningham for lots 7, 8, 9 block 128, Boise for $3000.[51] Others were sold to Elizabeth H. Parish for $475.[52]

May, 1907, John sold lots 2 and 5 of block 19 in his addition to former Rocky Bar, Idaho, brewery owner, Clarence H. Waymire, for $2,000.[53]

June of 1907, Lemp sold two pieces of real estate: to J. H. Oakes lot 6, block 19 of his addition for $350, and to Boise Inter-urban Ry. Co. a tract of 1.27 acres for the legal consideration of $1.[54]

END NOTES

1   Photocopy of the will, Probate Court, Ada County, Idaho. *Idaho Daily Statesman*, 22 July 1912, p. 3, c.1 & 2. *Sunday Capital News*, 21 July 1912, p. 11, c. 3 & 4.

2   Blaine County Judicial Records, Idaho State Historical Society, microfilm reel 31, original book, pages 533-536.

3   Bureau of Land Management, Land Patent Records. Accession/Serial # IDIDAA 043895. Document # 33354. The geographic name was Blue, and the description was Sections 5, 8, 9 of Township 14-N, Range 12-E.
4   *Wood River Times*, Hailey, Daily, 7 August 1906, p. 4, c. 3.
5   *Idaho Daily Statesman*, 15 April 1898, p. 4, c. 2.
6   *Idaho Daily Statesman*, 2 November 1899, p. 2, c. 3.
7   *The Evening Capital News*, 12 April 1901, p. 6, c. 2.
8   *Idaho Daily Statesman*, 26 September 1901, p. 3, c. 4.
9   *Idaho Daily Statesman*, 6 December 1901, p. 5, c. 1.
10 *Idaho Capital News*, 30 January 1902, p. 8, c. 2. The $1600 sale was to Carrie F. Bisby for a 1/16 of a section. *Idaho Daily Statesman*, 23 January 1902, p. 8, c. 2.
11 *Idaho Daily Statesman*, 29 January 1902, p. 2, c. 3.
12 *Idaho Daily Statesman*, 23 January 1902, p. 8, c. 2. *Evening Capital News*, 29 January 1902, p. 6, c. 3.
13 *Evening Capital News*, 27 January 1902, p. 2, c. 1.
14 *Idaho Daily Statesman*, 11 June 1902, p. 6, c. 2.
15 *Idaho Daily Statesman*, 11 June 1902, p. 6, c. 2.
16 *Evening Capital News*, 12 June 1902, p. 8, c. 1. 13 June 1902, p. 8, c. 2.
17 *Idaho Daily Statesman*, 7 September 1902, p. 8, c. 2.
18 *Idaho Daily Statesman*, 17 September 1902, p. 8, c. 2.
19 *Idaho Capital News*, 5 March 1903, p. 3, c. 4.
20 *Idaho Daily Statesman*, 16 August 1903, p. 7, c. 4.
21 *Evening Capital News*, 9 March 1904, p. 2, c. 3. *Idaho Daily Statesman*, 19 June 1904, p. 5, c. 4. The specifics were: To R. Winters, 4 lots, $900; To M.R. Fuller, 2 more lots, $525; To F.N. Ferrell, 1 lot, $175; To H. G. Bostwick, 2 lots, $350; To O. Burke 2 lots, $350; To C. A. Sargent, 2 lots, $525; To G. E. Matthews, 6 lots, $1300; To F. C. Bassell, 2 lots, $400; To F. W. Witham, 2 lots, $400.
22 *Evening Capital News*, 28 June 1904, p. 2, c. 2.
23 *Idaho Daily Statesman*, 9 July 1904, p. 3, c. 1-2.
24 *Idaho Daily Statesman*, 17 September 1904, p. 5, c. 2. 18 September 1904, p. 5, c. 4. *Evening Capital News*, 17 September 1904, p. 4, c. 2.
25 *Idaho Daily Statesman*, 7 October 1904, p. 7, c. 3 . 9 October 1904, p. 4, c. 5. *Evening Capital News*, 29 September 1904, p. 5, . 3. *Evening Capital News*, 13 October 1904, p. 8, c. 7.
26 *Idaho Daily Statesman*, 2 November 1904, p. 3, c. 2. *Evening Capital News*, 2 November 1904, p. 4, c. 3.
27 *Idaho Daily Statesman*, 5 November 1904, p. 4, c. 7. He was listed as Menzo R. Wentworth in *Evening Capital News*, 3 November 1904, p. 5, c. 2.
28 *Evening Capital News*, 4 January 1905, p. 2, c. 3.
29 *Evening Capital News*, 7 January 1905, p. 11, c. 3.

30 *Idaho Capital News*, 12 January 1905, p. 3, c. 3.
31 *Idaho Daily Statesman*, 15 January 1905, p. 8, c. 2.
32 *Evening Capital News*, 18 March 1905, p. 4, c. 2. *Idaho Capital News*, 23 March 1905, p. 11, c. 4. *Evening Capital News*, 9 March 1904, p. 5, c. 2. The first sale was to John Fisher for $400.
33 *Idaho Capital News*, 30 March 1905, p. 7, c. 3. *Evening Capital News*, 24 March 1905, p. 8, c. 5.
34 *Idaho Daily Statesman*, 2 April 1905, p. 8, c. 3. 8 April 1905, p. 3, c. 2. 13 April 1905, p. 8, c. 2. 19 April 1905, p. 5, c. 2. 30 April 1905, p. 3, c. 3. *Evening Capital News*, 11 April 1905, p. 8, c. 2. 28 April 1905, p. 8, c. 3.
35 *Idaho Capital News*, 25 May 1905, p. 7, c. 2. *Idaho Daily Statesman*, 19 May 1905, p. 4, c. 3.
36 *Idaho Daily Statesman*, 24 June 1905, p. 3, c. 2. *Evening Capital News*, 24 June 1905, p. 5, c. 2.
37 *Idaho Daily Statesman*, 25 July 1905, p. 2, c. 3.
38 *Idaho Daily Statesman*, 31 August 1905, p. 3, c. 3.
39 *Evening Capital News*, 18 September 1905, p. 5, c. 2. 21 September 1905, p. 1, c. 2.
40 *Idaho Daily Statesman*, 28 October 1905, p. 3, c. 7, and p. 5, c. 2.
41 *Idaho Daily Statesman*, 22 December 1905, p. 3, c. 3.
42 *Idaho Daily Statesman*, 30 January 1906, p. 6, c. 2. 4 February 1906, p. 7, c. 2. 13 February 1906, p. 8, c. 4. *Evening Capital News*, 17 January 1906, p. 6, c. 2. 26 January 1906, p. 2, c. 4. 31 January 1906, p. 6, c. 4. 7 February 1906, p. 2, c. 3.
43 *Evening Capital News*, 19 April 1906, p. 3, c. 3.
44 *Idaho Daily Statesman*, 24 May 1906, p. 5, c. 5.
45 *Idaho Daily Statesman*, 21 August 1906, p. 8, c. 2. 30 September 1906, p. 14, c. 1. 14 October 1906, p. 7, c. 2. 19 October 1906, p. 5, c. 1. 24 October 1906, p. 2, c. 4. *Evening Capital News*, 21 August 1906, p. 6, c. 3. 16 October 1906, p. 3, c. 3.
46 *Idaho Daily Statesman*, 11 November 1906, p. 8, c. 3.
47 *Evening Capital News*, 20 November 1906, p. 6, c. 3.
48 *Evening Capital News*, 28 December 1906, p.8, c. 3.
49 *Idaho Daily Statesman*, 8 January 1907, p. 8, c. 3.
50 *Idaho Daily Statesman*, 10 February 1907, p. 6, c. 1.
51 *Idaho Daily Statesman*, 24 February 1907, p. 8, c. 4.
52 *Evening Capital News*, 22 January 1907, p. 2, c. 4.
53 *Idaho Daily Statesman*, 4 May 1907, p. 4, c. 3. *Evening Capital News*, 4 May 1907, p. 3, c. 3.
54 *Idaho Daily Statesman*, 11 June 1907, p. 7, c. 1. 27 June 1907, p. 8, c. 4.

BIBLIOGRAPHICAL COMMENT

There is a small body of work that covers the lives of other North American brewers. University professor John T. Flanagan's *Theodore Hamm in Minnesota: His Family and Brewery* (n.p.: Pogo Press, 1989) and Moira F. Harris, *Louise's Legacy: Hamm Family Stories* (Saint Paul: Pogo Press,1999) cover that very famous beer baron of Minnesota. Stephen P. Walker's *Lemp: The Haunting History* (St. Louis: Lemp Preservation Society, 1988) gives a fine coverage of the often sad happenings in that star-crossed brewing family of St. Louis who were distantly related to John Lemp of Boise. Peter Hernon and Terry Ganey wrote *Under the Influence: The Unauthorized Story of the Anheuser-Busch Dynasty* (New York: Simon and Schuster, 1991) which at times seems intent on trying to sensationalize negative events in the history of America's most successful brewing family. Russ Banham, *Coors: A Rocky Mountain Legend* (Lyme, Conn.: Greenwich Publishing Group, 1998); Dan Baum, *Citizen Coors: An American Dynasty* (New York: William Morrow, 2000); and Russ Bellant, *The Coors Connection: How Coors Family Philanthropy Undermines Democratic Pluralism* (Boston: South End Press, 1991) all study the Colorado brewing family and its activities. There is a recent book on the Molson family of Canada.; Karen Molson, *The Molsons, Their Lives and Times, 1780-2000*. (Altona, Manitoba, Canada: Firefly Books, 2001). Another Canadian offering is Peter L. McCreath, *The Life and Times of Alexander Keith,*

Nova Scotia's Brewmaster. (Tantallon, Nova Scotia: Four East Publications, 2001). There are also brewing business histories that briefly cover the families involved. A good example would be Thomas Cochran's classic study *The Pabst Brewing Company: The History of An American Business* (New York: New York University Press, 1948) Idaho even has its own entry in the category of a family history of brewers. This is Edith C. Taylor, Philip O. Weisgerber, and Marie E. White, *A Man, His Family and His City* (n.p.: n.d. copyright Edith C. Taylor, 1982) which covers their relatives Ernest, John, Christ and Philip of the Weisgerber family of Lewiston, Idaho.

REFERRENCES

I. Books, periodicals, interviews, letters to the author, bylined newspaper articles, cd-roms, maps, dissertations and historical files

"Ada County Death and Cemetery Records," Idaho State Historical Society, Boise, Idaho.

Ambrose, Elaine. "Brewing Beer in Boise," *Boise Magazine*, Winter, 1999, pp. 58-111.

American Brewers Review, 1907.

Anderson, Eloise H. *Frontier Bankers: A History of Idaho First*

National Bank. Boise: Idaho First National Bank, 1981.

Anderson, Steven. "Boise's German Heritage: A Casualty of War." *Idaho Statesman*, 26 July 1993, p. c 1., c. 1-7.

Anderson, Will. *Beer, U.S.A. 500 Years of America's Beer Facts, Beer Lore, Beer Photographs, Beer Fun*. Dobbs Ferr Morgan and Morgan, 1986

Beal, Merrill D., and Merle W. Wells. *History of Idaho*, 3 vols. New York: Lewis Historical Publishing Company, 1959.

Bird, Annie Laurie. *Boise, the Peace Valley*. Caldwell, Idaho: The Caxton Printers, 1934.

Boise Idaho, Forty-Five Years of Progress. Boise, Idaho: The Illustrated Idaho Company, 1911.

Boone, Lalia. *Idaho Place Names: A Geographical Dictionary*. Moscow: University of Idaho Press, 1988.

Bradstreet Commercial Reports, vol. 87, Sep., 1889.

Butts, Mike. "Boise Polo Club," *Idaho Daily Statesman*, internet. November 2001.

Cemetery Records, Ada County, Idaho. Idaho State Historical Society.

Defenbach, Byron. *Idaho the Place and Its People, A History of the Gem State from Prehistoric to present Days*. 3 vols. Chicago: American Historical Society, 1933

Dick, Charles Edwin. "A Geographical Analysis of the Development of the Brewing Industry of Minnesota," Dissertation, University of Minnesota, 1981.

Dun, R. G. List of Idaho Businesses, 1904.

1850-1951 Marriage Index, ID, CA, Ariz, NV. Family Tree Maker. CD-ROM.

1851-1900 Marriage Index, Illinois. Family Tree Maker. CD-ROM.

Elliot, Wallace W. *History of Idaho The Territory: Showing Its Resources and Advantages*. San Francisco: Wallace W. Elliot, 1884.

Everett, George. *Champagne in a Tin Cup: Uptown Butte and the Stories Behind the Facades*. Butte, Montana: Outback Ventures, 1987.

Flenner, J. D. *Syringa Blossoms*. Caldwell: Caxton Printers, 1912.

Frederick, Manfred, and Bull, Donald. *Register of United States Breweries, 1876-1976*. Trumbull, Conn. Donald Bull, 1976.

Freidrich, Manfred, Bull, Donald, and Gottschalk, Robert. *American Breweries*. Trumbull, Conn.: Bullworks, 1984.

French, Hiram T. *History of Idaho, A Narrative Account of Its Historical Progress, Its People and Its Principal Interests*. Chicago: The Lewis Publishing Company, 1914.

A General Directory And Business Guide of the Principal Towns East of the Cascade Mountains, for the Year 1865. San Francisco: A. Roman & Co., [1865?]

Gibbs, Rafe. *Beckoning the Bold, Story of the Dawning of Idaho*. Moscow: University of Idaho Press, 1976.

Goulder, W. A. "How a Penniless German Boy Made It Go in the Early Days of Idaho," *Idaho Daily Statesman*, 15 November 1908, p. 5, c. 3 & 4.

Guetig, Peter R. and Selle, Conrad D. *Louisville Breweries: A History of the Brewing Industry in Louisville, Kentucky, New Albany and Jeffersonville, Indiana*. n.p: Mark Skaggs Press, 1995.

Gullick, Bill. *Outlaws of the Pacific Northwest*. Caldwell, Idaho: Caxton press, 2000.

Guttridge, Leonard. *Ghosts of Cape Sabine: The Harrowing True Story of the Greely Expedition*. New York: Berkley Books, 2000.

Hailey, John. *The History of Idaho*. Boise, ID.: Syms-York Company, 1910.

Hart, Arthur A. *Basin of Gold: Life in Boise Basin, 1862-1890*. Idaho City: Idaho City Historical Foundation, 1986

Hart, Arthur A. *Boiseans at Home*. Boise: Historic Boise, Inc., 1984.

Hart, Arthur. "Boiseans Flocked to German Club Events," *Idaho Statesman*, 12 December 1988, p. 3D, C. 1-4.

Hart, Arthur A. *Chinatown: Boise, Idaho, 1870-1970*. Boise, Idaho: Historic Idaho, Inc., n.d. (ca 2003)

Hart. Arthur A. "Beer King Ruled Boise," *Idaho Statesman*, 25 December 1872, p. 3-D, C. 1-4.

Hart, Arthur A. "German Beer Breweries Kept Idahoans Supplied," *Idaho Statesman*, 21 February 1983, p. 3C, c. 1-3.

Hart, Arthur A. "German Immigrant John Lemp Seeks, Makes Fortune in Idaho," *Idaho Statesman*, 9 February 1984, 5D, c. 1-6.

Hart, Arthur A. "Germans Cornered Market on Brewery Trade in Idaho," *Idaho Statesman*, 9 July 1979, 10A, c. 1-3.

Hart, Arthur A. "Germans Danced at 6th and Main," *Idaho Statesman*, 5 December 1988, 3D, c. 2-4.

Hart, Arthur A. " Lemp Helped Raise Funds," *Idaho Statesman*, 8 January 1973, p. 11, c. 1-4.

Hart, Arthur A. "Lemp Hailed as Investor," *Idaho Statesman*, 1 January 1973, p.10A, c. 1-5.

Hart, Arthur A. "Lemp Helps Boise Grow," *Idaho Statesman*, 26 July 1993, p. 2D, c. 1-2.

Hawley, James H. *History of Idaho, The Gem of the Mountains*. 3 vols. Chicago: S. J. Clarke Publishing Co., 1920.

Hawley, James H. "Hawley Manuscript, M52 H31," Idaho State Historical Society manuscript collection.

Idaho Death Index, 1911-1951.

Idaho Reports, (law book) Vol. 7.

Idaho State Gazetteer and Business Directory, 1903-04, 1906, 1908, 1910-11, 1912-13, 1914, 1916. Place Varies: R. L. Polk.

Idaho State Historical Society Biography file: John Lemp.

Idaho State Historical Society Manuscript File, 178. The John Lemp Family.

Idaho State Historical Society Photo file. Jacob Lemp. John Lemp

Illustrated History of the State of Idaho. Chicago: The Lewis Publishing Co,. 1899.

Illustrated History of the State of Montana. Chicago: The Lewis Publishing Co., 1894.

An Illustrated History of North Idaho. Western Historical Publishing Company, 1903.

"John Lemp," Idaho State Historical Society Reference Series, number 582, 1981.

"John Lemp: Foundation Builder of Boise," *The Idaho Magazine*, March 1904.

Langely, Henry G. *Idaho Territory Business Directory*. San Francisco: Langely Publisher, 1866.

Lemp, Karl, Sr. Letter to Author, April 2002.

Lemp. Karl H. Phone interview with author. 19 January 2002.

MacGregor, Carol Lynn. "Founding Community in Boise, Idaho 1882-1910," Dissertation, University of New Mexico, 1999.

MacGregor, Carol Lynn. *Boise, Idaho, 1882-1910: Prosperity in Isolation*. Missoula, Montana: Mountain Press Publishing, 2006.

Mangam, William D. *The Clarks: An American Phenomenon*. New York: Silver Bow Press, 1941.

Maxwell, H. James, and Sullivan, Bob, Jr. *Hometown Beer: A History of Kansas City's Breweries*. Kansas City: Omega Innovative Marketing, 1999.

Miller, Joaquin. *Illustrated History of Montana, 1894*. Chicago. Lewis Publishing.

Neil, J. M. "The Impossible Dream," *Idaho Yesterdays*, Winter 1999, p. 14.

"New Plants and Improvements," The Western Brewer: and Journal of the Barley, Malt and Hop Trades. June 1906, pp. 320-321.

1910 Idaho Census Index. CD-ROM, Family Tree Maker.

"Nez Perce War Letters," Orlando Robbins to M. Brayman, 7 July 1877. Fifteenth Bienniel Report of the Board of Trustees of the State Historical Society, Idaho, 1935-1936. pp. 109-111.

O'Connor, Richard. *The German-Americans: An Informal History*. Boston: Little, Brown and Co., 1968.

Polk, R. L. & Co., *Boise City and Ada County Directory*. Vol. VII., 1911. Vol. X, 1915.

Progressive Men of Southern Idaho. Chicago: A. W. Bowen, 1904.

"Pioneer Cemetery: A Self-Guided Tour," Pamphlet. Boise, Idaho: Idaho State Historical Society, n.d.

Ronnenberg, Herman. *Beer and Brewing in the Inland Northwest, 1850-1950*. Moscow: University of Idaho Press, 1993.

Ronnenberg, Herman W. "History of the Brewing Industry in Idaho, 1862-1960," Ph.D. dissertation, History Department, University of Idaho, 1989.

Ronnenberg, Herman W. "Idaho on the Rocks: The Ice Business in the Gem State," *Idaho Yesterdays*, 33: 4, Winter 1990, 2-8.

Ronnenberg, Herman W. *The Politics of Assimilation: The Effect of Prohibition on the German Americans*. New York: Carlton Press, 1973.

Ronnenberg, Herman W. "Researching Your Hometown Brewery: The Fire Insurance Connection," *The Breweriana Collector*, Vol. 69, Spring 1990, 22-24.

Rudin, Max. "Beer and America," *American Heritage*, June/July 2002, p. 28.

Russin, Don. Phone interview with author, 23 January 1999. St. Louis, Mo. to Troy, Idaho.

Salem, Frederick William. *Beer, Its History and Its Economic Value as a National Beverage*. Hartford, Conn. 1880.

Sanborn-Perris Maps, Boise, various years.

Schwantes, Carlos. *Railroad Signatures of the Pacific Northwest*. Seattle: University of Washington Press, 1993.

Schwantes, Carlos. *The Pacific Northwest, An Interpretive History*. Lincoln: University of Nebraska Press, 1989.

"Settlers Canal (Lemp Canal)," Idaho State Historical Society Reference Series, number 531, 1974.

"Those Were the Days: Growing Up in Style," *Idaho Yesterdays*, vol. 14, no. 3, Fall, 1970, pp. 28-9.

Van Wieren, Dale P. *American Breweries II*. West Point, PA.: East Coast Breweriana Association, 1995.

Vandracek, John Felix, "The Rise of Fraternal Organizations in the U.S., 1868-1900," *Social Science*, Vol. 47, Winter, 1972, p. 26.

"Visit the Blaine County Historical Museum," Pamphlet, Hailey, Idaho, n.d.

Walker, Francis A. and Seaton, Charles W. *Compendium of the 10th Census, June 1, 1880.* Washington: Government Printing Office, 1883.

Walker, Francis A. *A Compendium of the 9th Census, June 1, 1870.* Washington: Government Printing Office, 1872.

Washington, Oregon, Idaho Gazetteer and Business Directory, 1886-1887, 1892.

Wells, Merle. *Boise: An Illustrated History,* 1982.

Western Brewer, (Periodical) 1909.

Wright, Patricia and Reitzes, Lisa B. *Tourtellotte and Hummel, The Standard Practice of Architecture.* Logan, Utah: Utah State University Press, 1987.

II Newspapers

Boise Capital News, Boise, Idaho, 1935.

Boise Citizen, Boise Idaho, 1907-1908

Boise City Republican, 1881-1887.

Boise City Weekly News, Boise, Idaho, 1869-1870.

Boise News (Idaho City, then called Bannock), 1863, 1864.

Boise Sentinel, Boise, Idaho, 1897.

Caldwell Tribune, Caldwell, Idaho, 1894-1910.

Camas Prairie Chronicle, Cottonwood, Idaho, 1900-1910.

The Capital, Boise, Idaho. (aka, *Idaho Capital News, Idaho Evening Capital, Evening Capital News, The Weekly Capital*) 1899-1912

The Capital Chronicle, Boise, 1869-1870.

Capital Report, Salem, Oregon 1893.

The Commonwealth of Idaho, Boise, 1892.

Daily Evening Citizen, Boise, 1891.

Elmore Bulletin. Rocky Bar, Idaho, 1888-1892. Mountain Home, Idaho, 1892-1900.

Evening Capital Journal, Salem, Oregon, 1893.

Genesee News, Genesee, Idaho, 1891.

Hailey Times, Hailey, Idaho, various dates.

Idaho Democrat (aka, *The Weekly Democrat*) Boise, 1886-1897.

Idaho Falls Times, 1891 – 1893.

Idaho Herald, Boise, Idaho, 1872.

The Idaho Pioneer, Boise, Idaho, 1935.

Idaho Register, Idaho Falls, 1891, 1907.

Idaho Review, Boise, Idaho, 1915.

Idaho Scimitar, Boise, Idaho, 1907-1908.

Idaho Signal, Lewiston, 1873.

Idaho Statesman (aka *Idaho Tri-Weekly Statesman, Idaho Sunday Statesman, Idaho Daily Statesman*), Boise, Idaho, 1863 to 1917.
Idaho World, Idaho City, 1880-1882.
Ketchum Keystone, Ketchum, Idaho, 1884.
Morning Oregonian, Portland, Oregon, 1875.
Mountain Home Bulletin, Mountain Home, Idaho, 1888.
North Idaho Star , Moscow, 1891.
Owyhee Avalanche, Ruby City, later Silver City, Idaho (aka *Owyhee Daily Avalanche*), 1865-1871, 1914.
Owyhee Bullion , Silver City, Idaho.
Owyhee Tidal Wave, Silver City, Idaho (aka *Semi-Weekly Tidal Wave*), 1869.
Post Register, Idaho Falls, 1937.
Semi-Weekly Idahoan, 1877.
Semi-Weekly News, Boise, Idaho, 1870.
Soda Springs Chieftain, Soda Springs, Idaho, 1904-1920.
Soda Springs Sun, Soda Springs, Idaho, 1915.
The Standard, Ogden, Utah, 1892.
Teton Peak, St. Anthony, Idaho, 1899.
The Teton Peak-Chronicle, St. Anthony, 1905.
Tri-Weekly Herald, Boise, Idaho, 1871-1872.
Weiser Signal, Wesier, Idaho, 1926.
Wood River News Miner, Hailey, Idaho.
Wood River Times, aka *Wood River Times (Weekly)*, Hailey, Idaho, 1883-1906.
Yankee Fork Herald, Bonanza, Idaho, 1880.

III. Manuscript Material

Ada County Probate Court Records. Wills of:
Augusta Julia Margaret Lemp Grant
Edwin G. Hurt
Edward H. Lemp
Herbert Lemp
John Lemp
Katherine Lemp
Charles Leyerzaph
Martha Elizabeth Lemp Connor
Ada County Judicial Records, Judgement Books, Idaho State Historical Society, Microfilm.
Alturas County Patent Deeds, Blaine County Judicial Records, microfilm reel 31, Idaho State Historical Society.

Blaine County Judicial Records, Idaho State Historical Society, Microfilm.
Custer County Deeds, Idaho State Historical Society, reel 6.
Federal Tax Records, Idaho, 1865-1866, University of Idaho Microfilm 558.
John Lemp Family, Manuscript file # 178, Idaho State Historical Society.
Logan County Deed Records, vol. 13, Blaine County Judicial Records, reel 10, Idaho State Historical Society.
Owyhee County Deed Books. Idaho State Historical Society
Owyhee County Judicial Records, Idaho State Historical Society, Microfilm.
United States Census Population Schedules, 1860, 1870, 1880, 1900, 1910, 1920.

IV. Internet Sites.

Ancestry.com

"Boise, Idaho Elections 1867-1885." gesswho.com/idaho/boise-elections,html-10k.

"Boise City Mayors." Internet site. www.ci.Boise.id.us/city-clerk/re-cords-%mayors.shtml.

Booth, James. "James Booth Lockwood (1852-1884)." Online. http://freespace.virgin.net/peter.lockwoodl/james_booth_htm. 19 May 2002.

Brown, Cecilia. "Lemp, John." http://boards.ancestry.com/mbexec/message/an/localities.northam.usa.idaho.counties.ada/162. 28 September 2001.

Bureau of Land Management. Land Patent Records. Online. http://www/glorecords.bim.gov/search/detail_print asp?accession. 2 May 2001.

Butts, Mike. "Polo Team was Called the Four Horsemen." www.idahostatesman.com/news/history/archive/140489.shtml-18k.

Creas, Toennises, Mullins & McAllisters of Idaho—Descendants & Relatives.

Current Conditions for Secteurs is T.N.O. "May, 2002. Online. http://216.239.35.120/translate/hl=en&sl=fr&u=http//ourworldcompuserve.com/homepages/polarlys/97hym&pev.

Chapter Three Background Report. East End NeighborhoodPolicy Guide (Boise). www.cityofboise.org/pds/Neighborhood/East_End/Chap%203.pdf

Fortune Favors the Brave, (Story of the 644th Tank Destroyer Battalion) Internet site. http://www.644td.com/fortune.htm.

Free Space, Virgin.net/Peter.Lockwood/Jamesbooth.htm. "James Booth Lockwood (1852-1889)

Genealogy.com. "Matches in Genealogy Library—Family Books & 1850 Census." http://www.genealogy.com/cgi-bin/wizardresultscgi?&Category=GENLIB&UsearchD=990cla3165acad.583bff21121GaWG&FN 4 April 2002.

"German Americans in the Columbia River Basin: Historical Over-view," http://www.vancouver.wsu.edu/crbeha/ga.htm

"Hildebrand Family." hhttp://www.users.bigpond.com/t,whelan/personal/family/hildrnd.htm.27 May 2002.

Idaho Secretary of State, Election Division. "Constitution of the State of Idaho, Approved July 3, 1890." http://www.idsos.state.id.us/elect/stcon/articl121.htm. 8 November 2001.

"Idaho State Constitution Article XXI." www.idsos.state.id.us/elec/stcon/articl21.htm-20k.

Independent School District of Boise City. "History of The Boise School District." http://www.sd0.1.k.12.id.us/administration/dist1st.html 19 November 1901.

Morning Report: Chronological History of the 644th Tank Destroyer Battalion for the Calendar Year 1942. Declassified per executive order 12356, Section 3.3, NND735017. Online. http://www.644tf.com/morning.htm.. 19 November 2001.

The Nieder-Weisel Story. http://users.bigpond.net.au/haintz/village2.html. 27 May 1902.

New York Times on the Web. "Books: Ghosts of Cape Sabine." Online. http://www.nytimes.com/books/first/g/guttridge-ghosts.html. 19 May 2002.

"Nez Perce War Letters," Fifteenth Biennial Report of the Board of the State Historical Society of Idaho. 1935-36. Roots Web. Social Security Death Index.

Treasure Valley Hydrology. "History of Water Development." Online. http://www.idwr.state.id.us/tvalley/history_of_water_development.htm. 4 April 2002.

World War I Draft Registration Records. RootsWeb.com.ftp.rootsweb.com/pub/usgenweb/id/ada/adawwiadaLEE_LO.txt

INDEX

Page numbers appearing in italics refer to photographs or illustrative materials. Alphabetizing of entries is word-by-word. Therefore, John Lemp and Lemp family members are alphabetized before Lemp-named businesses or properties, e.g. Lemp Addition, Lemp's Dry Goods Store all appear alphabetically after the last Lemp (Lemp, William J.).

accidents and injuries. *See also* fires and firefighting
 construction, 45, 92
 drug related, 262
 employee related, 76, 78, 91, 94–95, 122, 169, 171–72, 207, 236, 250–51, 262
 equipment, 238
 falls, 44, 59, 169, 197, 201, 205, 206
 flooding, 56–57
 horse/wagon, 51–52, 76, 78, 79, 90–91, 92, 94–95, 122, 147–48, 165, 170, 171–72, 178, 212–13, 217, 236
 polo, 306–13
 weather related, 56–57, 69
Ada County. *See also specific town or location*
 elections, 12, 22, 40, 42, 46, 263, 277
 farming in, 78–79, 315
 federal land in, 28
 JL daughter named after, 33
 largest mortgage in, 169
 number of brewers in, 258
 proposed division of, 85, 145
 resolution on JL's death, 310
 tribute to JL, 312–13
Ada County Board of Equalization, 170, 213–14, 217, 270
Ada County Commissioners, 144, 176, 189kn, 211, 305, 310
Ada County Court, 235, 278, 301, 312–13
Ada County Fair, 214, 227
Ada County Grange, 309
Ada County Jockey Club, 24, 26–27, 31–32
Ada County Republican Central Committee, 40, 45
Ada County Sheriff, 12, 42, 46
Ada County Treasurer, 22, 40
Adams, Charles Francis, 67
Adelman, Jack, 267

Adelmann, Richard C. "Dick," 29, 46–47, 51, 58, 256, 277
Adolph, Eva, 148
Adolph, Joseph, 148
Adolph, Lilly, 148, 207
Adolph, Samuel, Jr., 148
Adolph, Samuel, Sr., 10–11, 34, 97n, 147–48, *159*, 297
advertising and publicity
Bank of Idaho, 261
beer, 41–42, 70, 124, 128, 153, 156, 157–58, *165*, 273–75
Boise Brewery and Saloon, 23–24, 84–85
in the Boise City Directory, 143
Boise City promotion, 124
Capitol Hotel, 151, 159–61
City Brewery, 13–14, *21*, 28
CL appears in sewing ad, 94
elections, 128
farm loans, 304, *306*
ice industry, 30
Lemp Addition, 145, 201, 208
Lemp & Co., 14, 20, *21*
Lemp Park, 260–61
Lemp Triangle, 247
Lemp's Dry Goods Store, 166, *200*, 201–4, *203*
liquor house/store, 52, 165
mining industry promotion, 130
secondary markets, 30
Agricultural Park Association. *See* Boise Agricultural Association/Park
Aikman, Robert, 277
Ailshie, C. J., 303
Alaska-Yukon-Pacific Exposition, 262
alcohol and drug abuse, 21, 262
Alcove Bar, 251
Alexander, Moses, 173, 213
alfalfa, 63, 79, 314
Algenbarger, Jacob, 53
Alkali Flats, 67

Allen, John, 52, 57
Alta-Johnson mine, 129
American Baseball League, 62
American Brewing Company (St. Louis), 233
Ancient Order of United Workmen, 70, 155–56, 158–59, 174, 275, 299
Anderson, A. B., 209
Anderson, C. C., 262
Anderson, I. W., 228
Anderson Ranch, 84
Andola, A. R., 128
Andricks, William, 142
Anheuser Busch saloon, 239–40
Annett (councilman), 242
Anti-Saloon League, 149, 231
Arc Light Saloon, 273
Arrowrock Dam, 84
Artesian Hot and Cold Water Company, 133, 143, 153, 206–7, 263
Artesian Water and Land Improvement Company, 133
Ashcroft, Henry, 316
Ashton, Walter, 314
assassinations, 242, 252
Astor, John Jacob, 80
athletic clubs. *See* Boise Turn Verein
Atkinson, John, 208, *237*
Augustine, Mr., 130
Austin, Mrs. A. A., 263
Austin, William C., 59–60
automobiles, 207, 257, 271
Avalanche (newspaper), 35
Avis, Misses, 267

Bach, Frederich, 230
Bach, Margarethe (Lemp) (sister), 5, 6–7, *25*, 139, 230, 276
Bair, Mrs. E., 94
Bair, William F., 94
Baker, D. F., 208

Baldridge, H. C., 310–11
Ballard, David W., 39–40
Ballentine, J. M., 49
Ballentine, J. W., 93
Bane, J. C., 166
Bank of Commerce, 198, 212, 251–52
Bank of Idaho, 257, 261
banking industry, 30–31, 32, 37–40, 147. *See also specific bank*
Bannock Indian War, 45
Barber (councilman), 217–18
Barbour, Clitus, 28
Barefoot Schoolboy Law, 147
barley, 3, 14, 18–19, 24–25, 37, 41, 79, 157
Barnes, William, 171–72
Barringer, Charles T., 272–73, 305
bartending, 52, 54, 57, 58, 89, 90, 147
  City Brewery Saloon, 28
  entertaining customers, 121
  fights, 144–45
  robberies, 146, 156–57, 173–74
  selling to minors, 172–73, 249
Bartholomay Brewing Company, 146
baseball, 62, 146, 236, 238
Baxter, Charles, 128–29
Bayhouse, George, 17, 18
Beal, Joe, 178
Beatty, James H., 120
Beck, Sarah M. *See* Kohlepp, Sarah M. (Beck)
Beckhardt, Fred, 34
Bedell, William, 59–60
Bee, Mr. and Mrs. W. F., 270
beer. *See also* brewery industry
  advertising and publicity, 41–42, 70, 124, 128, 153, 156, 157–58, *165*, 273–75
  bock, 153, 156
  extra pale, 273–75
  Falstaff, 273–75
  lager, 157–58
  prices of, 28, 29, 143
  Rainer, 149
  taxes on, 10–11, 13, 14–15, 30, 169, 214, 228
  Wiener, 70, 124, 128, *165*
Beer and Whiskey League, 62
Bender, Jacob. *See* Leyerzapf, George
Bengston, Olga, 202
Berry, Mr., 61
Bethal, Joseph, 223
Biederbick, Henry, 73, 74
"Big Jim" (horse), 312
Biggerstaff, W. B., 133
Bigham, Harry, 316
Bilderback, C. P., 40, 55
billiards, 52, 59, 77, 89, 142–43, 266
"Billy Lemp" (horse), 38, 40, 42, 45–46
Bird, Mounce, 48
Bishop, Edson, 145, 165
Black, Charley, 45
Black Law, 273
Blackinger, Frank, 171, 205, 239
blacksmiths, 250–51
Blaine, James G., 122
Blaine County. *See also* specific town or location
  commissioners of, 240
  mining industry, 121–22, 136, 138, 145, 147, 208, 217, 237
  ranches in, 278
Blair, Mrs., 241
Blesse, Frederick A., 319
Blitz, Dr., 211
Blumauer-Frank Company (OR), 207
bock beer, 153, 156
Boeck, Dr., 211
Bogart, James A., 123, 161–63

Boise (ID)
form of government, 273
founding of, 8–10
growth of, 143, 150, 234
Boise Agricultural Association/
Park, 38, 43, 53, 58, 60, 121
Boise Athletic Club, 53, 236
Boise Baseball Association, 236
Boise Board of Trade, 67, 72, 124, 132, 144
Boise Brewery and Saloon, 10, 23–24, 84–85
Boise business census, 14, 258
Boise Butcher Company, 174
Boise Canal Company, 80
Boise Central Railway Company, 120, 145, 157, 163, 165
Boise Chamber of Commerce, 238, 309
Boise City Council
 building codes and committee, 241–42, 264
 canal flume, 57, 145, 208–9
 elections, 14, 29, 31, 32, 40, 42, 45, 51, 55, 58, 62, 69, 93, 125–28
 laundry businesses, 209
 Lemp Triangle, 243–47, 245, 248, 301–3
 meetings, 60, 66, 89, 123–24, 130–31, 133, 145
 petitions, 43, 57, 123, 155, 207, 209, 241
 railway lines, 65–66
 Red Light District, 262
 resolution honoring JL, 276–77
 roads and sidewalks, 206, 216, 230–31, 233, 250, 253, 254, 268–69
 sewer systems, 205, 213, 233, 234
 special elections, 207
 statement on HFL's death, 309–10
 Sunday laws, 239
 tearing down Lemp brewery, 217–27
Boise City Directory, 124, 143, 304
Boise City Fire Department, 23, 37, 55, 60, 94, 123, 309
Boise City Irrigation Canal and Land Company, 212
Boise City Railway & Terminal Company, 234
Boise Commercial Club, 251, 303, 316
Boise Country Club, 309, 316
Boise Electric Street Railway, 125
Boise Gun Club, 249, 253
Boise High School, 248, 250
Boise Ice and Commission Company, 144
Boise Independent School District, 312. *See also* schools
Boise & Interurban Train, 254, 255, 260
Boise Library, 237
Boise Mayor's Office
 acting in absence of mayor, 88, 308
 Alexander administration, 173, 213
 Bilderbach elected, 55
 brewers elected, 299
 Eagleson administration, 66
 Good administration, 218
 Haines administration, 244, 253, 256, 303
 Hawley administration, 219
 HFL elected, 305–13, 318
 Hodges' administration, 301, 303
 JL administration, 37, 39, 40, 55, 259, 273, 276–77, 299
 land issues, 123, 161, 163, 224, 243–44, 301–2
 Pence administration, 185fk, 246, 262
 Pierce administration, 303
 Pinney administration, 62, 66, 127, 240, 303

power of, 303
Prickett administration, 301
Republican nomination for, 157
selling of municipal land, 253
street paving, 250
Boise Opera House, 92
Boise Pioneer Association, 120, 234, *237*
Boise public square, 41
Boise Railway Company, 68
Boise Rapid Transit Company
earnings and ridership of, 207
election of officers, 129, 142, 149, 154–55, 158, 166, 214
extensions and improvements, 129, 142, 214
Jaumann estate and, 159
sale of, 228
Boise school board, 48, 50, 91, 147, 154
Boise Statesmen (newspaper), sale of, 61
Boise Stone Company, 304
Boise Turn Verein
balls, 17, *20*–21, 26, 78
grounds of, 38, 82
JL funeral, 276, 277
officers and membership, 17–18, 27, 149, 232, 276
organization of, 16–18, 158
picnics, 121
Boise Water Works Company, 133
Boise Wesangverein, 18
Boomer, Mr., 54
Boone, Samuel and Mary, 143
Boot and Shoe Store of Spath and Lessman, 36
Booth, Hazel, 266, 267, 268
Booth, W. T., 242
Borah, William E., 125, 159, 161–63, 167, 216
Borll, Eugene, 76

Boston Grill, 254
Bostwick (officer), 221
bottling industry
cork-free breakthrough, 37
"crown top," 144
lawsuits, 303
lightening stopper, 37
new equipment, 240
piping of beer, 119
soda manufacturing and, 124
in St. Louis, 40
Boulder Consolidated Mining Company, Ltd., 138, 250
Boyle, Pat, 143
Bradstreet's Commercial Reports, 94
Brainard, C. E., 200
Brayman, Mason, 42
Breck, Francis, 46
Breen, Pat, 252, 291oh
Breen, William, 141, 142, 178
brewery associations, 32, 157, 258
Brewery Collectibles Club of America, 319
brewery industry. *See also* beer; laws and legislation; saloon business; *specific brewer*
awards, 146
baseball and, 62
Boise business census, 14, 258
brewers affiliated with JL, 334
at the Centennial Exposition, 40
competition in, 158, 205
consumption levels, 157, 158
coopers, 76–77
effects of depression of '73, 32
as family business, 297
in Germany, 5
health conditions in, 299
Horace Greeley on, 27
mining industry and, 297, 298
overall sales, 22
political affiliations, 299

prices, 28, 29, 143
profits and revenues, 13, 41, 69
religious affiliations, 299
San Francisco earthquake and, 248
taxes, 10–11, 13, 14–15, 30, 169, 214, 228
training for, 298
in the U.S., 19, 20, 25, 52, 54–55, 119, 158
at the World's Fair, 146
brewing process. *See also* bottling industry; ice industry
barley, 3, 14, 18–19, 24–25, 37, 41, 79, 157
fermentation, 30, 41
hops, 55, 157
odors from, 41, 173
pasteurization, 30, 40, 70
piping of, 119
production capacity, 10–11, 14–15, 71, 214, 240
refrigeration, 40, 54, 129
soda manufacturing and, 124
water and, 61
Briggs, Mr., 262
Brink, J., 142
Brisbin, Edward, 145, 165
Broadbent, John (building owner), 88
Broadbent, John B. (brewer)
brewery business, 58, 60, 218, 241, 269
Capital Hotel mortgaged to, 218
estate of, 68, 88, 147, 168, 231–32, 233, 240, 252, 256
foundry investment, 128
railroad industry, 68
serves as bondsman, 138, 231–32
water bills, 133
Broadbent, John R., 88
Brockbank, Isaac, 136, 164
Brodbeck, John R.

brewery business of, 26, 44, 52, 69, 79, 86, 89, 91, 145, 177, 178, 239–40, 241, 297
death of, 260
death of daughter, 62
foundry investment, 128
grandchildren of, 56
joins Home Guard, 45
participates in raffle, 47
political life, 52, 55, 88, 157
sells brewery, 178
social life and travels, 210
Brodbeck, Lena. *See* Kohlepp, Lena (Brodbeck)
Brodbeck, Sarah, 53, 56, 62
Brown, "Brother," 28
Brown, Jonas W., 21–22
Brum, J. W., 78
Bryan (judge), 255, 303
Bryan, William Jennings, 147
building construction. *See also* roads and streets; Settler's Canal (Lemp Canal)
accidents and injuries, 45, 92
additions, 40, 55–56, 57, 62–63, 121
bank, 125, 130
billiard hall, 142–43
Capitol Hotel, 119–20, 122, 123
city codes and, 241–42, 264
foundry, 128–29
Lemp house, 34, *41, 44*
movie theater, 204–5
new, 14, 27–28, 32, 35–36, 43, 44, 46, 60, 69, 70–71, 73, 77, 89, 92–93, 94, 207–8, 220, 250, 256, 258, 264–65
praise for, 143–44
repairs and improvements, 13, 52, 89, 92, 120, 133, 166, 174, 241, 303
schools, 49–50, 88, 312
Bunker Hill & Sullivan concentrator, 171
Bunnell-Eno Company, 169

Burblock, Jacob, 211
Burgess, Solon, 134
Busch, Adolphus, 30, 40
Bush, James H., 53, 78, 85
Bush, W. H., 12
business reports and listings
Boise business census, 14, 258
Boise City Directory, 124, 143, 304
Bradstreet's Commercial Reports, 94
Polk City Directory, 269
R. G. Dun Mercantile Listings, 69, 154, 232
Butler, J. H., 123, 149
Butte Brewing Company, 198
Butter Ball mine, 211
Butterbaugh, W. M., 270
Byron, William, 128

Cage, John W., 236
Cahalan, Thomas D., 44, 78, 140
Caldwell Tribune (newspaper), 153–54
Calkins and Beachey, 55–56
Call, Messr., 28
Campbell (sheriff), 174
Campbell and Hodgson architects, 133
canal systems, 212, 228, 242. *See also* Settler's Canal (Lemp Canal)
Canyon County. *See also* specific town or location
  creation of, 145
  farming in, 276, 315
  land patents, 124, 153–54, 241
  "Lemp Town," 201
Canyon County Fair, 215
Canyon County tax assessments, 278
Capital State Bank of Boise, 256
Capitol Hotel
  address of, 205
  advertising and publicity, 151,
159–61
  building of, 119–20, 122, 123
  employees, 123, 151, 169, 171, 205
  Equal Suffrage Club meeting at, 164
  fire insurance map, *160*
  lawsuits, 171
  leasing of, 149, 171, 239, 254
  literary history of, 151
  mortgaging of, 218
  tower near, 225
Carder, Tome, 77
Carey Act. *See* Desert Land Act
Carpenter, L. N. B., 228
cars, 207, 257, 271
Cartee, L. F., 60
Cartwright, George, 213
cash sale law (1820), 28, 132
Casmier Winter and Company (CA), 18–19
cattle business, 28, 130, 169, 217, 232, 269, 304, 315
celebrations
  Alaska-Yukon-Pacific Exposition, 262
  balls, 16, *17, 20,* 26, 32, 33, 53, 92, 122–23, 149, 155, 161, 234, 268
  Boise Opera House opening, 92
  Centennial Exposition (Philadelphia), 38, 40
  Fourth of July, 28, 29, 32, 38, 42, 44, 55, 77, 79, 87, 91, 93, 123–24, 146, 238, 257
  German-American, 210–11
  Idaho State Fair, 132–33, 166, 209, 227, 230, 233
  Lewis and Clark Exposition, 238, 240
  library opening, 237
  May Day, 53
  Memorial Day, 238
  President Taft's visit, 271
  raffles, 46–47

Thanksgiving festival, 38, 46
U.S. Centennial, 38
World's Fair, 146, 163, 229, 234
Centennial Brewery, 198
Centennial Exposition (Philadelphia), 38, 40
Central Brewery and Bakery, 15
Centre claim, 147
Chapin, Carrie, 50
Chapman, George A., 150
Charcoal Gulch, 211
charity work. *See* donations and charity work
Charles Carson & Co., 149
Chase, Eben J., 134
Checkmate mine, 230
Cheyenne Indians, 38–39
Chicago (IL), 28, 146, 208
children. *See also* schools
orphanage for, 130, 134, 139, 149
selling liquor to, 172–73, 249
Chillingsworth, George, 237
Chinese Masonic tong, 206
Chinn, Charles, 277
Chrichlow, Robert W., 319
Christe, Dr., 89
Christian, Joseph, 56
Christian Science Church, 231, 308, 309, 312
Christiansen, James G., 318
Cincinnati (OH), 37–38
City Brewery, 13–14, *21*, 28, 97q
civil rights, 35
Civil War (U.S.), 8–9, 77, 158
Clark, Anna L. (La Chappelle), 230, 269
Clark, Charles A., 165
Clark, Mabel (Foster), 206
Clark, S. J., 273
Clark, William, Jr., 206
Clark, William A.
children of, 206
health of, 239

home of, 292pv
marriage of, 230, 269
mining business, 7–9, 96j, 154, 247, 257
political life, 179
Clarke, Leo G., 319
Clarke, W. S., 247
Clay, Henry, 75
Cleary, Maud L., 271
Clemmens, D. E., 178
Cleveland, Grover, 122
Clifton, W. M., 258
Clinton (councilman), 242
Club for Women, 227
Coates (colonel), 165
Cobb, Frank, 142
Cobb, Lynn, 275
Cody (inspector), 225, 226
Coeur d'Alene mines, 131–32, 171, 242
Coffin, Frank R., 48, 58, 122, 277
Cohen, Hazel, 266, 267, 268
Cohen & McDevitt Store, 204
Cole, C. E., 169
Cole, Oric, 277
Cole's restaurant, 57–58
Collins, Felix, 10, 12, 97ab
Collins, James, 155
Collins, John, 53
Collister, Mr., 125
Colorado, 7–8, 32
Columbian Club, 232, 256, 262, 313
Commercial Club, 251, 303, 316
communications, 19, 24, 35, 262. *See also* telegraph; telephone services
Conant Brothers, 45, 51
Concordia claim, 88, 121–22
Congdon, J. P., 312
Connor, Amanda Brower, 95
Connor, Martha Elizabeth (Lizzie) (Lemp), *33, 43*
birth of, 25–26

census records, 21, 54
childhood, 38, 42, 53, 55, 61, 70, 93
death of, 314
JL's estate, 277
marriage of, 95, 275, 314
Connor, William Brower, *91*
JL claim against, 164, 166–68
jury duty, 207
Lemp's Dry Goods Store, 202, 209, 239
marriage of, 95, 275, 314
social life and travels, 215
Connor, Willoughby, 95
Consorting, Topp, 54
construction. *See* building construction
conventions. *See* Republican conventions
Cooke, Jay, 32, 63
coopers, 76–77
Coors, Adolph, 32, 119, 146
Corder, Mr., 66
cork-free closures, 37
Cottonwood Creek, 56–57, 145
courts, 85. *See also* jury duty; laws and legislation; lawsuits; *specific court*
Cowles, Calvin, 308
Cox, L. H., 237, 262
Coyle, Andrew, 61
Coyote mine, 211
"Craven" (horse), 306
Cremin, Thomas, 93
Crime Act of '73, 30–31
crime and violence
accusations of cow stealing, 251
arrest complaints, 169
assassinations, 242, 252
assaults, 90
embezzlement, 154
against German Americans, 5
hog stealing, 155

horse thievery, 53, 87, 250
human remains found, 269
involving employees, 146, 156–57, 172–73, 173–74, 219, 273
land disputes, 140–42
liquor licenses and selling, 172–73, 219, 249
martial law, 131–32
murders, 48, 59–60, 71–72, 242, 252, 273
peddler's licenses, 209
practical jokes, 203
prostitution, 205
public disturbances, 255
robberies, 24–25, 33–34, 47, 56, 125, 146, 163–64, 164–65, 173–74, 252, 263
saloon fights, 144–45
shootings, 59–60, 215–16
shoplifting, 164–65
stealing, 53, 87, 155, 156–57, 223, 250, 263
trespassing, 174
vagrancy, 232
vigilantism, 11–12
Crouch, Charles, 79, 141, 142
Crouch, Mr. and Mrs. Charles, 253
Crown Point mine, 79
"crown top," 144
Curtis, Henry, 163–64, 262
Curtis, T. J., 74
Curtis, William, 262
Custar, O., 35
Custer, George A., 38–39, 42
Custer County, 77, 163, 197, 215. *See also specific town or location*

Daly, John D., 242
Daly, Marcus, 179
Dangel, Fred, 37, 62, 130, 147
Daniel, Theodore, 277
Daniels, J. W., 83, 163, 175

Dauskin, John M., 48
Davidson & Stoutemyer (attorneys), 235–36
Davies, Joshua, 59
Davies, Mr., *237*
Davis (councilman), 243
Davis (judge), 315
Davis, Thomas, 57, 60, 125, 128
Davis, Tom, 80, 256
Day, Mr. (Chicago), 208
De Quillfeldt, Charles, 37
Deed, R. H., 48
Democratic Party, 126–27, 299
depression of '73, 32, 63
Desert Land Act, 124, 241, 261
Deuel, Charles E., 155, 174, 197
Deutschtum, 232
Dewey, William, 71–72
"Dewey" (horse), 216
Dickinson, President, 68
Diehl, Jacob, 37
Dill, Riley E., 166
Dillon, Sidney, 65
discrimination, 5, 27, 35, 42, 46, 71, 112ro
Dixon, Jake, 12
Dobson, Lynn, 315
donations and charity work
  Boise Washington statue, 41
  Camas Prairie residents, 120
  Chicago fire victims, 28
  education support, 145
  Franco-Prussian War refugees, 24, 28
  homeless children, 258
  Idaho State Fairgrounds, 53
  Irish relief work, 53
  JL's legacy of, 276
  listing of, 332
  Memorial Day, 238
  for mining road, 202
  orphanage, 130, 134, 139, 149
  Placerville fire victims, 172
  San Francisco earthquake victims, 248
  St. Luke Hospital, 265
"Douglas" (horse), 216
Dowd (detective), 252
Dreamland Moving Picture Company, 204–5
Dressler (councilman), 218, 219
Driscoll, Emily L., 201
drug and alcohol abuse, 21, 262
Dry Creek Ditch Company, 85
dry goods store. *See* Lemp's Dry Goods Store
Dubois, Dr., 79
Dubois, George, 84, 176
Duffey, George, 227
Duillo mine, 35–36
Dun Mercantile Listings, 69, 154, 232
Dunbar (justice), 252, 263, 278
Dunbar, W. C., 223
Duncan, J. G., 76–77
Dunton, Herbert, 236
Dunton, W. H., 167
DuRell, B. M., 39–40

Eagle Rock (Idaho Falls) orphanage, 130, 134, 139, 149
Eagleson, Ernest G., 66, 305
Eagleson, John W., 171
Early, John, 22–23, 33, 55–56, 87, 129, 138, 151–53
Eastman, Hosea B., 51, 66, 85, 87
Eastman water works, 61, 69
education. *See* schools
Edwards, Joe, 52
Elam, Laurel, 312
Eldred, B. B., 145, 190mf
elections, 125–31. *See also* Boise City Council; Boise Mayor's Office
  Ada County, 12, 22, 40, 42, 46, 176, 263, 277
  advertising and publicity, 128

Boise school board, 48, 50, 91, 147, 154
conventions, 29, 40, 56, 72, 79, 91, 93, 157
Idaho State Treasurer, 122
laws and legislation, 263, 275, 305
primaries, 163, 215
special, 207
U.S. Congress, 78
Electric Light Company, 88
electricity, 80, 86
billiard hall, 143
railways, 125, 239
street lighting, 88, 133, 268–69
transom lighting, 213
Eliot, J. B., 77
Elkington, H. N., 200
Elks Lodge, 300, 303, 309, 312, 316
Elliot, J. B., 147
Elliot, Thomas, 48
Elliot, Wallace W., 71
Ellis, Lester W., 312
Ellis, Messer., 141
Ellsworth, C., 94
Ellsworth, H., 271
Elmira Company, 80
Elmore County, 166, 217, 232. *See also specific town or location*
Emerson, R. E., 208, *237*
Emery "old man," 52
employees. *See also* bartending
  accidents and injuries, 76, 78, 91, 94–95, 122, 169, 171–72, 207, 236, 250–51, 262
  Arc Light Saloon, 273
  blacksmiths, 250–51
  bookkeepers, 165, 176
  canal, 212
  Capitol Hotel, 123, 151, 169, 171, 205
  Centennial Brewery, 198
  coopers, 76–77
  crime and, 146, 156–57, 172–73,
173–74, 219, 273
  Falk Mercantile Company, 278
  farm, 171, 262
  as future brewers, 297
  H.F. Lemp Livestock Company, 304
  Idaho Brewing, 198, 276
  labor strikes, 135, 144, 242
  labor unions, 78, 144, 252
  land disputes, 140–42
  Lemp Development Company, 313
  Lemp's Dry Goods Store, 165, 169, 170, 171, 174, 176, 201–4, 220
  mining industry, 135, 136, 138, 242, 252
  office managers, 301
  Oregon Short Line (OSL), 316
  overall in Lemp businesses, 214
  ranch, 76, 121, 122, 129, 177–78, 215–16, 217, 228, 232, 255
  Ridenbaugh Canal Company, 212
  Settler's Canal (Lemp Canal), 200, 209–10, 212
  wagon drivers, 32–43, 69, 78, 79, 91, 94–95, 121, 122, 173
  Wheeler-Motter Store, 203
Enebo, Peter K., 165, 176
Englehardt, George, 34
Ensign, Lew W., 203
entertainment. *See also* celebrations; sports
  movies, 151, 204–5
  music, 130, 139, 176, 201
  television, 151
Eoff, Alfred, 262
Epstein (Fourth of July committee), 86
Equal Suffrage Club, 164
Europe, 4, 24–25, 26, 28, 156, 232
Evening Citizen (newspaper), 126–28
Everett, Mr., 208

Exchange Bar, 270

Faine, Syril E., 319
Fairplay mining claim, 236–37
Falk, David, 134–35, 163
Falk, Harry, 305
Falk, Leo J., 138, 278
Falk, Nathan, 237
  on Boise City Council, 155
  as bondsman, 172, 201
  clothing store, 66, 204, 278
  death of, 217, 232
  foundry investment, 128
  Jewish heritage, 112ro
  memberships, 208
  mining business, 88, 121–22, 134–38, 145, 147, 165, 190mf, 208, 217
  railroads and, 66, 68
  Vienna Exposition, 85
Falk, Rosa, 136, 138
Falk, Sigmund, 277
Falk Mercantile Company, 66, 204, 278
Falstaff beer, 273–75
farms and farming, 32, 78–79, 177–78, 276, 304, 306, 315. *See also* alfalfa; barley; fruit farming; hog farming; hops; ranches and ranching; sugar beets
Faust's art store, 258
Fennell, James, 316
Ferguson, Mrs., 266
fermentation, 30, 41
Field, Marshall, 95
Fifer, Charles, 200, 212
financial panics, 32, 37–38, 63, 67
Finnegan, Thomas, 93
fires and firefighting
  barns, 90
  Boise City Fire Department, 23, 37, 42, 55, 60, 94, 123, 309
  Cole's restaurant, 57–58

  downtown Boise, 52
  Exchange Bar, 270
  former Lemp billiard hall, 266
  Great Chicago fire, 28
  insurance for, 58, 240
  insurance maps, *160, 162, 273*
  Lemp brewery, 217, 221–23
  Lemp home, 166, 238
  Lemp Triangle, 246
  lumber mill/yard, 13, 221
  Pabst Brewing Company, 247–48
  Placerville, 172
  railroad, 58
  Red Light district, 239–40, 241
  saloon, 89
  schools, 260
  stable, 86
  Valley Hotel (Payette), 161
  water sources for fighting, 154
  wildfires, 246–47
  wooden building, 22–23
First Church of Christ Scientist, 309
First National Bank of Idaho, 39–40, 40–41, 44, 53, 61, 119
Fischer, Herman, 44
Fisher, W. E., 178
fishing. *See* hunting and fishing
Fletcher, George, 277
Fletcher, Steen, 312
flooding, 56–57, 145
Florence (ID), 27
Ford and Co., 15
Forney, S. W., 317–18
Fort Boise (ID), 8–9. *See also* Boise (ID)
Fortman, John, 13–14
Foster, Mabel. *See* Clark, Mabel (Foster)
foundries, 128–29
Franco-Prussian War, 24–25, 26, 28
Frawley (county attorney), 213

Friedman Company, 229
Fritsch, Albert, 143
Fritter, Barbara, 171
fruit farming, 60, 79, 254–55
Fulton, Harry W., 223, 224, 246
Funsten (bishop), 262, 275, 277, 300
Furnell, Helen, 266

G. & S. M., 77
Gable Iron & Steel Company, 95
Gabner, O. L., 57
Gamble, Mrs., 267
G.A.R. Hall, 210–11
Gardiner, Wilfred, 203
Gardner, Lucille (Weaver) (Lemp), 235. *See also* Lemp, Lucille (Weaver)
Gardner, Nate E., 235
Gariner, Mr., 74
Garland, Edwin, 316–17
Garrety, Elizabeth. *See* Kohlepp, Elizabeth (Garrety)
Gateley, J. P., 165
Gaumer, A. I., 58
Gem mine, 131
Gem Saloon, 51
General Pettit mine, 163
Gerdiner, H. L., 73
German American Alliance, 211
German Americans, 4–7, 15–16, 28, 210–11, 232, 300
German language, 32, 46
Germania Singing Society, 139
Germany
 beer brewing in, 5
 immigration from, 4–7, 15–16, 28
 Turnverein organizations, 16–17
Gibbard, William H., 209–10, 242
Gibbons, William, 137
Giffen, Professor, 49
Gillespie, Dr., 97q
Girard, Dr., 92
Glantzman, John, 236

Glenn, Earl, 315
Glorieux, A. J., 161, 212, 234
gold standard, 30–31, 147
Golden Rule store, 169
"Goldfoil" (horse), 46
Good (mayor), 218
Good Templar movement, 21–22
Gooding, Frank R., 236
Gooding, John M., 236
Gordon (lawsuit), 166–68
Goulder, W. A., 56–57, 259, 260
Graham, George, 217
Graham, Harry, 251
Graham, J. M., 215–16
Graham, W. A., 215–16
Graham mines, 92
Grand Prize mine, 79
Grant (soldier), 163–64
Grant, Angus Roderick
 accidents and injuries, 165
 business of, 144, 206, 207
 marriage of, 144, 161
 social life and travels, 198, 211, 215
Grant, Augusta Julia Margaret (Gussie) (Lemp)
 attends sister's funeral, 231
 birth of, 29
 census records, 54
 childhood, 42, 53, 55, 93
 death of, 301
 death of father, 275, 277
 death of mother, 255, 256
 donations and charity work, 145
 marriage of, 144, 161
 social life and travels, 155, 157, 165, 198, 250, 265, 266, 268, 273
 grasshopper plagues, 120
Gray, Ben R., 137
Gray, John P., 215, 234
Gray, John S., 163
Gray Swan mine, 211
Great War. *See* World War I

Greathouse, Henry, 28
Greathouse, Ridgeby, 13
Greeley, Horace, 27
Greely, Adolphus Washington, 74
Green, R. E., 212
Green Meadow Corral, 161
Greene, John, 210
Grey Wolf mine, 211
Grigsby, Hazel, 257, 267
Grossman, Alzena, 313
Grove Street home, *41, 44*
  building of, 34
  burglaries, 125
  directory listings for, 205, 269
  fires, 166, 238
  Statesman description of, 214
  trees, 232, 276
Grunbaum, Julius, 207
Grunbaum, Leo, 174, 201, 218
Gumbert, George, 147, 217–18
Gun Club, 249, 253
Gurtling, George, 13–14
Gwinn, M. B., 135

H. F. Lemp Livestock Company, 304
Hailey (ID), 143, 147, 214, 229, 235, 283en
  breweries in, 58, 69–70, 242, 256
  electricity, 86
  government and politics, 91, 258
  mining industry, 61, 72–73, 77, 91, 94, 134–38, 149, 154, 228–29
  railroad industry, 64–65, 69–70
  telephone service, 69–70, 205
Hailey, John, 90
Haines, John H., 244, 249, 256, 303
Haines, Mrs. J. H., 265
Hale, Mrs. Eugene, 266
Haley, Dr., 172
Halford, B. F., 242
Hall (carpenter), 59
Hammell, Messer., 141

Hancock Lode, 88
Hanna, J. L., 242
Hansen, Walter F., 308
Hanthorn, N. M., 47
Harmony Society, 17–18
Harris, Bert, 257
Harris, Fred, 263
Hart, Jimmy, 60
Hart, Len, 250
Hasbrouck, Sol, 14, 41
Haug, Bert, 257
Haug, Frank, Jr., 173
Haug, Nicholas, 44, 47, 87
Hawley, James H., 47, 150–51, 178, 219, 268, 304
Hayes (D.A.), 141
Haynes, John, 213
Haynes, Loyal M., 319
Haywood, Big Bill, 252
Hedden, Dudley, 144
Heed, Judge, 62
Heinen, John, 312
Helfrich, Marguerite, 267, 268
Hemmel, Mr., 120
Henchkel, D., 32
Henderson, S. T., 77
Henry, Charles B., 73, 74, 75–76
Herrick, T. M., 171, 211, 216, 230
Heskett, Zo, 165
Hesse, Con W., 253
Heuschel, Mrs., 211
Heyd, Louis, 17
H.F. Lemp Livestock Company, 304
Hickey, J. A., 67
Hihn, Frederick "Dutch Fred," 59–60
Hildebrandt, Herman, 45
Hilt, George, 250
Himrod, Charley, 22, 24, 37, 51, 256, 277
Hirschburg, Peter, 305
Historical Society of Idaho

Pioneers, 155
History of Idaho, The (Hawley), 178, 304
History of Idaho Territory, The (Elliot), 71
Hodges, Arthur, 301, 303
hog farming, 41, 79, 155, 262
"Hogan"/Jimmy, 232
Hollister, Bishopric & Co., 94, 95
Holton, Dr., 140
Home Guard, 45
Hopper, Angela, 306
hops, 55, 157
horses. *See also under* accidents and injuries
  awards, 214, 227, 233
  blacksmiths, 250–51
  health of, 89, 216
  horseracing, 33, 38, 40, 42, 45–46, 52, 53, 77–78
  polo, 271–73, 303–4, 305–6, *307,* 308, 312
  wagon drivers, 32–43, 69, 78, 79, 91, 94–95, 121, 122, 173
Hot Lake (OR), 262
House, Frank G., 276
Howlett, S. R., 53
Howrie, Sam, 125
Hudson, W. H., 69
Hughes, Harry M., 234
Hummel, C., 211, 256, 303
Humphrey, C. B., 58
hunting and fishing
  fishing excursions, 166, 270
  frog hunting, 257
  HFL and, 303
  hunting excursions, 62, 93, 240
  on ranches, 129, 255, 257, 260
  women and, 129
Huntoon, John, 48
Hurd, James, 14, 98aj
Hurt, Ada Anna (Lemp), *39, 43*
  attends sister's funeral, 231
  birth of, 33
  census records, 177
  childhood, 55, 77, 147, 149
  JL's estate, 277
  marriages of, 159, 316–17
  social life and travels, 154, 198
Hurt, Edwin G., 159, 171, 212, 230
Huston, J.W., 65, 159
Hutchin, O. R., 46
Hutchins, Thurston, 169
Hyatt, Bryon E., 316
Hygh, Charley, 215–16

I. X. L. Grocery, 171
ice industry
  accidents and injuries, 78
  advertising and publicity, 30
  affects of weather on, 177
  in Boise, 26
  competition in, 158
  fires, 221, 226, 227
  harvesting of, 27, 30, 44, 53, 63, 78, 89, 119, 132, 144
  health related conditions in, 299
  man-made ice, 177
  new equipment, 46, 146, 177
  refrigeration and, 129
Idaho. *See also specific town or location*
  government and politics in, 51, 91, 93
  JL's daughter named after, 33
  map of, *2*
  number of breweries in, 54–55, 119
  origins of, 8–9, 122
  petition for military road in, 43
  population, 15, 54–55
Idaho Agricultural Park Association, 38, 43, 53, 58, 60
Idaho Brewing and Malting Company, 198, 238, 240, 254
Idaho Central Railway, 67

Idaho City (ID)
lawsuits, 10
mining industry, 10, 79, 87
name of, 96m
Odd Fellow meeting, 78
railroad industry, 65
telephone service, 205
temperance movement, 21–22
Wirtz estate, 216–17
Idaho Falls orphanage, 130, 134, 139, 149
Idaho Farms Company, 315
Idaho Gold and Silver Mining Company, 92, 129
Idaho Historical Society, 319
Idaho Life Insurance Company, 304
Idaho Midland Securities, 176–77
Idaho Mining and Smelting Company, 36
Idaho & Oregon Railway Company, 65–68
Idaho State Bimetallic League, 147
Idaho State Brewers Association, 258
Idaho State Constitutional Convention, 93, 242
Idaho State Fair, 132–33, 166, 209, 227, 230, 233
Idaho State Governor's Office, 48
Idaho State Life Insurance Company, 268
Idaho State Secretary, 48
Idaho State Sportsman's Association, 253
Idaho State Supreme Court
Gibbard *vs.* Lemp, 209–10
Lemp Triangle, 301–3
Lemp *vs.* Connor, 164, 166–68
Lemp *vs.* Pence, 150–51
liquor laws, 253, 255
local elections, 305
Morris *vs.* Lemp, 235–36

Settler's Canal (Lemp Canal), 251–52
Idaho State Treasury, 122
Idaho Trust and Savings Company, 235, 251–52
immigration, 4–7, 15–16, 28
Independent Order of Odd Fellows (IOOF). *See* Odd Fellows (IOOF)
Indian wars, 38–39, 46. *See also* Bannock Indian War; Nez Perce War
infrastructure, 85. *See also* electricity; roads and streets; sewer systems; transportation; water and water rights
insurance
fire, 58, 240
fire maps, 160, 162, *273*
life, 38, 70, 73, 153, 156, 174
International Mining Congress, 206–7
International Shoe Company (St. Louis), 319
inventions
"crown top" bottle closure, 144
fruit dryer, 60
lightening stopper, 37
investment strategies, 14, 28, 81, 201
Ireland, 53
"Ironclad" claim, 88, 121–22
irrigation, 63, 80–84, 201, 212, 249
IRS (U.S. Internal Revenue Service), 138
Isell, Marshall, 90
Island ranch, 59, 255

J. E. Tourtelotte & Co., 258
Jacobs, Cyrus, 58, 64–65
Jacobs Canal Company, 80
Jahn, Frederick Ludwig, 17
James, W., 20

Jaumann, Martha Elizabeth (Eliza) (Lemp). *See* Wolters, Martha Elizabeth (Eliza) (Lemp) (Jaumann) (sister)
Jaumann, Minnie, 54, 61
Jaumann, Rankin V., 189kn
Jaumann, William H.
  census records, 54
  death of, 158–59, 189kn
  political life, 127
  saloon business, 58, 69
  social life and travels, 29, 93, 124–25
J.B. White Drugstore, 94
Jeanette (steamer), 74
Jenkins, West, 12
Jenning, Isaac, 136
Jensen, Peter, 141, 142
Jewish residents, 112ro, 148, 173
Jimmy/"Hogan," 232
Johnson, F. F., 312
Johnson, Richard Z., 51, 128, 142
Jones, D. H., 300
Jones, Joel M., 77
Julia Davis Park, 256
Jung, Anna Elizabeth. *See* Lemp, Anna Elizabeth (Jung)
Jung, Anna Elizabeth (Jung) (mother), 5
Jung, Hanns, 5
jury duty
  District, 145, 328
  Grand, 27, 32, 44, 47, 53, 150, 328
  meals for, 159
  Territorial, 328

Kaffen, C., 211
Kahn (city attorney), 243
Kahn (councilman), 242
Kane, J. J., 142
Kane, Tom, 94
Kansas, 6, 21
Kaufer, C. E., 211
Keane, John, 172–73
Keegan, Frances, 211–12
Keegan, John, 211–12
Kelley, T. P., 161
Kellogg, Messr., 28
Kelly, Lois, 133
Kelly, Milton, 66, 121, 133
Kent, Messer., 141
Kentucky, 6, 33, 56
Keohler, Louis, 210
Kessberger, Edward H., 197–98, 212, 231
Kessberger, Ida Catherine (Lemp), *39, 43, 199*
  birth of, 33
  census records, 54, 177
  childhood, 77
  death of, 231
  marriage of, 197–98, 212
  social life and travels, 155, 161, 165, 166, 214, 215, 230
Khortz, Miss, 268
Kimberly, Louis A., 49
"King" (horse), 46
"King's Pride" (horse), 216
Kingsbury, W. S., 242
Kingsley (register), 142
Klein, Otto, 254
Kline, Jennie (Leyerzapf), 54, 212, 238
Kline, Martin, 212
Klinge, Jennie, 238
Klinge, M., 210
Knights Templar, 153, 275, 277, 298
Know Nothings, 6
Knox, Douglas, 47
Koehler, Charles, 211
Koelsch (attorney), 253
Koelsch (judge), 174, 242
Koelsch, Charles, 251
Koenig, Joseph, 71–72
Koeninger, Robert, 26, 176

Kohlberg, Gus, 20
Kohlepp, Catherine (Kate). *See* Lemp, Catherine (Kate) (Kohlepp) (wife)
Kohlepp, Elizabeth (Garrety), 72, 73, 86–87, 177, 253
Kohlepp, George (son of George), 56, 62, 177
Kohlepp, George (son of William)
  brewery business, 69, 297
  death of wife and child, 62
  horse racing, 38, 46
  immigration of, 15–16
  JL and, 143, 172, 264
  land dispute, 141
  marriages of, 53, 72, 86–87, 138, 253
  mining business, 72–73, 134
  political life, 42, 51
  social life and travels, 46, 47, 85
  Stadtmiller and, 58
Kohlepp, Henry, 129, 253–54
Kohlepp, Lena (Brodbeck), 53, 62
Kohlepp, Martha E., 15, 57
Kohlepp, Mary, 15–16
Kohlepp, Mattie, 121
Kohlepp, Sarah M. (Beck), 138
Kohlepp, William, 10, 15, 19, 27
Kohny, Albert B., 49, 236
Konrad, Henry, 211
Korts, Lennie, 267
Krall, Emma, 61
Krall, John
  brewery business of, 10–11, 15, 22, 98ap, 207
  foundry investment, 128
  fruit business of, 79
  ice industry and, 27
  joins Home Guard, 45
  memberships of, 18
  mining industry, 132
Kroeger, Gustave, 18, 263
Kurs, Ben, 210

La Chappelle, Anna L. *See* Clark, Anna L. (La Chappelle)
labor strikes, 135, 144
labor unions, 78, 144, 252
Lady Franklin Bay Expedition, 75–76
lager beer, 157–58
Lakotah Indians, 38–39
Lamb, Virgil, 48
land patents. *See also* mineral patents; property purchases and sales
  of ACL, 304
  Ada County, 28
  Boise County, 132
  Canyon County, 124, 153–54, 241
  Custer County, 197
  of J.C. Pence, 140
  of JL and CL, 265–66
  Lemp Triangle and, 243
Langdon, Kathryn (Lemp), 88, 182df
Largilliere, August, 26
Latham (councilman), 219
Latimer, James, 257
laws and legislation. *See also* Prohibition
  Barefoot Schoolboy Law, 147
  Black Law, 273
  building codes, 241–42, 264
  cash sale law (1820), 28, 132
  crime, 30–31
  elections, 263, 275, 305
  gold standard, 30–31
  land, 28, 124, 150, 241, 260
  local option, 261, 263, 275
  martial law, 131–32
  mining, 121–22, 145, 197
  refusal to grant liquor licenses, 255
  sale of liquor in the Red Light District, 162

sale of liquor near public works, 253
sale of liquor to minors, 172–73
schools, 51, 147
Sunday laws, 130, 219–20, 238–39
tax, 15, 29, 30
lawsuits, 328–30
ACL divorce, 230
BLL vs. Idaho Farms Company, 315
Bogart vs. JL, 123, 161–63
Boise City Irrigation Canal and Land Company vs. JL et al, 212
Boise City Railway & Terminal Company vs. JL et al, 234
bottling industry, 303
Capitol Hotel, 171
elections, 305
Fritter vs. JL, 171
Gibbard vs. JL, 209–10
HFL vs. Austin, 263
HFL vs. Western Bottling and Packing Company, 303
Idaho City (ID), 10
JL vs. Anderson, 209
JL vs. Bairs, 94
JL vs. Bane, 166
JL vs. Biggerstaff, 133
JL vs. Breck, 46
JL vs. Brockbank, 136, 164
JL vs. Butler, 149
JL vs. Connor, 164
JL vs. Fritsch, 143
JL vs. Idaho Gold and Silver Mining Company, 92, 129
JL vs. Keegan, 211–12
JL vs. Maxon, 85
JL vs. Moudy, 63
JL vs. Oldham, 43
JL vs. Olson, 55
JL vs. Riggs, 120
JL vs. Schaffer, 72
JL vs. Sparber, 236
Jones vs. JL, 77
Kohlepp divorce, 86–87
Kohlepp vs. Lemp, 172, 264
Lemp (St. Louis) divorce, 261
Lemp Triangle, 301–3
Lemp-Pence war, 140–42, 150–51
Medosh vs. JL, 171
mining, 136–37
Morris vs. Lemp, 235–36
People vs. John Lemp (1873), 30
Rankin vs. Jaumann, 189kn
Richards/Gordon et al vs. JL/Connor, 164, 166–68
Russell vs. JL, 163, 175
Sabin vs. JL/Early, 151–53
Settler's Canal (Lemp Canal), 82–83, 163, 212, 251–52
State of Idaho vs. Lemp, 170
Stuzernacker divorce, 14
United States vs. John Lemp, 70
Lawton & Torrence, 77
LDS Church, 227
Leeds, Messer., 141
Lemp, Ada Anna (daughter). *See* Hurt, Ada Anna (Lemp)
Lemp, Albert Carl (son), 43, 47, 169, 172
administers GWL's estate, 174
birth of, 40
brewing business, 214, 229
census records, 54, 177, 265, 315
childhood, 90–91, 92, 139
death of, 315
divorce of, 230
draft registration, 299–300
fines paid, 270
home of, 205
land patents, 304
Lemp's Dry Goods Store, 171
marriages of, 178, 197, 212, 230, 315
mining business, 137
on new municipal water system,

206
political life, 215
Polk City Directory listing for, 269
social life and travels, 166
as surety, 201
thwarts robbery attempt, 164–65
Lemp, Anna Elizabeth (Jung), 5, *43*, 170
Lemp, Augusta Julia Margaret (Gussie) (daughter). *See* Grant, Augusta Julia Margaret (Gussie) (Lemp)
Lemp, Bernard Louis (son), *43*, 85
attends presidential inauguration, 236
birth of, 84
businesses of, 315
census records, 177
childhood, 171, 178, 206, 207
children of, 265, 315–16, *317*
on closing of Capital State Bank, 256
death of, 315–16
draft registration, 299–300
EHL's estate, 300–301
JL's estate, 277–78
marriage of, 206, 248
Polk City Directory listing for, 269
Lemp, Bernard Louis, Jr. (grandson), 265, 315–16
Lemp, Caroline (Carrie) (Zeltman), 139, 155–56, 172
Lemp, Catherine (granddaughter), 309
Lemp, Catherine (Kate) (Kohlepp) (wife). *See also* Grove Street home
appears in sewing ad, 94
census records, 15, 21, 54, 177
childhood and family of, *15*–16, 98av
death of, 98av, 255–56
equal suffrage rights, 164
land patent filed, 265–66
marriage of, 16, 98aw
mining business, 136, 154
sister of, 34
social life and travels, 29–30, 93, 129, 145, 147–48, 150, 153, 155, 161, 169, 207
World's Fair contribution, 146
Lemp, Clarence J., 177, 236, 265, 300
Lemp, Edna (granddaughter), 315, *317*
Lemp, Edward H. (Eddie) (son)
accidents and injuries, 212–13
census records, 177, 265
childhood, 171, 172, 198, 207
death of, 300–301
JL's estate, 277
Polk City Directory listing for, 269
social life and travels, 250, 254
Lemp, Elisabetha, 5
Lemp, Frederick, 229
Lemp, George Tucker (grandson), 315
Lemp, George William Jacob (son), *22*, *33*
accidents and injuries, 170
birth of, 18
census records, 21, 54
childhood, 53, 61, 70
death of, 174, 275
land dispute, 141
manages Lemp farm, 171
social life and travels, 166
Lemp, Harold, 265
Lemp, Herbert Frederick (son), *43*, 75, 301–13, *307*, *311*
attends Idaho State Fair, 230
attends sister's funeral, 231
baseball and, 236, 238
birth of, 70
brewery business, 220, 223, 226, 227
business career, 204, 268, *302*, 303

census records, 177
children of, 251, 257, 317–19
death of, 306–13
directory listings, 304
draft registration, 300
EHL's estate, 300–301
gun club, 249, 253
home of, 270–71
on JL's building plans, 265
JL's estate, 277–78, 304
jury duty, 252
lawsuits, 263, 303
legacy of, 309–13
marriage of, 248–49
political life, 250, 251, 257, 271, 275, 299, 304, 305, 309–11
Polk City Directory listing for, 269
polo interests, 271–73, 303–4, 305–6, 312
resume, *302,* 303
social life and travels, 240, 262, 268, 270, 273
writings about, 304, 305
Lemp, Ida Catherine (daughter). *See* Kessberger, Ida Catherine (Lemp)
Lemp, Jacob (brother), 26
  brewery business, 297
  census records, 54, 85
  children of, 265
  death of, 161
  immigration of, 5, 28
  JL's business partner, 36
  marriage of, 85
  mining business, 36
  participates in raffle, 47
  in Payette (ID), 80, 85
Lemp, Johann Adam (brother), 5
Lemp, Johann Adam (cousin), 6–7
Lemp, Johann Konrad, 5, 233
Lemp, John, *4, 237,* 326–36. *See also* Grove Street home
  accidents and injuries, 44, 79, 197, 201, 205, 206, 212–13
  accused of stealing, 251
  birth of, 6
  birthday celebrations, 139, 145
  Bradstreet's Commercial Reports listing, 94
  census records of, 6, 21, 54, 177, 265
  death of, 275–79
  descendants named John, *300*
  Dun Mercantile Listing, 69, 154, 232
  early life, 5–10
  estate and will of, 21, 28, 38, 51, 71, 88, 147, 168, 170, 206, 232, 270, 276, 277–78, 323–25
  health of, 44, 57, 62, 73, 92, 129, 144, 161, 163, 170, 172, 173, 234, 236, 250, 251, 252, 262, 299
  immigration of, 4–6
  interviews with, 69–70
  investment strategies, 14, 28, 81, 201
  legacy of, 3–5, 276, 297–319
  marriage of, 15–16, 98aw
  Polk City Directory listing, 269
  religious affiliations, 299, 332–33
  stories and lore about, 58–59
  streets named after, *277, 298*
  writings about, 71, 137–38, 153–54, 174, 201, 214, 228, 259–60, 275
Lemp, John (descendant), *300*
Lemp, John, Jr. (grandson), *300*
  birth of, 251
  childhood, 269
  death of, 317–19
Lemp, John Emil (son), *19, 33*
  birth of, 16, 18
  census records, 21, 54
  childhood, 53, 92, 93, 121
  children of, 314
  death of, 155–56, 275

marriage of, 139, 149
revolver owned by, *157*
Lemp, John Frederick (grandson), *300*
  birth of, 149
  childhood, 150, 172
  death of, 314
  JL's estate, 277
  military service, 156
Lemp, John Frederick, Jr. (great-grandson), 314
Lemp, John Jacob (father), 5
Lemp, John Louis, *300*
Lemp, Julia (sister). *See* Leyerzapf, Julia (Jennie) (Lemp)
Lemp, Julia (St. Louis), 248
Lemp, Karl, *43*
Lemp, Katherine/Kathyrn Ida (granddaughter)
  birth of, 211
  childhood, 217, 266, 267
  divorce of parents, 230
Lemp, Krall & Co., 10–11
Lemp, Leona Caroline (Tucker), 206, 248, 265, 315–16, *317*
Lemp, Leona Marie (granddaughter), 315, 316, *317*
Lemp, Lillian (Mrs. Albert C.), 315
Lemp, Lillian (Mrs. Wm J., Jr. of St. Louis), 261
Lemp, Louise Bernice (daughter). *See* Simonson, Louise Bernice (Lemp)
Lemp, Lucille (Weaver). *See also* Gardner, Lucille (Weaver) (Lemp)
  divorce of, 230
  health of, 227
  marriage to ACL, 178, 197, 230, 315
  mining business, 211
  social life and travels, 214, 217, 230

Lemp, Margarethe (sister). *See* Bach, Margarethe (Lemp) (sister)
Lemp, Marguerite Ann (Nolan)
  children of, 251, 257, 313
  death of, 313
  marriage to HFL, 248–49, 308
  social life and travels, 265, 266, 270, 273
Lemp, Maria Elisabetha, 5
Lemp, Marie Anna (daughter), 129, *131*, 132, 147
Lemp, Martha Elizabeth (Eliza) (sister). *See* Wolters, Martha Elizabeth (Eliza) (Lemp) (Jaumann) (sister)
Lemp, Martha Elizabeth (Lizzie) (daughter). *See* Connor, Martha Elizabeth (Lizzie) (Lemp)
Lemp, Mary (Stirm), 85, 161
Lemp, Mary Catherine (granddaughter), 257, 265, 313, *318*
Lemp, Susanna, 5
Lemp, William (NY), 233
Lemp, William Adam (son)
  birth of, 51
  census records, 54
  death of, 59, *64*, 275
Lemp, William J. (St. Louis), 7, 11, 52, 131, 229, 248
Lemp, William J., Jr. (St. Louis), 229, 261
Lemp Addition, 145, 201, 208
Lemp Block, *160*, 276
Lemp brewery (Boise)
  closing of, 217–27
  fires, 217, 221–23
  maps of, 162, 222, 274
  photo of, *226*
Lemp Brewery (St. Louis). *See* William J. Lemp Brewing Co. (St. Louis)
Lemp Canal, 82, 198, 209, 210, 212, 229. *See also* Settler's Canal

(Lemp Canal)
Lemp & Co.
advertising and publicity, 14, 20, 21
brewery additions, 14
fires, 13, 22–23
profits and revenues, 13, 14
tax records, 10–11
Lemp Co-Operative Lateral Co. Ltd., 242
Lemp Development Company, 313
Lemp Lane, *277*
Lemp Livestock Company, 304
Lemp Park, 260–61
Lemp Street, *298*
"Lemp Town," 201
Lemp Triangle, 243–47, *245*, 248, 301–3, 312
Lemp's canal. *See* Settler's Canal (Lemp Canal)
Lemp's Dry Goods Store, 201–5
address, 205
advertising and publicity, 166, *200*, 201–4, *203*
business listings of, 232
contests, 201, 203, 204
donation for mining road, 202
employees, 165, 169, 170, 171, 174, 176, 201–2, 220
free lunches for customers, 202
liquidation of, 204
music concerts, 176, 201
origins of, 164
profits and revenues, 174, 204
shoplifting, 164–65
Lemp's Extra Pale Beer (St. Louis), 273–75
"Lemp's Island Ranch," 58–59
Len, Bob, 69
Leonard, E. R., 153
Leonard, J. C., 70
Leonardson, R. D., 312

Lewis, William, 84, 176
Lewis and Clark Exposition, 238, 240
Leyerzapf, Anne (Annie), 54, 212, 231, 238
Leyerzapf, Charles (Carl), 54, 69, 73, 124, 210, 238, 271
Leyerzapf, Christina, 74
Leyerzapf, Conrad, 73
Leyerzapf, Ernest, 73
Leyerzapf, George, 73–76, *75*
Leyerzapf, Jennie. *See* Kline, Jennie (Leyerzapf)
Leyerzapf, Julia (Jennie) (Lemp), 5, *23*, 54, 73, 170, 276
Leyerzapf, Lena, 54
Leyerzapf, Lizzie, 54
Leyerzapf, Phillip, 73
libraries, 237
life insurance, 38, 70, 73, 153, 156, 174
Light Company, 159
lighting. *See* electricity
Lincoln, Abraham, 8
Lincoln Public School, 173, 217–27, *222*, 274
liquor house/store, 44, 52, 59, *71*, 165, 174
liquor industry. *See also* laws and legislation; saloon business
competition in, 158
licensing, 219, 237, 263
prices, 29, 56
taxes, 15, 29, 30
training for, 297
Little, Andrew, 31
Little Big Horn, 38–39
livestock industry
cattle business, 28, 130, 169, 217, 232, 269, 304, 315
hogs, 41, 79, 155, 262
Local Option law, 261, 263, 275
Locke (magistrate), 219, 220

Locke, B. F., 169
Lockwood, James, 75
Logan (councilman), 218
Logan, Thomas E., 37, 48, 59, 64–65
Logus, Walter, 173
Lomkin, Harry, 49
Lomkin, Merritt, 49
Long, Robert F., 216
Lord Gage barley, 37
Louisa Lode, 138, 145, 165
Louisville (KY), 6
Lowe, Audrey, 267, 268
Lowe, Richard, 53
Lubkin, Mr., 58
Lucille mine, 211
Lucky Peak Dam, 84
Lugenbeel, Pinkney, 8
Luney, M. G., 48
Lusk, James R., 159, 236
Lusk, Minnie, 159

Magnetic Iuso Mine, 36
Magruder, Dr., 306
Maine, 22
Mallard Duck mine, 211
Mallon, Carl, 26
Maloney, Johnny, 256
Mandell, Frank C., 137
"Market"/"The Market," 175, 208
martial law, 131–32
Martin, W. C., 137
Martin O'Farrell & Brothers, 56
Masonic Lodge, 16–18, 34, 42, 56, 275, 276, 298, 309
Massachusetts, 22
Maxgut, Rupert, 198, 210, 211
Maxon, Arabella C., 85
Maxon, Hamilton J. G., 85
May, Charles, 48
Mayer, W. A., 147
Mayer, William, 54
Mayfield, Max, 172, 201

McAuley, E. H., 244–46
McCarty, J. H., 48
McCarty, Mr., 246
McConnell, William, 163
McDevitt, John, 316
McDonald, Harry, 207
McGee, J. A., 67
McGuffin, William, 277
McHendry, Al, 58
McHenry, Thomas, 27
McIntyre, Mr., 124
McKean, J., 57
McKennon, Pearl, 169
McKinnell, Charles L., 233
McLean, J. W., 241
McLennan, Donald G., 319
McMillan, John, 234
McMillan, Tom, 312
McMullen, Dave, 251–52
McNamara, John, 77
Medosh, Mary, 171
Meffert, C. C., 47
Meinke, Robert, 97q
Mendenhall, Mrs., 266
Meridian Irrigation District, 84
Meyers, John, 141, 142
Middle Slough, 63
Middleton (ID), 37, 54, 78, 80–81, 133
Middleton ranch
  accidents and injuries, 76, 170
  employees, 76, 170, 174, 216
  fires, 90
  horses at, 216
  hunting on, 129, 255
  Lemp Park, 261
  property value, 254
"Midget" (horse), 312
Miller, Joe, 80
Miller, O. L., 132
Mills, J., 209
Mineral Hill Mining District, 136
Mineral Patent-Lode Act of 1866,

121–22, 145, 197
  mineral patents, 333–34
  Blaine County, 121–22, 145
  Canyon County, 124
  the Centre, 147
  Concordia, 121–22
  "Ironclad," 88, 121–22
  Louisa Lode, 145
  "Star Quartz Lode," 134
  "Washington," 217
  mining industry, 6–10. *See also specific mine or location*
  brewery industry and, 297, 298
  employees, 135, 136, 138, 242, 252
  International Mining Congress, 206–7
  mining roads, 202, 212
  mining wars, 171
  monetary standards and, 30–31, 147
  organizations for, 147
  promotion of, 130
Minneapolis Brewing Association, 157
"Minnie Clay" (horse), 42
Mint Saloon, 251
Misseldt, Agatha, 44
Misseldt, Joseph, 15, *21*, 22, 42, 44
Misseldt, Mrs., 30
Missouri City (MO), 7
Mitchell, William L., 319
Mobley, Robert, 277
Mohr, Mrs., 85
money standards, 30–31, 147
Montana, 7–8
Moore, Asa, 41
Moore, Christopher W., 39–40, 48, 51, 128
Moore, Clinton H., 48, 50
Mops, John, 45
Morehouse, Miss, 267
Morgan, Waldo J., 172
Moritz, August J., 156, 210

Moritz, Moses, 17
Morris, Elias, 135, 136
Morris, Jack, 94–95
Morris, John, 235–36
Morris, William B., 47, 80–81
Morris Hill Cemetery, 300, 312
Morrison and Pence (attorneys), 210, 235–36
Moseley (sheriff), 156–57
Moudy, E., 63
Mountain Home, 92, 94, 167, 169, 185fk, 217, 232
movies, 151, 204–5
mugwumps, 122
Mullin, James, 252, 291oh
Muntzer, Henry, 178–79, 198, 205
music, 130, 139, 176, 201
Myers, Julius, 266
Mystic Shrine. *See* Shriners

Nagel, John, 210
"Nancy Brown" (horse), 216
National Baseball League, 62
National Irrigation Congress, 249
Native Americans, 269
Natorium, 128
Neal, B. F., 257
Neal, Miss, 230
Neiberding, H., 205
Neilley & Co, 58
Nelson, John, 209
Neptune (ship), 75–76
Neth, Peter, 54, 78
Nevada, 35, 54, 55
New Idaho Mining Exchange, 164
New York
  brewery industry, 54, 55
  Lemp family immigration via, 4, 6, 7, 15, 28
New York Canal, 177
Nez Perce War, 41–42, 45
Nichols, A. E., 136
Niederweisel, Germany, 4, 5

Nolan, Marguerite Ann. *See* Lemp, Marguerite Ann (Nolan)
Nolan, Mary Ellen, 313
"Norma" (horse), 45
North Carolina, 55
North Dakota, 95
North German Lloyd Steamship Company, 233
North Pole, 74–76
Northern Pacific Railway, 63–64
Notus (ID), 201
Nourse, Frank, 121
Nugent, E., 150, 151

O'Connor, Mabel, 201
O'Connor, Mrs. (sister 1), 267
O'Connor, Mrs. (sister 2), 268
Odd Fellows (IOOF), 16–18, *17*, 47, 55, 208
  anniversaries of, 256, 257
  article about, 146
  brewers as, 299
  builds Eagle Rock (Idaho Falls) orphanage, 130, 134, 139, 149
  JL elected "C.P.," 40
  JL elected treasurer, 16, 28, 34, 52, 63, 70, 72, 80, 88, 122–23, 130, 143, 149
  JL honored, 233
  JL installed "second W," 42
  JL's funeral, 275, 276, 277
  temperance movement and, 228
O'Grady, Thomas, 163–64
Ohio Lode, 134, 138, 145, 165, 190mf
"Old Capitol" (horse), 216
"Old Hickory" saloon, 248, 263
Old Ironside mine, 230
"old man Emery," 52
Olden, B. F., 198, 200, 212
Oldham, J. B., 43, 47
Oliver, Mae, 201
Olson, Peter, 55

Orchard, Harry, 242
Oregon, 55
Oregon Railway & Navigation Company, 64
Oregon Short Line (OSL), 64, 65–68, 88, 165, 256, 316
Oregon Trail, 8
orphanage, 130, 134, 139, 149
Ostheimer, Julius, 18
Ostner, Ed, 271, 272, 305, 312
Overland Hotel, 230
O.W. R. Manufacturing Company (Portland), 144
Owyhee Avalanche (newspaper), 35
Owyhee Hotel, 268, 273

Pabst, Frederick, 229
Pabst Brewing Company, 146, 247–48
Pacific National Bank of Boise, 304
Paine & Adelmann Saloon, 46–47
Painter, William, 144
Parker, M. S., 224–25
parks, 41, 243–47, 256, 257, 260–61
Parson, Frank H., 229, 277
Parsons, George M., 200
pasteurization, 30, 40, 70
patents (inventions), 37, 60, 144. *See also* land patents; mineral patents
Patteg, David C., 95
Patterson, Messr., 165
Paul, Phillip, 42–43, 76
Paulson, Thomas, 10
Pavey, Charles C., 228
Pavy, Dr., 76
Paxton, Mr., 42
Payette (ID), 80, 85, 161, 207
Pearson, Frank, 35
Pefferlee, Mr., 58
Pefly, P. J., 46, 51

Pence, J. C., 140–42, 150–51, 185fk, 187iu, 210, 235–36, 244, 246
Pence, J. T., 262
Pence, Mrs. J. C., 187iu
Perkins, Mr., 176
Perrault, Joseph, 53, 61, 133, 139, 234
Perry, A. L., 170
Peters, J. H., 204
petitions, 43, 57, 123, 155, 207, 209, 241
Pettingill, Ben, 240
Phelps, Charles, 249
Phylls Canal, 212
Pierce, Mrs. Georgia, 304
Pierce, Walter E., 143, 237, 251, 278, 301, 303. *See also* W. E. Pierce and Co.
pigs. *See* hog farming
Pinchot, Mr., 232
Pinkham, F. J., 304
Pinkham, Joseph, 122, 163, 256
Pinney, C. W., 137, 240
Pinney, James Alonzo, 62, 127, 266, 303
Pioneer Cemetery, *64*, 161, 255–56, 260, 277, *278*, 300, 314
Pioneers. *See* Boise Pioneer Association
Placerville (ID), 172, 238, 316
Plaisted, Frank H., 236
Plouhead Market, 235
Plummer, W. S., 60
political affiliations, 299. *See also specific party*
political conventions. *See* Republican conventions
Polk City Directory, 269
polo, 271–73, 303–4, 305–6, *307*, 308, 312
population, 15, 54–55
Populist movement, 164
Porch, Paul K., 319

Porcupine mine, 211
porcupines, 177–78
Post, John, 61
Post Office, 154, 201
postmaster, 154
Price, Lyttleton, 208
prices
  beer, 28, 29, 143
  liquor, 29, 56
Prickett, Henry E., 63, 77, 301
production capacity, 10–11, 14–15, 71, 214, 240
profits and revenues. *See also* taxes
  Boise Rapid Transit Company, 228
  brewery industry, 13, 41, 69
  canal system, 81
  hog farming, 41
  investment strategies, 14, 28, 81, 201
  Lemp & Co., 13, 14
  Lemp's Dry Goods Store, 174, 204
  Prohibition, 21–22, 95, 128, 149. *See also* temperance movement
property assessments and values
  decreasing, 270
  highest, 147
  increasing, 119
  JL's, 170, 206, 214, 232, 256, 270, 277–78
  property purchases and sales, 334–36. *See also* land patents; lawsuits; mineral patents
  to C. P. Rader, 214
  Canyon County, 124, 153–54, 241
  cash sale law (1820), 28, 132
  city park, 121
  delinquent assessment sale, 253
  Desert Land Act, 124, 241, 261
  to Fong Suey, 206
  to Idaho Trust and Savings Company, 235
  to Jacob Diehl, 37

to John C. Broadbent, 88, 231–32
to John P. Gray, 215
Lemp addition, 145, 201, 208
Lemp Park, 260–61
Lemp to Daly, 242
Lemp to McLean, 241
Lemp Triangle, 243–47, 245, 248, 301–3, 312
Leyerzapf to Klinge and Leyerzapf, 238
Locust Grove addition, 242
"Market"/"The Market," 175, 208
offers of, 119, 175
Oldham foreclosure, 43
to P. J. Pefly, 46
to Riley E. Dill, 166
for South Mountain brewery, 35, 36
to Western Surety and Trust Company, 207–8
Wolters, 229, 283en
property taxes
cattle business and, 217
delinquent, 170, 173, 253
highest, 51, 88, 206, 234, 240–41, 256
increases in, 217, 254
rebates, 210
special assessments, 228, 229, 233, 248, 250
Prossner, E. E., 90
Proteus (ship), 74–76
public education. *See* schools
publicity. *See* advertising and publicity
Purcell, Mrs., 263
Purdum, Adolphus, 81
Purdum, Christian R., 81
Purdy, O. H., 48
Pursell, Helen, 267
Pyles, P. A., 204

Quarles (justice), 168

Quilliam, L. R., 308

R. G. Dun Mercantile Listings, 69
Rader, C. P., 214
railroad industry, 63–68. *See also* telegraph; *specific railroad line*
Boise to Butte, 132
depression of '73 and, 32
electrification of, 125, 239
fires, 58
freight costs, 131
origin of, 19
shipping and, 40
time zones and, 131
Rainer beer, 149
ranches and ranching. *See also* horses; Middleton ranch
Boise River, 143
cattle business, 28, 130, 169, 217, 232, 269, 304, 315
Crane Gulch, 215–16
employees, 76, 121, 122, 129, 177–78, 215–16, 217, 228, 232, 255
fires, 90
hunting on, 129, 255, 257, 260
Island ranch, 59, 255
"Lemp's Island Ranch," 58–59
Mountain Home, 217
porcupine intruder, 177–78
Randall (magistrate), 144
Randall, Theo., 66
Ray, Mr., 205
Red Fox mine, 211
Red Light district (Boise), 239–40, 262
Reed, R. B., 58
refrigeration, 40, 54, 129
Regan, Alvin, 277
Regan, Tim, 171, 239, 256
Reiniger, Henry, 26
religion/religious affiliations, 112ro, 148, 173, 231, 299, 308, 312, 332–33

Republican Central Committee, 40, 45, 89, 122
Republican conventions, 29, 40, 56, 72, 79, 91, 139, 157, 215, 250, 257
Republican Party, 22, 32–33, 45, 78, 122, 125–28, 215, 275, 299
Revenue Act (1868), 15
Revenue Act (1872), 29, 30
Revenue Act (1890), 119
Reynolds, Dr., 148
Reynolds, Jack, 7
Reynolds, William, 141, 142
Rhea, Frank, 316
Richards (lawyer), 166–68
Richards, J. H., 256, 312
Richardson, J. H., 308
Ridenbaugh, William H., 47, 81, 85, 128, 144
Ridenbaugh Canal Company, 80–81, 212
Ridenbaugh lumber yard, 221
Riggs, Henry, 120
Riid, Alois, 26, 44
Rivers, E., 59
roads and streets. *See also* electricity
  from Boise to Atlanta, 72, 78
  lighting of, 88, 133, 268–69
  military, 43
  mining, 202, 212
  named after JL, *277, 298*
  paving of, 206, 216, 230–31, 233, 250, 253
  repairs, 89
  street sprinkling, 254
  travel difficulties and, 35
Robbins, Mrs., 236
Robbins, Orlando "Rube," 22, 42, 132, 165
Roberts (councilman), 218, 219
Roberts, George H., 236
Roberts, J. M., 271
Roberts, John, 79
Roberts, William, 40
Robie, A. H., 76
Robie, Henry, 77
Robinson, A. L., 65
Robinson, Jerre, 277
Rocky Mountain Bell Telephone Company, 205
Roeder (detective), 225
Rogers, E. M., 264
Rogers, Gordon B., 319
Rogers, John R., 164
Rogers, Will, 305, 307, 312
Roosevelt, Theodore, 228, 236
Ross, Charley, 89
Ross, D. W., 83, 84, 175–76
Ross, Mary Kenneth, 214
Rost, John, 89, 90
Rotary, 309
Roth, Dan, 49
Roy (employee), 121
Ruchdaschel, John C., 71, 90, 146, 209
Rudin, Max, 61–62
Russell, Alice, 203, 204
Russell, D. A., 305
Russell, J. R., 83, 163, 175
Ryal (judge), 141–42, 155

Sabin, R. L., 151–53
Salfer, John, 211
saloon business. *See also* bartending; brewery industry; liquor industry
  Anti-Saloon League, 149
  billiards, 52, 59, 77, 89, 142–43, 266
  closings of, 263
  fights, 144–45
  fires, 89
  music and, 130
  robberies, 146
  Sunday laws, 130, 219–20, 238–39
  training for, 297

Salt Lake Herald (newspaper), 206
Salvation Army, 205
San Francisco (CA), 69, 70, 248
Savidge, W. H., 145, 190mf, 250, 251
scarlet fever, 132
Schaffer, Fred, 72
Schin, Ai, 21
Schley, Winfield Scott, 75
Schmelzel, William G., 205
Schmidt, Jacob, 17
Schnabel, Charles A., 48–49
Scholl, Mr., 29
Scholl, Mrs., 30
Scholtz, Otto, 255
Schooler, J. E., 251
schools, 48–51
  Barefoot Schoolboy Law, 147
  Boise High School, 248, 250
  Boise school board, 48, 50, 91, 147, 154, 260
  building of, 49–50, 88, 312
  creation of Boise Independent School District, 51
  for the deaf, 260
  end of year activities, 61
  fires, 260
  laws and legislation, 51, 147
  Lincoln Public School, 173, 217–27, *222, 274*
  St. Michael Episcopal School, 50
  White Cross school, 175
Schriebe (coroner), 251
Schueler, Jacob, 32
Schwantes, Carlos, 164
Schweitzer, William, 56
Scottish Rite Masons, 309
"Scrambled Eggs" (horse), *307*, 308, 312
Seattle Brewing and Malting Co., 149
Seitzel, Louis, 62
Seller, Leo, 269

Sellers, H., 208
Sellers, Mr., *237*
Settler's Canal (Lemp Canal), 80–84, 139, 146, 175–76, 199–201, 228, 254
  employees, 200, 209–10, 212
  lawsuits, 82–83, 163, 212, 251–52
  transfer of ownership, 200–201
Settler's Canal/Settler's Ditch (Lemp Canal), 198, 209, 229
Settler's Irrigation District, 84, 251–52, 253
sewer systems, 61, 205, 213, 233, 234
Shackelford, T. N., 316
Shainwald Brothers, 88, 276
Sharing, Charles A., 35
Shaw Mountain mines, 132
Sheep Mountain, 84–85, 87, 129, 139
Shellworth, Harry, 203
Sheridan, Avice, 257, 266, 268
Sheridan, Ethel, 257, 266, 267, 268
Shevilin, Thomas, 141, 142
Short, Mac, 52
Shrader, George, 156
Shriners, 16, 169, 257–58, 277, 299
Shriver, Mrs. Charles, 266
sidewalks. *See* roads and streets
silver standard, 147
Silver Valley, 247
Simonson, Bessie (Johnston), 268
Simonson, John M., 268
Simonson, Louise Bernice (Lemp), *87, 249*
  attends sister's funeral, 231
  birth of, 91, 132
  census records, 177, 265
  childhood, 198, 206, 250
  death of, 314
  JL's estate, 277
  marriage of, 266–68
  social life and travels, 240, 253,

257, 262, 263, 265, 266
Simonson, Marshall (grandson), 314
Simonson, Marshall C., 266–68
Simpson, Bethel W., 319
Singh, Lee "Jim," 215–16
Smith (judge), 210, 219
Smith, Arthur, 237
Smith, B. F. "Picayune," 48
Smith, Dan, 267
Smith, Edward, 218, 306
Smith, Frank J., 235–36
Smith, N. G., 78, 88, 90, 146
Smith, William F., 54, 148, 307
Smith, William H., 81
Smith Prairie, 201, 269
soda manufacturing, 124
Sommercamp, William, 44, 71
Sonna, Mrs. Peter, 276
Sonna, Peter, 48, 58, 87
Sonnleitner, Charles, 138
Sons and Daughters of Idaho Pioneers, 313
Sons of Hermann, 211
Sons of Idaho, 309, 311
South Mountain Brewery, 35–36
Spanish-American War, 169, 214
Sparber, S. E., 236
Spath, Leonard, 36
Spiegal, Mr., 171
sports. *See also* Boise Turn Verein; horses
 athletic clubs, 53, 121, 236
 baseball, 62, 146, 238
 gun club, 249, 253
 hunting and fishing, 62, 93, 166, 240, 255, 257, 260, 270, 303
 polo, 271–73, 303–4, 305–6, *307*, 308, 312
Springer, Alice, 206
Springer, Dr., 213
St. Louis (MO), 11, 40–41, 52, 131
St. Luke's Hospital, 227, 306, 308

St. Michael Episcopal School, 50
Stabb, Messrs., 28
Stadtmiller, Joe, 58
stamps (tax), 13, 30, 228
Star mines, 72–73, 94, 134–38, 154, 228–29
Star Variety Theater, 130
Starr, R. O., 319
Starrh, Thomas A., 136
States, Ethel Velma, 315
Statesman (newspaper), 125–28, 244
Stayuer, Arthur, 135
Stearns, John L., 50
Steidel, Louis, 17
Steineck, W. E., 211
Steiner, Harry, 273
Steunenberg, Frank, 242, 252
Stevens ranch, 204
Stevenson (engineer), 82
Stevenson, Edward, 88
Stewart (school director), 225
Stewart, George H., 141, 142, 150–51, 157, 209, 235–36, 256
Stewart, H. M., 149
Stewart, J. (justice), 303
Stewart, James L. (Dr.), 308
Stirm, Mary. *See* Lemp, Mary (Stirm)
Stirm, William F., 85, 161, 297
Stockslager (judge), 166–68
Stoehr, William, 276
Stone, William, 250–51
stoppers, bottle, 37
Stout (neighbor), 60
Stoutemyer (attorney), 235–36
Strahorn, Robert, 67
Streb, John, 56
streets. *See* roads and streets
strikes (labor), 135, 144, 242
Stutzenacker, Elizabeth, 14
Stutzenacker, Peter, 14, 98ak
Suey, Fong, 206

suffrage, 164
sugar beets, 211, 237–38
Sugar City factory, 237–38
Sullivan (justice), 168
Sullivan, William, 257
Sun time, 131
Sunday laws, 130, 219–20, 238–39
Sunrise Lode, 134, 138, 145, 165, 190mf
Sunset group, 247
Sutton, H. W., 242
Sweet (councilman), 155
Swingle, A. L., 122

T. Wollstein & Co., 24
Taft, William Howard, 271
"Tag Day," 258
tanks ("Water Tanks"), 21
Tatro, W. C., 7, 256, 258
Tatro, W. C., Jr., 258
Tax Payers Party, 32
taxes. *See also* property assessments and values; property taxes
on beer, 10–11, 13, 14–15, 30, 169, 214, 228
German, 5
IRS officers, 138
on JL's estate, 277–78
laws and legislation, 13, 29, 30
liquor, 15, 29, 30
stamps, 13, 30, 228
telegraph, 19, 24, 35, 262
telephone services, 70, 205
television, 151
temperance movement, 21–22, 33, 40, 62, 95, 128, 149, 228, 231
Templars, 21–22, 153, 275, 277, 298
"The Market," 208
Thetis (ship), 75
Thomas, C. O., 272
Thompson, Amos G., 277
Thompson, Jeff, 8, 97n

Thunder Mountain mine, 202, 212–13
time zones, 131
Tipton, S. L., 150, 210
Torrence, John A., 138
Tourtelotte, J. E., 250, 256, 258, 303
transportation, 30, 35, 40. *See also* automobiles; canal systems; railroad industry; roads and streets
Tray, W. E., 170
Truesdale, O. B., 201, 207
Tucker, Edward, 316
Tucker, Leona. *See* Lemp, Leona Caroline (Tucker)
Tucker, William, 316
Turn Verein organizations, origins of, 16–18. *See also* Boise Turn Verein
Twogood, Jimmy H., 48, 50

Union Pacific Railway, 64, 67–68, 124, 129
unions (labor), 78, 144, 252
United States Brewers Association, 32
Updyke, Dave, 12
Urquides, Jesus, 169
U.S. Army Signal Corps, 74–76
U.S. Cavalry, 41–42
U.S. Centennial Exposition, 38, 40
U.S. Congress, 63
U.S. Food Commission, 309
U.S. Interior Department, 301–3
U.S. Internal Revenue Service (IRS), 138
U.S. Land Office, 140
U.S. Senate, 63, 67
Utah, 58
Utah Northern Railroad, 63064
Utter, Stephen, 271

Valley Hotel (Payette), 161
Vallisco Water Comany, 80

Van Door, Msser., 141
Van Pelt, J. H., 208, *237*
Van Valkenburg and Harris, 247
Vanderbilt mining claim, 136, 137. *See also* Star mines
Victory township, 240
Vienna Exposition, 85
Viggett, A. G., 137
vigilantism, 11–12
violence. *See* crime and violence
Virginian, The (Wister), 151
Vorberg, Herman, 242
Vorberg, Lizzie, 242
voting rights, 164

W. E. Pierce and Co., 143, 145, 201, 208, 240, 250, 262
Walker, A. A., 316
Walker, S. H., 58
Wannamaker & Brown (PA), 209
War Eagle Consolidated Mining Company, 176
Ward, Clarence T., 306
Warm Springs Mining District, 138
wars
  Bannock Indian War, 45
  Civil War (U.S.), 8–9, 77, 158
  draft, 299–300
  Franco-Prussian War, 24–25, 26, 28
  Indian wars, 38–39, 46
  Nez Perce War, 41–42, 45
  Spanish-American War, 169, 214
  World War I, 156, 232, 299–300
  World War II, 251, 314, 317–19
Washington mine, 134
water and water rights. *See also* Settler's Canal (Lemp Canal)
  article about history of, 262–63
  brewing process and, 61
  Dry Creek, 315
  firefighting and, 154

flooding, 56–57, 145
irrigation, 63, 80–84, 201, 212, 249
new flume, 57, 145, 208–9
new municipal system, 205–6
Phylls Canal break, 212
repairs, 208–9
water supply companies, 61, 69, 80, 133, 143, 153
"Water Tanks," 21
Waterbury (polo player), 271, 312
weather and climate
  accidents and injuries related to, 56–57, 69
  Boise Valley, 80
  effects on ice industry, 177
  flooding, 56–57, 145
  grasshopper plague, 120
  hail, 90
  snow, 120
  temperatures, 53, 55, 69
Weaver, J. L., 178
Weaver, Lucille. *See* Gardner, Lucille (Weaver) (Lemp); Lemp, Lucille (Weaver)
Weiler, I. S., 156
Weiser, Ed, 202
Weisgerber, Christian, 297
Weisgerber brewery, 19
Welch, Jake, 34
Wellington, Miss, 50
Wells, James M., 163
Wells, Merle, 67
Welsh, J. J., 46
Western Bottling and Packing Company, 303
Western Brewery, 7
Western Surety and Trust Company, 207–8
Weston, Thomas, 224
Wheeler-Motter Store, 203
whiskey prices, 29, 56
White Cross school, 175
White Swan mine, 211

Whitehead & Boomer, 94
Whitson, Mr., 48
Wiedeneck, S. T., 157
Wieland, John, 248
Wiener beer, 70, 124, 128, *165*
Wilcox, M. A., 254
wildfires, 246–47
Wilkerson and Thompson grading, 210
Willey, N.B., 130
William J. Lemp Brewing Co. (St. Louis), 11, 40–41, 52, 131, 229, 273–75, *299*, 319
Williams, Arthur C., 312
Williams, D. D., 156
Wilson, A. P, 169
Wilson, George, 236
Wilson, H. G., 128
Wilson, Ivy M., 271
Wilson Price Hunt party, 80
Winn, Barte, 60
Wirtz, Constantine, 217
Wister, Owen, 151
Wolcott, Col., 65
Wolf, Jesse, 135
Wolfkell, A. M., 84, 176
Wolley, H. Smith, 228
Wolters, Albert, *31*, 34, 134, 143, 176, 229, 236–37, 240, 283en
Wolters, Curtis A., 32
Wolters, Martha Elizabeth (Eliza) (Lemp) (Jaumann) (sister), 5, *31*, 276, 283en
  marriage to Jaumann, 93, 124, 170, 233
  marriage to Wolters, 240, 269
  social life and travels, 30, 93, 124, 145, 233, 269
women
  hunting and, 129
  saloons and, 130
  voting rights, 164
Women's Christian Temperance Union (WCTU), 33
Wood, Dr., 165
Wood, M. W., 138
Wood River mines, 55, 58, 61, 132, 134–36
Woodcock, Mrs. T.P. (Brodbeck), 260
Woodcock, T. P., 57–58
Woods, M. W., 234
woolen mills, 124
World War I, 156, 232, 299–300
World War II, 251, 314, 317–19
World's Fair, 146, 163, 229, 234
Worthington, A. C., 247
Worthman, Harry S., 210
Wright, J. B., 48
Wyman, Frank, 167, 210
Wyman, George, 230

Yeomans, E. W. "Walter," 278
Young, Bill, 42
Young, Charley, 58

Zeltman, Caroline (Carrie). *See* Lemp, Caroline (Carrie) (Zeltman)

www.ingramcontent.com/pod-product-compliance
Lightning Source LLC
Chambersburg PA
CBHW071656170426
43195CB00039B/2207